Voices *of* Truth

Conversations *with* Scientists, Thinkers and Healers

NINA L. DIAMOND

LOTUS PRESS
Twin Lakes, Wisconsin

COPYRIGHT © 2000 By NINA L. DIAMOND

ALL RIGHTS RESERVED. No part of this book may be reproduced in any form or by any electronic or mechanical means including information storage and retrieval systems without permission in writing from the publisher, except by a reviewer who may quote brief passages in a review.

Cover Design:	David C. Perry
Page Layout:	Linda Khristal
Author Photo:	Tim McAfee

First Edition, 2000

Printed in the United States of America
Library of Congress Cataloging-in-Publication Data
Diamond, Nina L.

ISBN 0-914955-82-9   Library of Congress Control Number
                            Catalogue No. 99-96593

Published by: Lotus Press
P.O. Box 325, Twin Lakes Wisconsin 53181 U.S.A.
e-mail: lotuspress@lotuspress.com
website: www.lotuspress.com

This book is dedicated to

the memory of

Gary Wilson,

Byron Frohman,

&

Rose Friswell O'Leary

*There are powers who take care
of you. If you're a doctor, you get sick people;
if you're a lawyer you get cases; if you're a writer,
the Almighty sends you stories.*

— Isaac Bashevis Singer

*We have sought truth, and sometimes perhaps
found it. But have we had any fun?*

— Benjamin Jowett (1817-1893), Greek scholar
and Master of Balliol College, Oxford

Contents

Acknowledgements

Small portions of some of the conversations in this book were first published in either Q&A format or as part of narrative feature articles, as noted on the Publications Acknowledgments pages at the end of the book. My thanks to those magazine and newspaper editors.

Special thanks to my *Omni* magazine editors Rob Killheffer, who also graciously provided the Foreword for this book, and Kathleen Stein, who was in charge of the magazine's Interview feature and Mind column.

My gratitude to Lotus publisher Santosh Krinsky and his executive assistant, Cathy Hoselton, for sharing my vision, to Lenny Blank for bringing this book to their attention, and to Lynn Franklin for early efforts on its behalf.

Much thanks to my literary agent, Frank Curtis, for his continuing guidance, David C. Perry for his beautiful cover and continued editorial feedback, and to Erica Meyer Rauzin, Gary Wilson, Diane & Eugene Eisman, Carl McColman, Mindi Rudan, Lisa Beane Goldman, and Mark Frazier for their support and helpful brainstorming.

The staffs, assistants and families of these 14 scientists, thinkers and healers have been so enthusiastic and helpful. I'm grateful for everything they've done over the years, from scheduling, providing information and relaying messages to fulfilling a multitude of requests on a moment's notice. Special thanks to Maja Fahey, John Winthrop Austin, Marge Jacques, Melissa Jaco, Mary Neville, and Arielle Ford.

James, Deepak, Caroline, Brian, Marilyn, Gladys, Pam, Arun, Charles, Brooke, Michio, Deborah, Christine, and JoAnn: Thank you for giving so much of yourselves as you shared your work, ideas and time with me, and now with everyone who reads this book.

Author's Note

If you don't read,
you can't write. And if you
can't write, you must work for a living.
— Linda Ellerbee

I have been very fortunate to make a career out of doing what I love. So have the people in this book. That's part of why I chose to include them here. They are committed and passionate about what they do, and it's not about a paycheck or a job description — what they do has evolved out of who they are, what's important to them, what they believe in, what they have to offer, what they're curious about, and what inspires them.

And, like me, they love a good conversation.

These conversations are drawn from the original transcripts of interviews conducted, in most cases, for articles I wrote for magazines and newspapers. Other conversations were conducted specifically for this book or as part of researching the material for *Purify Your Body: Natural Remedies for Detoxing from 50 Everyday Situations*, my book of natural health reporting that was published in 1997 by Crown.

For the last 20 years, I've followed my interests and curiosity when choosing the person or subject matter to write about. I never wanted to write about hard news or breaking news — crime, politics, accidents. Some journalists and writers want to be where the action or the power is. I've always wanted to be where the ideas, thoughts and creative expression are. So, that's where I went.

Drawn to areas you have knowledge of, experience with, an affinity for, and curiosity about, propels you to discover more, to expand your ideas, perceptions and perspectives. All the reading and the research, every interview or conversation, contributes to the writer's *own* evolution, not just professionally or creatively, but personally.

For the first dozen years, I focused on the artists, creators and communicators. Then, during the last decade, I went on to the scientists, healers, philosophers and cultural explorers. I've written more than 500 feature articles for dozens of magazines and newspapers, using both the narrative and Q&A format. I've written social commentary and humor essays, parodies and columns. I've interviewed more people than I can count, and asked more questions in a week than a "civilian" asks in a decade. But, I haven't asked *everything* yet, and so I keep going.

One afternoon, in the summer of 1991, I was in the newsroom of a newspaper, and overheard a reporter on the phone with a source.

"Did he have a gun?" the reporter asked.

When I heard that, time stopped. The room froze.

And I thought, "Now there's a question I've *never* asked."

I didn't note that to myself because I felt I was missing something and wanted to make sure I added that to my repertoire. Quite the opposite. I stood there in amazement at how different this reporter's life and work are from mine. It gave me a chill. The people and stories that live in his head, day after day, are gruesome, violent, bloody. That doesn't mean that I don't admire what these reporters do. It only means that *I'm* not the right one to do that.

When I interviewed Larry King, and asked him why he took the path he did, he said, "When news reporters cover a fire, they ask about the damage, how many people were injured or killed, what started the fire. If *I* were there, I'd be asking: 'So, what made you want to become a fireman?'"

Dave Barry expressed the same sentiments when I interviewed him a few months earlier, and, like King, also used the fire analogy. After his first job as a hard news reporter for a daily newspaper in Pennsylvania, Barry knew this was not for him. "Somebody's house would burn down, and you'd call them, and you'd say, 'Well, Mr. Jones, how many bedrooms *did* you have?'"

I came to understand why both of them chose the fire analogy. A few years ago, while house-sitting for a week for a vacationing friend, I had the occasion to call 911 when smoke suddenly started pouring out of the central air-conditioner's vents throughout the house. The firetrucks roared up to the house, and the firemen scurried around looking for the cause of this apparently flameless fire. They quickly discovered that what was pouring out of the vents wasn't smoke, but freon. A short in a wire had melted something that, in turn, burned a hole in the freon line. While they double- and triple-checked everything, I stood out on the front lawn talking with one of the firemen. After I answered all his questions, I had one for him. I was on automatic pilot, and as Dave Barry would say, "I swear I am not making this up." I also swear that I was not thinking about my interview with Larry King when I looked up at the giant bear of a man wearing a gazillion pounds of fireman outfit in the 92-degree Miami heat, and said, "So, did you always want to be a fireman?"

No sooner did those words escape my mouth... well, I began to laugh when I realized what I'd just done. He probably thought I was nuts standing there laughing on the lawn. I composed myself, he answered, and we began to talk about the difficulties firefighters have in extreme climates.

While his occupational hazards can be life-threatening, mine, at worst, are annoying: I end up interviewing everyone who crosses my path.

෨෪ ෯෬

*I*t was inevitable that I would write this book. Afterall, you can only complain for so long without finding a solution. Every writer ends up with wonderful stuff "on the cutting room floor," to borrow a film phrase, because magazine and newspaper articles can't be 40 or even 20 pages long. Even the lengthy Q&A Interview features I did for *Omni* were always well under 10 pages.

I hated knowing that in my file cabinets there lurked fascinating conversations with people that no one would ever read because magazines and newspapers only have room to print a fraction of the material that went into the article's preparation, or the Q&A. So, in the fall of 1994, while brainstorming with a friend, I decided to create this book. During the next five years, I chose those whom I'd interviewed who I felt represented the decade in their fields. It wasn't easy to narrow it down to these fourteen. In fact, the book kept growing. I began with eight. I didn't really want to stop with fourteen, but at 20–50 pages per chapter, I had to stop before the book weighed more than my aforementioned file cabinets. So, I'm now working on a sequel.

In conversations, you'll always uncover the philosopher inside everyone, as well as the historian, the humorist, the storyteller.

In Part One, you'll meet the folks I refer to, with all due respect, as "The Usual Suspects." That's because James Redfield, Deepak Chopra, Caroline Myss, and Brian Weiss are on everybody's list as leading the ever-growing pack in mega-best-seller publishing and on the natural health and metaphysical lecture circuit today. No book of this kind would be complete without a look at what makes these four tick, and what it is about the ideas they share that so moves people to run to the bookstore in astronomical numbers. Together, they've sold more books than God (as the old publishing saying goes) in any one given year. Quite literally. Redfield alone has outsold the Bible during a number of bookselling calculation periods. His first novel, *The Celestine Prophecy* is the best-selling work of fiction since the modern methods of calculation have been used. Go back a little further, and he's only topped by *Gone With the Wind*.

While modern publishing marketing has certainly made all four commercial successes, believe it or not, they don't write for commercial *purposes*. The information and philosophies they share are their motivation. They are not moved by some blind desire to be best-selling authors no matter what happens to be in the books they sell. For all of them, the information came *first*, followed by the vehicle by which to share it publicly. Their books could've garnered little attention, like so many other gifted authors who merely, by the arbitrary luck of the draw, weren't chosen by their publishers to benefit from a massive dose of publishing house marketing machinery. That their books happened to be chosen by the publishing powers-that-be to be among that teensy weensy percentage featured as lead titles surprised them (as it does every author when first chosen) and led to their instant household name status.

In Part Two, you'll meet another group of thinkers and healers who have much information to share, and as is the custom these days, also have published it in books. Arun Gandhi, grandson of Indian leader Mahatma Gandhi, is the founder of the M.K. Gandhi Institute for the Study of Non-Violence. In the critical 18 months leading up to India's independence, Arun, then only 12 years old, lived with his grandfather, and returned home only five months before Gandhi was assassinated on January 30, 1948. Conversations with Arun Gandhi are among my favorite kinds because it is through them that we have the sense of touching history. Charles Jaco, former CNN war correspondent, is one of the last of a breed of reporters for whom journalism was a *calling*, not a glitzy vehicle to become a celebrity. I'd like to believe that this kind of intelligent broadcast journalism is not on its deathbed, but I'm afraid that even the eternal optimist in me must concede that it's a goner.

Brooke Medicine Eagle is one of the most respected modern-day Native American teachers. Perhaps what makes her so effective today is that she's also a Baby Boomer trained as a psychologist and a veteran of The Sixties. More than 25 years ago, while still in her 20s, she returned to her roots and has been there ever since, learning ancient teachings from Native elders, and preserving them by educating both Native and non-Native peoples across the country.

Marilyn Sunderman has been an acclaimed portrait artist and painter for more than 35 years, and she shares her thoughts on the roles of creativity, inspiration, and karma in our expression of not only art, but every aspect of our lives. Pam Johnson asks the question, "Are you happier than you admit your are?" which may at first sound like just another one of those self-help mantras, but is actually an accurate sociological review of a negative society run so amuck that it is now politically incorrect to express the slightest bit of joy about *anything*. She also reveals a few things about freedom of speech that may surprise some.

Gladys Seymour Davis should be cloned a couple of billion times over so that she can hang out with every person on the planet simultaneously and talk some sense into them. Creator of a body sculpting treatment called the Seymour System, and an old-fashioned philosopher of the best kind — she doesn't have a degree in it — Gladys is, as trite as this may sound, a force of nature.

In Part Three, you'll see how scientists are expanding our definition of science, leading many to admit that science and mysticism are merely two different languages used to describe the same phenomena, and leading others farther out into space, and even other dimensions, than anyone ever dreamed possible. Michio Kaku has found what many believe is The Unified Theory. If so, this physicist will one day out-Einstein Einstein. His theory hinges upon the notion that we live in a universe that actually has 24 dimensions. The author of a number of books, including the best-selling *Hyperspace*, Kaku is the college physics professor you wish you'd had, and brings a good, strong dose of wit and scientific conscience (he was among an influential group of scientists protesting the Vietnam war and wouldn't use his talents and intellect to work on creating "Star Wars" and other defense systems) to his field and to the public.

Deborah Mash is a neuroscientist with the soul of a mystic. She coined the word *neuroshamanism* to describe the coming together of modern neuroscience with the ancient knowledge of the shamans — the healers and wise ones — of native cultures the world over. Her work as a highly respected mainstream scientist opens the door for her and many others like her to bring both worlds of knowledge together.

Christine DeLorey studies and interprets the meanings behind the numbers of life, and the natural cycles they represent. Picking up where traditional numerology leaves off, DeLorey is a cyclic analyst who focuses on free will and where our desire and goals can take us as we go through our own cycles of nature.

And, finally, as the highest-ranking female executive at NASA's Kennedy Space Center, JoAnn Morgan, who is also a seasoned aerospace engineer, has worked there for more than 40 years, since before NASA was even called NASA. She has watched the entire space program unfold,. Now, as Kennedy Space Center's Associate Director, she's got her eyes on Mars — for very personal reasons.

*F*OREWORD
by
Robert K.J. Killheffer

*N*ina L. Diamond and I have been friends and colleagues for many years, but I'm kind of a strange choice to be writing the Foreword to this book, which is, perhaps why I was her first choice. Although I was the editor who worked with her on many of her *Omni* articles, the ones that led to some of the chapters in this book were assigned and edited by another *Omni* editor who handled the Interview and Mind sections. Plus, I've often got a very different worldview from some of the people you'll find her talking with in the pages to come.

When it comes to philosophy, I'm a pretty staunch rational materialist. I go in for atoms and molecules, not life-force energy or vibrations. I don't believe in God, or god, or gods (though I *love* churches), nor mystics, an afterlife, or reincarnation (though I've always wanted to see a real ghost), nor even the existence of a "soul" as most people would define it. I haven't read anything by James Redfield except what Nina has included here, and, the same goes for Deepak Chopra, Caroline Myss, and Brooke Medicine Eagle. However, I'm thoroughly familiar with the work of physicist Michio Kaku, and I've followed the ideas of activist Arun Gandhi, NASA's JoAnn Morgan and neuroscientist Deborah Mash.

Okay, so what the heck am *I* doing writing this Foreword?

The answer lies in the very reasons why Nina and I have maintained our friendship over the years — the reasons why, whenever we get to talking, we're likely to go on for hours and hours (days and days, if we didn't start to get hoarse or called away to some other conversation). Despite the areas in which some of our views differ — perhaps because of them — I've always found talking with Nina to be a stimulating, entertaining, and provocative experience. And there's nothing I like better than a good conversation.

I believe she asked me to help introduce Voices of Truth because underneath that upper layer on which we can often see things differently, there's a deeper sense in which we're kindred minds. Though I prefer only material explanations, and Nina is comfortable digging deeper, right through to the metaphysical, what lies at the root of our personalities is *curiosity*. We want to *know*. We're always wondering, always questioning, and always exploring. And anyone who wants to know has to keep an open mind. Our differences fuel our friendship and editorial relationship because they provide a sounding board for our points of view. We can't get too complacent with each other there to remind us of alternate ways of seeing — and exploring — things.

And our similarities run deeper, because in the end we're digging for much the same thing, and that's not any specific fact or explanation, but *wisdom*. Wisdom is a practical knowledge, unbounded by theory, rooted in our subjective experience as human beings. Like science it draws on empirical data — experience — but unlike science, wisdom is not constrained by a need to fit into a larger framework of intertwined theory. Many people try to make wisdom do that — in fact, it's those theories that form the differences over which Nina and I debate. Chinese traditional medicine may explain the efficacy of its treatment by referring to a "wind" in the liver, or lines of energy coursing through the body, while Western science prefers to speak of chemicals and fields and cells and viruses. This is the stuff of different theories, merely two divergent explanations of the same treatment. Wisdom, on the other hand, consists of the treatment itself.

Wisdom is what you'll find in this book. For instance, I don't place much credence in Redfield's notions of a "birth vision" or the existence of a "pre-life/afterlife dimension." But that doesn't prevent me from finding in his viewpoint many worthy precepts — ways of seeing and ways of living that *work*, whether I agree with his theoretical framework or not. I think Redfield's absolutely right that our culture has overemphasized the simple acquisition of material things as a path to happiness, that it has discouraged other — often more important — elements that make up a joyful, satisfying existence. I think he's admirable in insisting that every person must be their own spiritual leader, must make their own journey of discovery, and find their own peace. He resists the temptation to turn wisdom into dogma, and that makes him rare in a world of self-proclaimed gurus offering thousand-dollar growth seminars. This is wisdom born of living and thinking and feeling and being. It is wisdom that can help others live and think and feel and be.

Another brand of wisdom, derived from a likewise rich but very different life experience, springs from Nina's conversation with reporter Charles Jaco. His perspective could hardly be more different from Redfield's — this is a man who has spent the past twenty years dodging bullets in Africa, ducking missiles in Iraq, and interviewing rioters in South Central L.A. But it's not the adventures of his life that stay with you most, it's the human insights, the openness, the profound optimism. For a person who's been present for some of the worst moments in recent history, Jaco maintains a stunningly hopeful and even idealistic heart.

That kind of optimism is another strand that binds all the conversations in this book together. It can be hard in our world of relentless marketeering, cynical day-trading, and raging hypocrisy to maintain any hope of improvement, but the people in this book — and the author who brought them together — share the gift, the courage, of believing in the possibility of a better world and a better life, both for individuals and for society as a whole. We need to hear voices like theirs. We need to believe in change.

And that, in the end, is why I'm writing the Foreword to this book. I may not share the metaphysical worldviews of some of its subjects, but I do share their passion for wisdom and truth and their hope for the future. Whatever your outlook, be it metaphysical or material, religious or secular, believer or skeptic, if you can approach this book with an open mind then you will come away rewarded. There is wisdom here, and hope, for those with eyes to see, and ears to hear.

Robert K.J. Killheffer
November 1, 1999
Brooklyn, NY

*Rob Killheffer is a writer, editor, and book reviewer
and the former Senior Editor of* Omni *magazine.*

Part One

One

James Redfield

*Western society is outraged if an
individual gives his soul as much daily
attention as his grooming.*

— Alexander Solzhenitysn

In the rain forests of Peru, an ancient manuscript has been discovered. Within its pages are nine key insights into life itself — insights each human being is predicted to grasp sequentially, one insight then another, as we move toward a completely spiritual culture on Earth.

So begins James Redfield's groundbreaking first novel, *The Celestine Prophecy*. Imagine an Indiana Jones kind of adventure, but starring an ordinary guy. And he finds himself trying to help a friend. And the next thing he knows, he's traipsing through Peru in search of a legendary, yet secret ancient manuscript whose self-empowering Insights are quite a threat to the Church's control. And, so, as he discovers each Insight — revealed to him by those he meets along the way — he's also trying to stay two steps ahead of the Church and local government officials who would like to see him dead (or at the very least permanently stopped), and the same for everyone else who could bring these Insights to the public.

Now, the how-to aspect of the novel emerges as our hero gets to experience the lessons of each Insight as he goes along, enlightening him and everyone around him to the true power of their spirits.

If you haven't read *The Celestine Prophecy* yet, the odds are great that you know someone who has, for the story behind the story is one of publishing's most unique — a spiritual/metaphysical/psychological/historical/environmental novel that packs the dual punch of adventure tale and spiritual how-to that spread by cross-country word-of-mouth among like-minded people and then, shock of all shocks, was embraced by the mainstream as well, propelling it to the number one spot on *The New York Times* bestseller list for what seemed like an eternity. In 1995 and 1996, it was the #1 book in the *world*.

Redfield, who has been writing all his life, keeping journals and publishing a bit, "but nothing major," was born on March 19, 1950, and raised some 35 miles out in the country from Birmingham, Alabama. He and his wife, Salle, lived not far from there for awhile, tucked away in a peaceful, rural setting by a lake. "We weren't at the ends of the earth," he jokes, "but you could see it from there." They now live on the water in Florida.

Always curious about spirituality and human interaction, Redfield majored in Sociology at Auburn University, then received his Master's in Counseling in 1975. After almost two decades working as a therapist to troubled and abused kids and their families, Redfield synthesized the best of interactive psychology, Eastern and Western philosophy, science, futurism, ecology, history and mysticism during the more than two years he took to write the book beginning on January 1, 1989, shortly after his first marriage ended. He worked on *The Celestine Prophecy* in such diverse places as the sacred sites of Peru, the high-energy locales of Sedona, Arizona, and a table at a Waffle House near Birmingham, Alabama.

He began shopping it around to publishers in 1992, but didn't like the few offers he *did* receive. "The publishing companies all wanted to take between a year and 18 months to get the book out," he says. "So, I hired a publishing consultant who used to work at Doubleday and decided to just publish it myself."

His risk paid off. He invested his savings of under $15,000 to finance his dream, which would go on to quickly sell millions of copies worldwide (plus calendars, audio tapes and the like) and make him a multi-millionaire. But, back to the beginning. He printed an initial 3,000 copies in trade paperback and in early 1993 began carting them around to bookstores specializing in new age, spiritual and human potential titles. Bookstore owners eagerly recommended *The Celestine Prophecy* to their customers, who, in turn, began buying copies for their friends and urging everyone they knew to read it.

With the help of a book distribution company, Redfield's books were placed nationwide. Word-of-mouth, not publicity, did the rest. Within months, 100,000 copies had been sold. Unheard of in self-publishing. Bookstores of all kinds around the country were reporting that they were selling more of this book than any other they'd ever stocked. They could barely keep it on the shelves.

In an Author's Note that appeared before the first chapter, Redfield introduces the book with a five paragraph explanation that includes the passage: "If it touches you, if it crystallizes something that you perceive in life, then pass on what you see to another." And pass it on they did.

It wasn't long before the big publishing houses in New York took notice and launched into a bidding war. By the end of the year, Warner Books had bought the hardcover rights for $800,000, and moved with record speed to bring the edition out with a March, 1994 publication date, which meant that the books would begin to hit the bookstores in February. The book quickly rose to number one on the fiction side of the *New York Times* bestseller list, and in its first two months the hardcover sold more than 500,000 copies. *The Celestine Prophecy* spent nearly three years on *The New York Times* bestseller list and has sold about 8.5 million copies worldwide. It has been published in an astounding 30 languages.

In April 1996, Warner published Redfield's sequel, *The Tenth Insight*, which also immediately snuggled into a spot on the *New York Times* and other bestseller lists. Warner has also published non-fiction companion books they call "experiential guides" to both novels in response to reader interest in further studying the elements presented in the Insights.

Redfield's own company, Satori Publishing, put out *The Celestine Journal*, a monthly newsletter, for four years before ceasing print publication — to save trees, of course — and incorporating its contents into Redfield's website at www.celestinevision.com in the fall of 1997.

Stressing self-discovery and experience as verification, Redfield's work places the responsibility for growth squarely in the hands of each individual, not a leader, guru, or religious or other institution. For this reason, perhaps, his books have struck a chord, more accurately a symphony, not only among those with spiritual, metaphysical or holistic interests, but among the many in the mainstream for whom these lines of thinking are brand new.

Redfield's critics have referred to his works as "Spiritually 101," but he scoffs at the notion that clarifying and tying together these philosophical, environmental and psychological themes in order to make them more understandable and accessible to people should be considered a valid criticism. For those who find his books too basic, well, his feeling is that a doctoral student might have the same complaint about a text meant for an undergraduate. However, that same doctoral student might just benefit from Redfield's work as a refresher course in how everything connects.

He says he did *not* set out to write The Great American Novel. He calls his fiction books parables, and indeed they are. The stories are simply told, and almost read like narrative versions of screenplays.

In our conversations, (which took place between 1994-1999), James Redfield discusses the philosophies in his books; his belief that we've all been born with a birth vision, a mission we've come here to accomplish (which is the theme of his second novel, *The Tenth Insight*); his views regarding the interaction of our three-dimensional world with the higher dimensional pre-life/afterlife dimension; the psychological and ethical aspects of the Insights, which stress the necessity of dealing with people without resorting to manipulation; earth's energy and the vital role of our forests; as well as his life and what compels him on his mission.

His life has changed since the success of his books, but he insists that he has not. He gives very few interviews, either print or broadcast, and although he is in great demand as a speaker, he limits his public appearances to only a handful each year and prefers to give talks as benefits for non-profit environmental groups and the like. He has not parlayed his popularity into cross-country workshops like other best-selling authors of spiritual, metaphysical, environmental and health books have done.

He and his wife, Salle, a therapeutic massage therapist and meditation instructor who has recorded a series of meditation audio tapes to accompany both *The Celestine Prophecy* and *The Tenth Insight*, keep a pretty low profile compared to other authors in similar arenas. Redfield has no desire to be anyone's leader or guru, and the message of his books makes that very clear: He believes that everyone needs to be the center of their own spiritual development. Alternately serious and playful, Redfield's manner is a reminder of his message: Life can be a spiritually responsible adventure of harmony with each other, nature and the universe, to be experienced with support, respect, joy, laughter and love. He intends to remain the mild-mannered, laid-back, easy-to-talk-to guy with the heart of Alabama in his voice.

James Redfield looks like one of those English professors who sport a corduroy jacket, jeans, and a close-cropped sandy beard in the not-quite-rugged manner of a poet who could also be a lumberjack if he put on 50 pounds.

But the same guy who meditates and gives intense thought to

interacting with higher dimensions, also enjoys outings with his two daughters (both from his first marriage), playing golf as much as is humanly possible (he's among those who consider it a transcendent experience), and hanging out with nature.

Indeed, success has had very little impact on the Redfields other than to enable them to travel more in conjunction with their Celestine endeavors, and provide him with the opportunity to support environmental and global causes, ponder and write full time.

In short, he's still a regular guy. Well, that is, a regular guy who probably has more mystical moments before breakfast than most people do in a lifetime. One who lobbies in Washington on behalf of Save America's Forests (he really, *really* loves those trees), and who, at the age of 23, stood in the Smoky Mountains in Tennessee and had his very own birth vision, "knowing" that one day he would write a book that would impact millions. Now, more than 25 years later, he says that the experience on the mountain was like "a daydream that went on and on. And once I got on the right path, it happened with the publication of *The Celestine Prophecy*."

Those who know him see an uncanny resemblance between Redfield and the unnamed lead character in his novels, a character he purposely does not give a name to so that he can represent an Everyman (or Everywoman), and so the reader can easily put himself or herself in the character's shoes. Redfield, like this mild fellow he refers to in conversations as "the narrator," tends to be aloof at times, one of the major personality traits Redfield writes about in *The Celestine Prophecy*'s Insights when he's addressing how someone's personality type leads them to behave in a particular manner that Redfield has dubbed "a control drama" (see Sixth Insight). This particular theme in his work leads to an exploration of how we all use our control dramas to manipulate others into giving us vital spiritual energy: essentially these are the power plays we all use.

Redfield's marvelous sense of humor allows him to laugh easily at the good-natured teasing he encountered during our conversations when his more aloof qualities surfaced from time to time, when I was looking for specifics and he was more inclined to be vague at the moment. In *The Celestine Prophecy*, his characters explain that one of the keys to breaking someone's control drama is to simply name it out loud to them. So, I tried it. I called him aloof. He laughed. Then he did his best to stop being aloof. At least until the next time he was in the mood to do it again.

Because Redfield spent so many years working as a therapist, he's a good listener, patient and kind. But it's not some kind of professional act. Even when he's in the mood to be aloof, he's awfully nice about it.

I first heard about *The Celestine Prophecy* late in the summer of 1993, just a few months after Redfield put out his self-published edition. Word was spreading, and over the next five months a number of people mentioned it to me, including artist and author Marilyn Sunderman and neuroscientist Dr. Deborah Mash, both of whom I'd been interviewing for magazine articles and the book you are now holding in your hands.

In the winter of 1994, just as *The Celestine Prophecy* was making its way into every bookstore in America in its Warner Books hardcover edition, I contacted Warner's publicity department and requested a copy of the book and an interview with Redfield for one of the national magazines I was writing regularly for at the time. As it turned out, over the next couple of years, I would interview Redfield more than a dozen times and would publish six articles and interviews on Redfield and the publishing phenomenon of *The Celestine Prophecy*.

When the book arrived, just a day or two after I'd requested it, I opened it immediately, curious about the publishing whirlwind it had created. I began to read, and didn't stop until I was finished, sometime in the wee hours of the next morning. I understood why everyone was recommending it to everyone else.

I expected that I might pick up a few tidbits of wisdom from *The Celestine Prophecy*, but I didn't expect what I found: a concise guide to connecting the dots among metaphysical experiences; good working definitions of how nature's energy and ours influence each other; a clear view of how metaphysics and human behavior are intertwined; a true energy definition of personal empowerment; and a historical context in which to place the inherent human quest for love, meaning and spirit. I was particularly intrigued by how Redfield uses synchronicities — meaningful coincidences — as treasure maps. Pay attention to them, follow their lead, his characters are taught by one of the

Insights. I'd been fascinated by, experiencing and researching synchronicity as far back as I could remember, just as Redfield has, and believe, as Redfield does, that they are important signs operating on many levels. They play a major role in his work, and also in his worldview.

Redfield's work means something different to each person who reads it. Perhaps that's another key to its success. It's just as effective for the seasoned mystic or philosopher as it is for the novice, and all those who fall somewhere in between.

Following his novels and their experiential guides, Redfield wrote *The Celestine Vision* (Warner, 1997), a non-fiction commentary on the Insights, spiritual consciousness, and a further exploration of the shifting worldview he's written about in his novels.

His first children's book, *The Song of Celestine*, was published in September 1998 by Little, Brown. In the fall of 1999, Warner published his third novel in the Celestine series, this one about the Eleventh Insight, titled *The Secret of Shambhala*, a journey to the mythic Tibetan Buddhist community where the ideal human culture lives.

In September, 1999, two months before this third in a series of Celestine novels was published, Redfield visited Tibet, where much of this novel takes place.

"The scenery, feeling, and ambiance in the mountains and high plains is spectacular," he said upon his return. "It's no wonder that Tibetan Buddhism developed into a belief system where nature is sacred. Tibet is conducive to that."

Redfield was appalled when he saw first hand what four decades of Communist occupation has done to Tibet. "Tibetan culture has been intentionally destroyed by the Chinese. But, there is hope," he said, adding that a free Tibet is among the global causes that he supports with his work and benefit activities.

Redfield is currently co-producing *The Celestine Prophecy* movie, and writing a book of non-fiction that traces the history of the consciousness movement, focusing particularly on the last 30 years. This book will be co-authored by Esalen Institute founder Michael Murphy, and published by Warner.

Material from this introduction includes information drawn from interviews that took place from the spring of 1994 throughout the late fall of 1999. The conversations presented here are divided into two parts, and took place between the spring of 1994 and the winter of 1999.

❧◦◦☙

The Nine Insights

For easy reference, here are brief descriptions of *The Celestine Prophecy's* Nine Insights, to accompany you during these conversations with James Redfield.

◈ **First Insight:** Surfaces unconsciously at first as a profound sense of restlessness. We become conscious of the coincidences and synchronicities in our lives. We have a sense of destiny, and with that comes a reconsideration of the inherent mystery that surrounds our individual lives on this planet.

◈ **Second Insight:** Puts our current awareness into a longer historical perspective. Understanding that we've been preoccupied with scientific progress and a more comfortable style of survival for the last 500 years, while putting spirituality on hold. Now we wake up from this preoccupation and reconsider our original question: What's behind life on this planet, and why are we really here?

◈ **Third Insight:** We learn to perceive the energy that forms the basis of, and radiates outward from, all things. We recognize that the physical world is a vast system of energy that responds to how we think.

◈ **Fourth Insight:** How humans compete for energy. We use this for power, to try to control each other by taking a manipulative posture and getting a psychological and energy boost out of controlling others. In effect, we're stealing their energy. This is the root of human conflict.

❖ **Fifth Insight:** We transcend the conflict, break free from the competition over human energy and instead receive our energy from another source. This is the experience the mystics have always described: receiving energy from the universe, from nature. Interacting with this energy is how we continue the evolution of the universe, propelling humans to a higher energy level — a higher level of vibration.

❖ **Sixth Insight:** To stay connected to this higher source of energy we have to get rid of our habit and methods of controlling and stealing people's energy. This is called our control drama, which we learned in childhood in response to family members who were pulling energy out of us. We developed a strategy to win it back. Everyone manipulates for energy either aggressively, directly forcing people to pay attention to them, or passively, playing on people's sympathy or curiosity. The *Interrogator* probes, looking for something to criticize. You become self-conscious. This drains your energy. He puffs himself up on the energy he's draining out of you. He pulls you off your own path and you judge yourself by what he might be thinking. The *Intimidator* threatens either verbally or physically. The *Aloof* person is engaged in a passive control drama in which he responds to an interrogator or intimidator in particular (and any other type) by being aloof. An aloof person also drains your energy when you work hard to get responses from him. The *Poor Me* tries to control and gain energy passively through guilt or by seeking sympathy. This Sixth Insight also shows you how to look at your family in order to determine your own spiritual path, your purpose in life.

❖ **Seventh Insight:** The process of your continuing evolution. Staying alert to every coincidence, every answer the universe provides for you. How to recognize the places and people who have messages or answers for you, and what dreams mean. What intuition is and how to follow it. If you let your energy get too low, your body suffers, and this is the relationship between stress and disease. Love is the way we keep our vibration up: love for people, for nature, for the universe.

❖ **Eighth Insight:** Using energy in a new way when relating to people. How to avoid addictions to people, which are really addictions to their energy. How to project energy to others. How to relate to adults and children without draining their energy and without creating control dramas. How to stay connected to the universal source of energy. To avoid someone's control drama, simply do not assume the matching drama, then the person's own drama will fall apart. How to bring out the best in others by sharing energy.

❖ **Ninth Insight:** Where human evolution is leading. How we will live a true spiritual life, guided by our intuition, preserving the environment, tapping into the universal energy, meeting our survival needs without the exchange of money and without overindulgence or laziness. How we will ultimately vibrate at such a high energy level that we can transcend our perceived three dimensions (and time) and pass into other dimensions.

—Adapted from *The Celestine Prophecy* © James Redfield

The Tenth Insight

For easy reference here are the central ideas from *The Tenth Insight*:

❖ There are levels of consciousness beyond our own in the spiritual dimension.

❖ We had a Birth Vision when we came into life.

❖ Collectively, we are awakening to the World Vision that has been held by our soul groups.

❖ We are realizing that we receive guidance from the spiritual realm.

14

✦ We are deeply connected to the people we have relationships with and some of the people we meet at turning points in our life.

✦ We are working to make the physical realm more spiritual.

✦ Together we're remembering that the worldview is based on the core elements of the ageless wisdom.

✦ We are learning to hold an intuition and to have faith that it is leading us to the next point on our path.

✦ What we want exists first in our minds and hearts and becomes a reality by holding that intention.

✦ After leaving the body at death, we will review every episode of our lives. We will clearly be able to see and feel how much love we were able to give others in every encounter.

✦ The ultimate goal for humanity is to merge the material and spiritual dimensions.

—Adapted from *The Tenth Insight* © James Redfield

⊰⊱

The Redfield Conversations: Part One

The conversations presented here in Part One were drawn from many conversations with James Redfield that took place between April, 1994, just weeks after Warner published *The Celestine Prophecy* in hardcover, and the fall of 1994.

What motivated you to write The Celestine Prophecy?

I think it was a long, long process of pulling loose ends together for myself. The actual writing of the book was like seeing the finished book in my mind and trying to get what I was writing to represent that. I started on January 1, 1989. In 1992, I started looking around for publishing sources. I felt that what was really happening out there was that we're bringing this new spiritual approach to life that's been generating for 15 or 20 years — at least in a mass way — into a clear focus. I wanted some clarity about how the many contributing fields to spirituality all tie together. It's something we're all doing right now. We're all trying to pull together a more common sense understanding of what's involved in approaching the spiritual life in this time period.

That's one of the book's biggest strengths. It's filled with common sense. It brings in spirituality and psychology and sociology in a way that no other book has because you lay it out so simply and give examples within the story of all the interactions.

That's the advantage of writing a story. Not only can one bring in one's own experiences, but one can also illustrate the concepts that have maybe only been discussed before in the abstract.

Part of what has made the book so successful and made it more appealing to the mainstream, landing it at number one on the *New York Times* bestseller list, which was unheard of for this kind of book, is that you presented it as an action-packed adventure that anyone can relate to. It's like an Indiana Jones movie. Did you do that on purpose?

(He laughs) *Well, sure, not just to make it accessible to more people, though, but to illustrate that what we're coming to in our clarity about spirituality is that it really is an adventure. It's not just a pious set of doctrines or a schedule of disciplinary procedures. Spiritual consciousness is, on the whole, very adventurous, and the Tao is about pursuing our deepest, most fulfilling dreams.*

Using that adventure metaphor in the book propels the characters to discover the Insights just as you'd discover spiritual truths in your own life.

And it always happens with mysterious coincidences that happen to us, that seem to be beyond chance. Like, why is this happening to me now? What does it mean? What does it indicate in terms of a particular direction that I can now go in my life with a sense of success and affirmation?

People are experiencing so many synchronicities, and they pick up the book, and the first thing they read is about these synchronicities. Everyone who reads the book asks, "How did he know this was happening to me?"

(He laughs) *Well, I think the synchronicities are very up right now because the level of spiritual awareness is at a point where we can really detect them. We're really tuned into them. And I think that what's new, though, here in the 1990s as we finish this century, is that we're now understanding how to get our egos out of the way enough to amplify this synchronicity, and to understand what the synchronicity is pertaining to. What about us is being drawn in a particular direction that is our spiritual growth, and what steps of clearing can we undergo in order to enhance this process?*

Many people say, "I know I'd like to live my life in an enlightened way, but what do I do about all the unenlightened people who are being manipulative?" They know they can't fix anyone. Well, you gave them useful examples showing how to deal with everyone's control dramas, as you've termed them, and you explained where they come from and how to make sure we don't do this to the next generation, to our children.

That's right, and I think this is something that's finally com-ing more into mass consciousness — how we subtly compete with and undermine other people. Even people who are spiritual or call themselves spiritual do this. We all unconsciously come from a place where we need to build ourselves up when we're in the presence of another person. We need to win and feel good about ourselves. And it's that process that can often become violent from a psychological point of view. We're all just trying to grow past this. I think that we need to be gentle with each other about it, but at the same time realize that we don't have to put up with people misusing us. We are now beginning to understand how this process evolved.

You go one step beyond classic spiritual and self-help books and show how people came to be playing their control dramas and give us tools to stop them from affecting us, all within the actions of the char-acters in the novel.

We've sorted through what works and what doesn't work, and we're reaching a point now where we know that we feel best when we're really connected on the inside with this force we've called God, this divine part of ourselves, with a universal ener-gy. At that point we're liberated from being manipulated by anyone. Understanding the process keeps us centered and on track.

You've defined energy very clearly. We hear a lot these days about power and empowerment. But because what we've been taught about power in the past is that it's external and it's control over other people,

18

we're confused about the concept of becoming personally empowered. You've showed in your writing that empowerment really is simply energy. Energy equals empowerment as opposed to control equals empowerment. And empowerment means not letting anyone steal your energy. And it also means that when you need energy, instead of stealing it from another person, you can absorb it from the universe, or in some cases receive it as a gift from another person.

That's right. I think my work is a synthesis of the best information from the East — that there is this universal energy, the chi *energy that we have within — and modern physics, which tells us that this is an energy-dynamic universe, and that we have to live in and negotiate all the energy dynamics that we run into. This is something that strengthens us individually and helps us stay centered in connection with the divine source of this energy, and that's within.*

Physics tells us that this is not really a material universe, it's really all about energy. *The Celestine Prophecy* uses that as a base and brings in Eastern and Western philosophy, physics, psychology...you've come up with your own kind of a Unified Theory.

(He laughs) *With this book all along people have been embracing something that they also believe in and that they want to pass along. My intention was to try to pull loose ends together and to set some ethical vision for the spiritual community.*

You've said that you don't want to be considered a guru, and I think that the very message of your book will keep that from happening.

Yes, and that's been my experience. The people who resonate with this book understand that we are our own center for our spiritual direction. I think that what is evolving is a true spiritual democracy. We're looking for truth all over the place.

Many people are buying this book for others.

That's one of the characteristics of the phenomenon. People want to pass it around. It's representative of the fact that this is a vision that we are all coming to at the same time.

What have your ideas been influenced by?

A book by Ernest Becker, The Denial of Death, *that really looks at how the modern age has denied the mystical side of life, is one (influence).*

Were you influenced by the 19th century Transcendentalist movement?

Oh, sure. A big part. That's such a rich part of American history. I was also influenced by the work of R.D. Laing, and Eric Berne, certainly from the side of interaction psychology. And from the point of view of modern physics, that's been a rich tradition of thought from The Tao of Physics *by Fritjof Capra to the work of Deepak Chopra on the mind-body relationship from the quantum point of view. And Gary Zukav's book* Seat of the Soul.

Zukav's book also addresses internal power as our spiritual energy versus the way that society has wielded this horrible external power.

That's right, and we're coming to a point where we're acknowledging and opening up to our own power and inner direction. Thank God, though, that we're understanding the importance of ethics in the spiritual journey instead of hoping we were spiritual and then going out and playing the same games and manipulations of other people unconsciously. We're becoming aware that there's an interpersonal ethic that's very important if we're to keep our own synchronistic unfolding moving along.

That's been one of the problems. We've been trying to play a new game by the old rules.

That's right.

For many people, the spiritual search begins out of some crisis.

*And it's usually a crisis of direction. There's a polarization —
on the one hand you have people becoming more and more frustrated because the old rules don't work, and (neither does) the
old view of the world that is materialistic and stresses the accu-
mulation of goods and status. These things don't suffice anymore.
The whole culture is raised to a level of awareness in which those
things seem petty. People are very frustrated and almost desper-
ate. They're shooting everybody and themselves all the time. The
other end of the polarization that's occurring is much more
unsung. It's people realizing that, hey, the old worldview needs
to be extended toward the path of fulfillment, in a spiritual
direction where life is seen for what it is: It's a birth/death process
and what we do in between is of historical significance. We're on
this planet to grow spiritually, and that's where we get most of
our fulfillment from once we tune in to how the process works.*

I imagine you were also very influenced by your experiences counseling children and their families because you saw lives being shattered
by playing by the old rules.

*Of course, and the whole level of emotional abuse in fami-
lies was a taboo covered up for years. I was working with these
troubled teenagers and one thing about abused kids is that their
challenge is to see life as something positive again, that has some
kind of opportunity, and that they can find some kind of fulfillment, and can transcend the trauma of what they've gone
through and find some reason to live that's exhilarating and
inspiring. It's really a passage that we all have to make. There
are always reasons to be bitter and resentful, but the real spiritual fulfillment doesn't take place until we can overcome that
skepticism and cynicism and experientially discover that if we
get out of our own way and open up, the world is designed for
our dreams to come true.*

It's a problem getting out of our own way and also keeping people from sabotaging our good intentions and our spiritual journey.

Once we cue in to how to avoid that, how to remove ourselves from it, and how to stay connected with the measure of connection — the energy, which is really love — then we can negotiate all of that without getting pulled in to it. I think that with most of the book it's experientially verifiable. One of the reasons why I wanted to tell a story and not try to create a new program is so that people could see the Insights investigated and then investigate them in their own time and test them out. People find that they're verifiable.

Was it difficult for you to come up with exactly what the Nine Insights should be and in what order?

It certainly was a result of my own experiences, but there's a psychic connection there somewhere. I saw the structure and then tried to put it into words. I think the Insights really represent archetypal stages that with just slight modifications can pertain to any culture in any historical period. They are archetypal shifts in awareness that any culture goes through or any person goes through as we move from a materialistic view of life to a more spiritual world view in a transcendent — even an ascendant — process. I think that's why they make sense to many, many of us. I have trouble taking credit for these in a sense because the process seemed to me that they were — as with any book — delivered to me rather than thought up by me.

These come from many sources that were germinating in your subconscious.

Of course, and it's a real Higher Self experience that leaves me awed by the result.

The Insight that addresses gaining our energy through nature, our environment and the universe is in keeping with Eastern thought as well as Native American and other native philosophies. Were you also influenced by Utopian philosophy and the notion of spiritual communities?

I've certainly been interested in spiritual communities and the whole idea of an Ecotopian vision. I wanted to integrate that in a broader sense. I think there's a place for Green technology. Certainly we're not going back to an Ecotopia that's non-technological.

We'll just learn how to integrate ecology and technology better.

Yes, and have it grounded in the traditions of the Earth, in the traditions of the energy dynamics of natural systems.

Do you think the thoughts that *The Celestine Prophecy* generates could become a catalyst for a movement of advanced spiritual communities, research communities like the one in the book that combine science and spirituality?

I really think that that's a step in our evolution, that we will start to produce models of community that are in harmony with natural and spiritual laws.

In *The Celestine Prophecy* these communities exist to further information and knowledge and conduct environmental, nutritional, scientific and medical research. The characters haven't formed a community devoid of purpose.

That's what keeps all of us energized — when we have a dream of discovery that we're all operating on. There's no such thing as being harmoniously at peace in the lotus position. In our world we participate in the Tao, and the Tao is a process of unfolding and self-discovery as we become more and more conscious of the universe. I was very much influenced by the whole idea of Taoism, and also the Zen experience. But, I guess my concern, my angle is (showing) that reaching a real connection

23

spiritually in the ideal of the east is not *then* doing nothing (he laughs).

You don't just get this enlightenment and then say, "I've got it, now I'm just going to sit here on this rock."

Yeah, that's only one aspect of this spiritual consciousness. The other aspect is the Tao of action that we participate in, which has always been much more represented by the West than the East, in my view. The West has always been about creativity and action, discovery and science. The unification in a true spiritual awareness is neither totally East nor totally West. It's the unification of East and West in terms of cultural traditions. And what comes out is a lived *spirituality that is involved in discovery. It's taking the ideal of the East, which is that we can reach a state of total union with our Higher Source energy, and joining that with the Western idea, which is that part of the human experience is discovering where we are and who we are in a biographical way. Once we connect on the inside with our highest spiritual sources — the oneness that the East idealizes — we then begin to operate in the Tao, so that our* actions *become centered and become* purposeful, *and the meanings of life become purposeful as we allow our destiny — who we are in the world and what we're here to do — to come forward. The genius comes out in the Western tradition.*

One of the drawbacks of the Eastern approach is the idea that you should just sit in a corner and revel in your oneness.

Their mistake is in thinking that the world is illusion. In my view, the world is a phenomenon that we can see deeper and deeper inside. Our adventure, then, in the Tao, is to follow our own course of discovery and add more truth to our understanding of what this human experience is all about.

Have you been influenced by science fiction?

Not really. I've read all the old classics, though, like Stranger in a Strange Land.

What made you want to go into counseling?

I've always been motivated by a need for clarity. I grew up in a little Methodist church that was very rural, love oriented, very community support oriented, and made up of great people who talked about love and grace and the spiritual experience, but just in very rhetorical terms. I was motivated by a need for clarity: What is this spiritual experience? How do we describe it to each other? How does one open up to it? What is the mindset that we have to get into to really open up to it? Those aren't things that people in little churches talk about.

In fact, they find that threatening, just as the organized religious leaders portrayed in your book do.

Yeah, because it shakes things up a little bit, and they'd rather just do what they have always done. For our whole generation, though, that wasn't enough. We really wanted to understand more about the spiritual experience and the purpose for life in a way that wasn't oriented just toward guilt, but that highlighted the more fulfilling and enhancing parts of spirituality and our spiritual connection. So, that led me to get a degree in sociology and then in graduate school into humanistic transpersonal psychology for a masters in counseling in 1975.

How did you come to astrology? You also do astrological readings with an interpretation geared towards control dramas and the other issues raised by the Insights in *The Celestine Prophecy.*

Around 1989 or so I began to become more interested in it. In the therapy I conducted through the years I did a sun sign/moon sign interpretation. I've always used astrology in my therapy work as a personality profile. Of all the ones available to a therapist, astrology is really the most accurate, and I've talked to more and more therapists who are using it. It's one of the most mysterious of the synchronicities: Planet position influencing personality. It has a 10,000-year-old tradition. And it's very helpful if you integrate your sun and moon signs. The problem with astrology is that it takes a couple of years to really learn how to do it right. Out of respect for that, I don't really call myself an astrologer. I just use some aspects of a chart to help my own assessments when working with people. It's about how astrology relates to their own psychology.

You went to Peru before writing *The Celestine Prophecy*, and while there you heard a rumor about an ancient manuscript that supposedly contained secrets.

There are rumors that there's an old manuscript in Peru or nearby. I created a story around an old manuscript. In reality, the rumor is that this manuscript exists and that it contains secrets into the true meanings of life. Edgar Cayce even prophesied that we'd find old documents like this. There are many prophecies about it.

So, in writing your novel, you played "What if..."

That's right. Peru is a spellbinding, beautiful, high energy place. People have been gravitating there for many years. I first went in the late 1980s.

Did you know about the rumor before you went?

I heard about it during my journey. I've also spent time in Sedona, Arizona, which is also considered a high energy place. Much of the book came together while I was in Sedona in November of '89 for three weeks. My interest is in sacred sites. There are sacred sites — high energy places — in all the states. I urge people to try to preserve them. They're disappearing as the wilderness gets developed.

What were some of your experiences at the high energy sacred sites?

The synchronicities became more frequent, especially concerning the book. I met everyone I needed to meet. In Sedona, one of the mythologies is not only the 15 or 20 strong vortexes there, but that there are energy spots that are high energy for each of us individually. I was sitting on a ridge near the Chapel Vortex and trying to work with the notes for the book. It wasn't coming easily. All of a sudden a crow flew out of the canyon and right over my head, and then flew back into the canyon. I continued to make notes. I was having some trouble getting the story to flow out. The crow came out of the canyon again and flew over me and then back into the canyon, so I went into the canyon, and when I sat down the book just came pouring out. I've also had prophetic visions in Sedona. Much of the Ninth Insight came while I was in natural settings at power places. The vision I wrote in the book about evolution that happened to the main character on the ridge top was based on a vision I had. While writing the book I felt like I was getting a story down on paper about what I had already seen. When I did revisions it wasn't content revision, but getting it to look like what I'd seen in my head.

How have the various psychological, spiritual and religious communities responded to the book?

I get letters every day from therapists who use the book. Clinical psychologists, too. It's opened up a dialogue with their clients about the control dramas they've been repeating. I get letters from Zen centers and ashrams that they're using the book in one way or another.

How have the Insights and principles you write about enhanced your relationship with your wife, Salle?

Salle came into the picture after I finished writing the book and while I was fine-tuning it. We're all learning that we have to be whole people before we're ready for a relationship. And we should hold out, heal, become okay alone and not rush into a relationship that just gives us an energy or that's just a repeat of an old pattern. Then we'll be ready for the one that's right for us, that won't pull us off center. This is a place many of us are coming to. We have to transcend our own negativity and vulnerability and work from our own security from within. We're aware now how relationships ought to be. People used to be able to hide their addictions — to people, alcohol, drugs and other things — but no more. It's a clearing.

It seems that you met Salle at just the right time — after your divorce and the couple of years you spent soul-searching and writing this book — when you, too, were finally ready for the right relationship.

Yes, and she's very much a part of this. She comes from a mind-body healing perspective, as a therapeutic massage therapist, and she also writes and leads workshops and contributes to our newsletter.

In your next book, *The Tenth Insight*, how will you follow how you ended *The Celestine Prophecy*, where as a result of the Ninth Insight the characters become "invisible" and transport into other dimensions? How do you top that? Is the Tenth about what it's like to be out there?

Well, that's exactly right! There's a lot of interest in the after-life dimensions, and it's an exploration of that from the point of view of what it says about how we're shifting this planetary culture to be more in sync with the culture that's already operating in the other dimensions.

What do you think is in the other dimensions?

A very rich culture of learning and interaction.

With us in our soul form?

Yes.

Moving around out there in dimensions that we have yet to be able to prove scientifically, but that physicists are now researching, like Michio Kaku, who wrote about it in his book *Hyperspace*?

That's right. In fact, those other dimensions are right here. In large part, much of what's in the other dimension is not on the other side of the moon somewhere, so to speak. It's right here, but we just vibrationally can't open up to it yet, which is the theme of the Ninth Insight.

Many believe it's those other dimensions we "go to" when we are in an altered state of consciousness like the dream state, or a deep pre-sleep state, or a deep meditative state. Will other books follow *The Tenth Insight*?

Yes, an eleventh and a twelfth.

❧ ❧

The Redfield Conversations: Part Two

While James Redfield was writing *The Tenth Insight*, his sequel to *The Celestine Prophecy*, we spoke at length a number of times about the themes he addresses in his second novel. In a classic synchronicity, I happened to be working on a publishing project about the afterlife/pre-life dimension at the same time Redfield was making this his theme in the writing of *The Tenth Insight*.

Science, mind-body medicine, and higher dimensions all take center stage in *The Tenth Insight*, in which three characters from *The Celestine Prophecy* return: the always unnamed male lead character, his friend Charlene, and his fellow adventurer, Wil. Redfield ties together reincarnation and the role of the afterlife/pre-life dimension into both the personal and spiritual quest as well as the global quests of groups to determine and literally create the future.

29

Who are we? Who have we been before? What did we come into this physical dimension to accomplish in this lifetime and what does that have to do with our "soul groups?" How can we remember our birth vision and how does that connect to the world vision?

How does experiencing the first Nine Insights make it possible to proceed to the Tenth? Where are our dreams really taking place? What is the role of our own personal vibrational frequencies, our energy, in all of this? Redfield tackles all of these questions within the plot.

Just where does James Redfield get these ideas and insights (with both a capital and lower case "i"), anyway?

Usually reluctant to speak much about his personal life, James Redfield wove telling childhood memories into our conversations about the role of the afterlife/pre-life dimension, the environment, our individual spiritual journeys and his own.

The conversations here in Part Two are drawn from conversations with James Redfield between the fall of 1994 and the winter of 1999. Shortly after we concluded this first round of conversations, presented in Part One, and just before we began these, Redfield asked me to appear on *Oprah* as part of a panel discussing the impact of the current wave of interest in spirituality, consciousness, personal growth and metaphysics. The panel, which included journalists and members of the healing arts and spiritual fields, opened the program in discussion with Oprah. Her in-studio interviews with James Redfield and authors Dannion Brinkley (*Saved by the Light, At Peace in the Light*), Thomas Moore (*Care of the Soul*), and others, followed. The program aired on October 28, 1994. In our conversations, Redfield also talks about what he learned upon first meeting these colleagues.

After the publication of *The Tenth Insight*, we continued to speak regularly to discuss not only the ideas he presents in his work, but also his continued projects.

ᘓᘓᘓ

The Tenth Insight delves into other dimensions. Why?

It has to do with an exploration of what might be called the Fourth Spatial Dimension, or the afterlife dimension, over there where people also have Near Death Experiences. It has to do with the culture of the pre- and afterlife dimension. That gives us insight into what's going on here, about the path of evolution we're taking here in this dimension as it relates to what's already happening over there.

How did you research this from both a scientific and a spiritual point of view?

Much of my research happens in a meditative state. A lot of information comes to me in what I would call visions, pictures of information. What I think is important is that we start to pull together things from other informational sources, like Near Death Experiences and Out-of-Body Experiences. Robert Monroe's (founder of The Monroe Institute and author) work is right on the frontier in terms of what one encounters out-of-body and the other dimensions one has access to.

Do you think the afterlife dimension is in the neighborhood of, or the same dimension people go, when they're having an Out-of-Body Experience?

Oh, it's exactly the same. Of course, there are vast reaches in this dimension.

There are different levels.

You shift into that dimension and you're right here on Earth, but you can also go to other places, into other regions that seem more purely spiritual and less physical.

31

So, the place where you go when you're having a Near Death Experience is a very different level of that dimension than someone might visit when they're having an Out-of Body Experience or they're meditating.

> *If you compare the literature, the difference is that an Out-of-Body Experience is more conscious, much more controlled, or can be, and in the Near Death Experience you're just sort of sucked into this other place all of a sudden.*

Where the other folks are the ones in control.

> *That's right. And then it's a matter of trying to figure out what's going on. It's obvious that we're met by guides in both instances, and we then begin the exploration of that culture, in terms of trying to make sense of where we are and what the game plan's all about.*

What have your experiences been in this other dimension?

> *My experiences have been as a witness more than as a traveler.*

Whose traveling are you witnessing?

> *Lots of traveling by many other people, and I seem to be getting a picture, like a clairvoyant view through a window.*

When you're in a meditative state, an altered state, what you're seeing is the doings of other people, rather than traveling yourself?

> *That's right. It's almost the same thing, but I'm vicariously there.*

Chicken! It's like you're staying home reading a travel guide while the other guy gets on the plane!

(He laughs) *It's more like I'm a fly on the wall.*

Who are the people whose experiences you're seeing? Do you know them?

Not really. I'm getting a snapshot of the culture in different ways. The thing about my work is that I have to pull it all together from my own experiences, and much of my role is looking at other people's descriptions and pulling it together into a clear framework.

So, in a sense you're a messenger.

Yes, and a popularizer in a sense. I take all this information and make it palatable and understandable to a wider audience.

In your experiences, you've had a glimpse into this other dimension. What's this place look like?

(He laughs)

Why the Halloween giggle that sounds like it's out of a Stephen King movie?

(He continues to laugh)

What have you seen over there that you don't want to tell me about?

I'm not going to tell you everything I know. (He continues to laugh). *I think the most interesting aspect of that culture is that most of what's going on over there is focused on what we're doing over* here.

They're monitoring us?

More than that. They're sort of identifying with us, and

33

almost put a supreme value on our dimension over their own.

Really? Is that because this is where all the hard work is done?

This is where all the action, fun and adventure and histori-cal importance are being played out.

And we'd tend to think that they're having all the fun over there.

This is the grand panorama.

You mean it doesn't get any better than this?

(He laughs) *I didn't say* that, *it's just that this is where the historical action is. What's most important is what's going on in* our *dimension. Everybody's focused on this dimension to try to make something happen.*

So, are those in the other dimension trying to assist us?

There are different groups. The ones that are most attuned and enlightened and advanced are certainly doing that. They're also working on themselves. And there are other groups that are just half-asleep and in worse shape than we are.

Why is that?

Because free will is operative everywhere, and it's easier to fulfill one's addictive dreams over there. Thought is instant man-ifestation, so you can have whatever you want. And if you're addicted to certain things, you can just get that over and over again. And you also get the consequences of the addictions as well. Hell is not a real place. Hell is a state of mind. And if you're in a state where you project awful things or expect awful things then that continues to go on for you over in the other dimension, although there are many people whose mission is to intervene.

So, there are some people over there who still aren't spiritually strong enough to grow, and instead they are as stuck as they were when they were here.

Oh, yes.

But, if they want help, there are people over there who will help them.

That's right. They're more attuned over there to knowing that anybody can "wake up" at any time than we are over here. We're just now getting the spiritual psychology down, to understand that we're all trying to "wake up" and be all we can be and to use our spiritual abilities. But, often we have to do this in a vacuum, by trial and error, because the people who are supposed to be right there to help us along the way are too shy or have something else that's gotten in their way, so they're not taking action. We're just learning that, for example, when we get an intuition to call up an old friend after two years, that that's an important thing to do. That intuition corresponds with that friend's need for us at that moment.

The other dimension is essentially where we are when we're not here. Before we come here and after we leave. How did you first get a glimpse of that place, and by the way, why won't you tell me everything you know?

Well, I don't feel totally confident that I have it fully in perspective. Part of the process of writing The Tenth Insight *is to pull it all together in the kind of picture I want to present, so I don't want to jump the gun there. The images and the picture window view that I get has always been in response to where I am personally in my own development. I started this whole thing from a psychological point of view. I started looking at growth and human potential and all the theories and at who's made the most sense and then integrated the spiritual point of view from spiritual visionaries. In the late '70s when Ruth Montgomery wrote a book in contact with Arthur Ford, a psy-*

chic who had just died, called The World Beyond, *my interest in that other culture over there was sparked. We weren't talking about abstract heaven and abstract hell anymore, we were talking about an afterlife/pre-life dimension in which something was going on. There's still not a lot of information about that except from* Robert Monroe *(of the Monroe Institute) and the* Near Death Experience *books. Part of my work is to make it common sense. We don't have the whole story, in terms of what is a better or fuller way to describe what we're doing here. We're not just growing. What else are we doing? That's what's next. To me, that's the Tenth Insight.*

Many people have had contact with those from the afterlife or pre-life, and a variety of other experiences that reflect deeper levels of consciousness. Maybe many of us have caught a glimpse of that other dimension and don't realize it, or perhaps we don't know what we're looking at. Tell us what the experience is like so we can determine if we've had it or not.

What I'm talking about I've always done. I didn't learn it anywhere. I've been able to tap into a picture window view that represented an answer to my question. I would see scenes and pictures of people who were making growth discoveries of purely a psychological nature when that's all I was curious about. And then I started studying the other dimension and started seeing pictures of that.

What does it look like to you?

A mental picture of scenes and snapshots. I understand what's going on without any dialogue. It's just a clairvoyant kind of thing. I'm seeing things on earth in which everything has a fifth dimensional perception. The thing about the fifth dimension (also referred to as the fourth spatial dimension when time is considered the fourth dimension) *is that it's right here right now.*

Physicists consider light the evidence of the fifth dimension.

Right. And everything is there except for synthetic items. When you create a porch swing out of organic materials, it exists not just in the three dimensions but in the fifth dimension as well. We have an awesome responsibility because we're creating in the fifth dimension as well as the third to a certain degree. Synthetic products can't cross the dimensions. They just don't quite work.

They're not vibrating in a way that allows them to cross over?

No, thank God. We don't have all the pesticides in the fifth dimension that we have here, for instance. When we die, it's like in the movie Ghost. *"Here I am. I'm still here, what's happening?" We're really just right here, because the fifth dimension is right here.*

You must spend a little more time "over there" than most people.

Not really. (He laughs) *I try to live life on the borders of the dimensions because that's where the third dimension becomes the most miraculous and the most beautiful. The only reason we don't look around and remain in constant awe of the incredible beauty of everything around us is because we're dulled out in the third dimension. All it takes is just a little bit of openness to the higher dimensions and you can just sit around and gawk at the incredible light and beauty and shape and form. That's one of the measures of how close we are to raising our vibrations and to another dimension.*

Your task in *The Tenth Insight* is to try to explain this to people and introduce a new vocabulary so they can understand what it's like to experience the fifth dimension.

That's right. It's all contagious in the sense that we have this collective consciousness and the more people get closer to it the easier it is for others to start to experience it and the better our vocabulary about it becomes, so that it becomes part of our everyday common sense experience and that's the sort of social evolution that comes from the daily dialogue we have with each other. Beauty and love just need to be clarified and described and told in biographical sketches so that we get more and more comfortable and affirmed by the dialogue and by the common sense. And that's what's happening out there. My role is just to create a new picture of life in which spiritual issues and spiritual descriptions are more talked about and valued. The short answer is I come back and forth just like everybody else and I struggle to stay in the higher spheres just like everybody else. I'm trying to make sense of it and describe it in a way that makes sense to others.

There are a number of ways to experience the higher dimensions and you experience it in a visual sense when you meditate, and others can tap into it in an energy sense, a psychic sense, a feeling level.

It has impact on all levels of experience. What we're doing is trying to map out all the barometers of this level of consciousness. For some a deeper level of connectedness is their ticket in. All the mystics talk about a deeper level of connectedness, but they also talk about a sense of expanded beauty, love, euphoria and creativity.

It's like living a double life. Some of us can live one life on this level and then you have all the practical things that require you to change gears in your head.

I think that where we're headed is where we don't have to change gears to deal with the practical aspects of life.

So, we're moving to a time when we'll all be more deeply connected so there's no gear-changing required when dealing with each other.

That's right. It's also about being able to say what you mean no matter who's listening, and that can still be intimidating now. None of us can do that all the time yet.

38

The Celestine Prophecy touched the mainstream and opened a door for people who ordinarily wouldn't have felt comfortable talking about all of this.

> *And they still don't know what to do with it, many of them, but I think that it's happening on the level of cellular memory. People read it and like it and don't know why they like it. They've never liked anything like that before. It was time for it. In the sense that it was given to me, it represents something archetypically that rings true for all of us in this historical time. I don't take credit for that, but it is very interesting to watch!*

Certainly your personal evolution continues, so what have you learned recently? What are some of the messages you've been given by the people you've met?

> *What I've learned more than anything is that we're all evolving, that even the worst sort of polluting chemical company you can think of has in place people ready to shift that company into a more positive direction. That there are no enemies at any level, there are just people who are afraid. That it's more important than ever not to meet conflict with conflict. Criticizing someone does nothing more than send an energy out to them that makes them more defensive, less secure and more apt to keep on doing what it is you're criticizing.*

We're just now seeing it working.

> *That's right. We're just now putting it into practice. It's difficult because we need to be very careful of even the most humorous criticisms we make of people. It has psychological impact. What I've learned is that at our level of spiritual power, thought is creativity in a much greater sense than we ever envisioned. When you send positive energy to everyone, and interpret everything in your life as having a positive message, it turns negativity around. One of the things I do in* The Tenth Insight *is show the people in the other dimension who are caught in this web of*

"expecting the worst so the worst comes and then they expect the worst again," that you have to break the cycle.

People think that expecting the worst is a wise thing to do, so they'll be prepared or won't be disappointed.

They've got it backwards.

It's been said that we teach what we most need to learn, so because you're teaching these principles they must be what you need to reinforce for yourself.

(He laughs) There's no doubt about it! I've known for a long time that a positive viewpoint works and I've been practicing that, but what's happening to me now is that I have almost instant manifestation, so I've got to be very careful! Until we use our power correctly, we're not going to be able to master it. The greatest power comes from good, and from the wise use of the power to manifest.

When you appeared on *Oprah* in the fall of 1994, you met Dannion Brinkley, Thomas Moore and Marlo Morgan, all authors of successful spiritual books. At this meeting of the minds, what did you learn?

Whenever you meet people who are well known, you come away thinking, "Well, they're just ordinary folks like me!" But, they're especially grounded and centered or they wouldn't be doing what they're doing. They all have messages, yet they all respect the messages of other people. They're not just "preaching," they're learning. They're open to broadening their views, and that's the profile of the spiritual person. We have to be totally committed to our messages and our mission, but at the same time be willing to amend them in the face of new information. We had an instant camaraderie. Dannion is very outspoken and carries himself with a sense of urgency. That was a message to me because I'd been thinking about doing benefit lectures and meeting him put a little more energy into the urgency for that.

Dannion, a man who's been struck by lightning, realizes that your life can change in one moment and you really can't waste time.

That's right. From Thomas it was a message for me not to neglect the little soul grooming that you need to do, the small things. Sit in a rocking chair and have a decent conversation. That's the best thing you can do for the world and your soul. Marlo really impressed me with how fully she came from the heart.

How has your life changed since *The Celestine Prophecy* became a bestseller?

It hasn't that much. What I need in order to stay creative and centered is a certain amount of distance from the crowd. You cease to be your best self if you're running too fast.

You've become active in environmental issues and encourage people to join watchdog groups to monitor polluters.

The government's never been very effective in preventing pollution or in cleaning it up.

Do you really think they want to?

I think they kind of want to, but all the power games and bureaucracy come into play and scratching the backs of campaign supporters, so no matter how socially conscious they profess to be they always pay somebody back. The recent environmental superfund that was supposed to be used to clean up toxic dumps — all the money has been spent in litigation, spent on attorneys for both sides.

They also aren't keen on requiring businesses to spend the extra money to do things in a way that's friendlier to the environment.

Sure, and some of that is hard to pull off. Government can't do it. They're just a bunch of bureaucrats going through their day and too often they do as little as possible. So, non-bureaucrats, people as individuals, need to get involved with the environmental problem. As government shrinks, more and more groups will form to do the watchdog function, the monitoring of businesses. I'd like to see more grassroots groups form in the inner city, too. Government also can't break the cycle of poverty. All they do is throw money at it and in fact reinforce it.

Also, the haves like it a little better when there are some have-nots out there.

Mostly people just want to forget about it and hope that somebody else will deal with the problem. And if they can think that government is dealing with it, then they don't get involved.

We don't really have a lot of work for people to do in this country anymore. Not much is manufactured here anymore. We use cheap labor overseas instead.

There are plenty of jobs out there that haven't been created yet. We live in the Information Age now. Very few people (in the future) will be in the business of manufacturing. People will be in the business of providing information to other people. It's a motivation and education problem. Everybody, no matter where they are, if they're motivated, can begin to educate themselves and find a niche in which they're valuable.

In *The Tenth Insight*, you address the environment, which is linked to spirituality.

As we increase our awareness in the physical dimension, we have to assume more and more responsibility for creating the future, for envisioning the future and having it be a self-fulfilling prophecy. The Tenth Insight is all about understanding the afterlife dimension and how the shift in energy is occurring and coming into the physical dimension, and how we can "awaken"

42

No, I never felt that way.

You didn't? You liked it here?

Oh, yea, I loved it and I was perfectly enthused and over-joyed about being here, like this was going to be great fun. Of course, I had my share of trauma in childhood, but not over-whelmingly so.

Not any more than the usual ups and downs.

Yeah. I recognized everything early on as being kind of a preparation.

Where did you fit into the scheme of things in your family?

I have one older sister who was very supportive. I think I got along with my sister very well. And I was born into an extend-ed family. I had a grandmother and grandfather right next door and an aunt and uncle in the backyard (we laugh).

This is *The Waltons.*

Exactly. It was a compound, it was Walton's Mountain. But it was not nearly as free of conflict as the more idyllic television program.

It was just you and your sister.

She's a hospice nurse now.

Both of you went into a healing direction. Why do you think that happened?

I think it was the influence of my aunt and uncle, who were very religious, and my mother, who was very, very spiritual. Her influence very early was that life is about finding some way to make the world better. And I think that rubbed off on both of us.

And how about your dad?

Dad was a cowboy who found himself in Alabama and always worked on making it okay within this very rigid Southern culture. He wore his cowboy hat and his boots out on Sunday. He was the rebel. So, I think I got some influence of "you don't have to accept what is" from him. He was an artist, a painter. Both of my parents are deceased. My mother died in 1989, my dad died in 1994.

So he did live to see the success of *The Celestine Prophecy*.

Yeah, but he was in bad shape. He had emphysema, but he certainly knew it was happening. My mother was only about 70 (when she died) and my father was 74 (when he died). They were both relatively young.

In your astral travels, do you run into them?

Not really. I get little sneak peeks. I don't get enough aware- ness over there to pick out particular individuals personal to me.

Do your parents come to you in dreams?

I do dream about them and daydream about them. I'll see them in a situation in a daydream that usually has a message of some sort.

What do you feel was your father's impact on you as an artist?

As an artist probably "follow your own path and don't let the cultural restrictions around you hamper your creativity."

Do you have a lot of his paintings?

*I don't have a lot of them. I have a few that I treasure great-
ly. Toward the end of his life he'd give them to total strangers* (he
laughs).

Was his work carried in galleries?

*A few. He wasn't wildly successful with that. He ran an art
school. He was a teacher of art more than maybe a successful
painter. But he was very good. He was a colorful, enlightened
realist in his method. Almost all landscapes.*

He didn't paint cowboys?

He did a few horses.

You had good role models for being a spiritual person, a creative
person and for not going along and conforming with whatever was
happening around you.

*There's no doubt about that, and I probably didn't appreci-
ate them enough for that.*

Having spiritual ideas from early childhood on must've made you
want to research this.

*That's right. I didn't want to do anything else. I didn't want
to go to school. I certainly didn't want to* work *for a living* (we
laugh). *I couldn't relate to* that *at all.*

There's a great quote from broadcaster Linda Ellerbee. She says,
"If you don't read, you can't write, and if you can't write you must
work for a living."

*We're all trying to do what we came here to do and not be
channeled into something because it's expedient.*

Or considered practical by society or your parents. If everyone did that we'd have no great painters, no great writers, no great composers, no great scientific thinkers or philosophers.

At least no full-time ones!

That's right — they'd all be doing it on the side. Who were some of your influences when you were young?

You know, that's interesting — I really wasn't learning from any people at an early age. I was wandering around in the woods, alone, sometimes at night, freaking everybody out.

You weren't sacrificing small animals I hope.

No, I skipped that part. But I was certainly totally entranced by the wilderness and the animals you can find in the wilderness. I was a hunter until I actually shot something and that ended that (we laugh). After that I'd just stalk around out there. Early reading was — it's really funny —there was a series of books about a friendly microbe, a bacteria that helps milk turn into cheese, I think, was his claim to fame. This microbe was an adventurer and he was very curious. He'd be on the edge of a glass of milk and somebody would come by with their finger and pick him up and then someone else would swallow him and he'd give these graphic pictures of the inside of the body and he'd be in someone's eye or up in their nose (we laugh) or he'd get passed around and he'd be on a leaf for awhile and an animal would come by and get him and he'd be riding around on an animal. It was fascinating stuff, giving an inside view of the way nature really works, and there was always sort of a mystical flair. So, I think that was one of my earlier models for the wild adventurer looking at the world in a new way.

Were you reading Thoreau?

Not until college did I read a lot of philosophy and then I started to devour the transcendentalists and went through all the comments about the history of philosophy and the philosophers, trying to see what the academic philosophy was all about and if they were talking about anything that people should care about.

Yeah, whether this was all abstract or had a purpose in life. As a kid, when you were pondering the universe, did your family understand what you were doing?

Not really. They were kind of fearful that I was never going to be self-supporting! I was in these Piscean daydreams for hours at a time. It was quite the joke.

Then when you were older you found out that it was called meditation.

(He laughs) *Well, what happened was that I just stayed the path because I really didn't have any choice. I discovered college, which is a great place to hide out. For years, I stayed in a little college town — Auburn — for ten years before I ever ventured out. I was on a quest for self-education. I didn't learn anything in school, but I sure ran into the people and the books that broadened my horizons!*

You ran into catalysts that propelled you on your own self-education. That's what college is best for, isn't it.

That's got to be a theme for the future. The problem isn't education, it's motivating kids to educate themselves. That's an awakening that's much more difficult and happens at a person's own pace.

How have your kids reacted to having you as a dad? You must be different than most dads.

I am and I'm not.

They certainly must feel from you an encouragement to discover who they are.

> *There's no doubt about it. I think they feel supported, they feel they can be anything they want. They've watched me go from this two-bedroom apartment and working very hard to having it pay off.*

They've seen that someone can take ideas and turn that into a line of work.

> *Right. I've tried to figure out what they're about, why they chose me as a father, what they had in mind. I try to talk to them in a way that acknowledges that we're all waking up and that they have to wake up and figure out why they're here, just like everyone else.*

Are they naturally curious the way you were?

> *I think they are. I think that one of them will either be a therapist or a writer and the other one will have something to do with animals. Who knows?*

Are you preparing *The Eleventh Insight*?

> *Yes. It's about an alternative community of people who are trying to live the Insights.*

Almost modeled upon the research communities in *The Celestine Prophecy*?

> *Yes, but less research and more actualization.*

How much was *The Tenth Insight* influenced by world affairs?

> *Oh, just tremendously.*

While you were writing it?

The same thing happened as it did with The Celestine Prophecy — *every time I'd get to a section it's synchronistic to what's going on in the world, and as I'm writing it I'm looking out at the world and wow — I see why this part has to be in here, because the world is putting out all the data that can then be clarified by the Insights. As you read* The Tenth Insight *you see one of the themes is the polarization that's happened: One of the reasons we become aware of our responsibility to create the future is because there's a reaction to the new spirituality made up of some very fearful and controlling people who have their own agenda for the future. There's not a lot of conspiracy theory in it, but that's the implication, which puts the urgency in place that we have to start to very consciously remember the future that we're trying to create there and do the things we need to do to create it.*

And your conclusion is that we can overcome all those negative forces.

Oh, yeah, and I treat it like a minor hindrance, well maybe not minor...

Well, somebody's got to be optimistic because in reality this does not look good and it's going to take something on the order of a massive spiritual energy shift to counteract what's going on out there.

I think that's already happened and all we have to do is focus it. I'll be doing benefit lectures with meditations and what we'll do is visualize the future we want to create. I'll do that to support the book and act in a way the book calls for.

You went to England after *The Celestine Prophecy* was published, and you've been fascinated by the mysterious crop circles there. Where do you think they're coming from?

I think they're dimensional signatures in the same way that the Bermuda Triangle gets out of control and reaches out and surges into the physical dimension.

I call that "Falling Through a Hole in the Script."

(He laughs) I think that's what happens. As the veil gets thinner there will be more of these areas. It comes through as a very high-energy signature with a message, much like a dream. If we can interpret some of those symbols there's some truth there.

Is it someone trying to communicate with us from another dimension, like we might try to communicate with other life in the cosmos, for example, by using radio wave signals?

Possibly, but I think it might be more structural than a group of souls would do.

You mean less like a specific message and more like leaving a calling card?

Yeah, even less than that. If we're talking about the veil falling between the two dimensions it may not fall all the way, it may just have little holes in it now.

Why can't anyone actually see these crop circles being created?

I think that they're instantaneous, that they're beyond time, so that in a blink of an eye they're there.

Which would be perfectly plausible if it's interdimensional.

Sure.

What recently has caught your attention?

The thing that continually fascinates me is how human evolution sings its own theme song. As we're awakening to our own sense of mission, all these tragic things are happening. And what comes out is that there are people who failed to act who could have stopped what happened. I think it's part of the message we're getting. People can't quite "wake up" all the way yet, but they can say, "Look at all these people who knew that Nicole was in trouble!" (regarding the O.J. Simpson murder trial) And sometimes people will come forward and say, "If I'd just taken Nicole over to this (support) group and gotten her involved, maybe this wouldn't have been played out." The same with O.J. There are reports about people who knew what was happening and didn't take action. And with the bombing in Oklahoma City, there were a bunch of reports about people who knew and didn't do anything about it, and there was another event recently where that happened...

There were reports that some people knew about the assassination of (Israeli leader) Rabin before it happened and didn't do anything about it.

That's what it was, and the fact that they even warned the secret police. (In all of these instances) there were people who could've stopped it and didn't. My theme in The Tenth Insight *is that for instance, there's no piece of ground anywhere on this planet that someone's dumping pollution in that somebody else doesn't know about it.*

Do you feel overwhelmed by people's expectations of you now?

I isolate myself so well that I don't even think about it. It's probably a defense mechanism that's working really well (he laughs).

Until you open all your mail, or your staff does.

It's at the level of 200-300 a day.

I know you don't have the time to read all of it, nobody would, but there must be wonderful things in there.

I'm sure. Occasionally I'll reach in and pull some letters out of the file.

What do you find?

> *Different things. Mostly "thanks for the book, and this is my story." Sometimes it's "Let's you and I do this project." Or "This is what you should write next," or* (he laughs) *"This is what you should've written."*

These people have been moved and motivated and now want to do something. Do you have the folks who open your mail sort these into categories? I mean, talk about the basis for a grassroots move-ment...you've got all these people in your mail bin poised and ready for action.

> *Then they need to look into their souls for that. I'm not the one to tell them what to do. I don't want to be.*

And in the newsletter you used to publish, which is now part of your website, they can look in the calendar and see all of the things they can participate in across the country.

> *Right. All along I've made it very plain that I didn't want to be the symbol or clearinghouse for all of this, that it was very important to me that it stay grassroots and that people who are moved to do something go out and do that with other people they synchronistically run into, not to look to me to help set that direction.*

Your whole message in all of your books is that people have to rely on what's inside of themselves. And you've stood by that. I would imagine that also keeps the criticism down.

> *I haven't heard much. The academics thought* The Celestine Prophecy *was clumsily written and all that.*

They'll say that about anything that sells a lot of copies.

(We laugh) *I know, and the spiritual elitists have said it's okay but soft-core.*

I've heard it called "Spirituality 101," but that's okay because someone has to put this stuff out for the mainstream.

Well, it is okay, but I also retort though that I wrote it for the spiritual leaders on the planet who think they know it all. Because in The Celestine Prophecy, *is an interpersonal ethic — the Eighth Insight — and it's something that the greatest gurus in the world don't practice.*

That's true. There's still all the power-play garbage going on.

That's right. No matter where you are. After attending enough conferences and being rudely treated by some of the "gurus," I realized that talking this is one thing, but we're not going to be able to live it until there's a new ethic that emerges in terms of the way information is exchanged with people.

Some of these egos getting in the way of people walking their talk.

Oh, yea, it's just like someone who wants to give to the poor, but doesn't see the world as they run around collecting money.

It's like the socialite who would never have any of these people in her home, but is out there raising money for them.

Yeah, exactly.

During the writing of *The Tenth Insight*, how do you think you've grown?

I guess writing is growth always. I've moved into another perspective of fuller awareness. I feel like the Insights are all coming to us at the same time and it's my way of personally coming to grips with the Insights.

Are the rumors still floating around that there really are ancient manuscripts of some kind out there?

Every day.

Do you put any stock in these rumors?

Sure. I think there are plenty of documents out there that reinforce the awakening that's happening on the planet. I don't think there's anything that's saying exactly what I'm saying because what I write is intuitive. It's something coming into our memories archetypically. But there's plenty of information that's starting to be found out there.

Two

Deepak Chopra

Nothing can bring you peace but yourself.

— Ralph Waldo Emerson

*Y*ou can sum up Deepak Chopra's life's work and beliefs in just two words, and he believes that these two words express it all so well that he even named his education company after them: *infinite possibilities.*

He speaks and writes about the universe's infinite possibilities whether he's in the role of physician, poet or philosophy educator. The theme is his passion as well as his explanation for life as we know it and *could* know it.

He draws upon the Hindu philosophy of his native India, as well as Celtic and other Western traditions, all of which he was first exposed to growing up in India, the son of a doctor.

Young Deepak wanted to be a doctor, too, but he loved literature, poetry and philosophy and also wanted to be a writer.

He chose medicine, and probably couldn't have foreseen that one day he'd become first a highly respected endocrinologist and Chief of Staff at Boston Regional Medical Center, then create the Chopra Center for Well-Being in La Jolla, California after he'd become a best-selling author many times over.

He's written more than 20 books, including the best-sellers *Perfect Health, Ageless Body, Timeless Mind; The Seven Spiritual Laws of Success; The Way of the Wizard;* and *The Path to Love.* He's been published on every continent, in dozens of languages, and ten million copies of his books have been sold in English alone. He's put out more than 30 audio, video and CD-ROM programs, and his PBS televised lecture specials, *Body Mind and Soul: The Mystery and the Magic, The Way of the Wizard, Alchemy,* and *The Crystal Cave* have been among the public television network's most highly viewed ever.

He's as well known for being a pioneer in mind-body medicine as he is for his writings about the wisdom of both the East and the West. He created his educational company, Infinite Possibilities, Inc., in order to present workshops to the general public worldwide (as well as accredited training sessions for health care professionals) on aspects of mind-body medicine, meditation, and spiritual awareness.

All of this has led to criticism that Deepak Chopra is too much of a commercial enterprise. He answers his critics in our conversation, and adds that he sees himself and his purpose in very simple terms.

"I want to make knowledge available to people who want it," he says.

When the U.S. government decided to fund research into alternative medicine, they created the Office of Alternative Medicine division of the National Institutes of Health (NIH), and invited Deepak Chopra, M.D. to join their Ad Hoc Panel on Alternative Medicine, a distinguished group convened to consult on research recommendations that launched the division in 1992. Five years earlier, he'd returned from a trip to India, where he'd been introduced to the intensive study of Ayurveda, the ancient mind-body medicine tradition of India. He went on to become the Founding President of the American Association of Ayurvedic Medicine, and served as the Director of an Ayurvedic health center near Boston while still maintaining his regular medical practice as an endocrinologist. He coined the term "quantum healing" to describe the underlying levels at which the mind and body interact to produce disease and trigger healing, and joined the ranks of the pioneers of mind-body medicine with a series of critically well-received books on the subject through the early 1990s, then widening his scope throughout the rest of the '90s to include books and lectures on spiritual philosophies and the bridge between science and spirit.

The accessibility of his message reached right to the boardrooms of top corporations whose leaders reported that they were profoundly influenced by his breakthrough book *The Seven Spiritual Laws of Success*, which had just as long a run on the business best-seller lists as it did on the general ones.

Deepak Chopra is one of the most articulate people I've ever interviewed, and one of the most prolific. He's a veritable idea factory, and gives full play to all of his creative and philosophical musings, which is how he can be involved in so many projects at once. For him, sticking his neck out to follow an idea to it's logical published or presented conclusion is not only the norm, it's in keeping with his belief in "infinite possibilities." If there were 48 hours in a day, he wouldn't run out of possible projects.

I first interviewed him in 1993 for a series of articles on alternative medicine that I wrote for *Body, Mind & Spirit* magazine. Then, in the fall of 1995, while I was writing *Purify Your Body: Natural*

Remedies for Detoxing from 50 Everyday Situations, my book's publisher, Crown, which also publishes Chopra, decided to publish a monthly newsletter, *Deepak Chropra's Infinite Possibilities* and asked me to help create the publication. For the next 18 months, as *Infinite Possibilities'* Founding Editor, I worked closely with Chopra on the first eight issues. During that time, Chopra and I also spoke about healing, metaphysics, philosophy and human potential in other conversations whose contents were *not* for use in the newsletter. The conversation presented here was one such conversation, and took pace in the spring of 1996 while he was writing his best-seller *The Path to Love* and pondering the nature of human relationships.

As you'll see here, he has a dry wit, the naturally patient instincts of a good teacher, and the kind of unbridled inquisitiveness that most people lose as adults. Chopra, however, manages to maintain a balance between the responsible groundedness that one would expect from a gifted physician, educator and businessman and the wide-eyed glee inherent in the spirits of curious and thoughtful children as well as all those who give free reign to their creative or artistic expressions.

❧ ☙

Why did you decide to write a book about romantic relationships and spirituality?

You look around and see that people are struggling with that. We need to have a deeper look at this subject. I see good books, like Men Are From Mars, Women Are From Venus, *that are psychologically based, but not spiritually based. That's something that needs to be explored from a spiritual point of view.*

People talk a lot about their karma in relationships. What's your take on karma?

Karma is not linear. It's much more complex than we've thought it to be. Because if every event leads to every other event, then every event has infinite versions and it takes the entire universe to conspire to create every event in my life. Now, that's an awesome thought.

Yes, and we all run around thinking the universe doesn't take notice of us.

Yes, and here I am participating in it by the choices I make. As soon as I make a choice, any choice, I introduce an event line in the web of infinity. And that event line is not a linear event line because there are so many things that are going to influence it. In fact, the entire universe. I was thinking yesterday just how miraculous this is. To go off the beaten path here...you know, you have two parents, four grandparents, eight great-grandparents, sixteen great-great-grandparents. If you go back 40 generations, it adds up to a few million ancestors. That's just 40 generations, which is not a long time, you know. If one of them had been missing out of that few million, you wouldn't be here (we laugh), and we wouldn't be having this conversation. It literally takes the entire universe for us to have this conversation.

And it takes the entire universe to conspire, in a sense, to even affect you getting in to the car and driving to the store.

Or just making a phone call. Yes, it does,. And, yet, there is free choice in this infinity of space time events that are all happening simultaneously. My choice influences the entire web, you know? So, when I understand the awesome complexity of karma — because karma is this whole process of choice-making — then two things happen, which I'm going to write about in the future in detail: one is that when you really, really begin to understand this, you'll begin to live in a blameless world. You become spontaneously non-judgmental. And, two is that you become so conscious of choice-making that it leads to evolutionary choices.

Do you think it leads to more responsible choices?

Yeah — responsible, evolutionary, life enhancing.

Because you know there are going to be very direct effects.

Every electron that vibrates — the universe is gonna shake! You'd better be careful! (We laugh.)

Of course, there are a lot of people out there who might be paralyzed by that thought, and might say: "Well, I'm not leaving my house today!"

I would be so awesomely struck by the power inherent in my choices.

Do you often look back on the timeline of your life, your karma — the domino effect?

No, it's too complex. And it's not dominoes.

Because it's also going sideways at the same time it's going forward.

It's sideways, upwards, backwards, everywhere.

When people aren't used to thinking this way, it's encouraging for them to take a look at how this affects their lives.

And this leads them to learn about surrender and trust and non-judgment. They all come from this, too. It doesn't come by saying, "Oh, I'm gonna surrender," or "Oh, I'm gonna trust," or "Oh, I'm gonna not judge."

What does it come from, then?

It comes from understanding. It's insight, changing the perception of who you are, changing the perception of what the world is — because it's an extension of who you are — and then they lead you to automatically change your behavior. And change your experience.

Even though sometimes people may interpret karma in a way that makes them believe that things are out of their control, at the same time you can say that karma means you can create your own reality because your choices are so powerful.

Oh, yes. Vivekananda said it's the ultimate affirmation of free will because you realize that you're the creator of the universe. It takes the entire universe to conspire to create every event, and every event conspires to create the whole universe.

And you do have an active role in all this because you're the one making the choices. We often say, "That was fate, that was out of my control." Well, no it wasn't because ultimately you made a choice that set that into motion.

Right.

You get a lot of letters, hear from so many people who've read your books, seen your PBS specials, gone to your lectures and workshops. So many of these people are from the mainstream now. Are we evolving?

Yes. The mainstream, the corporate world — they're getting involved in The Seven Spiritual Laws of Success.

That book was a big business bestseller.

And it still is.

What's the feedback been from business and corporate people?

That they're practicing it, that they're making it part of their corporate ritual, their corporate culture.

Does that surprise you — their willingness to give up some of their external power plays?

It did in the beginning, but I also think it's practical. It'll make for better, healthier corporations. We're going through a process in our own company, IPI, where we're seeing to it that we're collectively aligned to our mission statement. Our mission is basically to make self-knowledge available to as many people in the world, at a grassroots level, through as many outlets as possible, whether it's entertainment, non-fiction, fiction interactive media, a website, or whatever. Our goal is to make self-knowledge the most important knowledge in the world, and to ultimately bring about a paradigm shift in global consciousness so that this really becomes the most important thing in people's lives. So they can know who they are, or at least know more about themselves than anything else. Because the world they experience is going to be an extension of what they know about themselves.

What we've done at IPI is have everybody doing meditation twice a day, on company time, morning and evening. That's how we start the day, and that's how we end the day. And when we have a board meeting or something, we always start it with meditation. Group meditation. And at the end of the meditation, we also go over the Spiritual Law of the day so that we're consciously practicing the Seven Spiritual Laws. Today is the Law of Karma, by the way, so it's interesting that we should be talking about that. And another thing we're doing is taking weekend retreats several times a year as a group to discuss our spiritual insights. We want to make sure that we become the expression of the harmony and the peace and the self-knowledge that we're talking about.

Each day everyone at IPI studies a different one of the seven spiritual laws?

We start with Sunday, with the first law, The Law of Pure Potentiality.

And you just keep going week after week, repeating the seven.

The more you do it, the more it becomes a part of your life, and you also see the infinite possibilities inherent in each Law.

Does anything surprise you anymore?

Yeah!

Yeah? Like what?

Like, I'm alive.

Like, you're alive *(we laugh)*. Why, were you worried you wouldn't be?

No, it's just the miracle of being alive. I don't think you can get used to that. You breathe, you take in oxygen and it becomes hemoglobin in your body. That's amazing.

I think there are certain times that people just naturally tend to take stock of certain things in their life. And yesterday I turned 40, so that was one of those days. I looked around, and looked at all the things I thought I would do by the time I was 40, and where I thought

I would be, and what was important to me, and I think it's natural for us to do that at certain times, but what your book, *The Seven Spiritual Laws of Success*, makes us do is live that every day.

Yes.

To do a daily evaluation...

Right.

And not wait until milestone birthdays, anniversaries or other events.

It's good to say that.

Eventually we'll make that evolutionary leap and automatically practice this.

Yeah, but for the moment we need to put our attention on it.

Until it becomes second nature. Do you find that the corporate people are catching on pretty quickly?

Yes, yes. I was talking with some corporate people recently who want to create a coffee house that would be what coffee houses traditionally used to be — places where not only coffee was brewed, but where people from the art world, artists, playwrights, journalists, and politicians gathered to have intellectual discourse. Of course, we have a romantic notion that we can restore that, and we probably can't, but we can create a new version. A place where there's not just coffee, but learning and entertainment and discourse and enlightenment.

A place that encourages ideas.

And that's a shift in corporate consciousness, for sure.

That's the relationship between corporate culture and the consumer. And to get back to where we began this conversation, about your interest in addressing the spiritual aspects of our *personal* relationships, in particular our romantic ones, what are the most important components in that and how can we make the shift to thinking about our relationships more as spiritual expressions?

The first thing is to recognize that life is relationship, and we are a set of relationships. Even on a quantum level — there is no such thing as a particle. A particle, which is a basic unit of matter, is actually a web of relationships. Mathematical ghosts relating to each other, creating the appearance of matter. Matter itself is an expression of relationship. So, we are here because of relationship. As I said before, if you go back 40 generations we have 7 million ancestors, and if one of those, one guy in the primordial forest didn't have a gleam in his eye on one particular frosty morning, you or I wouldn't be here. Every relationship we have, at any particular time in our life, is precisely what we need at that particular time in our life to take us to another level of awareness. So, if we participate in relationships consciously, we can use every relationship, whether we interpret it as good or bad, to take us to the next stage of our own evolution. Relationship is an expression of who we are at that point in time. Totally and completely.

If we understand that we are holograms of the universe, we must recognize that all the qualities inherent in any relationship are also part of our own psyche. One of the best ways to understand our relationship is to examine both your social self and your so-called shadow self. Spirituality is not about moral, self-righteous behavior. Spirituality is about getting in touch with reality. And a part of reality is the fact that we're all the same, all the same, with very minor differences. Even very minor differences between the saint and the sinner. We are a conglomeration of ambiguities. When we are honest with ourselves, with no melodrama, we become spontaneously less judgmental. And then we spontaneously become more forgiving. And that leads us to spontaneously allow love to happen. If you don't deal with your emotions as they happen, they build up over a period of time. With painful emotions, they build up into remembered pain, and that manifests as anger and hostility.

And disease.

Yes, and disease. Anticipated pain manifests as fear and anxiety. Pain that you redirect within yourself manifests as guilt. And the depletion of energy as a result of all of these manifests as depression. If you take responsibility for pain, witness it, express it, release it and share it, you don't build that toxicity of remembered and anticipated pain and redirected pain. Relationships go through so many stages. Fantasy, reality, disenchantment. But you can transmute the disenchantment into real romance.

Provided you're compatible with that person in the first place. So often, the fantasy wears off and you take a look at the real person and that's when you decide, "Is this someone I want to be with?"

Yes, at that point you need to do that. Ecstasy is a primordial energy state, and ecstasy is not the end point but the beginning point of a new phase of your evolution.

You hear people who've had a Near Death Experience talk about what it feels like to be "in the light." And that same feeling happens between two people who have a very strong spiritual bond. They'll feel "in the light" when they're in the company of that person, and it's especially heightened when they're making love.

That's the whole idea of the gateway to universal love.

It's very hard to describe this feeling. I've found that the people who can explain it best are those who've been "dead," who've come back after Near Death Experiences. And even they have a hard time coming up with the words that can express to others what this feels like. That's just one of the ways of being "in the light." That's the ecstasy you're talking about.

Right, right.

It's what everybody searches for and few people find.

Right.

Probably because they're not approaching it from a spiritual perspective but only from a physical perspective, and they're with all the wrong people.

> *Right. Love is very confusing as an experience for most people. And yet, we know that all human beings need to love and to be loved. A baby will survive if it's fed and protected, but it will not properly grow and thrive without the nourishment of this abstract force which we call love. And that holds true throughout life. Let all of the other conditions of survival be secure, such as food and shelter and money, and the human spirit will wither in the absence of love. Therefore, one would think that we all know a great deal about this basic need of ours, but everyone knows this isn't the case. Love remains mysterious. Many people spend their whole lives without experiencing anything like the love they need. Relationships come and go. This is more true today than ever before.*

Relationships seem to be a place where we learn more about ourselves than any other area of our lives. Why do you think that is?

> *Because we are nothing other than relationship. We are a set of relationships. Our essential nature is that we're born of relationship. Without relationship we are extinct. It's what we thrive on.*

Do you subscribe to the theory of soulmates?

> *Not in the way that everybody else does. Because I believe*

72

that relationship is meant to take you from one level of evolution to the next. And having a soulmate would imply that you and this so-called soulmate are exactly at the same level of evolution and are also evolving at the same rate.

We know that's not true *(we laugh).*

Yeah.

Many people believe that love and romance is such a mirror for us, and changes our lives so much because we're going through something with this predestined person, this soulmate, or number of soulmates, and that those are the people we will have our greatest lessons with.

I think we have lessons with every encounter that we have, not just with someone special. And the more turbulent the encounter, the bigger the lesson. But there are lessons no matter what. And these encounters shape us into who we are today. And they aren't always the most pleasant encounters. There are certain principles that I build upon. One is that everything is spirit in disguise. The mind is spirit in disguise, the body is spirit in disguise, the physical world is spirit in disguise, and everybody that we meet is spirit in disguise. Therefore, I think that every relationship is a relationship with the soul. The soul is a ripple in the vast ocean of spirit or consciousness, so the soul has an individuality. No matter how superficial the relationship may appear, there is a karmic connection. There are billions of people on the earth and in any particular lifetime I'll have relationships with a small fragment of them, not with all of them. Any encounter is a relationship. Just the fact that I'm going to have a relationship with a very small fragment of all the people that exist right now means that there's a special karmic bond in every encounter.
If you look at the mechanics of karma — karma means experience and it generates something called memory. I have a cup of coffee, I go to see a concert, or I hear a certain musical note, or I meet someone, that's karma. That generates memory in my

consciousness. Basically, I'm consciousness or spirit. And that memory becomes the basis for desire. And that desire leads to karma, or experience, again because it's desire that motivates experience. In other words, karma, memory and desire are the software of my soul. And if you really look at this very carefully, they're all the same thing because without karma there's no memory, and without memory there's no desire, and without desire there's no karma. So, in seed form they're the same thing. Every thought you have is either a memory or a desire. There are no other kinds of thoughts. You can analyze this forever and you'll see that every thought you have is either a memory or a desire. Or an interpretation or a choice, which are the same as memory and desire. Interpretation is memory and choice is desire. Which means that every thought is spontaneously generated — that's why people who say "think positive thoughts" don't know what they're talking about because you don't consciously choose your thoughts, they come and go based on your past experience.

You can also have thoughts that are fears.

And fear is a memory.

It's a projection of the future based on a memory.

Yeah. And every encounter is generated by these mechanics of memory and desire. And every thought automatically leads to another thought through this association of memory and desire. Which means that the thought you just had was the result of all the other thoughts that you had. So, when you meet somebody, it's been conspired forever (we laugh). *And the whole universe has conspired to create that encounter.*

And people like that notion because it's so romantic — it's destiny.

It's statistical probability (we laugh). *But what I like about that is to me it makes a relationship sacred.* Any *encounter is sacred. It gives a different perspective to the relationship, and if you have that in your awareness you take things with sincerity and with authenticity, with the knowing that every encounter and every relationship is going to start weaving an event line that will extend into eternity. It's marvelous. When I'm lecturing to an audience, or I'm meeting people, or I'm interacting with a group, in my mind there is the awareness that I'm karmically bonded to these people. I have a special relationship to these people at this moment. And that specialness that you hold in your awareness changes the texture of the relationship. It sends signals to the other person on a subconscious level that alter the texture of the relationship. As spiritual beings, each of us is fashioned to be nourished by love, and I don't mean just that emotion we call love, but a universal force that upholds life. And unless love is part of our spiritual journey, we're not experiencing its complete truth. We might say to ourselves, "I'm in love," or "I really feel loved," or "This will only be a superficial experience without the spiritual dimension."*

And how do you define the spiritual dimension of a love relationship? People always analyze the relationship they're in. They ask, "Am I really in love, or is this lust? Is this just like? Do I just like the companionship?"

Do you have attachment? If the answer is yes, then the spiritual dimension is missing in the relationship. If you call someone and they don't return your call and you feel hurt, there's no spiritual dimension because you're just acting out of self-pity and self-importance, not out of love. To be able to truly love you have to be detached. We use the word love to camouflage our fears, our self-pity, and our anxiety about our ego.

If you take a look at some of the characters in literature that have always been portrayed as the greatest lovers, they also seem to be the most attached. Look at Romeo and Juliet — they were quite "attached to the outcome" of their relationship, to the point where if they couldn't be together they didn't want to live. So, we don't have very good role models for what true love is. Our historical and cultural role models are about attachment.

Correct. If I truly love someone, then my only concern is for their happiness and not my self-importance.

But, unfortunately, all the self-help experts tell everyone that this is the definition of co-dependence. They say that if all you care about is the other person's happiness, then you're co-dependent — you're putting their happiness above your own well-being and you're so focused on their happiness that you're not taking care of yourself.

You cannot be intending someone else's happiness unless you're happy yourself. That's a very important thing to recognize.

I happen to agree with you. I'm not bringing this up in order to challenge your concept. I think we're getting so many mixed messages from all of these so-called experts in various fields. And the spiritual idea of unconditional love is that your concern is for the other person's growth, spiritual growth, happiness and well-being.

And you can only have that if you are full in yourself. That's why the key to love is self-knowledge. Here's one sentence that I think holds the key: You know that you are fully experiencing love when you turn into love. So, you cannot give what you don't have. The co-dependence definition is pretty accurate: it's about these miserable people who use another person's happiness to sustain themselves.

They're like parasites.

Yeah, and that's not what we're talking about.

So, I guess what we're dealing with here is the language. There's a fine line.

Right.

Because unconditional love is about putting the other person's well-being out there as your primary concern.

Right.

But, that's also what a co-dependent person might do, too. But they'd be doing it out of neediness.

Yeah. And there is no neediness in true love. See, I think that our limited perception makes us see love as dependent upon out-side influences. Well, not everyone can be in love, or even in a relationship, at any given time. We have demands of life that pull us in different directions that have little to do with our love life. But, spiritually, love is a constant. A cycle of nature that never ceases to influence us.

I think we get bogged down, too, by the language we use. We don't have a very adequate way to describe these things, and it can be misleading.

I think the higher function of love is creativity. Every act of creation is an act of love. And, you know, we tend to limit cre-ation to acts of artistic value or the first creation, when God expressed his divine nature. But, this implies on the one hand that creation is separate from normal life, reserved for the cho-sen few. And on the other hand, that creation occurred only once, causing all mortal acts of creation to pale by comparison. But, I think that every time we create something that every act of creation is an act of love.

People need to be re-educated about what love is, what it feels like, what it isn't, and to bust all the old myths. So, if you were to do that, and to give someone a recipe, what would you tell them is in love?

I would say, first of all, that the very idea of a recipe is abhor-rent to me (we laugh).

What if someone made this salad, and you said, "You're calling this potato salad, but there are no potatoes in it. It's beans and rice." They've got this recipe they've been calling potato salad, but it's really beans and rice. And you say, "Here, let me tell you the components that are actually in potato salad." So, that's what I'm saying: what are the components that are actually in love?

> *I would tell them to step into nature's creative cycle directly from their heart, and see how it's process conforms to the stages of any creative act. There's "conception:" where you unexpectedly fall in love — you don't plan it — and there's the sense that everything old and ordinary in one's life is about to be overturned in favor of the new and extraordinary. So, you have that willingness to step into the new and extraordinary, a place of not knowing. Then there's "gestation:" which is the second phase of any creative act, where you begin to create new and powerful feelings of joy and longing and passion and sweetness. Then there's "delivery:" the birth of love occurs when the inner feelings are shared, the love is declared. And then "growth:" where relationship begins. And finally "maturity." Then, the cycle repeats itself. There is ultimately a beginning, a middle and an end to everything in the relative world, and one should know that, and one should not try to build something that's not true. And then there's renewal. Once the cycle comes to an end, it opens the way for the next — it's the cycle that repeats itself in nature again and again and again and again.*

So, if we want to look for the real components of love, the recipe, so to speak, if we look to nature we will see.

> *Absolutely.*

Because the components of love are the same as the components of creation.

> *Right, even in the longest-lasting love. Even though love remains constant and continues to ripen, the physical aspects of*

love that are dependent upon the body no longer hold. People age, and even though their existence is as one, there's an inward turning for each partner, and then there's death — the breaking of the physical bond inevitably arrives.

Love has its seasons and stages, just like anything else in nature and creation.

Absolutely. There are eleven principles to think about. They give you insights:

1) *Everything is spirit. Whatever you see, hear, touch, taste, smell, it's all spirit, but in different form.*

2) *The whole is contained in every part. By knowing some details, you can understand everything. By knowing your beloved, you can understand everything about life. Relationships are the key to understanding the totality of life.*

3) *Everything is a vibration. All of the emotions — anger, fear and jealousy as well as the higher emotions of compassion, sympathy, kindness — are just different vibrations of consciousness. The key is to be alert to the vibrations you're sending out and the ones you receive. The ones you receive are echoes of the ones you send out.*

4) *Change is the only constant. Whatever is going on in your life, you can be sure of one thing — it's gonna change.*

5) *Each thing contains its opposite. You may have the most exquisite pleasure in a relationship, but pain is also inherent in it.*

6) *Life expresses itself in seasons. Cycles, rhythms, seasons — there's a season for everything, even relationships.*

7) *Every event in any relationship has an infinity of causes and leads to an infinity of effects. So, when we say, "I'm experiencing this because you did that," or "This is happening because of that," it's*

far more than that. It's very complex.

8) *The creative energy of the universe is sexual energy. In every relationship or encounter, that element is always there, even if it does
not express itself. This is something our society has completely
avoided. But, the fact is, it is the primal energy of the universe,
and nothing would be alive without that energy.*

9) *Attention and intention are the keys to transformation. And relationship, too.*

10) *States of awareness project as states of experience. It's not that your
experience creates a certain state of awareness, it's that your states
of awareness create your experiences.*

11) *The core of every being, even the most evil person, is only love.
Even the most evil acts are motivated by love or the need to be
loved.*

To change the subject slightly, it's common practice in this country, unfortunately, that the media build people up so that it can then
tear them down.

Right.

And as soon as someone becomes successful, they're fair game, and
all of a sudden the media picks on you because you're earning money.
This has now happened to you. The media complaining that Deepak's
earning money. Well, how come they're not complaining that the head
of a Fortune 500 company is earning money for his hard work? How
do you answer these people?

*This is how I answer them: I look at the United States econ-
omy, and I see that most of this country's income comes from the
sale of arms and what's called the sale of entertainment in the
world. And what goes by the name entertainment is basically
violence and sex. I don't see anyone being defensive or apologiz-*

ing about that (we laugh).

That' true.

> *I see that there are other economies in the world that their entire income comes from the sale of drugs. I don't see anybody being apologetic about that. I don't see the tobacco industry apologizing or being defensive about making money. I don't see the alcohol industry doing that. I don't see anybody being defensive no matter what they're selling.*

Or these sports guys who make 80 million dollar deals just to speak on behalf of a soft drink or a sneaker. Nobody seems to pick on them. They congratulate them. Yet we pay teachers, educators and others offering information so poorly, and attack them if they do become prosperous.

> *Right, yes. But we're asked to be defensive about selling —— and we are selling —— knowledge that helps people. And they want to buy it. Nobody's forcing them to buy it. We are being asked to be defensive about selling knowledge that motivates and inspires people who want to be motivated and inspired. That, to me, speaks of the psychosis in our psyche as a culture. It's because we are still in our adolescence as a culture. When we become mature, we will realize, I hope, as some ancient traditions and wisdoms did, that philosophers, those that motivate those that inspire, will be the highest paid. And then we will have gone past our collective psychosis. As long as we are defensive about making money from doing good things, we will remain "poor." Poverty is a mental disease. And the very ones who complain about this are the ones who are afraid they're never going to make money. And the very ones who are defensive won't make money because their defensiveness and guilt about making money through helping people will interfere with their ability to do it. Spirit shows promise. In every seed is the promise of thousands of forests. Nature is lush with wealth. Part of this guilt that goes back so many years...*

Comes from the notion that there's something holy about being poor.

Yes. You should quote Oscar Wilde: "There's only one class of people who think more about money than the rich, and it is the poor. In fact, they can think of nothing else. And that is their misery."

He's one of my favorites. I have a quote of his framed and hanging over my desk. As a fellow writer, I think you'll appreciate this. It says: "I've had such a tiring day. This morning I took out a comma, this afternoon I put it back." *(We laugh.)*

He's great. I just did an interview with Time magazine, and the guy asked me, "Are you ambitious? You're very ambitious, you're doing all this stuff." And I said, "Oscar Wilde once said: 'Ambition is the last refuge of the failure.' I'm not ambitious, I'm successful." (We laugh.)

It can be difficult to reconcile the idea of money in our lives. We've been taught a very backwards way of looking at it. We're told to go be ambitious and make a success out of our lives, and then people throw guilt at us if we actually do accomplish our goals.

Yeah, well, basically money is a symbol for wealth consciousness. You can have a lot of money, you can have a billion dollars in the bank, but if you worry about it, you're poor. You can have none, and if you don't think about it, you're wealthy. It's a level of comfort with your own creativity. If you're really wealthy it has nothing to do with money, it means you sense that you can create anything you want. To me, money is an expression of knowledge, of unboundedness, of truth, of abundance, of harmony, of creativity, of flexibility, of transformation, that is inherent in the intelligence of nature. Nature's intelligence is without limits, and that's why we call our company Infinite Possibilities.

Are creation and abundance, or financial security, the same thing?

Exactly the same thing. All you have to do is look at nature and its creativity, and its infinite flexibility, and its ability to create again and again. Like I said, in every seed is the promise of thousands of forests, not one. So, too, in every desire you have is the promise of thousands of manifestations. Inherent in the desire is the ability to manifest anything. And that's why I wrote The Seven Spiritual Laws of Success, *because I believe totally and completely that the only way to create permanent wealth in your life is not though physical means, not through psychological means, but through spiritual means. Because the spirit is that part of your awareness that has no beginning and no ending, and is the source of infinite creativity.*

And when you look at nature, there is no such thing as a poverty-stricken plant.

No.

Or a very wealthy tree.

There are no poor people actually, there are impoverished spirits. That's it.

And people like to keep other people impoverished because that's their way to control them.

Right.

Three

Caroline Myss

*There comes a time when the mind takes a higher
plane of knowledge but can never prove how it got there.
All great discoveries have involved such a leap.*
— Albert Einstein, on intuition

*Everyone who is seriously involved in the pursuit
of science becomes convinced that a Spirit is manifest
in the Laws of the Universe.*
— Albert Einstein

Caroline Myss gave a keynote speech at the 1996 Institute of Noetic Sciences (IONS) annual conference that summed up the topsy-turvy trend of the '90s:

"It takes courage to look at how much we have woven both our culture and our lives around what our roles do for us. Being healthy is very appealing in theory but not in fact, for we can use sickness or a sick situation to gain so much social energy," she said. "Our new language of intimacy is what I call woundology."

The esteemed medical intuitive, lecturer and best-selling author of *Anatomy of the Spirit* (Crown, 1996) and *Why People Don't Heal & How They Can* (Crown, 1997), has also had a successful string of audios and an acclaimed PBS special. She is in demand, quite literally, across the globe, as an educator and speaker, and the wisdom she shared that day at the IONS conference comes from her phrase "your biography becomes your biology," one of the basic tenets of mind-body medicine.

"The idea that biography becomes biology implies that we participate to some degree in the creation of illness. But — and this is a crucial point — we must not abuse this truth by blaming ourselves or any patients for becoming ill. People rarely choose consciously to create an illness. Rather, illnesses develop as a consequence of behavioral patterns and attitudes that we do not realize are biologically toxic until they have already become so," she writes in *Anatomy of the Spirit.*

"I believe the quality of what we invest in emotionally turns around and becomes the quality of our cell tissue," she told the IONS conference audience. "First, we need to identify our wounds, and to 'call our spirit back' from them. Then we need a witness to whom we can say, 'That wound hurt,' and we can say this up to three times. But, by the fourth time we should be told, and we've also got to be able to say to somebody we really love, 'I've witnessed this wound long enough. Knock it off, because at this point it's costing you your cell tissue. You're indulging in self-pity and you're not progressing in your life.' Somehow we have got to recognize that healing is the courage to let go of the wounds. Once we have identified our wounds we need to stop using wound vocabulary. People rarely talk about how good they feel. When they talk about their strengths, their becoming strong is vi the privilege that a wound gave them. We have developed a whole support system around the healing of the pain we encounter on the journey of discovering who we are. This is like taking a boat across the river and forgetting to get off on the other side."

Yes, Caroline Myss doesn't mince words, if I may rely on a tired old cliché. And perhaps that's part of what has made her such a breath of fresh air in an overcrowded field of self-help experts. She is considered a pioneer in the field of energy medicine and human consciousness, but came to the work she does now via a route that took her from a Bachelor's degree in journalism and work as a journalist and publisher to a Master's in theology, reflecting her life-long study of spirituality, and then a Ph.D. in intuition and energy medicine.

With a rate of well over 90 percent accuracy, Dr. Myss can intuitively diagnose anyone, whether she knows them or not, whether they are in the room with her or on the other side of the world. All she needs to be told is their first name, age, and that she has their permission to intuitively "scan" them. She has worked closely with other pioneers, including Dr. C. Norman Shealy, M.D., Ph.D., founder of the American Holistic Medical Association, on whose cases she has consulted since the early 1980s. In 1984, she and the Harvard-trained neurosurgeon formed a partnership to further their research into the stresses that contribute to the creation of disease. Recently, the two founded the Institute for the Science of Medical Intuition.

Although she teaches seminars internationally, and has lectured at universities in the U.S. and abroad, including Oxford, the program at her Institute will focus on the extensive training of both medical intuitives and their teachers.

She is often asked if everyone has the ability to be highly intuitive.

"I offer this analogy to answer that: I can teach anyone to read music, but few people are Chopin," she says. "The essential difference between a strong intuitive and someone who isn't is the health of the ego. If you have a defensive ego, you can't be a clear intuitive because you have too strong an agenda. How could I possibly want to see you clearly if I want to see you in a way that serves my attitude about you? The nature of intuitive sight is dependent upon self-esteem and the refinement of one's ego. I would like everyone to be able to intuitive diagnose, and to also be able to manage their own power so they don't get sick."

Born and raised in Chicago in the 1950s, Caroline (pronounced Carolyn) Myss (pronounced Mace) is the middle child of three. She and her older and younger brothers were raised by a father who worked in banking and a mother who is a homemaker in a close knit family. Caroline was named after her grandmother, whom she describes as "very intuitive."

Growing up, she says, she had "an intuitive bent and natural observational skills. Periodically, I'd have experiences. Just a handful. My gut hunches formed instantly and were accurate. And then this ability 'went to sleep' in my 20s and resurfaced as a mature instrument in my 30s."

By then, she was a working journalist and the co-founder of Stillpoint, a New Hampshire-based health and spirituality book publisher. "My intuitive skills resurfaced, and I found that I could intuitively see the state of someone's health," she recalls. Word spread, and people began to seek her out for readings.

Invitations to lecture and speak at conferences followed. At one such conference she met Dr. Norm Shealy, and their long association began.

"He was interested in medical intuitives. He would call me with a patient in his office. I lived in New Hampshire and he was practicing neurosurgery in Springfield, Missouri. He'd give me the patient's name, age and permission, and I'd intuitively access whatever data I could. The more we worked together, the more the quality of the data matured," she remembers. Before her recent bestsellers, Myss co-authored two books with Shealy, *The Creation of Health: Merging Traditional Medicine with Intuitive Diagnosis* and *AIDS: Passageway to Transformation*.

From 1982 until 1995, Myss regularly did private readings. She now places her focus on teaching people to understand the psychological, emotional and physical reasons why their bodies have developed an illness as well as training others to diagnose intuitively.

"I use the language of energy," she explains. "I'm reading vibrational levels, energetic patterns. When I scan the body, I can intuitively see the energy of illness even before it shows up physically. To sense when something's wrong with someone is a natural part of the human design. What I do is just a little more refined and I have a longer antennae, so to speak. I don't have to be in the room with you to read you."

In her first best-seller, *Anatomy of the Spirit*, she explains the symbolic lessons we are meant to learn from managing the power of our seven energy centers (the chakras), reveals the spiritual and psychological basis of illness, healing and health, and discusses diagnosis though intuitive means.

"Your belief patterns become trapped in the cells of your body," she explains. And five of the biggest misconceptions we have about healing are addressed in her second best-seller, *Why People Don't Heal & How They Can*. "These five are: My life is defined by my wounds, Being healthy means being alone, Feeling pain means being destroyed by pain, All illness is a result of negativity and we are damaged at our core, and True change is impossible. These are myths. One of the biggest handicaps to healing is when we can't forgive. Forgiveness is the road to freedom. It'll heal you, and it's the best thing you can do for yourself," she says.

She goes on to highlight other tips that play crucial roles in her books and lectures. "We have to give up the need to know why things happen as they do," she says strongly. "Life isn't logical. So, we also have to remember to make no judgments and have no specific expectations."

Dr. Caroline Myss brings a fierce independence and low bulls***t threshold to her work, balanced by compassion, ironic wit, and the kind of visionary intelligence that enables her to see even beyond the big picture. I must confess that these are the qualities I most admire and respect, especially in a healer who is not afraid to be direct, to simply say, "Hey, wake up! Look at what you're doing to yourself!" While this method lacks subtlety, it should be noted that subtlety is a useless luxury when matters of life and death are at hand, and this alarm clock approach, tempered with humor, often works wonders. This probably accounts for Dr. Myss's critical acclaim and her success among readers, students and lecture audiences. It also makes for a lively interview, especially when both parties are rather fond of being direct and using humor to make a point.

I first spoke with Caroline Myss in the spring of 1996, about five months before *Anatomy of the Spirit* was published. Crown was also just about to publish my book *Purify Your Body: Natural Remedies for*

Detoxing from 50 Everyday Situations, which followed three months after Myss's book, and I was working on another project with the publisher, a monthly publication, *Deepak Chopra's Infinite Possibilities*, for which I was the founding editor. I interviewed Dr. Myss for that publication, but the material you read here is drawn from *other* extended conversations that took place in both the spring of 1996 and January, 1999. Dr. Caroline Myss is now based in Chicago and is at work on another book.

એ.કૃ

You use the Kabbalah, the chakras and the Sacraments for their symbolism. If you look at any form of religious scripture symbolically, it becomes very valuable. But, if you try to live it literally it actually can become judgmental.

That's right. If you take it literally, it's used as a way to divide your tribe from the other. But when you look at them all symbolically, you realize that they are all identical. And then you see the wisdom in it, and it becomes nothing but a source of empowerment.

People have been taught to view scriptures and religious teachings literally, so they need to re-learn and view them symbolically or mystically.

We've only now been given access to symbolic reasoning. We never had it before. There were two events that brought mysticism into the mainstream. One of my favorite lectures to give is the symbolic or archetypal interpretation of historic events. Let's take this event literally: In the late 1950s, the Chinese invade Tibet. Big deal. The Dalai Lama leaves. Big deal. But, what does that mean symbolically? It means that the mysticism of the East went into the mainstream. And Buddhism went into the mainstream.

It had to leave its formerly protected little environment.

Precisely. Symbolically, it was released into the global brain. What's the counterpart in the Christian tradition? Vatican II. All of a sudden, all of the teachings of Christian mysticism went mainstream. So, all of a sudden, the general population had access, for the first time in our evolutionary history, to the sacred texts and the journey to empowerment. Everything I am teaching now was standard knowledge in monasteries. Not in convents, not in priesthoods, but with the mystics. In the mystical traditions this is all well known. Not in the language we're using, because we're using psychological therapeutic language as mystical sub-text, and therapists are surrogate spiritual directors. What has symbolically happened is that all of a sudden the rich journeys that one would once upon a time have to be a hermit to discover, we are now doing full time while holding jobs.

Yeah, no one's a professional mystic anymore. You're a mystic and an accountant.

That's right (we laugh)! So, all of a sudden, these incredible teachings are available to us. Some of us look back and say, "you didn't teach us that!" That's because (until these past few decades) it wasn't permitted to be taught. We are the generation that's beginning the management of the mystical texts while living full-time in the mainstream. We are that generation.

Where do you see us progressing in our evolution? What's our next evolutionary leap?

Oh, we've got a long way to go before our next one! (we laugh.)

A lot of people think it's right around the corner, as symbolized by the year 2000.

Oh, well, they're crazy. What do you say to people who don't have 2000 on their calendar? Go to China and ask them. (The emphasis on the year 2000) is to me symbolic of the fact that we are in a different energy zone: we are now two energetic cultures simultaneously. There is the energetic culture that is fundamentally five senses, homo sapiens, and then there is homo noeticus, humans of multiple sensory systems. We are in a time when both of us are living simultaneously on the same planet, with two different vocabularies, two different structure systems, and the energetic culture homo noeticus is going to dominate.

So, it's just a matter of time before one gives way to the other, through evolution.

Yes. And what we're looking at is the complete dismantling of the first culture.

And, like previous evolutionary changes in humans, this will take generations before it's completed.

Precisely. Everything that's based on a five-sensory power is being dismantled because it's not working. And everything that's based on multi-sensory power is...

Now beginning to come into its own.

It's beginning to come into its own. Correct.

Maybe this symbolic fascination people have with the year 2000 is just a point where...

The newer energetic culture becomes 51%.

Right. That it's so very noticeable that this evolution's underway, but not that we've hit the peak yet.

That's right. And what does this look like physically? What's going to change? What's going to change is this: everyone around the world has to start using global language, and do global politics, and global reasoning, and global thinking, where the tribe is the planet now. Like it or not. Where we have to admit that we're in this together. We can see it symbolically, and we may like that symbolically, but what does it mean literally? It means that I can't use as much fuel in my tank because of what it does to the air for the rest of the world. It means applying literal global rules to our everyday living environment. What we're going to see over and over again is the failure of ordinary tribal reasoning to manage solutions to what are now global problems. Ordinary tribal reasoning will never work again. There will never be a problem that can be solved by an individual "tribe" making a decision for itself without taking into consideration the consequences in the global arena. Our weapons are global, our crises are global, therefore our solutions have to be global.

How do you do an intuitive medical reading on someone?

When I do a reading on someone I use three levels of sight. I take a look at the archetypal impressions I receive about somebody. For example, I might get a very strong rescuer impression. And the next question I go through in my mind is, "Where does she act this out?" And that brings me into her internal column, and that tells me the way in which she reasons, the way in which she views things, and the types of people she applies the rescuer to, because she doesn't do it all the time. It's very specifically oriented. That tells me how she manages her heart, her emotions, her mind. And that converts to the choices you make — the fifth chakra — and then that tells me what her physical life looks like as a consequence. And, then that tells me where you're losing your power and what part of your body is paying the price.

You're working from the outside in.

Absolutely. And I teach my students how to reason this way so they can look at themselves. I feel it's important for me to teach students to reason on their own, to be able to sense where they're losing their power, and to begin to ask themselves, "Why am I doing this? Where am I losing power? What other choices can I make so that this doesn't happen."

When you start with these archetypes, how do you know which ones to choose from? How many are there? Are there basic ones that we're all going to fit into?

No, no. You want to look at archetypal reasoning. Archetypal reasoning is symbolic thought. Underneath that, we can throw universal archetypal symbols in. If I said to you, "That woman's a natural mother," you'd know exactly what I'm talking about. Everybody would. That's a universal archetype. A warrior is. A hero is. We can take every situation in our life and turn it into an archetypal journey.

So, archetypal reasoning is a level of perception that you can apply to every single situation in your life. I think people can get obsessed with trying to find meaning. People think they're looking for archetypal reasoning when they're really looking for a personal reason as to why things happen as they do. Archetypal reasoning is very detached. It's where you say, "I went through a situation, and it's to teach me something about power." And it's as simple as that. Any culture's mythologies contain the archetypes we're subject to. In Anatomy of the Spirit, *I talk about how the essential language that people need to think in terms of is the management of power. How am I managing power? What is power? Power is your spirit. And that's what I've found so essential to teach people. That no matter what choice you make, no matter what you do, you are acting out a management of power. What do you use as a reference to learn how to manage power? Spirituality. That's what spirituality is all about. It's the management of the power of your own spirit. And I found myself returning to scriptural language to explain this from a symbolic point of view.*

Not a literal one. This isn't about any particular organized religion.

Not a literal one. All of a sudden I saw the scriptural message in a whole new dimension. Instead of it being used as tribal ritual, like the sacrament. I suddenly realized that this was the literal management of power — to keep the person's power within the tribe — versus the symbolic, which is to say to think at a much more sophisticated level, spiritually sophisticated, and that's the message that I put in this book.

And from there people can apply it to the situations in their lives, see where they are leaking power. How do they determine the correspondence between the power leak and the particular part of the body that's affected?

The reading of energy is not a gift, it's a skill. It's a skill that requires a maturation process. And the part of the person that needs to mature is their level of reasoning. Human reasoning is determined to find a specific cause and effect in the immediate moment. It's very challenging for people to understand that the human energy system has all of these energetic functions in all seven chakras simultaneously. And what we need to do is use all seven, all the time, and to reason that way. The only reason people lose power is because they want to control something. It's as simple as that. So, what's your reason for losing control? Fear. Fear of what? Everybody has the same fear: fear of being raped physically, energetically, financially. Fear of not being recognized. You're going to have some level of human fear that deals with being out of power. So, what I teach people is a much more symbolic overview of the management of their spirit, the management of power. And then I take them into how to look at the power significance of the scriptural teachings that told us thousands of years ago that there were seven stages of power that we were going to move through, evolve through. To look at the Christian one, you ask, what is the symbolic meaning of Baptism? From a literal point of view, a tribe gets a new baby and they baptize it, and they say, officially, "This is now one of our members, and we'll raise it according to our traditions." It's very physical, active acceptance of a life. But, from a symbolic point of view, the empowerment of the sacrament of baptism comes when an individual says, "I baptize my family," which means, "I fully accept the family into which I was born, and the whole of the life, environment and learning experience that goes along with it."

It's actually something you do for yourself, rather than them doing to you.

That's right. And think what that does when you can do that. Where are most peoples' crises? They begin with the family, and arguing, and looking for human reasoning as to why they ended up in the "family" they did. And when they can suddenly reach a point in their growth where they can say, "I'm taking my own family too seriously, and too personally. The real test for me is to look at this with gratitude and say symbolically, 'I chose this because it was the best learning environment for my spirit. What am I supposed to learn here? I'm supposed to learn lessons of power. What kind?'" And then you articulate that for yourself. And once you get to that point, all you have left over is appreciation for the souls who, in this lifetime, were the players in your life's drama. And that is the archetypal meaning of baptism. When you look at things symbolically this way, and with the lessons of power, we all go through that. Every one of us goes through the issues of power. It's an illusion that our lives are different. They may look different.

The circumstances may be different, but we're all playing the same game.

The power issues are identical. Baptism corresponds to the first chakra. Then comes the sacrament of Communion, which corresponds to the second chakra. What could be more literal than communion — with union? And the second chakra is the part of our body that we connect one-on-one with. Baptism is tribal, (where our tribe has much power over us) that's the first chakra. And communion, the second chakra, is how to go from fear and trying to control people from that essential fear of having our power taken from us, so that we can get spiritually close with someone in a spiritual union. The third chakra corresponds to Confirmation — to have a personal honor code. If you honor your own honor code your digestive system will get stronger. This honor code you make with yourself, where you say, "This is what I will do; this is what I won't do."

It's a time when you're confirming your beliefs.

That's exactly right. With yourself, symbolically with yourself. And until you are strong enough to do that, your tribe does it for you (confirmation usually comes in the teen years). Then, with confirmation, you begin to make your journey where you say, "Let me make myself. Let me build myself." So, you deconstruct your tribe's honor code, and you make your own. And that's the journey to selfhood. Then comes Marriage, which corresponds to the fourth chakra. What are we symbolically recognizing? That until we can love ourselves, have our own honor code, we virtually cannot love others.

This is why if you marry before you've worked through your "confirmation," no matter at what age it comes, and create this honor code of self-identity, the marriage isn't going to work.

Precisely.

Because you're not really who you're supposed to be yet.

Precisely. If you understand the symbology of what this journey of consciousness is all about, it's about becoming symbolically alive.

I'm sure glad you figured this out.

Yeah, so am I! (we laugh.) From the fourth we go to Confession, which corresponds to the fifth chakra. What is the symbolic meaning of Confession? It's to call your spirit back from choices that you made that do not serve you or life. To become aware and conscious of where you have directed your will, and to choose consciously to direct it with wisdom, and with love.

So, it's a process of recognizing...

The false missions you've sent your spirit on out of fear.

It's about recognizing this and forgiving.

That's right.

And does a re-confirmation of your code come with this?

That's exactly right. You say, "Wait a minute, what choices am I making? Do they honor my code?" You create your own reality. And you do it with conscious choice, and you have to say to yourself, "Am I sending my spirit into a fear? Am I commanding my spirit to believe a fear? Am I commanding my spirit to judge someone else? Am I sending my spirit on a mission to hold a negative thought of someone else, and what are the consequences if I do that?" People apply this beautiful truth that we create our own reality to how to get a job! (we laugh.) It's the strongest spiritual tenet of the next millennium and we've reduced it down to how to get more for ourselves.

To just acquire.

To acquire and acquire and acquire. That's why it's failing us left, right and center. Because we're not using it at the level of maturation that really wakes it up.

We're just using it to get more goodies.

That's right.

From the fifth chakra, Confession, we go to...

Ordination. That corresponds to the sixth chakra. And what's ordination? Literally, it means priesthood. But, in the old days, Ordination meant that your tribe looked at you and said, "You have a special gift." Whatever that gift was, whether it was, "You are the most nurturing person that we have, and therefore we're going to make you the tribal nurturer," or "You're the most wise person we have, so we're going to look to you for wisdom." When the tribe recognizes a gift in you, it's saying, "Put that gift on lead. We're asking you to accept that gift on our behalf." And you say, "Okay, I will." And that's ordination. What does it mean to enter Ordination symbolically? It means to recognize that "I have a special gift. What is the gift people see most in me?" First of all, you have to let your tribe see you clearly. Secondly, you have to accept the gift they turn to you for the most. In my case, I insisted upon being a publisher. And there was not one member of my publishing tribe that recognized any power in that choice. And what did the tribe come to me for? They said, "Caroline, teach us." So, I finally agreed. I said, all right I'll leave publishing and I'll accept my ordained role as teacher.

And the irony is, through your "ordained role as teacher," you went right back into publishing, but from a different aspect. Not as publisher, but as an author. It's like you were on track with this publishing thing, you just had the wrong role. You were supposed to be an author.

That's right. And what mythology plays itself out there? Abraham and his son, Isaac. God asked me to sacrifice the most precious thing I had, and I said you've gotta be kidding me, it's all I've got. But, I said, if this is what you want me to let go of, I will. I was as poor as a church mouse when I left Stillpoint (the publishing house she co-founded), and I had no place to go, and I had no idea what the future held. And in return, I got all of my version of Israel. Again and again you can see the archetypal truth in the teachings. Then, what's the last one? Extreme Unction, which corresponds to the seventh chakra. Extreme Unction — the release of your dead. Stay in your present time. Don't carry your dead with you. Your dead memories, your dead thoughts that no longer serve you. Stay in present time.

It's a path, and each one of these is corresponding to an area of the body. And you can't hopscotch. You have to go through them in that order.

> *You really do. If you can't get to the point where you can accept your family (you don't have to like them, just accept that they are the way they are), and you can't accept spiritually the meaning of Baptism, and the truth that comes in when you do, which is all is one, you're not ever going to be able to see the beauty in the one-on-one relationship symbolically, which is the Communion. Nor will you be able to make a personal spiritual honor code with yourself — the Confirmation — because it'll be contaminated.*

And people think that by saying accept your family that it means you have to like them or associate with them. We just have to accept who they are, and if they are toxic to us we don't have to be around them.

> *It means even seeing it less personally than that. It means saying, "What difference does it make whether I incarnated here or down the block? I have these lessons to learn."*

People who are in abusive relationships and find it so hard to leave them, sometimes misunderstand when someone says, "Accept what is happening to you." Accept doesn't mean "Stay there and take it." It means, "Don't make excuses for it anymore. Accept that this is the way it is, and then do something about it — leave."

> *And where people lose their footing along the line is that they apply human reasoning to that vocabulary, instead of spiritual.*

So the way that someone in a toxic relationship of any kind should be viewing it is without the human logic and the reasoning, which is what makes people stay in them very often. They say, "Well, I can't afford to leave," or "I don't want to break up the family," like this toxic family is so terrific?

> *Mmm-hmm...they're using human reasoning. They're using physical, external reasons for why they can't spiritually progress.*

And what they should be looking at — no matter what it is, whether it's a job that's toxic, or a relationship, or whatever — is the spiritual, power reasons behind it, and the fears in order to progress. In order to say, "What am I supposed to learn from this?" and to say, "I don't have to sit here in the muck in order to recognize my lessons and move on."

That's exactly right.

Is the goal to stop being a particular archetype if it's not healthy for you?

No, the goal is always to learn, "Where am I losing my power, and why?"

So, it's possible to be a rescuer or any of the other archetypes in a way that will not harm you?

Yeah! The real choice is to look at it and say, "I am losing my power. Why am I doing that? It's okay to help people. What I have to be aware of is: What's my motive? What's my agenda?"

What about people who want to empower someone, people who don't have an unhealthy reason for rescuing?

That's different. Then you have a healthy rescuer.

And that would be you, for instance. By teaching your students, by writing.

Actually, that's true.

By writing your books, you're a healthy rescuer. You really genuinely care that these people progress to the point where they don't need your "rescuing" and teaching anymore. Or, if they do need you, it's just for a "check up" once in awhile, rather than you trying to keep them sick in order to keep them around.

That's exactly right. And as a prelude to my workshops, I say: "You are now in my laboratory. I'm giving you the best of what life has taught me. Take with you only what serves you, and leave the rest in this room...and I don't want to hear from you again. Don't follow me, don't write me, don't call. Because I won't be there for you. I'm here for you tonight, in this room, as a teacher. And then I'm outta here. I will not have groupies, I will not have devotees, I will not have that." Because then, I'm contaminated, from my point of view. That is real important to me, because if I can't teach you to walk on your own, if I teach you to think that you can only walk if you're with me, then I'm in trouble.

That's not a teacher. That's someone holding someone hostage.

That's exactly right. So, I do not have an organization. I will not have any of that kind of stuff.

Ancient Chinese doctors used to be considered successful or good doctors only if their patients hardly ever needed them.

That's precisely right.

If their patients were all well, and just needed to check in from time to time, that meant you were a good doctor.

That's exactly right.

And now, the definition of a good doctor is, "How many sick people do you have?"

That's right. "How many can you produce for the hospital. What's your quota?"

How do people learn what parts of their bodies are expressing their particular symbolic power leaks?

First you ask, what causes me to lose power? Then you articulate that, and identify that for yourself. Like, I lose power when I get involved in getting attached to the outcome. That has to do with lower body energies. You have to say to yourself, my task is to do the best I can and then let go, and whatever happens happens. If I don't let go, I'm gonna pay a price. Where am I going to pay a price? Where do I have pain in my body?

So it really could be anywhere?

Yup.

So, it isn't that people who do "X" will end up with troubles with their "Y."

Well, there is a certain relationship. But not always.

Give me a few general patterns.

Okay. Let's look at a senator who just got booted out from his power zone. What does he have now? Prostate cancer.

It always seems to hit men at about retirement age, whether they retired voluntarily or involuntarily.

That's right. And why?

Because they see that as a loss of their external power, and their reproductive area is where they believe their power lies.

Precisely. Where do men think their power is? In their, excuse me...balls.

Literally and figuratively.

They have the vocabulary for it.

When you say to someone, "You've got balls," he takes that as a compliment to his power.

> *What do we mean when we say, "It's broken my heart?" We know exactly what we're talking about. We're putting the grief in the chest area. Now, for women it will often go the breast because they see that as the more nurturing thing.*

Women have more breast tumors and men have more heart attacks.

> *That's right. Look at the pancreas. It's the organ that stores all the stress we have about issues of responsibility. They're going to "burn out." That's the language we use. You burn out and you enter some kind of hypoglycemic condition or diabetes.*

Is that why a lot of adults out of nowhere get diabetes in their late 30s or early 40s, the vast majority men?

> *Right. They're burning out. This is a pattern. The other extreme is just as prone to create a pancreatic disorder: when you feel that you're not responsible for anything. And you manipulate and maneuver everyone else to take care of you.*

So, as soon as we've recognized what our life problems are, we can then reverse, correct or heal the physical disorder that's accompanying it.

> *Yes.*

For a man who has prostate problems or prostate cancer — if he can stop feeling like he's lost his power, he stands a much better chance of being able to heal.

> *Yes.*

And if he can tell himself years before it ever happens to not have that kind of attitude, the prostate won't suffer at all. Not every man has prostate problems.

That's exactly right.

What about women who have harmless fibroid cysts in their breasts. How does that differ from what causes a malignant breast tumor?

The issues that women go through are the loss of their feeling of attractiveness, or feelings of being rejected by male energy. Another one that's really common is when a woman realizes that she's not attending to her own needs, but rather has negotiated her personal needs in order to maintain a physical stability in her life, usually security.

And all of this results in the cyst or the malignant tumor?

Both. It depends upon how serious the issue is.

If you have a mild case of any of these issues, you may end up with a cyst. A severe case and you end up with cancer. And that would be the case no matter where it was located in your body.

Right. One of the reasons why breast cancer is so prevalent now is because you have so many women that are now aware of two worlds simultaneously: one the traditional world in which they are the homemakers, and the other is the world in which they are individuals. And we have yet to have a model in our society where the empowered woman can also have a personal life. But, a model that also says that it is as much a successful choice to say, "I just want to be a mother." So many women think of themselves as failures — so many times in my workshops I hear women introduce themselves by saying, "I'm only a housewife." As if they have to apologize for that. We are completely screwed up in what we expect from females.

And what we expect form everyone in general. We have an all or nothing mentality in this country. If you're not at the top, then we've decided you're not worth s**t.

Yup.

You're either the most successful superwoman or we think there's something wrong with you.

Yeah, and look at what we've created as our model of the successful woman: you cannot age, you cannot gain any weight, you have to be a perfect work-out person, you have to be extremely attractive, very bright, you have to earn a huge income, you have to be creative all the time, you have to be the perfect entertainer, you have to be a gourmet chef.

You also have to be the perfect Mom.

You have to be the perfect Mom, and you have to have "quality time." If I ever hear that phrase again...You have to be an absolutely sexy lover, you have to be all of this. And where does this modifier "perfect" come from anyway? Since when does being perfect mean anything?

Since advertising came along. It's the only way they can sell us anything — if they give us the promise of something.

And it's get your eyes lifted, get your cheeks lifted, get your this lifted, get your liposuction. What is this crap? Oh, I can't tolerate the images.

What we're saying as a society is that the only way we can feel good about aging is if we don't look like we're actually aging. If at 80, you can still look like you're twenty.

That's right. There are no images of, "Welcome to the wisdom years, ladies."

"If you're gonna be a crone, then dear God, don't look like one."

Yup.

Now, how about addiction. From a spiritual point of view, how do you view it?

It's very simple. Everyone who experiences an imbalance between the mind and the heart — and that's virtually everybody — deals with this: Where's the mind? Sixth chakra. Where's the heart? Fourth chakra. What's in the middle? Fifth chakra, your will. Picture mind as Daddy, heart as Mommy, will as child. If the mind and heart are not in unison, who is monitoring the child? Neither parent. So, the will, the child, is free to go it's own way. And it has to find a parent, and that will be an addiction. It'll get itself attached to a substance or behavior.

It'll attach itself to something rather than attaching itself to a mind or a heart.

That's right. It'll find itself an external. The most addicted people I see aren't addicted to substance, they're addicted to power. They're addicted to getting their way. They're addicted to their routines. Or they use their weaknesses to wield power. It's all power plays. We'll be addicts until the mind and the heart are commanding our energy system. When we use our will to command our externals instead of our internals, we're missing the point, we've not matured spiritually enough.

Now, how many people get to the point where their mind and heart are in harmony?

What is growth all about?

It's about striving for that.

That is the journey.

The irony is that when you finally get everything worked out, it's time to check out.

Yeah.

All of your life it's going to be a constant growth process, and you may get to weigh stations along the way and say, "Okay, I've tackled that one," but you've got ten more coming up.

And you know where I see so many people losing their power? People are motivated by the Promised Land mythology. That there is one choice, one person, one thing that they can do that'll finally make everything okay. Life is a continuum. It's not about reaching the Promised Land. You don't arrive at the Promised Land, you just keep going. Somewhere along the way you may make a connection where your heart and your mind are in unison on one point, and you think, "Boy, does this feel good," and you think the journey's over. No, you connect a dot, you get a little reprieve, and then it starts over again.

So, can we ever really, truly be healthy? As long as we stay on top of these issues that trigger illness, we should have relatively decent health.

That's right. We can say, "Now, I understand it at the energetic level. I don't have to let the components incarnate into a physical condition in order for me to make a decision."

So, we can say, "Now I see that this isn't working in my life. How long am I going to put up with it? Until it gives me a physical symptom? No, let's get rid of it now."

Precisely.

So, you have to stay in an emotionally and spiritually preventive mode. Prevent the thing before it manifests.

That's right. And you also have to have the faith to say, "I don't need to get attached to anything physically. I can let change happen. Where people lose their power and their spirit is that they want to stop change. They want to control the speed at which change happens in their life. And then they begin to commit their spirit into the management of a circumstance.

So, how do we reconcile this with natural, healthy desires for various things?

Well, it's very simple. Simple, but not easy. You say, "I want to be conscious, and included in that I want love, wisdom, I want to live well with my family. What does it take to do that?" It takes learning how to love without control. My task is not to command my spirit to control others, but to study the responses that they generate in me. Strong will is not the capacity to run 28 miles a day, it's to command my spirit to come back when I feel like judging somebody, or when I feel frightened by something and I say, "No, I'm not attaching to that fear, I will not do it. I'll attach to faith." That's what it is. And no matter where you are or what circumstance you're in, it's to decide, "I don't know what's going on here, but I'm going to trust it's for my best," and it's to stop using pain and pleasure as the measure of whether or not God (or spirit) is in your life.

Four

Brian Weiss

*For those who believe, no explanation
is necessary. For those who do not, no explanation is possible.*
— Anonymous

*The distinction between past, present,
and future is only a stubbornly persistent illusion.*
— Albert Einstein

*T*reating patients by guiding them through recollections of their previous lives is just about the last thing Dr. Brian Weiss thought he'd be doing.

A prominent South Florida psychiatrist, who before the age of 35 was the first Chief of Psychiatry at Miami Beach's prestigious Mount Sinai Medical Center (a post he held for 11 years), and a teaching professor at the University of Miami's medical school, Brian Weiss, M.D. had always taken the traditional path.

Born in Brooklyn in 1944, and raised in Red Bank and Kendall Park, New Jersey, Weiss was the oldest of four children in a Jewish household headed by an industrial photographer and his wife, who worked in an office at Rutgers University. Brian Weiss was an overachiever who graduated from South Brunswick High in 1962 as class valedictorian, then Magna Cum Laude from Columbia University in 1966, an then received his M.D. from Yale in 1970. Ivy League all the way.

He says he was always "the well-grounded one" among his family, friends and colleagues. He was publishing papers and becoming a nationally recognized expert on psychopharmacology — the use of drugs in treating psychiatric patients — and considered himself the kind of guy who only believed what he could see and prove, one who rarely gave much thought to anything mystical, philosophical or spiritual.

One patient changed all that.

Weiss calls her Catherine in his first best-selling book, *Many Lives, Many Masters*, which was published by Simon & Schuster in 1988, eight years after he began treating the young woman. He'd been using routine psychotherapy techniques to treat her garden variety phobias and anxieties, and after 18 months with little improvement Weiss finally put it very simply to her one day while she was under hypnosis: "Go back to the time from which your symptoms arise," he instructed her.

She did. Back to the year 1863 B.C. when she was a 25-year-old named Aronda.

He was shocked to say the least. A flood of memories poured in from other lifetimes as well, and Weiss soon discovered that the causes of her problems were the events and relationships — many traumatic — that she'd had in *previous* lives.

He didn't accept this notion right away, of course. Only after ruling out schizophrenia, split personalities, psychosis, drug use, neurological illnesses, sociopathic tendencies and just plain acting would he come to believe that Catherine was actually recalling events.

"My gut reaction was that I had stumbled upon something I knew very little about — reincarnation and past life memories. It couldn't be, I told myself; my scientifically trained mind resisted it," he wrote in *Many Lives, Many Masters.* "Yet here it was happening right before my eyes. I couldn't explain it, but I couldn't deny the reality of it either."

During the next three years, Catherine's anxieties, phobias and panic attacks were cured by her process of vividly recalling significant events from dozens of past lives she'd led in many times and countries. People in her present life always popped up in her past ones.

Reincarnation, however, was only part of what Weiss encountered during Catherine's treatment. He also met "The Masters," highly evolved souls who weren't presently inhabiting bodies, but who spoke through Catherine while she was under hypnosis. The messages they delivered were about the nature of the universe, God, levels of consciousness, intuitive powers, and the soul, which they said passed from one body to another, from lifetime to lifetime.

At first, Weiss thought he was hearing just some New Age mumbo jumbo, until "The Masters" talked about Weiss's late father, and the medical condition that caused the death of Weiss's three-week old son years before — information that Catherine didn't know and would have no way of knowing.

Brian Weiss's life and career would never be the same again.

In 1990, two years after *Many Lives, Many Masters* was published, Weiss left his post at Mount Sinai Medical Center (although he has since been named Chairman Emeritus of the Psychiatry department) to devote himself full-time to his patients and his work in the field of past-life regression therapy.

Beginning in 1992, we would have many conversations as I wrote a number of magazine articles about his work throughout the '90s, including the featured Q&A-format Interview in *Omni* magazine's April, 1994 issue. He has since moved his office nearby to South Miami, but during our first conversation, in April, 1992, I met with him in the suburban Miami office where he based his practice then.

A few framed paintings and drawings were the only adornments in his private office, which held a simple desk and chair, a credenza overflowing with books and journals, and two soft, vanilla leather recliners that swallow up anyone under six feet tall.

I got lost in one of those recliners to have a past-life regression before we began to discuss his work. He hypnotized me, but I did not experience past life recall. Instead, I had what Weiss calls "a mystical experience," in which I saw two separate scenes. In the first, a woman who vaguely resembles me stands in a garden, then swirls about in a flowing white dress while a man peeks out from behind a stone wall that she cannot see. In the second scene, the same man stands upon a rocky shoreline, gazing at the sea, while the woman from the garden, now invisible to *him*, watches as *his* guardian spirit. She, too, is behind a stone wall that no one else can see. From my description of these people, and the detail of each scene, it's clear to Weiss, and me, that these scenes are symbolic of the relationship I was having then with a man Weiss believes I've also known in many previous lifetimes, and just as importantly, in between in "the sprit state," as illustrated by the scenes in these visions. We have always been, in effect, each other's guardians. Sometimes, as in these scenes, one of us is having a three-dimensional lifetime on the Earth plane, while the other is in spirit state and watches, providing guidance.

These scenes I saw under hypnosis would become even more intriguing 13 months later, in May, 1993, when I first saw the work of painter Marilyn Sunderman, as you'll read in the introduction to my conversation with her in Chapter Eight.

After this hypnosis session, Weiss showed me copies of his first book translated into Icelandic, Italian and Japanese. It has since been published in more than two dozen languages. "I didn't realize it would be this popular," he says in a voice as light as a feather, the same tone he uses whether he's hypnotizing you or not. "But, I found that intuitive things are much more common than I expected."

Patients have come to see Weiss from all over the world, he's in demand as a speaker, and has done interviews in all the media, although he is extremely selective and guards the integrity of his work.

Since treating Catherine, he has researched not only reincarnation, but Eastern religions, mysticism, quantum physics, intuition and everything in between. He exudes an air of calm, wise counsel, but he does not come across as some kind of guru, nor does he want to be one. He's simply a doctor, he says, who's become enlightened.

Much to his surprise, Weiss's work has been taken seriously by many in the medical community. Shortly after his first book was published, the former president of the Dade County Psychological Association told *The Miami Herald* that "those of us who do hypnosis are not all that shocked by Dr. Weiss's book. Many have had patients who have gone back to something — I'm not prepared to say it was a previous life. I think we are very interested and very afraid to talk about it...it's like an underground thing." One that during the 1990s peeked its head above ground some more.

In Weiss's second book, *Through Time Into Healing*, published in the summer of 1992, also by Simon & Schuster, Weiss writes about many of his past life therapy cases since treating Catherine, the work of other doctors and researchers in the field (of which he is now considered one of the pioneers), the history of reincarnation beliefs, and regression techniques.

The 1990s brought together the widespread media, publishing and medical community attention that made him the leading psychiatric practitioner of past life regression therapy. He has even lectured at Yale, his alma mater, giving talks at both their Divinity School and their Medical School's psychiatry department.

Only Love is Real: A Story of Soulmates Reunited, his third book, was published by Warner Books in 1996, and met with the same success as his first two. His fourth book, with the working title *Sacred Steps*, will be published by Warner in the winter of 2000, and he calls it "a practical guidebook about the energy of love." He says it will focus on the role of past lives, the after death Life Review, and soulmates on our relationships, and will include both case studies and practical exercises.

Brian Weiss's office is now in South Miami, but he spends a great deal of time lecturing and presenting workshops worldwide, including specialized training for therapists. He says his work with past life therapy has helped not only his patients and readers, it has also helped *him*. Yes, it's the last thing he thought he'd be doing, but it has led him to explore a great body of knowledge, and to look inward as well.

The conversations presented here took place in the summer of 1992, in 1994, and in late 1998.

❦

Are we simply vessels that hold the soul?

Yes, exactly. We create these bodies which function in this three-dimensional world here in time and space so that we can express ourselves and learn, which is the ultimate purpose. But that part of us, the soul, the spirit, that inhabits these bodies, moves on from body to body, from time to time. Much like your car. You're very fond of it, and it gets you places in this world. But when it dies, when it gets old, when it's in an accident, you, the driver, the controller of the car, get out and say, "Well I need a new car. For me to make this journey I have to get another car." So, you get a new car. We are vessels, and we contain this eternal and immortal, much more knowledgeable part of ourselves. Now, probably as you get more mystical you find out that these souls, as well as the bodies, are connected to everyone else's, because really everything is of the same substance. And I think that's the job of physicists — to prove in the next decade or so how these connections are made, how the whole world is dependent upon every person in that sense. We have to get this before we completely screw up this planet. That's the danger.

Why do people find reincarnation a difficult concept to accept?

It's fear. The fear of the unfamiliar. Actually, people don't have to be afraid. This is very reassuring and comforting. People fear the unfamiliar. If only they would keep an open mind. Not just scientists, but everybody. Just observe it, watch it. Meditation can teach people to do that. If they can let go of their fears.

That's the secret, isn't it — letting go. But that means changing your whole life, and that's scary.

Yes, it's very scary. But it's totally safe. Yet it's so difficult to let

*go of the familiar and the old, even it it's harmful, restricting
and blinding it's still familiar. If you reject the finding that the
earth actually revolves around the sun, you stay in ignorance,
and you reject it merely because it isn't familiar. But it doesn't
change truth: the earth has been revolving around the sun all
this time anyway, no matter what man believed or didn't
believe.*

What do you say to scientists and others who believe that we're a
totally biological process, and there's nothing mystical about it, that
we're born, live and die and that's the end of it?

*That's a very common belief among biological scientists,
psychologists and psychiatrists. They're grossly missing the point.
There's so much evidence and data that we're more than just
machines or biological beings. A part of us is, though, and that's
what gets confusing. If we go back to the metaphor of bodies
being vessels, carrying around souls...we still have the bodies. So,
someone can say, "Oh, I see a body, it has all of these chemicals
and electrical activity and biological processes and structures."
Well, of course. I'm not saying that we aren't bodies, but we're
more than that. Let's go back to the car analogy — what they'd
say is "We are only cars, and I can prove that because there are
carburetors, batteries, oil and gas, and that's how the car runs."
And I don't disagree with that. But without the driver, it
wouldn't run at all. It wouldn't have any direction or know
which road to take on its journey. They're only seeing a small
portion of the self, and to subscribe to that theory blindly, they're
missing so much. It doesn't explain where these past life
memories come from. They're not passed biologically because the
person in a past life may have died as a child, or died childless,
and yet the material is still passed on. There is so much more to
it.*

Where did the concept of reincarnation come from?

It's so far back that we really don't know. I suspect that it's from the same place as it comes from now: people who are psychic having visions of it, other people through dreams or déja vu and memories, meditation, came upon the same knowledge.

Philosophers and mystics in earlier times incorporated reincarnation into their explanations of life, and Plato wrote about soulmates.

Yes, Plato wrote about reincarnation. So, the Greeks believed in this, too. The ancient civilizations believed in this.

Reincarnation shows up in all religions. Where did this knowledge come from?

It comes from so far back that we don't even know where it comes from. We only lost it recently. I think we lost it for political reasons mostly. In Judaism, belief in reincarnation or gilgul, is not just ancient, but existed until early in the 1800s, and it was only with the migration out of Eastern Europe to the West, and the age of enlightenment and science, and the need to be accepted, that the belief went underground. But not in the Chassidic (Ultra-Orthodox) populations. They still believe in reincarnation. In Christianity it went underground much earlier, in the 6th century at the Second Council of Constantinople where reincarnation was officially declared a heresy. Christianity was becoming a state religion, and the Romans felt that without the whip of judgment day people wouldn't behave, they wouldn't follow. They would think, "Well, I'll do it next time around." And so reincarnation was consciously made a heresy. But this was at the Council, centuries after Jesus.

Why is Jesus the only person we hear about who supposedly died and then walked again? Is it just a metaphor, and could they have meant that his spirit went on, as opposed to his body?

If you step back and look at this as a metaphor, it's a wonderful metaphor. It fits very much into what we've been

122

talking about, being a vessel, and the body housing the soul or the spirit. We get resurrected all the time — you do, and I do. We leave one body and we go into the next. This is the whole idea — that we are not our bodies, we are not our brains, we are not our minds. We are something far greater, and we get resurrected endlessly. Also, we are all the sons of God, we're all God, we're the same substance. God is in everybody. And I think that was the message of Jesus, Krishna, Buddha and wise beings in all religions. We are spirit, immortal and eternal. Jesus was an incredibly spiritual, talented person, a highly evolved soul. What the Hindus would call an avatar. Much like Krishna. He and Jesus were of the same magnitude of soul — coming back as a teacher to point the way, coming back in troubled times to show the way, and to change things.

How is the length of time between lifetimes determined?

People who die violently, or children who die, often come back faster. And people who live longer lives and die more peacefully, there can be much longer time between lives, a hundred years or more.

How many past lives do people generally have?

That varies, but the numbers that come up most (in my work) is about 100. Not the thousands and thousands that the Buddhists talk about.

Is there an infinite number of souls or a finite number?

To me it doesn't matter because ultimately we're all connected.

Are new souls being created?

I'm not sure, but my inclination is to say no. We're probably all ageless and have been (around from the beginning).

Are there people here now who are experiencing their very first life?

> *Theoretically, I would guess yes. Maybe they "transferred in" and they're here for the first time, but I suspect that most of us have been here other times. If we're one of thousands or millions of worlds...it's like asking where did all those children go to junior high school before the new one was built? Well, they were elsewhere. We shouldn't delude ourselves into thinking that we're the only place.*

Are there people who've been around more, so-called "old souls?"

> *I think there are people who've been around here more, but I don't think this is the only place. I know that's somewhat controversial, but I think that there are other places that we go to learn, too. I don't have a name for it. It's not like Jupiter or Pluto, or a different solar system, but perhaps another dimension. And I think that there are different levels. And, again, this is in all the religions. All the mystical traditions talk about other worlds. They may be other levels, too, such as different levels of heaven — that's where that expression "I was in 7th heaven" comes from, as being an ultimate. Catherine, the woman in* Many Lives, Many Masters *talked about seven dimensions.*

Judging from the number of souls who subliminally recognize one another in this life, considering the total number of lives they may have had and the places they may have lived, it seems highly improbable that any two souls would meet again.

> *It seems like an energy attracts — you're pulled into a situation where you need to be, to learn. Perhaps even from the time of birth, in choosing one's parents. It's not random — you choose because of the opportunity to learn. You may make mistakes. Everybody has free will, even your parents. They may not turn out the way you had hoped or envisioned, because they have the free will to not do that, to not reach their potential. I*

124

was doing a workshop once and we were talking about this, and a mother in the audience said to her daughter, "See? You chose me, so stop blaming me!" And her daughter turned to her and said, "Then I must have been in a hurry."

Are families more spiritually connected from life to life than strangers?

Yes, and I do think that people come around in groups. I think that's for the working out of debts and responsibilities, what the Eastern people call karma. These are the people that we're learning with and growing with and have relationships with. I even put love at first sight, or hostility at first sight into that category, too, a kind of recognition of souls. I keep finding that over and over again in my patients. You know the old saying: blood is thicker than water. Well, I mention in Through Time into Healing *that spirit seems thicker than blood. That's what really pulls us together. Sometimes genetically, biologically, yes, but sometimes not. You may be best friends. You may be father and son in one lifetime but lovers in this lifetime.*

So people can be male in one lifetime and female in another, and vice versa?

Yes, there seems to be frequent switching. You may have a preference, but you've tried out the other to see what it's like. This is also true of races and religions.

How do you explain souls that occupy bodies that are biologically damaged?

If this is all to learn — and this is what my patients tell me over and over again — to grow, to become more and more God-like, then whatever the experience you're having, this is a learning experience. Sometimes, though, it's a teaching experience as well, so you may come back into this for others, maybe as an act of charity.

Could it also be punishment?

Yes, that, too. But, it's really learning. For example: if you're a plantation owner in the mid-19th century and you're mistreating blacks, and you come back as a black man in modern day Harlem, to me that's learning. You learn about compassion, what it's like to be a minority, or to be abused because of skin color or race or sex, or whatever. I don't see that truly as a punishment. I see it as a learning opportunity. Maybe you've been a cruel person who's tortured people — you come back handicapped to learn what it's like to have an impaired body.

How do pre-determination and free will co-exist?

Someone told me this once: Life is like being on a bus. It has a certain route — that's pre-determined. But the person you sit next to, how you act, what you say, that's all the free will part. With lots of choices.

The choices you make can affect the outcome for every other individual on that bus.

Yes, and they can affect you, but the route is still set.

It's free will but it's like a maze: you can go anywhere you want, but you're still going to come out that end.

It is. It's still somewhat difficult to comprehend but they can coexist. The simplicity is that what you really need to learn is about love. So, wherever you look you can always learn that.

Do you think people are reluctant to believe in this because it implies a lack of control, that even with free will it implies we're on this ride, plugged into the big picture?

Sure. That's another fear. It still comes down to fear. Fear of

126

not being in control, when actually you are more in control because of this guidance of a higher wisdom, whether you call it a higher self, or a subconscious mind that really protects you, that guides you. This is not a haphazard, coincidental or chaotic place. There's a plan to it.

Why don't we automatically, consciously remember our past lives?

There are so many levels to this question. For one thing, more and more people are remembering. Through these therapeutic techniques such as hypnosis, but also through dreams, spontaneously, through meditation, déja vu, and when they're in a place they've never been before and it seems so familiar and they know their way around. This may be an evolutionary shift. I don't know why we don't all remember. The Greeks had a myth that when you were born again you drank from the River of Lethe, so you'd forget your previous lives.

Do you think that if we were given the knowledge of our past lives it would be cheating, just like taking a test with the book open? Each time we have a life, we're not supposed to consciously remember our past lives so that we can learn from this one without benefit of our previous lessons.

I agree. Yes, this is a kind of test of learning. For example: if you've learned all about charity, and in between lifetimes you say, "Yeah, I've got it now. I've spent 10 lifetimes learning about charity. I know all about it, it's in my head. I'm a charitable person." Okay, now comes the field test. You're born, you're put into a situation. Is it really in your heart? Is it ingrained so deeply in you that you don't have to act charitably because of a specific memory, but because it's part of your nature now, it's gotten into your soul? There's a kind of deeper learning that goes on, and it is like a field test, to see if you've really gotten it, if you've learned it.

So you think some of us are born with certain values and ideals?

Yes, that's the whole purpose. That it gets ingrained at a deeper level. Not at the level of the brain, but at the level of the heart, the level of the soul — that's where the real learning takes place. So that you're not dependent just on what your parents teach you, which is kind of superficial when you think about it. If one's parents were bigots, and the child is able to overcome that, to become a compassionate, understanding, charitable, un-bigoted person, this is a degree of independence that transcends what we're taught. This is your soul saying: "You know it's not right to be a bigot, despite what your parents are telling you, despite what the church, temple or mosque is telling you. You know better. Follow your heart." And when you're doing that, you've really learned it. This is the soul memory. In addition to specific talents or abilities or whatever else the soul might bring back with it. This is so important for the world. This is our real lesson here: to learn of love, and all the ramifications of that — truth, compassion, generosity, mercy. That's part of our purpose. To overcome the animal, biological part and to see that sharing brings you a treasure far greater.

What is the reward for the lessons learned?

It's difficult to answer without getting into God's mind, and even to say that God has a mind is anthropomorphizing God. We're learning to love, to be wise, but there may be much more than that.

Religions and philosophies say that the goal is perfection, to become "one with God," or the Creator, or the Higher Being.

Yes, that's part of it. But it's like if you ask a third-grader, "What are you learning in this arithmetic course you're taking?" And he says, "I'm learning about addition, long division and the multiplication tables." And he can't even comprehend calculus, geometry and advanced mathematics. So, we're limited by what we know. I suspect this has to do with love, with merging with this higher consciousness. But it may be so far beyond what we can comprehend now that it's hard to put into words. You can sense it when you're on target — you do something compassionate and a tear of joy comes to your eyes. You don't need to come back an infinite number of times once you learn, once you get it. You don't have to come back, unless you come back voluntarily to teach or to help out.

The Hindus also include animals in reincarnation. Have you seen that in patients?

I haven't found that myself in doing this work.

Do the Native American Indians have reincarnation in their culture?

Yes, many Indian cultures do. The Eskimos in particular. They'll look for birthmarks which may be sights of old injuries and wounds (from a past life). So, they try to identify who the baby is, in terms of who they may have been in the past. Dr. Ian Stevenson (a physician, and Chairman Emeritus of the Department of Psychiatry at the University of Virginia who has researched more than 2,000 cases of children who have had past life memories) looked for birthmarks, too, and he found them, at the site of old mortal wounds. I've had a few patients with birthmarks from old wounds. I think it has something to do with how bodies are formed. The physical form is on the basis of the spiritual. It gets carried over. Stevenson found ones that people didn't even know about because their hair was covering it. There are cultures that mourn births and celebrate deaths. Because they're so fundamentally tied to this concept of "this is a field test, the challenge, the hell, so to speak, and then we go home. Home is light and love and reunions, and whatever. You're freed up, you're a spirit again. You're not limited by the body. You know so much more."

When we're "out there," will we be with all the people we knew here?

I think so, and even with those who are still here. The vision is better coming from the other direction. They're aware of more because they're not limited by a body and the brain. But we are.

Most people are so busy with their daily lives that they don't have or don't take the time to think about the universe or ponder things. And others have found answers in organized religion and feel no need to question anything.

That can hold you back because it gets in the way of having an open mind, which is really the key. In a way, any fundamentalist or anyone who is unwilling to see the beauty and truth in all religions, is missing the point. It stops you from true joy. Being at peace isn't enough, unless it's a true peace. The Nazis might have been "at peace" because "they thought they were right." And yet, that was false.

A scientist once said that he would never have a firm belief in any one particular thing because it would limit him. He would much rather entertain all notions.

If he finds peace through that, that's great. If someone finds peace through Catholicism, for instance, that's great, too, as long as it's the open-minded kind that says: "It's the same God (as everyone else's), I'm just going this way for me, but I realize that there's truth and beauty in all religions."

What's the state of reincarnation research today?

There are other physicians doing this. Raymond Moody is now writing about his research with past life therapy. He's the psychiatrist who coined the phrase Near Death Experience. He's a welcome addition to this field. There are a few others doing it. There's a national organization called the APRT, the Association of Past Life Research and Therapy. Some of their members are doing research in this field also. It's a group to disseminate information, and they publish a journal. It's a mixed group, so it's hard to characterize them as representative of the scientific community.

Where do you see yourself within the research that's going on?

One patient called me a travel agent. And I like that. A travel agent, because I helped her on these "trips" that she made to past lives. So I think part of the answer is that I'm a bit of a travel agent. I'm also an encourager. I've encouraged Dr. Bob Jarmon, a New Jersey physician, to go public, and now he's had 15 or 20 cases, some of them well-researched, fascinating cases that he's had published in a journal. I'm doing my own research, and joining the other people who are doing this work.

How can reincarnation be validated? Do you look for information to support the past lives?

That's what Dr. Ian Stevenson does with children. He has more than 2,000 cases now, from all over the world. He's documented the cases of these children, many exhibiting xenoglossy (the ability to speak a foreign language you've had no exposure to), or who know details about other places. There are others who do that. Dr. Jarmon has a patient he's followed up through a past life that involved World War II, and a midwestern university. He's documented this. I don't think any one individual, by their story, is going to prove reincarnation. I think it's the weight of the evidence: hundreds of therapists with thousands of patients where this happens. Children, non-believers, skeptics, all who come out with these details of past lives.

It's very difficult to prove reincarnation scientifically because of what we consider scientific. As a psychiatrist I'm vitally interested in my patient's clinical improvement, in their welfare, so I look at two levels when I do this work: the level of therapy and of helping people, and then the other level, that of validating, or proving. Both of which are vitally important. But I function more these days in the therapeutic level. There's no question in my mind, or in the minds of all of these physicians and psychotherapists who are writing to me, calling me, that this has a tremendous therapeutic effect. It really helps people. It's quick, it's vivid, it's relatively inexpensive, and people get better. It's more expensive and difficult to get into tracking down and validating evidence. And yet, this is important, too. And there are people such as Dr. Stevenson who do track these cases down. When I get the chance I try to track down certain details, but right now I'm accumulating evidence that this therapy works and that people, whether they believe in reincarnation or not, are able to come up with details that they didn't know, from the recent or distant past.

What other research projects have you been involved with?

I've been involved in a research project with the Physics Department at NYU. They're studying healers. They're bringing people over from China who are experts at what we would call healing, what they call chi energy. The physicists are trying to measure it. And eventually, I guess, to build some sort of machine that could generate the same frequency and maybe induce more rapid healing or cellular changes. So they're studying the effects that these people have on viruses or bacteria, on people with certain ailments, and measuring the energy at the same time. They talk about reincarnation, and the physicists are not familiar with this, so I've flown up to New York. On the last trip I regressed one of the Chinese physicians. He was more interested in that than in the research. To him the healing research wasn't proving anything because he already knows it works. He was interested in being regressed, so I did that through an interpreter, and two lifetimes came up. That's not why I was going up there, but he was so insistent.

This energy — we can't see it, but some can feel it, and we can't explain it.

That's why you need a physicist. It may not have a name yet because we haven't "discovered" it, but it is going to be discovered. To give an example, a dog whistle — it doesn't mean because we can't hear it that there isn't a sound wave being generated, and we know that because dogs hear this, and maybe an occasional person with a wider spectrum of auditory acuity can hear it, too. It has a name. If 100 years ago I told you that we would be able to turn on a kind of box that had a glass front, that captured invisible waves out of the air and turned them into an instantaneous picture right in the box, with sound, and that you could see what was going on simultaneously in Moscow from Miami, and that this would be plucked out of the air by a metal rod on the side of our house, you'd say, "This guy is out of it! What would you call that wave?" And I'd say, "Well, I don't know yet what you would call it." But it doesn't mean the wave isn't real. It's the same thing — it's just that we don't have names yet for all these wave/particle phenomena. Our range is still too limited. I think we'll also use our minds, still probably the most amazing machines of all, to begin to become aware of and generate these same energies or wave/particle phenomena. Afterall, how does this psychic energy work? How can a person have a vision and see what's taking place simultaneously at a great distance? What wave, particle or energy carries that information?

Physicists are doing research now where one subatomic particle/wave in one location senses instantaneously, what's happening to another particle/wave somewhere else. Is this the same basic principle of psychic phenomena?

Yes, and physicists have proof that these particles exist, that they travel at the speed of light, and time is relative, and can stop. It's just that we have difficulty in letting go (of our old concepts). If I told you that you're really, physically, a mass of electrons, protons and neutrons and energy, and wave/particle phenomena, you would say, "but I'm solid," and I would say, "Yes, but that's not really true, because at a deeper level you're energy." And we know this because some enterprising physicists could probably build a bomb out of you some day if they could

*harness that energy. The body is something that is not what it
seems. But that's true of all reality.*

In *Many Lives, Many Masters* you said that your work with past life
therapy and research has made you a more intuitive person.

*I had been shutting it off. I kept a very closed mind. But
when you're relaxed and open up to it, you become more
intuitive. It's probably a talent that was there all the time.*

Why does reincarnation and other things in that realm keep coming back to psychic ability?

*I think that all of this is connected. It's energies that are
either beyond our five senses or our limited range right now. It's
hard to talk about reincarnation and not talk about knowledge
that comes "in other ways," such as out-of-body experience or
precognitive dreams.*

Is the simple explanation for everything that we're all inter-con-
nected? Isn't that what religion and science and the mystics have been
trying to tell us?

*Yes, of course. We know that it's true, but we don't act as if
it's true, and that's the part that needs to evolve. We need to act
as if we believe this; even though we know it intellectually, we
have to still let it get into our hearts and in to our behavior.*

Scientists talk about things being connected on a sub-atomic level,
and instantaneous communication — what we would consider ESP
— between these subatomic particles. Since we and everything in the
universe are made up of these, does this explain how people can have
intuition, communicate telepathically or other abilities that are considered paranormal?

*Yes, that summarizes millennia of mystical knowledge, and
solves the problems of the universe! It's true. I'm being serious. We*

need to practice, we need to develop the skills. How to do this, how to be aware. Mystics have been saying for thousands of years that there is no time, it just appears that way to us. And when you start talking about other states, there is no space, there is no time. It's all happening now. This is our conception of God and of nature beyond the three-dimensional. That's the fascinating correlation that physics is starting to prove: what the mystics and religious people have been saying for many, many centuries. But this has been considered esoteric knowledge. That's why the Kabbala, the mystical part of Judaism, is supposed to be hidden until after you're 40 and have attained a certain degree of knowledge. In mystical Christianity, Buddhism, Hinduism, this is all part of the esoteric tradition: There is no time, there is no space, we are part of everything, we're all connected. And now physics studies this. (A tremendously loud bolt of lightening hits close by and thunder engulfs the room, just as Weiss finishes this sentence. Weiss gives a look that wonders whether this is a sign of divine agreement with his comments, and then laughs as a storm begins brewing outside.)

Do you think people resist this on a scientific level because they consider it an invasion of their emotional and mental privacy — the notion that someone could read their mind?

I think that's part of it. It's all part of fear. But there are other fears, too. Fear of the unknown, fear of somebody, or some thing or some knowledge shaking up their foundations that they grew up with, what they're comfortable with. But this has to happen because it's too important.

You've commented that physicists are the mystics of the '90s. Do you believe that ultimately they will find that science, mysticism, spirituality, religion and parapsychology are connected though quantum physics?

Physicists are the mystics of the '90s and the next century.

They've begun to study consciousness, time moving backwards, all of these phenomena that used to be called occult or esoteric. I believe they'll be found to have their roots in nature, in science. As we begin to use more of our brains through meditation and other ways, we're going to find that these things do have their basis in science, in nature. We'll be able to prove it scientifically. Some of these concepts that seem strange to us now won't be, as we understand more of the underlying physics of them. That's why I make the point in Through Time Into Healing *that people like Gallileo have been threatened with ex-communication. This has always been the case. People discover that actually the earth is revolving around the sun. This is called heresy. This flies in the face of the knowledge they had at the time. And of course, it's true that the earth is revolving around the sun and within a hundred years we know he's right. We're in the same situation now, with the same outcries as there were centuries ago: "This is heresy, this is nonsense, this isn't knowledge." To discover the truth you need to have an open mind. You have to throw out your old assumptions and old knowledge. So that when you make an observation you can do it without any coloring. And then you can test it without bias, without prejudice from the past. And this is where a lot of scientists get into trouble: They're not able to throw out their old assumptions.*

You wrote in *Many Lives, Many Masters* that the most important lesson you learned with past life therapy is that there is no death. How has this changed your life, and how can this change everybody's life?

When you stop fearing death you start to live more. What I value now that I perhaps didn't value as much before are love, relationships, family — not just in the genetic sense, but in the larger sense. And what I value less now are material things. You can't take it with you. That's a cliché, but it's true. What you can take with you are your values, what you've learned, some of your personality, your deeds, your thoughts, your heart.

How do our past life experiences and relationships affect our present life?

They affect us in every way. Many of your most meaningful relationships are not new. That's how you connect. Past lives also affect us in symptoms, both emotional and physical. Certain fears and anxieties carry over from other lifetimes. Physical symptoms, where one may have been wounded or hurt in a previous life frequently come up. It affects us psychologically, emotionally, even in obesity. I've had about a dozen obese patients where I've found that two patterns frequently emerge from a past life: one is that the person once died emaciated. And the other is sexual abuse from a past life. The woman decides "I will never be attractive to men again," and keeps the weight on in this life as a form of protection.

Are there some conditions that are easier to treat using past life therapy?

Yes. Phobias, fears, specific things that may have their roots in a past life. It's very effective for that. And other conditions like migraines.

You've said that whether past lives are real or not, if past life therapy helps the patient then that's all that counts.

For me that's so important. That this is very healing. To the body, to the mind, even to the soul. The mind in its wisdom will select those experiences that we need to address. I think also that it's real and we'll be able to prove it.

Sometimes people who have never given reincarnation a second thought will go under hypnosis during traditional therapy and come up with a past life.

Yes, and frequently that's how therapists, physicians, psychologists and others have gotten into the field or first discovered it — spontaneously, seemingly by accident. It doesn't seem to come from an altered state. Many of the memories are quite spontaneous. When you have a child, for example, who, non-hypnotized, starts speaking about details of another time and place, sometimes even speaking a foreign language they've never been exposed to. That's a memory.

So we can remember past lives without entering a hypnotic state.

Of course. Many children, especially around bedtime, when they get a little drowsy, in the hypnagogic state, come out with details. Adults, too. The hypnagogic state is very fertile for bringing out memories, when the normal filters are relaxed. Dreams are another way, sometimes it may actually be a memory fragment and not a Freudian distortion or a wish, symbol or metaphor. Sometimes it's a strange talent or affinity that doesn't make sense in terms of what you've learned in this life.

Have you had patients who, while reliving a past life under hypnosis, had detailed or technical knowledge about something they know nothing about in this life?

Yes, that happens a lot. One of the best cases is one of Dr. Jarmon's cases. He let me write about a few of his cases in Through Time Into Healing, *and this is in there. A woman was seeing him for hypnotherapy for weight loss. He didn't believe in past lives. This was his first case, (with a past life) and it happened spontaneously. This woman was in her 30s, a Jewish woman, and she started to develop another symptom while she was seeing him for weight loss. Her periods had stopped and she developed lower abdominal tenderness, and she was becoming more anxious. He was becoming alarmed, and he thought she might have an ectopic pregnancy, which is a pregnancy not in the uterus but in a fallopian tube, which can be dangerous because it can burst. So he referred her to a gynecologist. But there was no evidence of pregnancy, these tests were negative. She continued to see Dr. Jarmon, and they were working on her anxiety, and he said, "Go back to the time from which your symptoms first arose." The same question I'd asked Catherine, but Dr. Jarmon hadn't read my first book yet.*

His patient went back to the Middle Ages, she was five months pregnant with an ectopic pregnancy. In that past life she was Catholic, and she was with a priest who wouldn't allow abortion or surgery, and so she died. And just before she died she repeated the Catholic act of contrition to the priest, word for word. Dr. Jarmon is Catholic and recognized it. It's what Catholics say to atone for their sins. The woman, though, in the present, is Jewish and she had never heard of the Catholic act of contrition. This happens all the time — I hear details of dress, culture, how to make butter, cheeses, how to put on roofs, herd goats, things like that. But again, it's hard to prove. Because you can say maybe they read this in school, maybe they picked up a book, maybe they learned this while they were overseas.

Talents can be carried over from a past life, too?

I believe so. I've found this in therapy many times. I found a young boy who knew the specifications of World War II bombers. He'd never studied it, he just knew it. He says because he had flown them when he was big. Children often say that: "Don't you remember when I was big?" That's very compelling to me, when you have children of three or four, who haven't been indoctrinated, they haven't read it, they're not brainwashed, and they're coming out with this. There's a story in Through Time Into Healing *about a girl who was almost hospitalized because her mother had come back with some antique coins and the little girl got all excited, pointed to a coin and said "Look, look, Mommy, don't you remember when I was big and you were a man, we had lots of those." This is a four year-old, and she kept going on and on about it, and the mother became alarmed. The daughter started sleeping with the coin, and talking about more details from this time. And this was a healthy, normal child, so the mother eventually got to a child psychologist, who referred her to a psychiatrist to start medicine, maybe hospitalize her.*

Well, she wasn't delusional, she was having a memory emerge. She got to me finally, over the phone, so I took a history. I don't treat children myself. But I told the mother I really think this is a memory, I don't think your daughter is ill. I don't think she needs psychotropic medicines. Just let her talk about it. If you don't want to talk about it, just say, "that's nice, dear," and go on with your life. And sure enough, eventually the daughter stopped. The mother was reassured once she knew that it happens to other children as well.

Some people have mystical experiences while under hypnosis. Are these just as valuable in understanding ourselves as the past life memories?

Yes, they're very important. A past life is not necessary for everyone to remember. The subconscious directs the traffic. If it's important and it will help you get rid of a symptom, of course, but if it's not then you may not remember the past life. Or you may remember only five of your 80 or 90 because those five are related to what you're working on in this life. The deeper mind is very wise that way. Mystical states sometimes are what is necessary. There was the man who had lost two young daughters to a congenital heart disease, and when I regressed him I thought he was going to a past life. He was high up in a beautiful alpine meadow, way above a city or a town below, which I thought might be in Switzerland. But it turned out not to be. It was one of these mystical places. His daughters, who had died at three and four, were now nine and 10, and came to him, along with his mother and his grandmother, both of whom had also died, and they took his hands, they were hugging him, and telling him how much they loved him, and that they were fine, and that he shouldn't worry and shouldn't grieve so much. He was crying with tears of joy from this experience. Because it was so real to him, and so vivid. It was a beautiful meeting place of the dimensions, where he had this reunion. I can't prove that this actually was a meeting, but it sure helped him. He felt so much better. That was what he needed.

Do you use reincarnation in family therapy?

Yes. Families come back again and again, not necessarily in the same relationships. Family therapy is something in which this type of therapy is extremely valuable.

What's the range in ages of your patients?

I was never trained in child psychiatry. I took courses in it, but I don't see younger patients. I see people between 18 and 99. I'll take the stories and listen to people under 18, but I'm not doing therapy with them.

Is there a particular age group that responds better to past life therapy?

No, it's not the age so much as the person. However, I do see more women then men, by about three to one, but that's true of all psychotherapists. More women come to therapy. They're more open to this and they're less afraid.

Since you started past life therapy have you relied less on medication for your patients?

Yes, I use medicines less. If someone is severely depressed I still use anti-depressants. Not only does that help the depression, but they also make the person more accessible. They're able to focus and concentrate better. The medicine brings them back to a state in which I can work with them.

Have you ever measured the brain waves of a person under hypnosis experiencing a past life?

I started to do that with a person, so I did that once, but I don't know if that's enough. And others have. In hypnosis you find very relaxed alpha and theta brain rhythms. But in past lives you find all different brain patterns: alpha, beta, theta. You find visual waves because the occipital cortex, which

controls vision, is stimulated as a person is seeing things. I've
measured brain waves using an enhanced EEG, and we got a
whole smorgasbord of brain wave patterns.

Are there misconceptions about reincarnation?

Probably the most famous misconception is that everyone was
Napoleon or Julius Caesar. But most of us have been living
pretty ordinary lives where we've been learning. There are even
more misconceptions about hypnosis: that it's the only way to
have reincarnation memories. Hypnosis is only a state of focused
concentration. You're not sleeping, it's not a dream. Your mind
is still there, you know where you are. That's why I wrote
Through Time Into Healing because I had thousands and
thousands of letters after Many Lives, Many Masters with these
questions. I wrote this book in part to clear up all the misconceptions. No, I'm not the only one doing past life therapy. Lots of
therapists and physicians are doing it. There's nothing to fear,
you don't get stuck in a past life or under hypnosis. You can come
out any time you want — just open your eyes. You aren't
harmed, you don't have heart attacks, you don't actually re-
experience the physical pain or disabilities. You're aware of it,
but it's not like it's happening fresh. You can float above it, or
stop it at any time. You're always in control.

Have any patients taken a turn for the worse as a result of past life
therapy?

I still haven't found one. I have a feeling that has to do with
the wisdom of the subconscious mind. It will not let something
out that harms a person.

If we can go back to past lives, can we go forward to future ones?

There are people who are doing this work, such as Chet
Snow, the president of the APRT Society. He's a psychologist. I
haven't found it, and probably the reason is I'm not looking for

it. Mostly I'm doing therapy and it seems to have some residue from the past.

If you're going to the origin of a problem, it makes more sense to look back.

Just like in traditional therapy, in this lifetime, we look back. However, at another level, and the physicists tell us, too, there probably is no time. It's all happening simultaneously. It just feels like there's time. As if there's a flow to it, from past to future.

Would you like to try going into the future?

I tried that with Catherine, right off the bat. And it wasn't allowed — that's what she said. I think there's a lot of truth to that. Our subconscious minds or our higher wisdom really directs the traffic. The past — yes, it's already happened, you can learn from it. But the future — that's a series of probabilities.

How about parallel lives, if there are parallel universes?

I think at some level we probably can, but then you're getting into the future again. To me, parallel lives or universes represent those choices, the alternatives. So it's like climbing a tree. The higher up you get, the more you're committed to a particular branch, and you're not on the other branches but the other branches are still there.

Are there an infinite number of parallel universes?

Yes. But it's only our mind that balks at the idea of infinity. We're always doing that. We limit God. We limit God into being a person. And we limit ourselves the same way.

God is looked at by many as an outside force, something outside the universe that regulates everything.

Instead of within. I say, "Why limit God?" Perhaps God can listen to all of our prayers, all at the same time and pay infinite attention to it, because God isn't a human being.

So, you're saying that if there are an infinite number of possibilities, then nothing is impossible, and therefore, God can be everywhere.

Yes, and we can all be part of God, and yet be separate, in terms of our own perspective. But we really are all connected.

So, if we're all connected to everything, then by definition aren't we connected to God, too, since God, or a higher being, created all of this?

Yes. Now you're approaching my very simplistic way of viewing everything. That God — love — is an energy that is in everything. Intelligence, wisdom, love, compassion, all of these traits, and more, and that's all that we're made of.

Is the biggest reward from death access to all knowledge, and to finally get some answers?

Yes, but let's look for that in life. We can start to find some answers, and through different means such as meditation, contemplation, giving up fear, relaxing, using these altered states not with drugs but through visualization, maybe we can come up with these answers even while we're in bodies. We certainly will afterwards.

How has working with reincarnation therapy affected your own religious beliefs?

If I were filling out a form I'd still write Jewish, but I'm much more a part of all religions now. I'm feeling and trying to act more spiritual than ritualistic. To me there is one God. One because God is in everything. God is the same God in all religions. I don't think one has to change one's religion to find God or truth or wisdom. I'm hoping that the distinctions and differences among people disappear, and that we all realize that we're connected, that we're brothers or sisters, that we shouldn't be separated because we've separated ourselves by religions, we should be brought together. So, I would be much happier if there were just one religion, a religion of love and spirit, hope and wisdom.

How has your work affected your political and social beliefs?

It has a great deal. It has to do with values. I'm much more aware of the environment now. We have to live on this planet, and we may have to come back here and live again, so what we do isn't just affecting our children, it may be affecting us as well! I'm much more aware of making the world safer. With the rise of nationalism now, it's taking people and separating them — it's worse than religions do — instead of bringing them together. And this is sheer madness. I don't want to use words like liberal and conservative, because they've lost all their meaning, but I'm certainly for that which promotes peace, love, the environment and brotherhood.

When you stumbled upon past life therapy with your patient Catherine, were you seeking something in your life?

I wasn't seeking at that time. As a matter of fact, things were going very well. I was Chairman of Psychiatry at Mount Sinai, and the youngest professor at the University of Miami medical school that they ever had in psychiatry. I was publishing papers, getting national recognition in my field. I was earning a lot of money, my family life was going very well. At that time it was like I was just floating along, not paying much attention, and here comes something to shake you up and turn you upside down. It was more like that. It didn't come out of a spiritual crisis, it came out of a time of comfort and affluence. Like I wrote in Many Lives, Many Masters, it really hinged on the *conversion which took place through this patient. The intellectual pursuits, studying psychiatry took me in a different direction: how the mind works, that's all there is. Very mechanistic view of things. Freud to many psychiatrists replaces God. My religion didn't fill the gap either. It was more ritualistic and lacked certain spiritual roots. It really came about through this patient and then subsequent patients, and my reading and interacting with these people, and others, meditating, too. These changes took place during the last 10 years. And it's in a completely different direction from my earlier background.*

Why did you decide to go public with your work by writing your first book, *Many Lives, Many Masters*?

That was a very difficult decision for me, and it took me four years to go public, even after I finished treating Catherine. I sat with the tapes I made of the sessions collecting dust in my closet because I was afraid. Afraid for my reputation. I'd spent twenty years going a very formal way: Ivy League education, Columbia, Yale, publishing. But I kept finding more people having these experiences, and I started to research it, read, met people, had more patients come in, and it really was the fear of death that seemed so pervasive, and here I was finding out that death is not what it appears to be, there's more to it, and in fact we don't really die. Yes, our bodies do, but we go on. It seemed too important. I knew that if I went public, I would reach more people than just those coming into my office one at a time. So in a way I started to feel guilty that I had all of this information and I wasn't sharing it. I think one of the reasons Simon & Schuster took my book was my credentials.

In your second book, *Through Time Into Healing* you write about the past life therapy work of other doctors as well as your own. Were they reluctant to go public?

The doctors that I've talked to have been quite reluctant to go public. There are exceptions though, and I'm encouraging them to go public. I've gotten more than 100 letters from physicians in the U.S. and elsewhere who are doing this work in secrecy. They always tell me the same thing: "I've been doing this work for 10 (or 15, or 20) years, but in the privacy of my office." They always preface it: "Don't tell anyone, but..." And then out come these beautiful, wonderful stories of their case histories.

Do you treat other doctors and members of the medical community?

Oh, yes, many. These doctors, while they'll tell me privately, are still reluctant to go public.

Have any of your patients claimed to know you in a past life?

Just Catherine. Our meeting had something to do with the carryover from a past life. I was an uncle to her and a teacher in a Greek lifetime.

Tell us about your past lives.

The first time I remembered was during an acupressure massage. I had an old neck injury that was flaring up and I went for treatment. At that point, Many Lives, Many Masters *has been written, but wasn't published yet. And I wasn't telling a soul. I was afraid for my reputation and career. So I mentioned nothing to the therapist. I would go into this very relaxed, almost meditative state, and during the third or fourth one-hour session I saw this image. It was me, taller, thin, wearing a multi-colored robe, standing in a very large geometric shaped building. I knew I was a priest of some sort, very powerful, with the ear of the royal family, and I was misusing the position. I had some psychic abilities in that life, too. And I was misusing it to gain more power, sex, greed, things like that. It was a very good life!* (he laughs) *Very easy, but wasted. I had* spiritual knowledge but wasn't teaching it. I was using it for my own personal gain. The word ziggurat kept ringing in my head. I had no conscious memory of every coming across that word. It doesn't prove that I didn't, in college or something, but I didn't remember it. I didn't say anything to the therapist, went home and looked up ziggurat. It's a word for architectural structures, temples of the Babylonian era, like the hanging gardens of Babylon.

I had another experience years later. I had this dream of being imprisoned in a European dungeon, my arm chained to the wall. I was being tortured for teaching about my religious beliefs, which included reincarnation. And I died in that dungeon for teaching this. I became aware, as I died, of a message: "When you had the chance to teach it, you did not." I knew that was referring back to that episode with the ziggurat. "When you didn't have the chance, you did." And I knew that meant that I should have taught about love. I didn't have to teach about reincarnation and get killed for it. I went too far. The implication was: "Now you can have both. You have the chance, and you can teach about it." It's as if those two were the important past lives.

How did your family react to your past life research?

My wife does this work, too, so Carole's very involved and believes in this. She believed in this way before I did. Not in reincarnation — I don't think either one of us ever talked about that — but in psychic phenomena and parapsychology. In the '70s, she and another couple wanted to go see a psychic. They thought it would be a lark. And I wouldn't go. I said, "Why do you want to waste your money? We can go to a movie, do something real." So they didn't go. That's how closed I was to it. My youngest brother is an oncologist in St. Louis, and he is now finding incredible stories with his dying cancer patients. Mystical experiences, out-of-body experiences. A lot of doctors are having these experiences, but they're afraid to talk about it. Peter now talks about it and some of his patients are in my new book.

Who are The Masters?

> *This is what Catherine, the woman in* Many Lives, Many Masters *described as the source of the information that was coming to her. She would hear them, and then tell me. It would come through her. But she had no memory of it when she awakened from hypnosis. When she was in-between remembering past lives she would go into this state. She said this was coming from the master spirits, so she called them The Masters. And out came this knowledge that was very unlike her. Even the phonetics, grammar and style were completely different. And she wasn't an actress or a multiple personality or schizophrenic. I've had other patients tell me things — it's coming form a more pure source that's not contaminated by our brains. I've had much contact with the masters, but they're not identifying themselves by that name anymore. Through Catherine the messages from these masters, these spirits, was so beautiful, so spiritual.*

In the beginning, perhaps to get your attention, The Masters came out with your late father's Hebrew name, and your infant son's cause of death, information that Catherine didn't have, and had no where to look up.

> *I think that was The Masters' way of getting my attention, and it did! There were facts that she had no way of knowing. This is described in detail in* Many Lives, Many Masters, *because it moved me so much. That was the turning point, when I started to believe it, rather than think it was imagination or fantasy.*

The Masters' messages of peace, love, understanding and God was all basic spiritual knowledge we've also heard or read elsewhere.

> *I think that's really the underlying message. But there's a great deal of complicated physics and laws of nature that are between that message and us.*

Are we all connected to The Masters?

Are The Masters different from our higher selves? And if they are, aren't we still connected at some other level? I'm not sure. I'm still getting these essays (while meditating) and other messages, such as the ones at the end of Many Lives, Many Masters, *and a few in* Through Time Into Healing. *I've had a few other patients who are coming out with incredibly wise and spiritual knowledge, sometimes involving physics, and yet the patient doesn't have that kind of education and knowledge.*

When you spoke to The Masters through Catherine, did they make any predictions?

The only prediction they made is that we better get things together on this planet because we're reaching a point where it could become irreversible. For people, for survival. And this was in the early 1980s, before the ozone hole and the greenhouse effect.

Many people think: "What's it to me? I'm going to be off this planet in 50 years," but if they thought they'd come back and have to live here again, then it's a different story.

That's right. You can say your children, grandchildren and loved ones will be here, too, but if that's not enough for you, so will you! There's more of a shared responsibility for taking care of your home.

Do you think past life therapy is the next great leap in psychiatry, and if not, what do you think might be?

I'm not sure it's the next great leap, but it's going to be a magnificent leap. There are still some marvelous breakthroughs that will come with the biological understanding of the brain, with Alzheimer's, other memory disorders, schizophrenia, manic depressive illness. Past life therapy is also extremely important,

*and while it may not be the next great leap, it may be the most
important.*

What do you think of other alternative approaches in physical and
mental health?

*I do feel that there may be validity to many of these
approaches and we need to study these. That's why I was
heartened to see that the National Institutes of Health created a
division that deals with alternative and holistic approaches (the
Office of Alternative Medicine, created in 1992). The
government is funding and supporting this. There's a tremendous
amount to gain, both in healing and direct physical and mental
health, but also because it will save so much money. We spend so
much money treating heart disease, effects of hypertension and
stress-related disorders, ulcers, so many other illnesses that have
their roots in stress, in immune system dysfunction. We can't
afford to overlook these alternative therapies, many of which have
much validity: hypnosis, biofeedback, to name just two, are
extremely valuable. Visualization techniques have already been
shown to help certain immune system dysfunctions. Cancer,
autoimmune disorders and other physical illnesses may have their
roots in impaired functioning of the immune system. We can't
afford to overlook these therapies. We shouldn't minimize their
importance.*

Now the NIH's Office of Alternative Medicine is in full swing and
books about spirituality are all over the bestseller lists. When the
mainstream finally caught on to mind/body medicine, holistic health
and personal spiritual growth, they pushed ahead with it very quickly.

*And it's still moving very quickly. That's one reason why I go
on these television shows, Oprah and 20/20 and all the others,
and conduct workshops, because it helps to tell people it's all
right to talk about these things, that it's not weird, it's not
strange, it's not crazy. When people talk to other people it ripples
out like a pebble in a pond.*

Give us an example of a dramatic turnaround with a patient.

A woman who couldn't button the top button of her blouse recalled a past life under hypnosis and learned she'd been guillotined. This had affected her present life's relationships and her ability to trust. And once she remembered the guillotining, it all began to clear up. She was able to close the top button right away and that set off a chain reaction.

The skeptics haven't given you a hard time, so what's the worst thing that's happened as a result of your work with past life therapy?

I think it's people taking advantage of it. Suddenly there are so many past life therapists.

Trying to cash in on what they consider the latest trend?

That's right. Some have training and they're good. Others have no training and they hold themselves out as experts. Some have fake degrees. It's been disappointing.

How should people go about finding a good past-life therapist?

They can write to me. I've been interviewing therapists and screening them, and I know many of them, so I can give out a list. And the list keeps growing!

What makes a good past-life therapist? Since this field is relatively new, where can they get training? Or are they self-taught like you originally were?

Some of them are trained. I conducted a week-long training workshop for about 25 doctors from all over the country. And I brought in some other therapists who'd also been doing this a long time, to train the others. What's required are people with good clinical training. They have to be able to handle what comes up. Just like in going back to childhood. It's the same

thing, but the arena is much larger. The therapy is important.
You have to have the training, whether it's a Ph.D. or an M.D.

Part Two

Five

Arun Gandhi

*Past the seeker as he prayed, came the crippled and the
beggar, and the beaten. And seeing them, he cried,
"Great God, how is it that a loving creator can see such things
and yet do nothing about them?" God said, "I did do something.
I made you."* — Sufi teaching story

*Peace comes not from the absence of conflict, but from the
ability to cope with it.* — Anonymous

My life is my message. — Mahatma Gandhi

$\mathcal{M}$ohandas Karamchand Gandhi was born in India on October 2, 1869, the youngest of four, the son of a prominent local politician. In keeping with Hindu tradition, Gandhi was married at only 13 to Kasturba, a girl of the same age.

At 17, Gandhi went to London to law school, and then returned to India to practice law. At 24, he took a job in South Africa, unaware of the discrimination against Indians in this white-ruled, British-ruled country., So, he booked a first class seat on the train there, boarded, and was shocked when he was thrown off the train. That nightmarish experience led him to stay in South Africa and actively oppose their racist laws and policies, and the following week he began by organizing a meeting of Indian immigrants. This was the early 1890's, and Indians in South Africa were not allowed to vote, own property or be on the streets after dark. There was much work to be done if discrimination was to be successfully challenged.

In 1906, when Gandhi served in the Boer War as a stretcher bearer, he got a first-hand look at the extent of British domination throughout South Africa, and that same year he became political for the first time when he gave a speech and led his first non-violent protest, this one triggered by the law that required Indian women to be strip-searched as part of registering for their required I.D.

Gandhi called his non-violent strategy "satyagraha," coining the phrase by combining two Sanskrit words that created the powerful new phrase: "The pursuit of truth." And it worked. When South Africa declared Hindu and Muslin marriages invalid, a national strike led to the repeal of those marriage laws.

In 1915, Gandhi returned home to India to challenge Indians to resist British repression, exploitation and rule, just as he had done in South Africa.

In 1919, he led the non-violent protest of repressive new laws by calling for a labor strike. And when Indian troops under British command then massacred hundreds of Indians at a protest gathering, Gandhi's plea for his people to resist taking violent revenge led Indians into their first mass movement for equality in their own country, a movement bearing the hallmark of non-violence. His methods were simple, yet proved effective, but they worked only because their power was created by the participation of millions of Indians. For instance, Gandhi spent at least one hour each day spinning his own yarn, and urged Indians to spin their own, too, and then make their own simple clothing and not wear the Western fabrics that just contributed to British economic and cultural control of India.

Salt was also a very lucrative industry for the British, who had made it illegal for Indians to make or sell it. In 1930, by then 61, Gandhi, nicknamed Mahatma ("Great Soul"), led his people in a non-violent revolt against these salt prohibitions, a strategy whose drama would make the world take notice.

In his Salt March, he simply led Indians to the sea to make salt. To build momentum, he walked 10 miles each day, and gathered more and more people as the march passed through village after village. The world did, indeed, take notice, and this act of what was dubbed "political theater" captured headlines across the globe. It took Gandhi and his growing legion of freedom marchers 24 days to reach the seashore, and when they arrived the massive group was hundreds of thousands strong.

Indians openly made and sold salt in the aftermath of this history-making march, and thousands were jailed for doing so, including Mahatma Gandhi. International pressure led to his release, and he was then invited to meet with the Viceroy to negotiate with the British government in India.

The following year, in 1931, Gandhi traveled to London for further meetings. He would not accept special treatment, and traveled third class, staying with the poor once he arrived in London.

When he appeared before the King of England, he did so wearing only a loincloth, his traditional clothing, having long since abandoned wearing anything more than that, and the occasional robe, believing that he should dress no better than the poorest man in his land. He was criticized for daring to present himself to the king in what looked like nothing more than his underwear, but he amusingly replied, "The king is wearing enough for both of us."

While in London, Gandhi called for no less than India's complete independence from Great Britain.

His visit captured the attention of the world, which by now revered him for both his spiritual and political leadership and message of non-violence, equality and freedom. But that freedom would still elude India for awhile, and Gandhi's calls for it more than ten years later, in 1942, in a speech given in India, would land him in jail for two years. In 1944, he suffered an even more personal blow when Kasturba, his beloved wife of more than 60 years, died in his arms.

For the next three years, serious negotiations were finally underway between Gandhi and Great Britain for India's freedom. It was during this pivotal time in India's history that Gandhi's 12-year-old grandson, Arun, came to live with him in 1946 for an 18-month stay that led well into 1947.

On August 15, 1947, thirty-two years after Mahatma Gandhi began his non-violent revolution in India, the country's independence was granted by the British.

The celebration was overshadowed by the growing tensions between India's two main religious groups, the Hindus and the Moslems, over their roles in a free India. To resolve this, India was partitioned, and the country of Pakistan was created. Civil war broke out as Moslems fled into Pakistan from India, and Hindus fled into India from the area that was now Pakistan.

A half a million people died.

Mahatma Gandhi was heartbroken, believing that his non-violent message had ultimately failed, despite its ability to win India its independence. To protest the violence of the civil war, Gandhi went on a hunger strike, and again, the world watched. A week later, the violence against Muslims in India's capital, New Delhi, ceased, but it continued across the rest of the country. So, Gandhi did what he always did best: he walked from village to village, calling for peace.

On January 30, 1948, five months after India's independence, Mahatma Gandhi walked to his daily prayer meeting in New Delhi. It seemed like any other day, until a Hindu man came up to Gandhi, bowed, and shot him three times.

Gandhi's last word was Rama, Hindu for "God."

Mohandas K. "Mahatma" Gandhi was cremated in a public ceremony attended by hundreds of thousands of Indians who chanted "Gandhi is immortal." His ashes were taken by a third-class train to the shore and scattered in the ocean.

In December, 1999, Time *magazine named Mahatma Gandhi one of the top three most influential people of the century.*

꙳ ꙳

ore than 50 years after his death, Mahatma Gandhi's quest for non-violence continues, not just in India, but around the world. Arun Gandhi, Mahatma's grandson, now in his sixties, has been running the M.K. Gandhi Institute for the Study of Non-Violence since he opened it on the campus of Christian Brothers University in Memphis, Tennessee on October 2, 1991, the 122nd anniversary of his grandfather's birth. Through the Institute, Arun Gandhi also lectures around the world on aspects of non-violence, equality, and many of his grandfather's other teachings about conflict resolution.

"People have a narrow concept of non-violence," says Arun Gandhi, a philosopher, activist, and writer who was a journalist with *The Times* in India for 23 years. "They think that it's just used in political situations. But you can use it to deal with conflicts at all levels, starting with the self."

Only in this way can true peace be achieved, according to the teachings of Mahatma Gandhi.

In 1934, Arun Gandhi was born on Phoenix Farm at the Phoenix Institute founded by his grandfather near Durban, South Africa. Although Mahatma Gandhi went back to India to work for its independence after he'd spent 21 years working against discrimination in South Africa, Manilal, the second of his four sons, stayed with his wife and three children in South Africa to continue his father's work. In 1946, Manilal and his wife, Sushila, thought that their 12-year-old son, Arun, born and raised in South Africa, would benefit from a year living with his grandfather in India, particularly at this time, when Mahatma Gandhi was in the throes of India's negotiations for independence.

So, the young boy went off to India, where he lived with his grandfather from 1946-1947, the crucial 18 months that led up to India's independence, and its immediate aftermath, just five months before Mahatma Gandhi's death.

Living with Gandhi was not simple.

"He used to be on the move all the time, all over India. He never traveled alone, he had an entourage of 15 to 20 people traveling with him all the time," Arun recalls. "He taught me, and arranged for teachers. Every day, at 5:00 p.m., he'd stop everything, and for one hour he'd go over my lessons. He scheduled his day exactly to the minute."

During their travels, "everywhere we went, hundreds of thousands were waiting to meet him," Arun remembers. "Communication was bad in those days under British rule, but people in remote villages somehow found out that his train would pass through, and they'd walk 10 or 15 miles just to see the train go by."

Arun would often wander in and out of Gandhi's meetings with high level British and Indian politicians during the final stages of the struggle for independence.

"Grandfather had a tremendous energy about him. He was a simple man, dressed in that robe, and he'd sit on the floor, yet you were drawn to him and hung on to every word he said. But he wasn't the kind of person who demanded things of you. He welcomed other points of view and arguments."

On August 15, 1947, India was granted independence from the British Empire, and one month later Arun went back to his home in South Africa.

Five months later, on January 30, 1948, at the age of 78, Mahatma Gandhi was assassinated in New Delhi while on his way to a prayer meeting.

"I was surprised," says Arun. "He was such a loving, dynamic person. I couldn't imagine anyone wanting to kill him. My second reaction was to go out and throttle the man who killed him."

The assassin was arrested and tried. Found guilty, he was sentenced to be hanged. In the Gandhi spirit of non-violence, "my father and the family pleaded with the government not to do it, but the government said they had to follow the law."

The assassin was executed.

"Toward the end of his life, my grandfather suspected he'd be assassinated. He said he wanted to die with the name of the Lord on his lips, and that's exactly what he did," says Arun.

As a young boy, Arun also got to see the lighter side of Mahatma Gandhi, who he says, "had a tremendous sense of humor. He was outwardly smiling and joking, even though serious events were unfolding. He could be a child with children, and a statesmen with politicians. He had an inner peace that enabled him to be calm."

Asked if there's anything we'd be surprised to know about his grandfather, Arun grins and replies that the revered leader known for his lengthy hunger strikes, "loved to eat, especially sweets."

I first met Arun Gandhi in October, 1991, the month that he opened the M.K. Gandhi Institute for the Study of Non-Violence. That fall he also spent a few months lecturing in Florida at a university and to the public.

At the time, he and his wife, Sunanda, were writing a book about Mahatma Gandhi's wife, Kasturba. Six years later, *The Forgotten Woman* was published by Ozark Mountain Press.

During this first conversation, Arun Gandhi's wife, Sunanda, sat at the dining room table of the townhouse they were staying at in Palm Beach Gardens (a pretty seaside town not to be confused with Palm Beach, the exclusive island of the rich, famous and notorious, a 20-minute drive south), working on stacks of research for their book, while Arun and I sat in the living room casually chatting about his legendary grandfather. Dressed in a T-shirt, jeans and sandals, he looked just like anyone else spending a day at home. As you can tell from the conversations you'll read, he has a relaxed, easy-going manner, a clever wit and laughs easily. Must be genetic.

The Gandhis have two children: their daughter Archana is a librarian in the U.S., and their son Tushar works in publishing in India. And, at last count, Arun and Sunanda had four grandchildren. As you will also read in our conversations, the Gandhi family has an inventive way of dealing with challenging moments between parents and children that has been part of Mahatma Gandhi's legacy.

Before we began, Arun Gandhi handed me a list that his grandfather had published. Titled *The Seven Blunders*, this list of no-no's creates violence and turmoil, and formed the backbone of everything Mahatma Gandhi worked to prevent:

The Seven Blunders
1) Wealth Without Work
2) Pleasure Without Conscience
3) Knowledge Without Character
4) Commerce Without Morality
5) Science Without Humanity
6) Worship Without Sacrifice
7) Politics Without Principles

Our conversation that day, and the one three years later, in October, 1994, naturally gravitated to issues that in one way or another touched upon all seven of these, as well as Arun Gandhi's memorable year and a half living with his grandfather, and the legacy of the many years that followed.

ॐ

Did your grandfather's children follow in his footsteps?

Manilal, my father, was the only one who dedicated himself totally to non-violent work. He defied apartheid in South Africa and spent a lot of time in prisons there, and whenever his father launched a major "battle" in India, my father would go to India and participate in that and go to prison there also. He ended up spending about 15 or 16 years of his life in prison.

Did your father ever talk about how he felt about being the son of someone who was so revered in the world? Did he feel that it paved the way for him to continue his father's work, or did he feel "How could I ever live up to my father?"

He did recognize the responsibility. He felt that he had to live up to his father's image and expectations and that he needed to do as much as he could. He recognized the fact that he might not be able to achieve as much as his father had achieved, but at least he would achieve a small percentage of it. And he tried his best to do that.

He could continue to carry the torch.

Right.

How did you feel growing up? Before you spent that year with your grandfather, were you aware of just how important he was?

Not until I went to live with him. We were away in South Africa and we would periodically visit him in India. I first visited him when I was three or four years old. When I went and lived with him at the age of 12, and spent those 18 months, then it really struck me how popular he was and how the people revered him all over the country. And it made me feel very proud that I was so close to him. So close to a person who was so widely respected and revered.

What was the biggest impact your grandfather had on you personally? What's the biggest lesson you learned from knowing him?

There were many lessons, and almost every day he taught me something. I think the biggest lesson that he taught me, and that I learned, one that I feel ever grateful for, is how to deal with anger. He taught me positive ways of dealing with anger, instead of the normal negative reactions to anger.

What did he teach you about that?

Well, he told me, first of all, that anger is like electricity. That just as electricity can be very deadly and destructive if we abuse it, anger, too can be very deadly and destructive. But, if we use electricity intelligently, we can bring it into our homes and factories and businesses and use it for the good of human beings. Similarly, anger, too, can be used positively and for the good of human beings.

To use anger as a catalyst for change rather than just a method of expression?

Right, right.

Did he have any psychological tips, behavioral tips about what people should do when they feel angry?

One of the things he asked me to do was every time I felt that surge of anger, if I could walk away from that situation and take time out, and go and write. He asked me to write an anger diary, go out there and pour my feelings and all the anger out into the diary. And then, in a moment of calm and peace, go back to the diary and read what I'd written and see how I could've used that energy in a more positive manner. He also taught me that there may be some occasions when you can't walk away from the situation. Then you have to face it at that moment. But in those circumstances, don't react in anger, count to ten, or say under your breath, "Calm down, calm down." Just repeat it like a mantra until you feel in control of your senses. And then do whatever is necessary. He also said that we are not governed by logic, so we can't eliminate all violence. There may be some violence necessary in our lives, but as we become more and more civilized we should be able to reduce the level of violence as much as possible.

How did he personally deal with people whom he could not get through to by trying to reason with them, people who were stubborn and cruel? Did he have a certain way of talking to these people?

He was very calm. I don't remember him ever losing his temper with people. He would treat them with respect and make them sit down and go on telling them over and over again, over a period of many days and sometimes even weeks, to convince them about it. I don't think there were many cases where people remained stubborn with him and wouldn't listen to him. He had a knack for getting through to people. He was so sincere and so open that it was difficult not to believe him or accept what he what saying.

Did he use his sense of humor when dealing with people?

Oh, yes. He had a tremendous sense of humor and he would use it all the time. I remember once when I was testing him after he taught me about anger. I wanted to see if he had control over his anger. There were hundreds of people every day seeking his autograph. And he had decided to sell his autograph instead of giving it free because he needed funds for all his social work, especially among the untouchables. So it was my duty to go out and collect all these autograph books and bring them to him, and the money also. And one day I thought, "Well, if everybody can get his autograph, why not me?" And I put my autograph book in the pile, and when he came to that book he looked at it and said, "Where's the money for his?" and I said, "This is my book and I don't have any money." So he said, "I don't make exceptions for anybody, even my grandchildren, so if you want my autograph you'll have to go and earn the money and pay me and I'll give you an autograph." And I said, "No, I'm going to make you give me one free." And I challenged him and said I'm going to pester him until he gives me one. And he laughed and said, "Okay, let's see who succumbs to this." And from that day onward, every day for weeks I would barge into his room when he was in the midst of some very important meetings with British politicians and Indian politicians — you know this was in 1946 on the eve of India's independence — and I would go in and pester him for the autograph. My reasoning was that when he was in the midst of such important things he would want to get rid of me, and he would sign the book and give it to me. And he didn't. But he never got angry, he didn't tell me to get out of the room. In fact, every time I became too insistent, and too boisterous, he would just put his hand around my mouth and press my head against his chest and go on talking politics (we laugh).

Oh, that's great!

He never did give me the autograph. And never got angry with me.

Was there anything that occurred during the year and a half that you were with him that really surprised you? We tend to think of people like your grandfather as being larger than life, and so when we see the human side of him, and realize that he's just like everybody else, there's a sense of surprise in that. Like, did he secretly read comic books? What did he do that was just like the rest of us, but we would not have expected from him?

(He laughs) *Well, he used to enjoy spinning very much.*

Whenever we sat down to talk we would both spin on the spinning wheel. And I remember on many occasions I would challenge him to see who did the best or the most spinning in that hour. We would really race each other (we laugh).

Were you spinning cotton?

Spinning cotton, yes. And the race was to see that we had the largest amount of thread, and the thinnest thread. I would always beat him in that (we laugh again). He acknowledged that in a letter to my parents.

Did he write to your parents often to tell them about your progress while you were there?

Yeah, and his letters were often very short. Just one paragraph. But in that brief space he would give them a list of whatever I was doing, and whatever he thought about it.

Did you have any idea at that age what kind of work you wanted to do?

No, I had no idea whatsoever.

Did he try to encourage you in any particular direction?

No, I don't think so. He did encourage me to learn my lessons — history, geography, and mathematics and all that. I was not interested in any of these lessons at all, and I never really paid much attention to it. I know that in some of his letters he had complained to my parents: "I just can't make Arun learn anything, he's too playful and doesn't concentrate on his lessons." He sounded a bit exasperated (we laugh).

What do you think was the best part of living with him?

I think I just enjoyed the glory, the attention that he got and the reflected attention that I got. Hundreds of people, and thousands of people coming and just wanting a glimpse of him, and here I was so close to him and so intimate with him. It made me feel real proud.

Did any of his other grandchildren come to live with him at times?

Yes, everybody did, but you see, the difference was because we were away in South Africa and we came only once in three years to see the family (in India), we stayed for a longer period (in India), whereas the others were all living nearby in India, so they would come for a few days and go away and come back. They didn't have that kind of concentrated period that I had — 18 months exclusively with him.

How many grandchildren did he have?

Fourteen.

Where did you fit in, among the oldest or youngest?

I was in the middle.

Are any of his other grandchildren following in his work?

All of us are doing something or the other in different fields. I am involved in the Institute and teaching the philosophy of non-violence. The others are doing it in social work — I have a cousin involved with children and women's affairs — and I have another cousin active in politics, my sister has been a member of the African National Congress and she was under house arrest for fifteen years

Are you one of the few Gandhis who managed not to be arrested?

(He laughs) Yeah. Among the grandchildren, actually none of us have really spent time in jail.

Your family is one of the few where people can actually be proud of having been in jail.

(We laugh). *Right!*

It means you were doing your job!

Right! No, I take that back. Some of the older grandchildren — two of them, I remember — they went to prison on a number of occasions during the freedom struggle in India. During that time many of us were very young so we couldn't go to jail.

Do you feel that your grandfather's presence is always felt within the family, that there's never a moment when you're all not aware that you're related to Mahatma Gandhi?

Yeah, it's difficult to put that away! (we laugh).

It's so much a part of everybody's life every day.

Yeah, yeah, even when we go out and people come to know the name Gandhi, they immediately want to know if we're related. And sometime they confuse us with Prime Minister Gandhi, Indira Gandhi. And then we have to explain that there's no relationship at all. We're different families.

Is Gandhi a popular name in India?

Well, our Indian names are originally caste-based. And caste is profession-based, so whatever profession you were involved in you got that name for the family name. Gandhi is grocer, someone who sells food grains. So, all people who sold food grains were known as Gandhi. It's a very common name. So somewhere along the line, I don't know where, somebody must've been selling food grains in our family. So we got that name and it's been there since then. For nearly five generations before me nobody has been involved in selling food grains! (We laugh). *So, it's got to be way, way back.*

What was the family business in the home that your grandfather was raised?

They were prime ministers of the states they were living in. These were princely states that were owned by royalty in ancient India and they needed prime ministers to take care of the administration of the states. My great-great grandfather, and right up to my grandfather, everybody was in that work. It was during my grandfather's time that they gave that up. The two states were Rajkot and Barbandar. Barbandar was where my grandfather was born.

Growing up at the Phoenix Institute in South Africa, you worked on the publication that the Institute published.

It used to be called The Indian Opinion *when Grandfather started it, and it was meant for the Indian community there, to teach them about non-violence. But then, later on, when my father took it over, we enlarged the scope of the paper and dropped the word Indian, and made it just The Opinion, and distributed it to all the different races, the whites, the blacks, the Indians, everybody. It was published until around 1979 or 1980. My father died in 1956, in South Africa, and then my mother took over. I had gone to India to perform the last rites for my father. And then I met my wife, Sunanda, who was a nurse, and decided to get married, and the South African government wouldn't allow me to bring her back with me to South Africa. It was a ploy to keep a Gandhi out. So, I was forced to stay in India. My mother and my two sisters continued to edit the paper every week until 1980. By then, they'd run into a lot of financial problems with the paper. It wasn't paying for itself and Mother couldn't continue. Her health wasn't good enough. So we decided to close it. I was living in Bombay, then.*

What happened to The Phoenix Institute after that?

The Institute was destroyed in 1985 during riots between the African and Indian community that were engineered by the apartheid government to keep the communities divided and oppressed. The white government kept the others fighting all the time. In the past it used to be contained. Just small pockets of violence. It would last a day or two and everything would subside. But, this time, in 1985, it become more violent and also the government saw the opportunity to get rid of the Institute, which was a pain in their side for a long, long time. So, they instigated the blacks to target that area and they just watched — literally. The police sat on the outskirts of the 100-acre area of the buildings as the place was plundered, broken and set on fire. When my sister went and asked them to do something about it, they said: "We can't do anything because this is private property and unless we get written permission from all the trustees, we can't enter the property." So, they just sat there and watched, and the whole place was destroyed. And then the land was taken over by about 30,000 squatters. The Gandhi family lived on the property. Worked and lived with other families. At the time it was destroyed, there were about 10 families living there. All of the archives and possessions were destroyed in the fire. That was my grandfather's first Institute, first commune that he build in South Africa. All his original furniture, printing machines and all sorts of things were all gone, up in flames, destroyed or looted."

Where else were Gandhi's historical documents and things stored?

In South Africa, that was the only place. In India, there are many places. The main one is in New Delhi, where they have the Gandhi museum and there they have preserved much of the collection from India.

Where did your family go when they had to leave Phoenix?

> *My two sisters remained there, living in Durban, about 18*
> *miles north of Phoenix. My mother came and lived with me for*
> *awhile in India, but she was so heartbroken that by 1988 she'd*
> *lost interest in living and died in December of '88 in South*
> *Africa. She was 83. My older sister is Fita, and my younger*
> *sister, Ela, was a member of Parliament then in South Africa.*

You'd been working as a journalist in India, at *The Times*, and then as the editor of a monthly magazine there. And in 1984, the year before the Phoenix Institute was destroyed, you came to the U.S.

> *I decided to come to the U.S. because I wanted to write a*
> *book about caste systems, South Africa apartheid, and U.S. race*
> *problems. On a grant I came to the University of Mississippi*
> *with a fellowship. In 1988, I began doing lectures at universities*
> *across the U.S. Then when I visited my mother in South Africa,*
> *just before she died, I saw the remains of the Phoenix Institute*
> *and I decided to open an institute in the U.S. attached to a*
> *university. To raise the money for it my grandfather's personal*
> *letters to the family were sold at an auction in London which*
> *raised $56,000, and then more funds were donated by friends.*
> *We've also been doing a lot of fundraising. I believe, as my*
> *grandfather did, that we are now faced with the option of non-*
> *violence or non-existence. So, at the Gandhi Institute for the*
> *Study of Non-Violence, we develop programs on how to deal*
> *with conflicts in a non-violent manner. We don't have to kill*
> *people and do all the ugly things we're doing.*

You've said that your grandfather couldn't have accomplished all that he did without the support of your grandmother, who is the subject of your book.

> *Right. I was very young when she died, but from what I*
> *gather from people who knew her and who lived with her, she*
> *was a very strong person. She wasn't one who could be ordered*
> *around. She wanted to be convinced about everything. Even*
> *when Grandfather wanted some changes in her attitude or her*

feelings or whatever, she wanted to know why. She wasn't going to do something just because her husband said so. She wanted to be convinced about it and wanted a proper explanation. She was a very dynamic woman. She was quite the strong-willed person. And she supported him when she appreciated what he was doing. But she wanted to be informed about all of these things.

They married when they were very young, didn't they?

Yeah, they were 13 years old, which in those days was considered to be very old! (We laugh).

And so, when they married at that age, they were still in school.

Oh, yes.

So did they live with their parents or did they set up their own home?

No, they lived with the parents. In India we still have the giant family system, and so people continue to live with their parents, even after they're married, for various reasons. Now, of course, in some of the big cities this family system is breaking down a little, but by and large in India we still have the family structure and people live together.

When did your grandmother die?

She died in 1944.

A few years before your grandfather did.

Yes

How old was she when they had their first child?

*She was 16, going on 17 when the first child was born, and
the child died I think a day or two after birth.*

Did she actively work along side your grandfather?

*Oh, yeah. In the commune, the ashram they had set up, she
was the Universal Mother, and my grandfather was the
Universal Father there. She was in charge of everything.
Otherwise, she did what wives did. The women took charge of
the kitchen. It was a communal kitchen where everyone would
come and eat together. All the women together would cook the
meals. The duties were all divided, and, of course, sometimes
they did work that was traditionally to be considered men's work
and the men did work that was traditionally considered to be
women's work. The men helped in the kitchen. It was a way to
break down the old traditions, the unnecessary traditions and to
make everybody equal.*

Did she have any particularly unique talents?

*She had a tremendous talent for resolving conflict between
people. She had that inborn knack in the way she handled
people.*

It seems to be the official Gandhi way. *(We laugh.)* Do any of you
guys fight with each other? *(More laughter.)* When you were kids growing up, I can imagine that your parents would've been appalled if they
ever found out that their kids ever fought. *(Even more laughter.)*
"Uh-oh, you're a Gandhi, you're not supposed to hit your sister!"
(The laughter continues.) Did you feel pressure when you were a kid
growing up, that you had to behave a certain way just because of the
family name?

*Yeah, there was a little bit of pressure sometimes, in the
young days when you're very impetuous and all that sort of thing
it was a bit of a problem. But, right from our childhood we were
never scolded, beaten or whacked or anything like that. There*

was no violence used in our family at all. In fact, every time we did something wrong or misbehaved, the parents took the punishment instead of the children.

Really?

Yes.

You mean on your behalf?

Yeah, well, the parents would say that you did this because there was probably something wrong with the way I brought you up or explained things to you, and so for that mistake I must punish myself first.

Oh, my, that certainly doesn't happen today, does it?

No, it doesn't. And so the parents would punish themselves. They would skip a meal or fast for the whole day or something like that.

I'll bet that probably worked really well because it made the kids feel really guilty.

It did (he laughs). *I remember one instance when I was sixteen years old and my dad wanted to go and attend a conference in a town that was 18 miles away. And he didn't feel like driving that day, so he asked me if I was free and if I could drive him into the town, and I said fine. And Mother gave me a few chores to do there, a little shopping and all that. And I drove Dad into town and he told me that since I had the whole day, I should get the car serviced, the oil changed and all that, and then I should pick him up at 5:00 in the evening at a particular intersection. And I said okay, and I went and did all the work I had to do, and I found that I had several hours left in the afternoon. So I went to see a movie. And I didn't realize that it was a double feature, and I got so engrossed in the movie that by the time I got out from the movies it was about 5:30.*

And I ran back to the garage and picked up the car and went to where Dad was waiting, and it was a quarter to six by the time I reached there. And he was naturally really concerned and upset, pacing up and down. The first question he asked me when I reached there was what happened, why were you late? Instead of telling him the truth, for some inexplicable reason I lied to him, and I said that the car wasn't ready, that I had to wait for the car, not realizing that he had already called the garage to find out.

Oh, no! *(we laugh)*. You got caught!

I got caught (he laughs)...red-handed! And he was very disturbed by that, and he said that he'd probably done something wrong in the way that he'd brought me up that I didn't have the confidence to tell him the truth, and I lied to him. So, he said, 'I'm going to walk home now. I'm not going to ride with you.' It was 18 miles. He started walking at about 6:00 in the evening. Half of those 18 miles was through dirt roads and sugar cane fields, no pavement, no lighting or anything. I couldn't leave him and go away, I had to drive the car in a crawl behind him all those 18 miles. I can still remember that day. I have not forgotten.

How long did it take you to get home?

Five hours (We both laugh).

Yeah, I'll bet you do remember that day!

Uh-huh!

Yeah, that works, that's good guilt. That works real well.

Real well (he chuckles).

Did you use that method with your kids?

Yeah.

Did it work?

Oh, yeah!

When you talk to people about this today, what kind of reaction do you get from parents? These ideas would be very hard to convince American parents to use, even though they would probably work very well. How do you get people to change their way of thinking?

Well, I talk to them and explain the whole concept, which is built on love and respect for each other. The reason why it worked in our family is because there was so much love and respect for each other. The children respected the parents, the parents respected the children. We loved each other, so if we did something wrong it pained everybody. And that's what we need to bring back now. We have destroyed the family unit, we've destroyed relationships, and there's no respect for anybody.

It's all one giant power play now.

Yeah, yeah, so that's the price we pay for it — through violence. If we want to turn things around, then we at least have to rebuild some of these things: some respect, concern, love and attention to relationships must be there.

Are people asking you now to comment on the O.J. Simpson case?

No, not yet (he laughs). *Nobody has asked me that question.*

The idea of family violence and the violence between husbands and wives.

They ask about general violence, and youth violence, but

180

nobody's specifically asked about the O.J. Simpson case.

Well, let me be the first to ask *(we laugh)*. Let's talk about violence between husbands and wives.

> *All violence is unnecessary, whether it's between husband and wife, or children and parents, or children and children...violence is something we must avoid. It's not the right way of resolving conflict. We must find more peaceful ways of doing that. And it's not that we can't do it. I think that we can. But, the problem is that in all of our relationships we become so intolerant of each other, so self-centered and selfish that we don't care what happens to other people. That fragments society, and eventually fragments the nation. I think that's happening on a vary large scale in the United States.*

Unfortunately, there isn't a quick fix for this.

> *No, there isn't a quick fix, but there is a fix.*

What is it?

> *The fix is that we bring about a change in ourselves, and a change in our attitudes. There isn't a magic wand that we can wave and get the whole nation to change at one time. It has to be a process that begins with the self and builds up from there.*

For people to stop focusing on the competition for power.

> *Right. Power, economic power or political power, or whatever power.*

Or personal external power within relationships.

> *Yes. There have to be some limitations. We can't go for power or go for money at the expense of our relationships.*

Do you think your grandfather's approach and methods would work today? If he were alive today, what do you think he'd be doing?

He would have been involved with all of the conflicts we have. He would have continued to work to help bring about change. He was experimental, he was never dogmatic. He never believed that whatever he said was the ultimate truth. He kept changing. In fact, many people accused him of being inconsistent. And he said: "How can anybody be consistent in this world when truth keeps changing every day?" What appears to be true today, is not true tomorrow, and so we have to change along with it, and search for truth. So, he was a great experimenter, and I'm sure he would've brought about some profound changes in his thinking and attitudes to conform to the needs of this present time.

Do you think we're likely to see someone like him again?

Well, I don't know. At the moment I don't see any signs of anybody coming up to that level, but you never know. Somebody, somewhere might be motivated to do something and rise to the occasion.

Do you think that if he were handling things today in the same manner in which he did more than 50 years ago, that the fact that we are so instantly connected worldwide by the media now would change his approach at all, or change the effectiveness of what he did? Maybe he would have made more progress quicker because the whole world is so connected through the media, so the word would've spread and maybe he would have accomplished things more quickly today.

Right, right.

Do you think his approach would have been different today because of the times we live in?

No, I think his basic approach, his fundamental principles would've remained the same. The way he would've approached conflicts and problems may have changed a little, but fundamentally he was against the rampant greed that we display today. He always believed that there is an inverse relationship between materialism and morality: that when one gains strength the other becomes weak. We see that in our lives today. We have become so materialistic that we are willing to do anything to get what we want. We fling morality aside. There are no ethics, no principles, just a quest to make money or get power using whatever means possible. So, that's what's causing all the heartache, all the violence.

That seems to be what's at the bottom of the violence even between kids, when you hear that they're shooting each other over a pair of sneakers.

Right, yeah. Once we get rid of that greed and become more human...you know, my grandfather didn't totally reject materialism. He believed we could find an equitable level at which we could live comfortably with materialism and morality in our lives. And that is the balance we need to find. We've just given up that balance and we've gone so rampantly for materialism that it's crazy.

Would he be disappointed if he could pop back here for a day? In looking around, would he think: "I died 50 years ago, and I would've thought that by now everyone would've learned from everything we went through in those days and that things would've gotten better, not worse!"

(He laughs.) *Yes, yes, certainly he would've felt that. He had a humorous exchange with a journalist, and when this journalist asked him "What do you think of Western Civilization?" And he responded: "It's a good idea."* (we laugh.)

I like that. That's very good *(we laugh some more)*. When you were living with him, did he talk to you a lot about his spiritual views?

Well, not to me specifically, but he was always talking about it in the mornings and evenings during the prayer meetings, and after the prayers he would give a short sermon. And in that he would always insist that all of us have an openness in accepting other religions and other faiths and other beliefs, and in incorporating the good from all of them into our own beliefs.

He was Hindu, right?

He was born Hindu, but he was not the type of practicing Hindu that you have today, in the sense that he didn't go to temple, and he didn't believe in all the Hindu rituals that people practice. In fact, he held his prayers every morning and evening outside in the open when the weather permitted, or in a big room when it was raining. And he incorporated hymns from Christianity, Judaism, Islam, Buddhism, and Hinduism. It was a half an hour prayer service with universal prayers. He respected the beliefs of all the religions. He had that kind of openness.

Did he believe in reincarnation?

I think he did.

Did he ever talk about where he thought his soul was going to go, where he was going to go in the afterlife, what he thought it might be like?

No, I don't think he dwelled on that very much. He said he was interested in this life, and that he wanted to do as much good as he could do in this life. He believed that heaven and hell existed here on Earth, that we didn't carry any baggage with us to wherever we go after this life, that whatever we have to pay back or suffer is all in this life.

What do you think his idea of heaven on Earth would be?

Oh, that's a difficult question to answer.

Obviously, a place with no violence.

Yeah, where there was no violence, where people lived in harmony, peace, and brotherhood and sisterhood.

Did he have any artistic talents, besides spinning? *(we laugh.)*

No, none that I know of.

How about music?

He didn't play anything, but he did like listening to it, but his time was taken up by so many things that he rarely had the time to relax and listen to music. His music was during prayer times. They sang hymns.

When the two of you would get together to discuss your lessons, did he take a practical approach with you since you were a child, or did he talk to you as if you were an adult, and talk philosophically?

No, he would treat me as a child, and try to explain things to me. He had a knack for explaining these profound philosophies in a very simple way, using simple anecdotes and incidents that happened during the day to illustrate the points that he was trying to make.

When you picture him in your mind, how do you see him?

I always have that last image of him, wearing that loincloth, barechested, and with that toothless smile. If you've seen the photographs of him taken during the last few years of his life, that's the image I have of him.

You know, everyone wants to know what was under that robe.

(He laughs.)

When I mentioned these interviews to a few of my fellow journalists, and asked them if there was anything in particular they wanted to known about Gandhi, one of them said, "I want to know what was under his robe." I said, "You mean that of all the things you could ask Mahatma Gandhi's grandson, you'd want to know what was under Gandhi's robe?" Well, he laughed and said, "Well, no one ever told us what he wore under his robe!" *(we laugh.)*

Yeah (he continues to laugh).

So, here's your big chance to tell us what was under that robe!

(He's laughing so hard he can hardly answer). *Well...what do you think was under the robe?*

More robe? You know, we have this image of him in that loincloth that looked like a giant diaper, so I figured it was probably just more diaper under that one! *(We both continue to laugh.)*

Yeah...well, it was just a piece of cloth that he wrapped around him. Even today, a lot of people wear that, but of course they wear it down to their ankles, not up to their knees like he did. But, under the robe he didn't wear anything. And he didn't wear any clothes above the waist. When he got cold, he'd just wrap that shawl around himself.

What was his reason for dressing that way?

Because of the poverty in the country. He said: "Because the poorest person doesn't have more than this, I don't have any right to wear anything more than the poorest person." It was just his way of identifying with the poor people.

Did all of his robes and loincloths come from the cotton he spun or that was spun there?

Yeah, either he spun or grandmother spun or somebody in the family spun and gave it to him. He wouldn't wear it otherwise.

You've said that in the end he thought he would be assassinated.

I guess he had a sort of premonition in the last few months of his life.

I would imagine that for most of his life he had to have been in some kind of fear for his life because he knew that they regarded him as "public enemy #1," and there probably wasn't a day that went by that he didn't think, "Today's the day they could send somebody to kill me."

Right. Yeah, I guess so. But more so in the last few months of his life when things really became angry, when the Hindu-Muslim issues became very touchy. That's when he realized that he was going to be assassinated.

I imagine he would be quite pleased with the turnaround in South Africa, to see Nelson Mandela become president.

Yeah, he would be pleased, but I think he would also be a little disappointed, as I am disappointed, but I guess that's part of life.

Disappointed that there has not been further progress?

Disappointed in the sense that I think about all the violence that came out of Mandela's release from prison, especially with the Zulus and other people, and all that. I think much of that could have been avoided if Mandela would have taken a leaf out of Gandhi's life. Gandhi, when he went back to India, after 22 years in South Africa, was advised to go around the country (India) for one year, not to make any political pronouncements, but just go meet the people and talk to them, and understand their problems and build bridges with the people and the leadership that had emerged during his absence. And then get involved in politics. And he took that advice and it served him well because he was able to mobilize everybody from the commonest person to the leaders of the country. He was able to carry all of them through the struggle in India.

Whereas, Mandela came out of prison after 27 years of total isolation, when he was not even allowed to think about politics, never mind talk about it, and instead of coming out and emerging as a statesman —the world had given him the opportunity to be a statesman; he could have risen above being just an African National Congress leader if he had spent two or three months, even one month, going around the country meeting people and talking to them and re-establishing his link and coming to his own conclusions about the situation in South Africa instead of depending upon the briefings that he got in the last few days from his ANC executive committee...if he had gone and met with (the other leaders) and all the people and built bridges with them, I think he would have been able to forge a much stronger unity with the entire non-white, and even some white, people in South Africa and avoided much of the violence that took place.

That's not a method that people use these days, is it?

And that's the trouble, that's the trouble.

They don't do the one-on-one, quiet gathering of information. Everything is quick, boom, boom, boom, put together a group of people, go on TV.

Exactly. Then, you pay the price for that.

There seems to be no room in our modern world for someone who is a gentle soul.

Right.

They tell you, "No, that's not the efficient, political way to get things done."

The greed for power is so overwhelming, yeah.

What would you most like to do on behalf of your grandfather?

Like my grandfather told me, "You should remember that you'll never be able to change the whole world, but if you're able to change a few people during your lifetime, that will be a great accomplishment, and those few people will carry on the work and change other people." And so I've used that as my guideline. And I'd be very happy if I'm able to change and affect the lives of a few people during my life, and if that change can spur further changes that would be the ideal thing.

Do you get feedback from the various programs and lecturing that you do? Do you hear back from people later on that they've applied some of the principles that you talk about and that they've worked?

Yeah, a lot of them do write back, and many of them say that they've been affected by what I've said and that they're trying to use that in their lives.

Do you speak a lot at schools, to parents or children?

Yes. In fact these stories that I've told you are now making many of the sermons in churches around the country. I was taken aback.

Have you been able to make the Institute as visible as you want it to be?

I have been able to make it very visible. In fact, I'm very satisfied.

Have you been to meet with people in Washington over any

189

issues?

Yes, I've even done a workshop at the National Security Agency (he laughs).

They want to know how to handle national security without violence? *(We both laugh.)* Now that would be a neat trick.

Yeah (he laughs). *I did a workshop and there were about 150 of the people in the agency participating, including the director, and I have a medallion from him to testify to that* (we laugh).

Is that the most unusual place you've ever presented a workshop?

Yes, I was shocked. I was absolutely shocked when they invited me. You never know...things come from the most unlikely places.

You worked at *The Times* of India in Bombay. Do you ever miss writing all the time?

I miss writing, yeah, and sometimes I miss journalism. It gets into your blood after thirty years.

You told me a few years ago that you began by covering the crime beat. That's pretty ironic *(we both laugh)*.

Right. That was standard practice. All junior reporters had to go through the beat.

Did you ever find yourself bringing your grandfather's non-violent perspective to your reporting on crime?

(He laughs.) *I didn't have much of an opportunity, but then gradually I started writing more and more on social problems and eventually they pulled me off the crime beat* (he laughs).

It finally occurred to them that Gandhi was not a byline for crime stories *(we laugh)*.

Right! And then I started writing a lot about women's issues, and children's, and general social problems.

Do you still have family in India?

Oh, yes. We still have a close attachment to the extended family.

So, they're scattered between South Africa, India and the U.S.

In South Africa, I just have my two sisters and their families. Uncles, aunts, cousins and others are India.

Do you ever have a Gandhi family reunion?

No, we haven't had one for a long, long time. And I think that's primarily due to the fact that we're scattered almost all over the world. There are a few of us here in the United States, and a couple in England. Travel is such an expensive thing, and unfortunately, Grandfather didn't allow us to accumulate wealth (we laugh).

Yeah, there's not a giant Gandhi family trust fund out there.

Yeah (he laughs).

It must've been a big culture shock going from Bombay to Memphis.

Oh, yeah (we laugh), *a very big culture shock.*

Is living in the U.S. like what you thought it would be?

Yeah, in many ways it is. In many ways it was a good and

pleasant change. Life has been easier here and more comfortable, with so many things available and all that. In India, life was hard and it was a struggle. You get up in the morning you stand in line for milk, then you have to stand in line for bread. Then you go to work and you have to push yourself into an overcrowded train. It was a big hassle. It was a hard life.

It's a little more low key here.

Much more low key, much quieter, more sedate and peaceful.

Especially in the South.

Especially, yes.

It would be very different if you were in New York. You would feel like you were back in India again.

Oh, yeah, that's why I don't like to go to New York or any other big cities. I've had my share of living in big cities.

Do you like Memphis well enough to stay for a long time?

We've been very happy here. The people have been very nice, very warm and affectionate. There's no reason why we would want to run away from here. We are quite happy.

And you've just created a new brand of cooking. Indian Southern cooking. Fried chicken curry.

(We laugh.) *Right!*

When you're bringing Indian culture and mixing it in with Southern culture, what does that create? Does that really create Fried Chicken Curry? *(We laugh.)*

Yeah, and you know it's strange, we think that the people in the South are very conservative and a very closed society — that's the general impression people have everywhere — but I was surprised that the people in the South who have gone to India and lived there for many years and learned Indian culture and come back and have become greater experts in those fields than many Indians are.

Americans are very fascinated by all kinds of Eastern philosophy. You hear of people going over to study in India, people with more intellectual curiosity that want to go do that. Plus, Americans always think that the "grass is greener on the other side."

Yeah. I always thought that people from the West Coast or the East Coast were more open and that they would want to go to India to study. I had never imagined that a young woman from Birmingham, Alabama, for instance, would go to India to study. And there are some who have done that. And now they really are experts.

Americans feel that there is a richness and tradition in Eastern philosophy that's missing in the West. So people always go there to look for the answer to the meaning of life.

Right.

People come to America, though, to make money. They don't come to America to look for the answer to the meaning of life.

No. (We laugh.)

We leave here and go to the East for that.

I didn't think that the American people were so into making money, even though I knew that a lot of Eastern people were coming to the United States to make money. And I thought that...well, I would always say that the Easterners are so narrow-minded, that all they could think of was making money, and making a new life in the U.S. Then, after coming here and living here I got a little bit of a shock to see that everybody was into making money (we laugh).

Surprise, surprise!

Yeah.

What do you think is the best part of living here? Besides cable TV.

Well, I guess the comforts that are available. The essentials of life are so easily available, except health care.

What do you miss the most about India?

I miss the warm relationships. I miss the extended family. I miss the warmth of people spontaneously coming and participating and enjoying and living together and all that. Here (in the U.S.) it's more formal in the sense that it's difficult to go and visit people unless you make prior appointments with them.

Just to drop in and visit with a friend, you have to plan that two weeks in advance because everybody's too busy.

Right, yeah. And in India we just do it spontaneously.

It didn't used to be that bad, even as recently as ten years ago. You could just pop in on your friends and not think twice about it. But, now, you're lucky if you can see them once every few weeks. And you've gotta make an appointment.

Mmmm, yeah. In India we would do so many things spontaneously. You'd come home from work and the children would be playing, and you'd say, "Let's invite some friends and have a potluck." And we'd all get into the mood and call up all our friends and say, "Whatever you've cooked, bring it over, and we'll all sit together and eat." And they would do it. We would all do it. Spontaneously.

Yeah, I miss that, too.

We would all go to somebody's home, meet there and eat and have fun and come back home again.

I think that another reason that's so difficult to do here now is that nobody lives close enough anymore. Even when they live in the same town, it could still be a half-hour away, and then you figure traffic.

Right. Yeah, but then I see here near a university campus that people live much closer to each other, but it's even worse. I was in Oxford, Mississippi on the university campus there for four years, and all the Indian faculty and so many others that we met all lived across the road in that small area, but it was the same thing there — you couldn't go and pop in or have spontaneous parties or anything. We had to call a few days in advance because their programs were set a week earlier, you know, and much of it was just to put up a big show of being so busy and all that (he laughs).

Considering the schedule you have now, do you plan a vacation any time soon?

At Christmas we're going to see our daughter and her family. And they know I'll hardly leave the house.

I guess every crusader needs a rest.

Oh, yes!

Six

Charles Jaco

Life is full of little injustices.
Either they bother you or they don't.
Me, they bother.

— Anne Bancroft in *Garbo Talks*

*C*harles Jaco is not welcome in Baghdad. Panama declared him an Enemy of the State. They don't like him much in Haiti, either.

He's quite proud of this, as he should be. Dictators, bad guys and corrupt governments are never very fond of war correspondents, and nobody would expect them to be. Afterall, what self-respecting thug wants a crusader getting the real story out?

Getting the story out has been Charles Jaco's mission for more than 25 years, on radio and television, in the U.S. and every major hot spot abroad. He became a household name back in January, 1991, when, as one of the first correspondents on the scene, he was the first to report live for CNN from Saudi Arabia the night The Gulf War began, as scud missiles exploded overhead.

He stayed for the entire war, and finally, at it's end, in early March, "when I saw Charles Jaco standing in the streets of Kuwait City, I knew we were free," a Kuwaiti resistance fighter told *TV Guide* in 1991, adding that the CNN correspondent had become a symbol of resistance to the Iraqi invaders.

Jaco is that kind of guy. Gets into the thick of it. Like a character in a movie, he's from the old school of war correspondents who don't give a damn about hair spray and don't let a little danger (okay, a *lot* of danger) get in the way of getting at the truth and bringing it to the public.

Let's take a peek at his official bio. and see just what he's gotten himself into:

In 1979, Jaco covered the Sandinista overthrow of Somoza for NBC Radio. Five years later, he was back inside Nicaragua, this time traveling with Contra troops as they sought to overthrow the Sandanistas. Between a diet of roasted iguana and plantains, and weeks spent slogging through the Nicaraguan jungle, he reported and produced a series of award-winning documentaries.

In 1985, Jaco was off to Africa. He covered the famine and civil war in Ethiopia. He spent two nights pinned down in a village in Tigray province, as Ethiopian warplanes bombarded suspected rebel bases inside the hunger zone. He sneaked across the border from Sudan in a convoy of food for starving villagers in Eritrea province, only to have the Ethiopian air force napalm a truckload of lentils. All the food was lost. He walked away from a plane crash when a DeHaviland Twin Otter carrying relief supplies landed on a dirt runway that had been torn up by air drops of food. The plane went from landing at over 90 miles an hour to a dead stop, flipped on its nose, in three seconds.

He also covered the war in Angola, riding with South African tank columns as they were outflanked, and eventually defeated, by crack Cuban troops. He covered the war in Mozambique, in a devastated countryside held hostage by adolescent boys with AK-47s. He also covered the slowly cracking apartheid system in South Africa, and was stabbed while doing interviews in Soweto.

The Africa series yielded two award-winning radio documentaries — "The Politics of Starvation," about Ethiopia, and "Race Against Time," about South Africa. They became the first works by a single journalist to win both first and second place in the Edward R. Murrow awards competition.

In March, 1988, Jaco was severely beaten by the Dobermans — Panamanian riot police under the control of Manuel Noriega. After knee surgery, he returned to Panama in October, 1989, to cover elections there, even though he had been forbidden to enter the country because of a series of newspaper articles he had written on Panama. He managed to get in anyway, and his coverage on CNN of Noriega's blatant theft of the elections led to Jaco being declared an Enemy of the State.

Jaco went into hiding with a U.S. intelligence officer, driving through the tear gas-filled darkened streets with a loaded .45 on the center console, as members of the so-called Dignity Battalions kicked in doors, looking for Jaco and others declared enemies of the Noriega regime. He was finally smuggled onto a U.S. air base, and out of Panama.

The next month, Jaco covered the rebel offensive in El Salvador. Salvadoran army helicopters in which he was flying were shot down twice, damaging his knees even further. One of his cameramen was shot through an artery and a vein, and lived only after three major operations.

Having spent Thanksgiving day pinned down by gunfire in Salvador, Jaco spent Christmas of 1989 back in Panama, for the U.S. invasion. He and a U.S. trooper poked through the Comandancia, which had once been Noriega's headquarters and was now a pile of smoking rubble. In a sub-basement, they found Noriega's office. While the trooper made off with a Noriega passport and business cards, Jaco found the watch Noriega wore when wearing his combat fatigues as head of the Panama Defense Forces. Jaco still wears the watch.

Jaco has been chased from a Bolivian town by campesinos angry with the United States for eradicating the coca leaf crop. He has, at various times, been declared persona non grata by the governments of Cuba, Iraq, and Sudan. He was almost killed by Tonton Macoutes in Haiti, who tried to shoot him and his camera crew. He has been detained by Cuban police for interviewing dissidents. He and a cameraman were almost killed by a mob during heated elections in Jamaica.

In the United States, Jaco was camped in Waco for the entire eight weeks of the Branch Davidian siege. He covered the Rodney King riots in Los Angeles, becoming one of the few reporters willing to travel into South Central to interview gang members. He has infiltrated the American Nazi Party in Chicago, and slept on the streets of Phoenix and Washington, D.C. for a series on the homeless. He has reported from the center of three major and five minor hurricanes. In Washington, D.C., he covered Congress, the White House, the State Department and various intelligence agencies.

Immediately after Iraq's invasion of Kuwait in August, 1990, Jaco was one of the first American journalists in Baghdad. Jaco bravely bypassed Iraqi censors for interviews with the human shields and Kuwaiti hostages. As a result, he was declared persona non grata by Baghdad and ordered out of the country.

Jaco became known throughout the world for his dispatches from Iraq, Saudi, and Kuwait during the Gulf Crisis and Gulf War.

Overseas assignments have taken him to Iraq, Iran, Kuwait, Saudi Arabia, Jordan, Syria, Egypt, Trinidad, Cuba, Haiti, El Salvador, Nicaragua, Guatemala, Panama, Honduras, Bolivia, Columbia, Peru, Chile, Argentina, Kenya, South Africa, Mozambique, Angola, Ethiopia, and the Falkland Islands.

He has won a Cable Ace award, two George Foster Peabody awards, two Edward R. Murrow awards, six National Headliner awards, and three dozen other national and international journalism awards. He has written for dozens of magazines and newspapers, from the Chicago Tribune and Miami Herald to Rolling Stone.

In his novel, DEAD AIR, Jaco raises serious questions about chemical and biological poisoning in the Middle East. Does Saddam Hussein pos-

sess weapons of mass destruction because American companies shipped him chemical and biological agents? Did the U.S. government try to cover it up? And is that why the Pentagon still denies that Allied troops were exposed to chemical weapons during Operation Desert Storm? Jaco raises these important questions in his book, DEAD AIR, published by Ballantine in March, 1998.

❧ ✦ ❧

*M*y, he's been busy. Like everyone else, I was glued to CNN during the Gulf War back in the winter of 1991. One night, while watching one of Charles Jaco's harrowing live reports, I said out loud to the screen: "I want to hear your war stories."

Jaco is a writer and a philosopher and a man of wit, irony and searing truth. His live shots and his taped reports reveal that and more. He's a character. He's got some Mark Twain in him, and some Dennis Miller. He's smart and irreverent. My favorite kind of interview.

Because of Jaco's globe-trotting, he was based out of CNN's Miami bureau. We first spoke in November, 1991, just months after the Gulf War ended, then followed that with interviews in January and August, 1992, and the spring and summer of 1998. During those early '90s conversations, Jaco was living forty minutes north of Miami in a condo filled with the stuff of his travels. It would barely be an exaggeration to say that it looked like the Egyptian room of a museum — pitchers, plates, bowls, rugs, pillows — yet it was welcoming and comfy. The ideal setting to hear about mideast adventures.

Charles Jaco thought we'd go to war in the Gulf as 1990 drew to a close.

"The deadline was firm," he says. "I knew that if Saddam didn't pull out of Kuwait, something was going to happen quickly. We looked at the almanac and the moon would be dark from January 16th through the 18th. The deadline was the 15th. We knew that the airstrike would be best with no moon."

Jaco was in Saudi Arabia for CNN. The first thing he did was learn the gas masks and chemical suits. Then the antidotes.

"We were given sets of injectors with two-inch spring-loaded needles," he recalls. "One was the antidote and the other was a tranquilizer because the antidote would drive your heart rate up to 300."

Starting on January 9th, Jaco began to get physically ready to cover combat. "I did intense physical training for a week. I have a bad left knee from Panama, so I put it in ace bandages and did the training — walking, running, sit-ups, push-ups," he says. "It wasn't grueling, and I worked out between filing stories."

Based in Dhahran, in a hotel right between two main runways of the Dhahran Air Base, journalists had U.S., British, Kuwaiti, and Saudi air forces all around them.

On the night of January 16th, the handful of other CNN correspondents were out in the field with the ground forces news pool. Charles Jaco happened to be the only one in Dhahran. It was just reporter's luck that he happened to be in the right place at the right time and able to go live first with the mayhem in Saudi, and one of the war's most terrifying moments for CNN viewers.

"I'm asleep, it's 2:30 in the morning and Jim Miller, the producer who'd set up our whole coverage operation in Saudi, calls me up. 'You'd better turn on your TV — it's started,'" Jaco remembers.

The coverage Miller was referring to was the memorable Peter Arnett-John Holliman-Bernard Shaw coverage from the Iraqi city of Baghdad under fire.

"I went to our live shot position on the roof of the hotel," he says, "and the sirens in Dhahran are going off. What you couldn't see on the broadcast were the Saudi and U.S. soldiers in MOPP — Mission Oriented Protective Posture — gear, right next to me, just off-camera. And we were just standing out there on the roof with our masks on. I took my mask off as the camera rolled and we went live, and immediately began talking. There were planes taking off behind us, and soldiers kept telling our crew to get out of there and into a shelter. All of a sudden the lights go out, the camera and power go off. They'd turned the power off in the city."

But, viewers didn't know that. All they saw was a screen that suddenly went dark, and then static.

If you were watching Jaco's live coverage on the roof, well...

"It looked for all the world like we'd just swallowed a missile. But we hadn't."

Jaco and his crew scrambled to the shelter and put their masks on.

"They told us to breathe slow and easy. I was tired, so I went to sleep."

A couple of hours later, the All-Clear sounded and they left the shelter.

"The shelter was in the basement, and since gas *sinks*, this was a bad place to be. We decided not to go down there anymore. I went in there just once more, to ask a question, and they locked me in briefly. I got them to let me out, and they said: 'We can't be responsible for your safety.' I said: 'Hell, *I'm* not responsible for my safety!' I had on my chemical suit and I left the shelter."

During the first week of the war, he broadcast live on CNN, gathered his information, and managed to catch 90 minutes of sleep in bits and pieces during the day.

"I had my best 45 minutes of sleep on a pile of chemical suits using my gas mask as a pillow," he laughs.

The Patriot Missiles were stationed close by, though Jaco and his crew didn't know that until the war began. "They didn't tell us. The Patriots were good at knocking the Scuds off course. Only a few times could they totally destroy a Scud, but they gave us a feeling of security, and by knocking them off course they saved a lot of lives."

That first week of the war, Charles Jaco was the only CNN correspondent in Dhahran. Then he split up the work with the correspondents who returned from the ground pool, including Carl Rochelle, who normally covered military affairs in Washington, D.C., and Brian Jenkins, who normally worked out of the New York bureau.

But, during that first week, when he was going solo, Jaco says the best part was "the rush. It was lots of play-by-play, but little context. Just a cascade of images, but the speed of events was so great that there was no time for context. We also had no idea how many people were watching."

After the end of the first week, though, they saw the ratings and numbers in the computers. The Gulf War had brought CNN its highest viewership since its birth a decade earlier. Their live war coverage would make CNN the network of record from then on.

During the second week of the war "we started receiving press clippings about the ratings, and then fan mail. Lots of it from military families thanking us. People sent cookies and other things."

After awhile, Jaco says "the Saudis asked us to edit our tapes of the Scud missile impacts so their locations wouldn't be revealed. We couldn't say Dhahran or show it live. The other networks weren't under such restrictions, and we were told that was because 'His majesty doesn't watch the other networks.'"

Jaco and his crew were catching on to what the outside world had been seeing for weeks: CNN's meteoric rise.

"The Governor of the Eastern province of Saudi Arabia couldn't get through when he tried to call Larry King on the air. That was one of the reasons an international call-in line was added," he laughs.

In February, three to four weeks into the war, the Iraqis attacked the city of Khafji, just north of Dhahran, and "shot it to pieces," he recalls. "I had been there 12 hours before the attack, reporting on an oil spill."

After the attack, Jaco flew to Khafji on a C130 transport. "The Saudis took us in a press pool to do a story on Khafji being liberated from the Iraqis. The bus was rattling around as B-52s were dropping bombs. And I thought, *something's* wrong here. We got there and all the lights were out. The Saudis were saying this was a great victory and that they'd liberated the city, but not only were the Iraqis still bombing north of the city, but the city wasn't secured. There were lots of Iraqi snipers. And there were mines all over the place left by the Iraqis. We set up a camera, and I look over and there's half of a dead Iraqi solder. Later, I kicked something, and I was afraid it was a mine. It was the soldier's head."

After an hour and a half there, they got back into the bus and left.

"The military said that it would be safer to leave. We were in the desert going west and suddenly the bus stopped dead. The radiator was overheated. It's the middle of the desert. Iraqi tanks are on their way. We had U.S. soldiers on board the bus. We needed to save our water because we were in the desert, so we couldn't put it in the radiator."

The drivers asked all of the men to "water" the radiator organically. They did, and the bus was up and running again.

But, not for long.

"The drive shaft broke. It was night and very cold," Jaco remembers. "We were on our way to see Iraqi POWs."

They didn't get to see those POWs, but they did get out of the desert some five hours later when a Saudi truck picked them up. Jaco and the crew flew back on a C-130 to Dhahran. Once there they found out that during their desert foray Iraqi tanks weren't bearing down on them afterall. After a day and over night, their harrowing Khafji expedition was over.

Now, it was on to the next information gathering adventure.

"We knew the ground war was getting ready to start because new press pools were being formed in a hurry," he says. "CNN had an ancient truck and a generator they bought. The whole press pool system broke down, so a group of us from CNN just headed for Kuwait."

Jaco, reporter Brian Jenkins, producer John Towress, videographer Jane Evans, videographer/editor Dan Morita, among others — about a dozen in all — loaded up the portable satellite uplink into the truck, got some jeeps, and set out on their own for the tiny, ravaged country.

"We had to pass through checkpoints. One Saudi at one of the points wouldn't let us through," Jaco recounts. "So, Jane has tea in a tent with the guy. He said he needed something in writing in order to let us through in front of his men. Someone Kuwaiti who was with the crew wrote a permission note so the guy could save face in front of his men! Then he let us through."

They were detained again by the Saudis, this time at the Kuwait border, where U.S. Marines were also on patrol.

"There were three U.S. Marines there at the border post. This was the night the Scud hit the reserves barracks back in Dhahran. Anyway, we put the border post Marines on the air live. They'd been out there since August. I gave them our satellite phone so they could call home. One of the marines gave me an Iraqi battle flag."

The next day, Jaco and the crew headed north into Kuwait City.

"It was *raining* oil. It was pitch black at three in the afternoon. And at night it's the darkest thing you've ever seen. And there are minefields on either side of the road. The muffler kept falling off the truck. We were towing the generator. We had four jeeps in front. From the air we looked like a military convoy. We had flash panels made of orange fabric and these identified us as allies. They were on the roof of each vehicle. But the oil loosened the adhesive and they all blew off."

This made for a very nervous ride to Kuwait City.

When they arrived, they hadn't slept in three days. The war had been going on for about six weeks.

"When we got into Kuwait City, the buildings were black. The Iraqis had burned everything. Trucks were on their sides. Abandoned tanks everywhere. We stopped under an overpass to unload our video equipment."

Graffiti on the overpass said it all:

GOD BLESS GEORGE BUSH

WE LOVE YOU ALL

GOD BLESS CNN

It was the night before Kuwait City was officially liberated. A tense night despite the war's imminent end.

"I opened a can of beef stew and warmed it in over a skillet — it was my first real food in three days — and the Kuwaiti resistance fighters showed up," he recalls, "with their AK-47s."

The armed men set up a perimeter around the CNN crew to protect them.

"We needed gas for our generator, and one of the Kuwaitis brought us gas. We said we could use a drink, and he came back with scotch and gin," Jaco chuckles.

He began broadcasting this night before liberation, but only live by phone at first. Finally, two hours after their arrival in the city, their live video was broadcast at 9:50 p.m. during *The Larry King Show*.

"Everyone was moving quickly, there was gunfire in the background. We'd discovered that we were on the main road into the city, so we got the first video on the air of the convoy of allied troops coming into the city, and went on with it live," Jaco says. "The Kuwaitis treated us like Gods. The Iraqis had tried to take down all the satellite dishes and antennas in Kuwait during the war, but they didn't get them all. The Kuwaiti resistance would put blankets over their TV sets and watch CNN."

After Kuwait's liberation, Jaco spent two weeks in Kuwait City. CNN set up their headquarters at the Kuwait International Hotel, but Jaco slept at the nearby townhouse of one of the Kuwaiti resistance fighters.

Finally, in mid-March, Jaco came back to the U.S. and spent the next three weeks visiting with his mother, who was recovering from colon cancer surgery.

Although he had seen plenty of mayhem before, and in nearly every part of the globe, this concentrated war of a couple of months had a tremendous impact on him.

"The CNN staff included some of the bravest men and women I've ever known," he says quietly, with plenty of reverence in his voice. "They weren't the ones you see on camera, but they made our coverage possible."

As for those in battle, "the men and women who fought this war were magnificent," he continues. That unity of purpose unfortunately evaporated over the next two years after the war. The soldiers had come back to no jobs, the economy was terrible, racial tensions were escalating again. The question keeps coming back to every one of us who were in the Gulf, as either a journalist or in the military: *What's going on here?* Women and men of every race and creed joined together during the war and, to paraphrase the Nike ads, they *Just Did It*. They come home and things are just a mess. Not just economically, but philosophically and spiritually. It's absurd. People who went over to the Gulf as part of the National Guard or the military Reserves came home and their insurance was canceled because they weren't home to write checks! Then the military was downsized and these people are suddenly out of jobs! Everyone who was part of it will always be proud of what they did, even though the Gulf War became instant ancient history."

But it's legacy lives on in most unfortunate ways: Thousands of U.S. men and women who served in the war have mysteriously become ill since returning home with what has been dubbed Gulf War Syndrome. And suspicions are high that these illnesses are the result of exposure to chemical weapons and vaccines during the war, exposure that many fear the U.S. government would rather not address. And then there's the revelation that "the U.S. had a role in propping up and arming Saddam over the years," says Jaco, who makes this the central theme of his first novel, *Dead Air*.

War, Jaco believes, often brings out the best in people.

"During the war, there was no petty office politics, no ethnic politics or racial politics out there. The military did their job and we in the media did ours. It shows you that normal people are capable of great things. You can understand why guys came back from World War II saying it was the greatest time of their life," he says. "The heroes were people you didn't see on camera. I forgot who said this — the definition of true courage is being scared to death and doing it anyway."

Charles Jaco was more affected by The Gulf War than any other he's covered, he says, "because of the scope. Others were disorder on a grand scale. This was war."

The 10 weeks he spent there covering the entire war and its aftermath were a "a high point in my life emotionally and spiritually," he says, labeling it "another cauldron of human experience."

Understanding human experience and human nature has always been one of his passions.

Born in poplar Bluff, Missouri on August 21, 1950, Charles Jaco is the only child of a truck driver and a homemaker, and the grandson of farmers.

"I always wanted to write," Jaco remembers. "I was a voracious reader. By the time I hit first grade I was reading at a fourth grade level and I was precocious to the point of being thoroughly obnoxious."

His family had one of the first televisions on the block, and Jaco remembers watching coverage of the Korean War before he was even old enough to go to nursery school. "The only TV station we could get was CBS," he says, "and I watched Murrow and Cronkite. They were *gods*."

He says that "curiosity and a desire to write" propelled him into his life's work. That, and the fact that "I'm a nosy son of a bitch!"

He graduated from The University of Chicago in 1973 with a bachelor's degree in English, then worked as a freelance journalist writing for newspapers and national magazines, including *Esquire* and *Rolling Stone*. After receiving his Master's in Journalism from Columbia in 1976, Jaco went into radio news, spending most of the next dozen years with NBC radio and winning more than 40 major national awards for his international reporting. He joined CNN in 1988 and continued his award-winning coverage of controversial and political hot spots — now with video — until he left the network in March, 1994. He moved to St. Louis in 1995 and in February of that year premiered his daily interview and discussion program,

Newsmakers, on KMOX radio, a CBS radio affiliate.

In our conversations, which took place in 1991, 1992 and 1998, Jaco spoke eloquently about the nature of war and its seemingly ironic goal — peace. We discussed the changing role of the media in the last two decades of the 20th century and his experiences both before and after independent news reporting became compromised by corporate ownership conflict of interest and the rush for ratings by newly profit-oriented news operations. Our 1991 and 1992 conversations took place in the wake of the then recently ended Gulf War, and those are represented in this chapter's introduction. The conversations presented below took place in the spring and summer of 1998, right after the release of *Dead Air*, his first novel. His second novel, *Live Shot*, was published in December 1999.

❧ ❧

Is writing well the best revenge, as the old saying goes?

I may have had that thought in my mind at one point while I was writing Dead Air, but that's not what it's about. I wrote about how big media operates, how war correspondents operate, and were the men and women in the Gulf poisoned and did the government cover it up. With the network owner in the book, I thought, "Let's go over the top and make the guy evil."

How do you like writing fiction?

I love to write, and I'll always write. I have two more planned. Live Shot *will be published in 1999, and the story is set in Cuba.* White Balance, *about a race war in the U.S., will follow in 2000. (The titles of all three novels are broadcasting production terms.)*

When did you begin to write *Dead Air?*

I began with notes right after The Gulf War, late in 1991. That was the genesis of it. I seriously began writing the novel in February 1995, which was when I also started the radio program.

Your radio program, *Newsmakers*, is the kind of program that once flourished on commercial radio, but is now most often heard only on public radio, like NPR affiliates. How would you describe the format?

The show is what we make it, whatever we choose. We had Phil Collins on for an hour on one show because he's a bright guy. And while the Pope was in Cuba, we were the first radio program to go live and uncensored from Cuba. I've also carried live news conferences on the air and then followed them with interviews. I do the issues of the day. I always choose the ideas for the show. It's a two-hour program every weekday, and my primary purpose is that once during each hour, I want people to say, "Hmm...I didn't know that," or "Gee, that's something to think about." We take the high road. I'm just doing what I know how to do — I'm a journalist.

If you were still globe-trotting on dangerous stories, what would you have liked covering since you left that in 1994?

Every so often, reinvention is good for the soul, so I haven't missed any of the war coverage. I've taken the natural progression from one kind of work to another. But, I'm glad I could go to Cuba when the Pope was there.

I want to talk to you about that, but, first, what do you like best about radio?

That it's personal. Think about how you listen to radio. TV is communal, but radio is individual: I'm talking to someone in their car, at their home while they're doing something. I appreciate that because of the individuality. I'm talking to a person and I'm telling them a story. TV is passive, but radio makes you use your brain while you're listening. With TV you don't have to do anything, but radio makes you use your imagination to visualize and sense what you're listening to.

Back in January, 1998, you went to Cuba to cover the Pope's visit, and unlike everyone else in the media, you did not come running home when the Monica Lewinsky story broke. Tell me why you stayed and how you managed to pull that off.

Well, it was partially high-mindedness, and partially a guess on my part, which is how a lot of journalism comes to be created. The high-mindedness was that this was something that was tawdry and may or may not have involved the president having oral sex in the oval office with someone thirty years his junior, and then lying to cover it up. And, weighing that against the Pope visiting Cuba, and maybe effecting the same profound changes there that he started in places like Poland — because the Pope was considered the match that lit the fuse that blew up Communism in Eastern Europe — I wanted to observe that. And the guess was even if this story (Lewinsky) had legs, it would take months or maybe more to develop, that the president wasn't going to be quitting immediately, although I did speak to some people at the Cuban Foreign Affairs Ministry who were up all night trying to figure out how they might deal with a Gore administration (we laugh), so that became part of it. So, I didn't want to jump out of a phone booth wearing a set of red tights with a "J" on my chest for journalist; I'm not that grandiose about it. It's just that if I weighed the importance of the two stories to cover, and their long-term effects on everybody, then the choice would be fairly self-evident.

About how many journalists, besides you, stayed in Cuba?

There were a number who were there to provide spot coverage, but all the major anchors — Rather, Brokaw, Jennings & Koppel — and their support staffs left immediately. Jose Marti Airport looked like the fall of Saigon — they were falling all over each other to get out. What made the difference was, as far as the TV networks were concerned, without their major anchors there this was no longer the major story, it was no longer the focus.

And they certainly were no longer devoting the air time to it that they had been earlier in the week.

No, it kind of evaporated very quickly.

And they all canceled the specials they'd had planned for over the weekend.

Yup. But, I felt that from a kind of tiresome high-mindedness that (staying) was the right thing to do. And, in a more immediate sense, what we had lined up for our program was something that had never been done before, which is ordinary, average Cubans who spoke English — and they could be from any walk of life, and we managed to cull a fairly good random sample of about eight — speaking to regular Americans who were listening to the program, and exchanging ideas, exchanging questions. "How is life in your country?" a Cuban might ask, "Is it true that you'll die if you don't have health insurance?" and "How is life in your country?" an American might ask, "Is it true that you'll go to jail for years for criticizing the government?"

The callers were calling into your station in St. Louis, and a Cuban you were interviewing in Havana was able to answer their questions.

To answer their questions and talk to them. One of the most interesting interchanges we had was with one of the Cubans, and we had a live satellite hook-up with a St. Louis area congressman who is on the House of Representatives National Security Committee. And they got into a very interesting conversation during which this conservative Republican congressman admitted that Cuba was in no way a national security threat to the United States, and serious consideration should be given to lifting part, if not all, of the U.S. embargo. Well, that was the kind of stuff I was looking for. Not that specific statement, but committing journalism where not only was it entertaining and informative, but you might, if you got lucky, have some sort of policy breakthrough. And I think it was informative, I think it was entertaining, I think we did achieve a minor policy breakthrough in that regard.

And I did what I was sent there to do, which was the best job possible being the first American radio program ever to broadcast live and uncensored from Havana. Nobody had ever done that before. So, that was the other thing. It was like going to the top of Mt. Everest. I was the first one here and there will be others, but this was the first. So, from a programming point of view, it would've made no sense to run back to the United States to cover Lewinsky and the president. From a journalistic point of view, it was more of a metaphor than I cared to see for the state of journalism. None of this is new, I mean if you consider this kind of the end of a new gilded age. Well, we went through this kind of stuff a hundred years ago when William Randolph Hearst, the publisher, said to his newspaper photographers, "You provide the pictures and I'll provide the war," and he did, and on through the more salacious aspects of yellow journalism before and after, so none of that is new. But what is new is that the media — and now I'm talking about the broadcast media, although print media is part of this, too — the news on the broadcast media have become profit centers, starting when 60 Minutes *was able to turn a profit, the first news program in history to actually make money.*

Before that, nobody ever even expected news to make any money, and it was the farthest thing from their minds.

So, several things happened. The FCC was de-fanged and became completely impotent. Telecommunications was de-regulated. And major corporations started buying up everything in sight. So, in ways small and large this has meant that because all of this stuff is now commercially driven, that the news product you see on the tube and listen to on the radio, and to some extent read in the newspapers, has become more and more trivial because they're aiming for a mass audience and they're trying to sell more of whatever it is they're selling.

Print media — newspapers have tricky graphics, slick-looking headlines, nice color pictures, and larger headlines have summaries to explain the stories. And that means that the news hole where it actually goes shrinks. Every newspaper in the country has been dumbing down for years as their circulation has fallen. Their assumption is, "Well, it's fallen because people are getting stupider, and if they're getting stupider, lets draw this with Crayola so they'll understand it." Now, radio news was a bastard child for years anyway, and now you find more and more radio news operations being completely pillaged. Very few radio stations even have news directors anymore. Very few radio stations have news departments. As corporations have gotten bigger, they've consolidated what news departments there are, so you get fewer sources of information. As of August 31, 1998, the NBC radio network and the Mutual radio network news staffs have all been fired. Here's where corporate takeovers of the media become particularly incestuous, and this is just one timely example. In 1988, NBC sold the NBC radio network, deciding it wanted to get out of the radio business. They sold it to a company called Westwood One. They licensed to Westwood One the use of the name NBC Radio News and the peacock logo. Westwood also owned the Mutual Broadcasting System, so what eventually happened is that NBC's news became subsumed by Mutual's news so that you had the same people doing two different newscasts, same sources, same reporters. What's going to happen now is that CBS in the meantime has purchased 25% of Westwood One. CBS these days is driven by nothing except an eye on the bottom line. So now, the news for NBC radio network and the Mutual radio network is going to be provided by CBS, so you're getting, once again, fewer sources of information — all in the name of corporate greed and saving a few bucks.

We're going to have a monopoly in about two weeks.

It's not going to take very long at all. Another example in radio is Jim Hightower, who used to be the Agriculture Commissioner in Texas, a raving populist, he used to have a talk show on the ABC radio network. He criticized — on his program — the Disney buy-out of ABC, railing against these corporate oligarchies that were reducing the number and quality of sources of news that people could get. Jim Hightower was dumped by the ABC radio network I think about a week later.

So much for independent voices.

216

Yeah, and in television the situation is actually more pernicious. Remember in the film Network *everybody thought it was funny twenty, twenty-five years ago when it is explained to Howard Beale by the president of the network that he's a fool, that there are no sovereign governments, that there is only Exxon and IBM and General Motors — and today one might add Microsoft — that is the reality. And about the same time that the movie* Network *came out was the time when the first consultants decided that male and female anchors need to giggle at each other a little more. It was the '70s. You got happy talk, fluffy news. Chop it up and put more stories in the same newscast. Make 'em shorter, make 'em less in-depth. It's been pointed out endlessly that in 1968, during the campaign, the average television sound-bite of the average presidential candidate was around 35-40 seconds. And in the 1996 political campaign, the average sound-bite of the average presidential candidate was down to about 5 or 6 seconds, certainly less than ten. It started with the local news: it became more and more trivial. Real journalism was replaced with "News You Can Use."*

Yeah, it became almost like a consumer guide.

Because it was easier, and they figured, well, that's what these people want, they don't care about anything unless it's right in front of their stupid noses, so we will deal with it. People who run broadcasting have utter contempt for the audience they're supposed to serve, they think they're stupid. And if anyone doubts that, I invite them to get to know any given group of broadcasting executives. Now, it is not true 100% of the time, but it's true, I think, about 70% of the time.

Probably about one of the only places it isn't true is at National Public Radio (NPR) because they're target marketed to a more intellectual audience.

Yeah, except NPR runs ads now. Everyone is being forced

into this. Every time I hear the announcer do a 20-second shpeil that this is underwritten by Archer Daniels Midland, "Supermarket to the World," I wonder if, push comes to shove, if NPR is going to do any hard, close questioned reporting on ADM and its relationship to food production and power politics. Maybe they will, maybe they won't, but the question is raised, and since this has been happening all over, since the news is now a commercial enterprise, it means it is a trivial enterprise.

And it also means it can't possibly claim any objectivity because it won't bite the hand that feeds it.

Generally not.

And now a handful of major corporations now own every major media outlet in this country, whether it's print or broadcast. And you can't expect a journalist now to give unbiased reporting that might be biting the parent corporation of his outlet.

Of course you can expect it.

You may not get it *(we both say at the same time)*.

You have every right to expect it because it's what we're supposed to be doing. There are a lot of people who are getting out of the business. And it may be kind of pathetic for a bunch of crusty, old farts to be pining for the way things used to be.

But, it's quite valid. It's not just nostalgia.

In the long-term historical perspective, the media in this country has been — more times than not — biased, one-sided, politically partisan, censored, etc. There have been a few golden eras, and a few shining moments when we've done our jobs specifically as we were supposed to be doing.

Maybe we had that for awhile in the 60s and 70s so that people thought, "Wow, this is great, we've got journalists being the conscience."

> *Remember that Fred Friendly quit as President of CBS News because instead of running Senate hearings on Vietnam, the network chose to run a sitcom rerun. I can't imagine any news executive quitting on a point of professional honor like that today when the heads of CNN of course kept their jobs after the Tailwind debacle. What's happening is that this pernicious drive for mass marketing and ratings and profits — and I have to say here that I am a committed capitalist, so don't get me wrong about this — because the news has become a profit center and because there's an underlying drive for the biggest audience, means that what you get is either completely trivial pap or sometimes scurrilous and quite often completely wrong information that is rushed on the air because what has happened is not only is this a profit center, but you have major news organizations that run 24-hours a day, cable news operations and Internet sites, and because of that, stuff gets thrown on the air without any fact-checking whatsoever.*

They have to fill up the time.

> *Stuff has to get on the air. I would rather get it on last and get it on right than get it on first and get it on wrong.*

And the drive right now is "Get it on first, fill up all the time we have with something." And lately we're not seeing news reporting as much as we're seeing speculation reported. All the reports we hear are people speculating about what they think may have happened when they don't know what happened.

> *The public, for years, has created this self-fulfilling prophecy. The public now may have trouble telling the difference between* Hard Copy *and* The CBS Evening News, *and between Rush Limbaugh and Peter Jennings. Information is information. It's*

the ultimate in value-free, non-judgmental irony that if a respectable news organization can put this stuff on the air then everyone is exactly the same. And that's essentially what happened. I mean, my God, Matt Drudge now has his own show on the Fox News Channel, and on one show he had Lucianne Goldberg (Linda Tripp's former literary agent) and Dick Morris as guests making it — as one columnist in The New York Times *put it — effectively, the first TV news equivalent of the bar scene in* Star Wars *(we laugh...a lot). And they're absolutely right. If you take a look at the people going into the business...Well, kids going into the business have never been taught the difference between journalism and marketing. Schools of mass communication have become just that — mass communication. My alma mater, Columbia, thank God, has gone against that trend. A marketer is paid to spin and massage the truth. And a journalist is paid to find out the truth. So, you have two antithetical groups of people right from the beginning. But, if highbrow academic institutions can get sucked into this morass, then it's everywhere.*

It used to be that we could count on journalists to play the role of detective. They were going to go out there and do their damnedest to ferret out the truth, no matter what it took. But that isn't what they do now, unfortunately. And if they do manage to get the truth, some-one stops them from putting it on the air because it's stepping on cor-porate toes.

A lot of what happens now is not necessarily some great corporate cabal, but what they've done in the drive for ratings and sizzle is hire some good looking but fairly vacuous people who are not trained the way they should be trained. And who don't have the stomach to do the sort of stories they should be doing. You've got a lot of fluff on the air, and the fact-checking is not there simply because the corporations will not pay for the bodies in a newsroom to check the facts. There is not that much in the way of filters, so indirectly, yup, there has been this corporate cabal that has screwed everything up and made it trivial and in many cases downright unbelievable. I am not sure that there is a corporate conspiracy as such to eviscerate the news.

There are checks and balances set up that keep the corporations from becoming damaged. Look what happened with CBS and the tobacco report that was crushed. And that's just one of many examples. We're never going to see something like Watergate again.

I think we will see something like Watergate, but it may not have the same effect of bringing down an administration. All of this is transitory. If someone 30 years from now picks up this book, they're going to wonder, "What's he talking about? What is Tailwind? Who is Monica Lewinsky? What is all this foolishness?" Well, that's my point exactly: What is all this foolishness? Because none of this has a lasting impression. Journalism is supposed to be the first draft of history, and it gets corrected as time goes along. But, that first draft is supposed to bear some resemblance to the truth. In every story that is done about you, you will find at least one thing that is wrong. Now, maybe it's a minor thing that nobody notices and nobody cares. Maybe it's a major thing — you're completely misquoted, things are taken out of context, or the story is twisted and spun. It happens. The way I look at journalism is: it's not a photograph, it's more like a painting — it's an approximation of reality. Because of deadlines, of the pressures of the sheer volume of stuff that comes in, you can't be expected to get everything right 100% of the time. That's why on radio they go on the air every hour, on TV they go on the air nightly, and newspapers publish daily. They can correct things when they're pointed out to them.

What has always driven you as a journalist, and has that changed?

Curiosity. What is the truth and what is supposition? How do things work? Why are things the way they are? What's wrong with this picture? That sort of thing. And that hasn't changed. The circumstances in which everybody works have changed.

You're no longer risking life and limb to ferret out that truth.

No, I'm no longer risking life and limb.

What drove you to be a war correspondent, or if you fell into it, what kept you there?

Genetic deficiency (we laugh).

Ah, yes, back to the old Neanderthal male brain, huh?

People are the way they are because of life itself. People are the way they are, but even more so, in times of incredible stress or tragedy. And you could not get more stress and tragedy than in war. And here the human condition is boiled down to a few paragraphs. In the space of a hundred meters, in the space of a hundred seconds, you will find stories of incredible bravery, selflessness, sacrifice for others. You will find cowardice, greed, venality, brutality. You will find redemptive hope, and you will find crushing fear, and you will find overwhelming evil. All in front of you. In a very short physical distance, and in a very short span of time. War is the essence of human life, boiled down and distilled. And if you want to know about the human condition, you can find out more by observing human beings in war in a week than you could find out by observing everyday human life in ten years, simply because everything is so much more intense. The things that are at stake are very basic issues of life and death.

So, therefore, it is going to simultaneously bring out the very best and the very worst in people.

Exactly. It always has.

What did you learn about the human spirit while you were covering wars? You've told me some amazing stories.

The thing that I've learned is that we are all precisely alike. And that we are all astonishingly different. No matter where you are on the face of the earth, a smile means the same thing, tears mean the same thing, raising your voice in a gruff tone means the same thing. And, yet, the faces are different, the languages are different, the food is different, the customs are different, the way of looking at the world is different. And nowhere is that as evident as places like Ethiopia or Bosnia or Kuwait, or anyplace where the ultimate — that is, life — is at stake. And this goes on, constantly, somewhere in the world. And I think that the reason we all need to be made aware of what's going on is, number one, as the world becomes smaller we all have a stake in everybody else's community. And, number two, you never know when something like this could strike closer to home. And, number three, they're damn fine stories. What does the person who is listening to or watching a report I might file get? At least once a story I wanted someone to go away from the TV set shaking their head, saying, "I didn't know that." It's the same as I want to do now, once an hour on the radio program I want someone to say, "I didn't know that." And what I think people come away with knowing, that maybe they didn't know before, is that these people who are going through all this aren't that radically different from them. And that therefore, maybe, just maybe a little more compassion than we normally show during the course of our daily lives is in order. And maybe, just maybe, a few thoughts about something in your own house, your own block, city, your own country is in order. And that's why I did it.

You told me a few years ago when we first spoke about your experiences covering the Gulf War, that it had changed you more than any other war you'd covered. You took a fresh look at what's going on here when you came back, and said you saw that people who put their lives on the line came home to the same old racism, and job problems, and that it really put into perspective how crazy things are here or maybe how crazy they always were.

I still believe that's true. And tempered by distance now, I would say that people who were willing to pay the ultimate price...You know a man or woman in uniform makes a very interesting bargain. The bargain is we, the government, the people of The United States will pay you a couple of grand a month in exchange for which you agree to lay down your life for your country if asked to. I always found it interesting to come back to The United States, both with a little disgust at how self-centered Americans can be in their worst moments, and with more than a small measure of relief to come back to this country, and these people, and this place after seeing what people go through in other parts of the world with a political system not as good as the one we have...

Yeah, every time you're tempted to bitch about the U.S., you can say, "Well, it could be Bosnia..."

Yeah, and yet things change in The United States, but things change very slowly. Who would've thought when we were talking the first time that the man responsible for the biggest act of domestic terrorism in American history would've been a Gulf War vet? (Timothy McVeigh, who bombed the Oklahoma City federal building on April 19, 1995.) *Simply because that in wars there is sometimes artificially and quite often from a real sense of the heart a unity of purpose that one hardly ever finds in any other endeavor: "We need to conquer this land because these people are somehow bad," or "We need to defend our land because the people who are trying to take it are bad," or "We, the Catholics, Protestants, Hindus, Muslims or Jews are in the right because God is on our side." This may, in many ways, seem, like the ultimate deluded fantasy, but in the middle of the situation, in the middle of war, it's one of the things that keeps you going, and because of that it's very interesting to see how human beings do what they do when they are put into a situation where there is a moral imperative: "This is something we must do, this is something that needs to be done," as opposed to teenagers in the United States who kill themselves on street corners every hour, and who kill others on street corners every hour for crack cocaine, or somebody's sneakers, or methamphetamine, or for a perceived snub or slight. That trivializes human life.*

Teenagers who kill themselves or each other in uniform fighting for something, are on a different level altogether. And the cynics may say, "Oh, that's absurd, that's romantic drivel." But, I've been exposed to too much of this to have any romantic fantasies about it (we laugh). *It makes more sense — if people are going to kill each other — to kill each other over something they believe to be true, rather than some material gain. When on "the highway of death," north of Kuwait City, thousands of Iraqi troops were incinerated by the Allied air forces, what seemed absurd about that when we got there was that this was a giant street gang, these were looters — they had everything from fire trucks to television sets to babies' incubators to duct tape, you name it, they took it.*

Who were they?

These were Iraqi soldiers. You die in battle to do something. You die trying to get away with as much booty as you could get your hands on — that's when it became sick because it was like something that would happen on the streets in the United States when people get mowed down while they're looting a liquor store. In war, people — mostly not through their own choosing — are put into a position where they long for something else, and that something else is peace. And they long for it so desperately that they'll kill to get it. And that is why human experience in war is significantly different and significantly more interesting than everyday experience.

The more spiritual among us may say, "Well, this is absurd. There is the face of God in every child on every street." Well, true enough, true enough. But, people who have never been exposed to a situation where everything is at risk tend to go through their lives in slow motion, somehow — and this is gonna sound awful — not really alive, because they have never experienced that moment where they literally don't know from one moment to the next if they're going to live or die. If I were listening to myself say this and I were in the middle of one of these situations again, I would say to myself, "What, are you nuts?" (we laugh), "Are you out of your mind?" But, no, this is the way it works. And that's why I felt compelled to cover this. I know this is a very long answer to a very short question. It's the type of human experience that has density, that has huge substance.

It also gives you a view of human nature that you would not ordinarily get.

Mmm-hmm...which is why when you find people dealing with news departments like they were just so much excess baggage, and being driven by next quarter's profits and nothing larger, you find it amusing, you find it disgusting because it seems to be a dishonor to every journalist and civilian and member of anybody's armed forces I've ever served with who has either been killed or severely wounded in the course of this sort of thing. A guy for whom I once worked once was upset that I had gone to a cocktail party with a bunch of people from this other broadcasting organization (network), and he was practically foaming at the mouth.

Because you were consorting with the enemy.

He took that metaphor and made this absurd metaphor about "They're the enemy, and this is war, and ratings and profits are at stake," and I said, "With all due respect..." and you and I know that when somebody says that there is no due respect involved..."I don't want you to say that again because as far as I know, and please correct me if I'm wrong, you have never been in combat, you have never worn your country's uniform, you have never been anyplace near combat, you've never covered combat, you don't know anyone who has been seriously injured or died as a journalist, civilian or combatant in combat, and you have no idea how distasteful this metaphor

226

is." These empty $5,000 suits in their glass-encased corner offices, sit around very proudly thumping the table that their corporate organization is based on their having read The Art of War. *These people would last 30 seconds, maybe less (near combat), because they have no idea what the real stakes of human life are, and the real stakes of human life are human life.*

That's right. Not ratings, not money.

It is not ratings, it is not cash. And yet, they dress it up in this way, and they trivialize it (war).

Isn't this no different than when they were little boys playing with their little plastic army men? And this ratings war is the closest they'll ever get to doing that whole macho war thing, so they create war out of commerce.

Yeah, you create war out of commerce and look what you get. One of the things that's also interesting is how political currents work in war. And I think it's the best exposition of any political system: how it wages war. Because people are either treated like dirt and shoveled into the fray, or they're actually treated with some consideration. Sometimes you go overboard. I think the Gulf War showed us that the American public may not have the stomach for large casualties, and if a public does not have the stomach for large casualties then that public is not prepared to actually go to war. On the other hand, look at how Saddam Hussein treated his people. He took all the conscripts from villages that were politically unreliable and put them on the front line of Kuwait because the American B-52s were going to pound them into dust. So, for someone to take metaphors for something like this and apply them to something as trivial as commerce is flabbergasting because the idea behind war is to learn from it so that the mistakes that led to this will not be repeated again.

If you take a look at the careers of various journalists, you can see a pattern. You can see where their passion is. Some people like to cover the political game, some people love economics. In your particular case, you kept following injustice around the globe. And in the U.S. Infiltrating the neo-Nazi party, covering apartheid, anyplace you smelled injustice, there you were. What does that say about you?

I think that gives me more credit than I actually deserve. I mean, I was not thinking of anything as grand eloquent as covering injustice.

But you were drawn to it. Look at your resume: you're not hopping around doing politics, economics, entertainment, religion or whatever.

The thing about war and the things attendant to war is that somebody is getting screwed someplace, and it's generally the little guy. Now, how does this play out, and what are the stories to be told?

Infiltrating the Nazi party. That wasn't war, but obviously it was important to you to do something like that.

Well, I sure as hell wasn't in a position to infiltrate The Black Panthers (we laugh). *But, looking supremely Aryan, I was able to pull that off, so I thought...*

You wanted to go in and see what makes them tick?

How does this work? Why is this? Are these a bunch of comic opera buffoons, or are these people actually dangerous? And the answer to both questions is: yes. Any journalist should do this. The old saying: "Our job is to comfort the afflicted and afflict the comfortable." Every journalist should be about that, whether you're covering a city council meeting, no matter what beat you're handed — the society beat, for God's sake, or even the sports beat. If you want superb prose read Red Smith or Grantland Rice. These are sportswriters, and some of the best

bits of journalism. It doesn't matter what part of journalism you're in, there are good stories to be had, there is meaning to be found. Any journalist worth their salt does the same thing, covers things the same way. The idea is the same: the truth is out there. There are facts to be deduced, and then the effects of all this on people. I happened to choose an area of it that's perceived as, if not glamorous then as something more than it is. Yes, (war) is the distilled essence of the human condition. But, I would've been just as happy if I'd turned into the best business reporter, or the best sports columnist.

You would've brought the same intensity, skills and curiosity to it.

Yeah, it's the curiosity. We are alive, therefore we are curious. We are curious about others like us, about why the sky is blue, why the Serbs are slaughtering the Albanians in Kosovo, why there are terror bomb attacks at U.S. embassies, why Mark McGwire when he follows through on his home run swing swings with one hand rather than two. We are curious about things, and that's why we're in the business. But, what's happened to the worst of us threatens to happen to the rest of us, which is to take that curiosity and put it into the service of someone's corporate agenda in order to get a paycheck. And a certain amount of it is the ratings, the next quarter's profits, and money. Well, my God then, if it all just comes down to money, then why didn't you get a business degree and go into business? We are not a priesthood, you know, that's what Charles Osgood, one of the most respected journalists around said to somebody in the elevator at CBS when they complained that Osgood was doing commercials on his daily radio commentaries. And he said, "Look, we're not a priesthood anymore." Well, I'm not sure we ever were.

Maybe certain people during certain decades aspired to that or even perhaps viewed their jobs that way, but certainly it was never the mandate.

Journalism was always — until the last 30 or 40 years — one of the ways that the working class, such as moi, *would follow a skill or a profession. And I've always looked at it that way. I don't put myself, or others in my trade — which is what I consider it — on the same level as...I'm not a doctor, I will not operate and save a child's life; I'm not an attorney, I will not give an impassioned argument and therefore an interpretation of the Constitution will be changed for future generations; I am not someone out doing good in the world by helping the weak, helpless and oppressed.*

But, you are uncovering the truth, which is a good service.

I look at it as a good electrician, a good plumber, a good automobile mechanic. I'm very proud of the craft I've chosen. I'm very proud of this trade. There are some of us who are damned good at it. But, I think it's very dangerous when we sell out for the bucks, look at ourselves as stars, get our teeth capped or our hair implanted, boobs fixed, and go on to become superstars, and why? So we can make more money. And at the same time, hob-nob with the people we're supposed to be covering. And rub elbows with them, and go to the same cocktail soirées, and become part of that social elite. When this stopped being an entrée for working class kids who had experiential fire in the belly because they knew what it was like to stand on the outside and watch the bourgeoisie soak up all the gravy, journalism got worse because instead of those kind of kids, we've ended up with upper-middle class kids coming into newsrooms.

What you're getting is privileged kids looking to make a lot of money and become celebrities.

Right. And they don't have anything in their gut that tells them, "This needs doing. Why? Because I've seen it with my own eyes, growing up." So, this business has turned into something that I'm not as proud of as I once was.

230

Many people going into journalism these days, look at it as their ticket to lead the glamorous life and become a part of the elite, rather than as the outside observer.

Right. Journalists are supposed to be outsiders. That's the whole bottom line. We are not supposed to be part of "it," whatever "it" is. We are not supposed to be part of the ruling elite. We are not supposed to rub shoulders with these people, we are supposed to cover them toughly but fairly. We are not supposed to suck up to them.

Seven

Brooke Medicine Eagle

*The invariable mark of wisdom is to
see the miraculous in the common.*

— Ralph Waldo Emerson

*T*he debate rages on: What Is The Meaning Of Life? How Did The World Get To Be Such A Mess? Can We Save It From The Ravages Of Humanity? Hey, wait a minute...Can We Save *Ourselves* From The Ravages Of Humanity?

From there we progress to What Are We Doing Here In The First Place? Where Do We Go When We Die? How Do We Understand The Body, Mind And Soul?

If you think you're eavesdropping on a bunch of Baby Boomers as armchair philosophers, think again. These are questions that every generation has asked since time began.

Being a highly egocentric species, humans place a tremendous amount of importance on themselves and their surroundings. Every generation in every decade in every century thinks simultaneously that their way is the best way and that life sucks; that they have all the questions and that they have all the answers; that the weather has never been as strange as it is now; that the world has never been as violent as it is now; that the world can't possibly ever get better; that society and science has reached its pinnacle.

Well, you can't blame them. Afterall, the times they are living in are, by definition, the only times they've ever lived in (let's not get into reincarnation now, that's another subject for other discussions, and besides, even with reincarnation you're not born with complete memories of all your previous lives), and all they have to compare it to is *history*, which they consider to be at best subjective and at worst incomplete. Perhaps if we had some video of The Spanish Inquisition, we'd have to admit that our 20th century atrocities aren't too much different and we moderns aren't so civilized afterall.

What we're lacking, say teachers like Brooke Medicine Eagle, is context and continuity.

What people are seeking, what best-selling authors like Brooke are writing about, is the need to recognize a non-denominational spirituality that expresses itself in the respect of human life and the life of the planet, and our innate ability to heal ourselves and each other, and to live without judgment, fear, power struggles, racism, violence or economic control.

A popular saying these days reminds us that we are "spiritual beings having a human experience." And the human experience by itself, when disconnected from its spiritual source, its awareness that all things in nature are connected, leads us to react from a mind-set of fear. Fear always leads us to try to control others.

And so we get: Nazi Germany, The Irish "Troubles," The 2,000-Year-Old Middle-East Conflicts, Bosnia, The Ku Klux Klan, The Aryan Nation, The Spanish Inquisition, The Roman Empire, The British Empire, Attila the Hun, Child Abuse, Rape, Battered Women, Gangs, Addiction, Torture, Ethnic Cleansing, Political Assassination, Intellectual and Cultural Persecution, Colonialism, Civil Wars, Starving Children, Homophobia, Prejudice, Indian Reservations, U.S. Japanese Internment Camps, Repression, Poverty, Civil Rights Violations, Lies, Riots, Disinformation, Scams, Dictatorship, Disease, Repression of Scientific and Medical Information, Pollution and Environmental Destruction, Slavery, Consumerism, the list unfortunately goes on and on.

Is it any wonder we'd all like some peace around here?

Raised with the traditions of her Native American people as well as the 20th century's advanced technology and education, psychologist Brooke Medicine Eagle began intensive studies and personal transformation among her native peoples when she was in college.

"I began to understand what was missing. The wholeness of the person wasn't being addressed. So, I began to look at my own people's work in body, mind, spirit and emotions," says Medicine Eagle, who was raised on a reservation in Montana, is now one of the world's most respected earthkeepers and teachers, and is the author of the acclaimed *Buffalo Woman Comes Singing* (Ballantine, 1991), a very moving account of Native American wisdom and healing in practice. "Western medicine covers the body, but in order to heal you need to look at a much larger level. People are turning to so-called alternative medicine because mainstream isn't working entirely. That's because it only concerns itself with symptoms. People are yearning for wisdom and they have no wise ones around them anymore to pass it down."

Her work is spiritual and psychological. "The psychology of our experiences is no longer distinct from our physical healing. I live by the motto: 'Embodying Spirit,'" she says. "We are whole and we are holy. It's not that we don't know these deep truths; it's that we haven't embraced them in our bodies and daily ways of living."

She believes that those who aren't Native American are now studying and embracing these traditional philosophies and practices because "they work. Being in harmony with all things is an eternal truth, not just a Native American truth."

Brooke Medicine Eagle has been teaching for more than 25 years and makes her home in Montana, although she spends a great deal of time on the road conducting workshops around the country. She is a fixture at the most prestigious gatherings of philosophical leaders and healers and bridges the gap between modern Western culture and traditional Native American teachings. She is equally well-trained in both.

Her second book, *The Last Ghost Dance* will be published by Ballantine near the end of 1999. She explains the significance of the title: "The Old Ghost Dance was used to create a renewed world by lifting themselves up in spirit," she says, "and this book is about lifting ourselves to the next level of being human."

She is also "paying more attention to my Celtic roots," she says, "and teaching about the connection between the Native American and Celtic traditions." Her heritage is a rich mix of Lakota, Crow and other tribes, plus Scottish and Irish. She frequently joins with other cultural leaders to not only teach, but hold ceremonial gatherings they've called "Confluence," in order to "create a feeling that you can do something and make a difference," she says, "like we did in the 1960s and 1970s."

I first spoke with Brooke Medicine Eagle in 1993 when I interviewed her for a series of articles on alternative medicine for *Body Mind & Spirit* magazine. The conversations presented here took place in 1993, 1994, and late 1998.

༄ ༄

One of the things I'm sure that people are curious about is the nature of a vision. How do you describe a vision, whether it's part of a vision quest or if you have it at any other time? Is it comparable to a dream, a daydream, an insight, a hallucination?

Visions are difficult to describe, yet there is always a numinous quality about them — an extraordinary quality. The basic nature of our mind is that we are constantly running images and thoughts and daydreams through it; thus when visions come, they're arriving on what seems like the same channel. It's like TV: you can see something illuminating or something junky on the same channel. Yet, there's a special internal quality about a vision.

A knowingness? A vividness?

Yes, it strikes you in the gut and heart. You say, 'Hmmm...that was something special.' Even if you don't understand it, it feels extraordinary. This brings up one of the challenges of vision questing. When some people come down from their questing place, they initially may not think they saw anything special. Everything is unusual since they are sitting quietly on a mountain fasting, rather than living their ordinary lives, yet the moment-to-moment experience may not seem extraordinary. However, when they look back at the experience, it's like looking through a different lens. I'm able to help them see the larger and deeper metaphors, and it all takes on a mystical quality.

So, they can often feel like mystical dreams or mystical daydreams, but when you're having them in a physically and mentally unusual environment, like a fasting vision quest, you can often get more perspective on them after the fact.

Yes, and there are also other times when we're not on a formal vision quest that we can receive higher guidance. Someone could be sitting in an office looking out the window, daydreaming, and all of a sudden something important will come through. There's a certain way that our system opens up to feel and perceive the deeper levels of experience when we're not trying. That openness is vital, yet one of the things we're not trained to allow in life is surrender. And we need to surrender in order to open up to those numinous places. Someone who goes up on a mountain for a vision quest straining to have a vision often doesn't have as powerful an experience as someone who simply opens up to what Creator has to offer. I teach processes of opening and clearing so people can have an uncluttered space to receive something new and useful. Like a dream what comes might be simple or very meaningful and in double Technicolor!

Most of my dreams are like visions. That's why I wonder what label to give certain experiences. Do most visions come when awake, asleep, or in the state just before falling asleep or waking up?

Wherever and whenever the Great Spirit catches one off-guard enough so they're not holding on to their normal consciousness, normal state, normal way of being and thinking, there is the possibility of a meaningful vision. It most often happens in those pre-sleep and post-sleep in-between states when we're not focused on our usual reality.

In your book, *Buffalo Woman Comes Singing*, you write about an incredible vision you had in an emerald healing cave. Did that happen when you were awake, asleep, or in-between?

On a formal vision quest, as I was participating in, one is usually fasting, and thus in a somewhat altered state. I would say that I was in an altered state, although it didn't necessarily feel unusual at the time since I was simply resting there on a mountain, dozing and allowing my mind to wander. When it's totally quiet, and there's nothing else going on, an altered state comes quite easily and naturally.

You're at the very least in the alpha state.

Yes, yes, at the very least. That's a wonderful state that allows you to tap in to these kinds of things. It's the same state you're in when daydreaming or staring at water, or something like that. So, you're in a different state, with a different kind of receptivity. You know, everyone has the thought, "Am I just making this up?" That went through my mind, too. Yet, I recognize that whatever the consciousness brings to the surface is important to reflect on at length. I could have had that dream of the emerald tablet, and said, "That was a neat dream," and just let it go, but...

But, instead, you found meaning in it, and it enhanced your spiritual growth and enhanced your daily life and your understanding.

Yes, and speaking of that reminds me of our need to pay more attention to every part of our consciousness. Illumination and guidance can come from working with our dreams, our daydreams, our imaginings, as well as what we would label as visions. Unfortunately, we're not usually taught to do anything with those aspects. I often give this as an example: When he was nine years old, Black Elk, who eventually became a Lakota holy man, was given a profound vision. It was very strange to him — filled with many colors of people he had never seen, so he didn't speak about it for a long time. Yet, his elders eventually did encourage him to speak about it. That is certainly different from American culture today, whose general attitude might be expressed with "What are you doing sitting up on that hill when you have math and science homework to do? Get out of your spacey head and get into the real world here!" But, Black Elk's elders paid attention, listening carefully to his vision of the four colors — races — of two-leggeds coming into harmony. Two-leggeds is the phrase for people.
Then the elders literally danced those metaphors "into the

ground." They got out four colors of horses and also painted themselves different colors, and did a ritual performance of the dream to make it real in the world. It's important to work with the people on setting up their own symbol system in order to provide a basic framework through which they can understand and find meaning in their lives. Each may choose which of many different systems to work with, just so they have something. It's also useful to clear out things that no longer work for you. Here's an example: different animals, birds, trees and other natural things are given meaning by many primary peoples. If you understand one of these, a crow flying past you reminds you of particular teachings or themes and gives you a deeper message than if the crow didn't mean anything to you. This way, your consciousness and the Great Spirit can speak to you through natural happenings.

That's what Native Americans call an animal's "medicine."

Right. And I tell people in my classes, "If you think that Creator/God is going to speak to you only by coming out of the clouds as an old man with a white beard in a long robe, then you're likely to receive a very limited amount of guidance! But, if you realize that The Great Spirit, The Great Master, is alive in everything, and thus each and every thing could carry a message to you, then Spirit can use many things to speak to you. In this way, you have unlimited possibilities for what you might receive."

This can come from literally anything and anywhere.

You could be sitting by a big tree and receive profound guidance from it, or from a cloud, or a child's voice. You know how often children say something to us that's incredibly wise. There's spirit and meaning in everything and we need to wake up to that fact. It's not that life and experience doesn't offer us guidance and vision, it's that we don't often acknowledge and work with what does come, or allow ourselves to grow from the

241

experience.

We see things and get messages all the time, and it's just a matter of whether we're going to follow up on it, understand what it means, and then do something about it.

Yes, I think so, and the more we have a symbolic system to help us get the message, the better.

Can you create your own system, just keep it consistent where each symbol always means something in particular?

Yes, even though I use a traditional tribal system, I let my own experience add even deeper meaning and more personal symbols to it. Your mention of consistency reminds me of something else. I advise people to have continuing contact with the dream/vision/inner symbol aspect of self. We live in a TV world that says, "Well, that program's done, what's next?" so we're likely to also say, "Well, that dream is finished, what's next?" when we have an interesting dream. Instead, we could take this approach — "Something about that dream with the bird is really intriguing. I'd like to know more about what this means for me." Then, later that day take time to sit down, bring up the image again, and internally ask that bird what it means, or ask it to transform into something that makes even more sense to you.

Inviting it to teach you more.

Right. And inviting it to come into another dream, or inviting another dream that makes more sense to you. Really working with those things your consciousness brings forward. In the old days, among tribal peoples, if someone had a really powerful dream of a blackbird, for instance, the person might go find a blackbird feather to keep on their altar or special place. Then, each time they saw the feather, it would bring back that energy and help deepen the meaning of the dream. Many of the medicine bundles were created in this way. For generations, people carried those bundles that contained things that were symbolic and had personal or tribal meaning. This continuity over time was very empowering.

It's not unlike what people do — although they may not think of it in spiritual terms — when they keep a box of mementos, or a scrapbook, or a shelf with their favorite pictures. We're already in the habit of being collectors and savers, and this would put a new spin on that.

Right, and keeping consciously active with these symbols creates an ongoingness of the experience, which is qualitatively different than having a thing that reminds you of an experience. My elders remind me that we don't receive that many numinous experiences because we haven't paid any attention to any of the ones we've already been given. A deeper level of knowing says, "Why bother bringing visions in if they're not even going to be acknowledged and used in a beneficial way?" One of the challenges we have in this modern life is that many, many of us are without elders, without older wise people in our lives. We're without the shamans and spiritual people who used to be available to everyone — and still are among primary people and nature tribes. So, where can we get any guidance? I think humans really need that wise assistance. We need some help to wake us up because we get into patterns and we can't see ourselves very well.

And, also, these kinds of elders traditionally served as a bridge between people and nature. Our modern world severs our connection with nature, so now more than ever we need to be reminded that we are part of that, we're not separate from nature or our own planet.

Yes, shamans have traditionally bridged, not only the ordinary world and the spirit world, but also humans and the exquisite wisdom of the rest of the natural world. This reminds us of however important it is to be aware of symbols, metaphors and teachings from nature because we are certainly lacking in that kind of guidance.

Do you find that the people coming to study with you are more serious about it now, rather than it just being the latest fad?

It's clear to me that the people who come are very serious about learning, deep in their hearts, although they might have superficial ways of approaching it. For example, some native people say to me, "You're giving away Indian secrets!" Well, I feel like I could pour magical, powerful secrets out on the ground, and very few students would bother to pick them up and truly use them. I've seen many people in my workshops who are listening to the words, but have a glazed look in their eyes — they're not letting themselves get into the experience.

You're teaching people how to open up to the connection that's already there — the connection between people and every other living thing on earth, or what Native Americans call All Our Relations.

Yes, to really open up and honor that. And I give them a lot of ways to do that. That's a theme of my work now, not just a cooperation but a partnership with everything in the Circle of Life. That is the ancient message that comes down to us. One of the things I teach is Creator's Law, the one Law given by Creator in the beginning when we were all created: to be in good relationship with each other and all things. It's easy to think that we should all just meditate and be mellow and groovy, but it's something much more than that. It's about being actively involved in connecting with life around us. More and more people realize they can do that. Certainly, it is vital to truly be in cooperation and good energy with people we're living and working around. Yet, we must also realize that actually communing and working in cooperation with the plants and all life around us is good not only for us, but for All Our Relations. For instance, it seemed like a good idea to use cars, yet all the pollution and damage caused are very unworkable. We must learn to come up with those things more in harmony with

nature. Our ancestors have sent down information to us —
eternal truths through which we can look ahead seven
generations and deepen our sense of what will work down
through time. This perspective will create much more wisdom in
our actions.

Where do you go, and what do you do when you need to retreat
and tap into the wisdom of some of the elders? Who are you learning
from?

*A couple of the elders I initially worked with have now
passed into Spirit, so I commune with them in meditation.
Recently, my sister, Heron, and I did a quest gathering called
Lodge of the Wisdom Women in a sacred valley in Montana. It's
focus was on the wisdom of the ancient grandmothers, who often
came to guide us in our work there. Something tremendously
powerful came out of our work last summer. Many of the
profound lineages carried by all our ancestral lines were broken
within the last few generations, so the wisdom of the
grandmothers and grandfathers has been lost. Those ancestors
are calling out to us to connect with them through meditation,
dreams and vision — to bring forward the wisdom that has
been lost, for the good of all the children of Earth. This is a
powerful reason to open to these avenues of guidance — there is
so much to bring forward that couldn't be handed down person-
to-person. The elders also taught me to go directly to Mother
Earth and Father Spirit — to go into the quiet, especially if I
can get myself into a natural place, which, around my home, is
relatively easy. That's one of the things I teach other people and
practice myself — to go directly to Source in that sense, more
than to people. Go to that quiet space where you listen deeply to
the voices of all the Earth life, Mother Earth herself, and Spirit
as it speaks through all of those. That's a very powerful way,
which helps us move past human foibles and confusions.*

*We have to remember that our intention makes all the
difference in what we receive. You know, when we are open to
higher guidance, we'll find it in many places. I'll pick up a book*

somebody recommends, and find enormous riches there, like they're speaking directly to me. Many people now are getting useful and important messages, and these people are then speaking out in different ways, so sometimes I can find profound insight in the writings of some contemporary person who's received information that makes sense to me. And because their words are different than those I'd have gotten, it deepens my own perception of what's going on.

More so than ever before, this is available in books now. What we need seems to show up at exactly the same time we need it, if we're open to it, and if we are sensitized to know to pay attention to it.

And what's helped lately is doing a practice of being grateful for whatever challenges come my way, whatever pushes my buttons, because until we're aware of something, our consciousness can't work with it. When a challenge is brought right in my face, I have to deal with it now. And that's an opportunity for me to get through it rather than have it hanging around. I also do a lot of prayers about these things. I say, "Okay, now that I see this, I really need help. Because obviously if I'd been able to change it, I would have already done so." I take a warrior stance and ask for every bit of help possible, whether it's from inside myself, from outside, from a book, my best friend, a little kid, a bird flying by — I don't care where it comes from.

It's like you're putting out an APB, an All Points Bulletin, for help.

Exactly. And I really feel like the help comes through then. Too often, we panic, freeze up and think we can't do it. That may be the very first thing we think; "I can't handle this because I don't know how." But, if we knew how it wouldn't have come up in the first place. So, we need to say, "Oh, good, this has come up, and now I can invite some help so I can learn from deep inside myself and also from outside myself." And it's so fun to see what starts to come around, like a conversation or dream you have, a book you pick up — it can come from anywhere. A vital thing to remember is that where you put your attention is where the action will result. The way the universe works is that when we attend to something — focus our attention on it in a positive way — that's where the energy goes to make it work. It's like this: do we put gas in our pick-up truck or our car? If you put gas in the pick-up, that's the one that's gonna run. It's a very simple thing. And that's where the possibilities are — where the energy is. I was taught by one of my elders that even the energy behind our doubts can pile up and go towards making something happen. Doubts aren't a problem, they're just another kind of emotional energy that we can add to the pile.

That's a basic universal law common to all native peoples' philosophies and all metaphysical philosophies.

Right, and one of the things I talk to my students — and therefore, myself — about is our concept that someone —the magic shaman, the savior, or whomever — outside us is not going to come along, put a hand on our head, and then everything's gonna be all right. We forget that we generate these things inside us. We don't need that outside person for this. When I'm totally clear about wanting something — no ifs, ands, or buts — it happens very quickly. It requires work, though. And part of the work is that we have to cast away the doubts and fears so we don't have anything in the way of our intention.

Or else you end up manifesting the very things you're afraid of.

That's right. Our work now is not so much to manipulate and force things, which never has good consequences anyway, but to get clear of all the workable stuff. You have to be willing to let go of anything that holds you back.

That's difficult for many people to do because society has told us that happiness is a luxury, and that's conditioned people to believe that it's not our birthright, it's not logical, it's silly, it's emotional, it's ideal-istic, and that we shouldn't think happiness should be an adult priority. The faulty message is: "Who are we to believe we have the right to be fulfilled and happy?" Well, we do have the right to make choices and changes to be happy. Forget what society teaches: that we have to settle for this or settle for that.

Right. When we're willing to be happy, we're healthier, more creative and we get more done. Even in the midst of things that aren't the happiest of circumstances.

It's such an uphill battle getting that point across because people get so much negative influence from society to reinforce the idea that they don't have the right to be happy. That being happy is frivolous, emotional stuff, 'girl stuff.' If we listen to that, we're only living half a life.

We think we're using logic when we believe that kind of thing, but we're not. It's not logical to think being happy is wrong. It truly doesn't make sense.

It's completely illogical to choose unhappiness over happiness. The ultimate logical thing to do would be to go for what makes us happy.

Yes. Listening to our intuition, the guidance of our dreams, our heart's calling — all those help us break through this sense of limited logic that we've had, and open us up to a much larger knowingness that connects us to ourselves and everyone else. People are yearning for it.

Even the very people who fight it are yearning for it.

Yes, they are, but they just don't have any idea what it is because we've been taught such weird things in our modern society.

People are inherently afraid of the unknown, and this is unknown to them, the idea that they can be guided by what's inside them.

Yes. Even though I'm a very hopeful person, I think we're in a time when we're in really dire straits. We've pushed our planet and ourselves into a very stressful and critical situation. But, like the pendulum that gets too far out and starts swinging back, there's evidence of balanced energies emerging now. We're turning a corner in our consciousness. I really do believe in critical mass. There's a certain amount of energy and attention given to something, and then it starts to awaken and bring that energy forward for everyone. My new book, The Last Ghost Dance, *is about these energies, and how we can use them to create a golden time for ourselves and All Our Relations.*

Let's talk about healing from the Native American perspective. This is something that we can all be a part of.

It sure is. The words healing, health and wholeness all come from the same Latin root word. One of the things that's special about primary peoples' view of healing is that they understand it is about wholeness. True healing isn't about cutting something out in an operation or anything like that. It's about becoming more whole, and that extends to all levels. One of the things I found missing in my study of modern psychology and other things was that wholeness. As I re-awoke to my native roots in my late 20s, I came to understand that healing is spiritual, as well as physical, emotional, or mental. We must look at the whole being rather than just one part. We have to do this in as many ways as we can. This means within the person, within the family, within the community, and within the whole of All Our Relations. This is what I've been studying and teaching for more than 20 years now. Many of our challenges come from not functioning well in the larger whole — in what I call an ecologically sustainable sacred walk of earth. The larger view of how we're healed and healthy is a very vital one in our current critical situation. So much of our water and food is poisoned, we have immune deficiency diseases. We've wanted to heal individual people, but we've really lost sight of the fact that the health we need is going to come from healing the larger whole. So, that's where I put my emphasis.

We weren't put on a planet that didn't have everything we needed to survive, so it makes sense that we continue to investigate herbal and natural medicine, and look to nature for all our needs.

Exactly.

A lot of the knowledge that has been lost over the years is now being rediscovered.

There are so many people who devoted their lives to studying and teaching herbal and natural healing, so I try to turn people's attention to them whenever I can. And we have to remember the real healing, which is to create harmony and sustainability in our world. The native peoples, in the old days, didn't just use the things around them, they also sustained them. It's not just about going to the earth to get materials.

We need to make sure that we put back what we remove.

Right. And we need to commune with the life around us. One of the keynotes is a sacred ecology. That's a much more intimate, deeper wholeness with nature. The trees breathe out this air that we breathe in. That's an intimate nose-to-nose dance with the trees. And we can begin to love them just for what they are, not just for what they have to offer. This caring tends to be missing even when we turn our attentions towards nature and the land.

Do you consider yourself a healer?

Well, that's an interesting question. At the deeper level I do because in every bit of work I do, I'm working for wholeness. When I say I'm a healer, though, people think they can come to me and I'll lay my hands on them and fix it. But I'm certainly not that kind of healer. I do bodywork, and I do touch people, and I do believe I have a healing touch. I would like to develop that part of myself more. One of the other words that applies to health and wholeness and healing is holy. My definition of holy, which I've been given through guidance over the years, is the quality of attention we pay to everything in the Circle of Life. It's not about a white-haired guy in the sky. And it's not about a lot of other things. It's not about a certain day of the week when we go and act a certain way. It's an intention in every moment, if we can hold it, that says: 'I am respect and care for the whole Circle of Life as I walk.'

One of the reasons healing energy is so powerful for people is because of that holy connection. We will actually ascend to a higher plane of living when we truly balance the physical body and awaken our spiritual body. To be fully human — truly whole and holy — we must have our spirit body as alive and fully awake and active and useful to us as our physical body. I'm certainly just on the path of learning myself. I'm not a master of any of this, yet I'm being strongly "invited" by spirit and my teachers to urge all of us to wake up at this level and understand what incredible capacity we have once we do. Our native teachers down through time fully understood that. And every high spiritual tradition there is, whether it's Native American, Tibetan or East Indian or whatever, works on this aspect of things where we're able to quiet the physical self and awaken a part of us that is not bounded by space and time. Because when we move into that — the place of spirit or the invisible — then we are truly out of time and space. Our elders have told us for a long, long time that we can move through and beyond space and time. So, we can become a part of things if we want to know them, rather than scientifically killing them, tearing them apart, and dividing them down to look at the cells. We can know a tree by becoming it. This, of course, gives us a profound and actual connection with All Our Relations.

At that level — where we're in the place of wholeness and connected deeply with the spirit of things — we're in a holy place, a sacred place of harmony and good relationship. We're more aware of the whole thing, so we have not only knowledge and facts and connections that way, we also have wisdom.

And that's the key.

I feel wisdom is what's been missing in our larger culture. Too often, we look at a single, isolated thing, then make up a solution that ends up being terribly damaging to the rest of the cycle of life. Stepping up to that level — the spirit level — allows us to look at a much broader plane. When we learn to make decisions from there, we make wiser decisions, ones more in line with what I call sacred ecology. We're honoring and respecting the life of everything then, and, in fact, being ecologically sound. That's who we look toward creating a truly sustainable future.

What's the focus of your work now?

The best way I know to describe my work is the embodiment of Spirit. Many of us have had the initial experience of needing to sit quietly and focus specifically to touch the spiritual aspect of things. Yet the Old Ones understood — our ancient lineages tell us — that we can learn to hold that energy in our everyday life and thus walk in a sacred manner. The practice is called using the third attention, and it's literally about paying attention to the whole thing — to be able in our daily life to experience that connection that helps us be in good relationship with All Our Relations — and to hold in mind seven generations of children coming after us.

You seem to be synthesizing many different cultural and traditional viewpoints, which would not be surprising since you have both a strong mainstream and university education as well as one in your Native American heritage, and studies of other cultures including your Celtic heritage.

I've always had a very global view. My real interest in life and in my teaching is in helping us to become fully human, fully integrated and in good relationship. It only makes sense to me, since wholeness in our time certainly has global implications. You asked before about the quality of people's interest and attention. This reminds me of some other things I want to say about that. First, I'm just appalled at how little many people today really see and pay attention. I know a butcher's son who doesn't understand that you have to kill cows to get beef! Many people are simply hooked into TV and other media, believing everything that is said. That's often where their attention is focused. What we're getting through the mainstream media is certainly not often about truth and wholeness and holiness or good relationship with the Circle of Life. So, on some levels, there is a tremendous amount of ignorance and unconsciousness.

At another level, among people who've been paying some attention, doing a bit of personal homework, and trying to awaken their spirit, I see a fabulous thing — that we are graduating to another level. I used to have to teach all the basics every time, but now my classes can jump well beyond those into using our combined energy toward something powerful and positive. It's what I call apprenticeship, rather than simply learning, and that's very exciting. That's where I feel I can do my best — to help hone and lift and continue working with those who are truly willing to take those steps — to attend and to wake up at higher levels of personal joy and service. As a certain percentage of us do that, we lift the energy enough to help everyone else wake up, even if they have not had much intention toward that so far. That's what encouraged me to bring forward a new way of gathering together that's focused that way — the Confluence.

This is also what is called critical mass. Are we moving toward tipping the balance, then?

I feel like we are. One of the things that's helping with the spiritual upliftment and with our personal awakening is that we're coming to a time that all peoples' prophecies say is a time of more light, more consciousness, more vital life force. It will bring about a parting of the ways. Those who have no caring or honoring or respectfulness — who focus on competition, divisiveness, force and warring — will call to themselves a very difficult time. But, those people who want to live in harmony and balance and holiness — to share and care and cooperate — will be lifted up to another level of life. Some people call it the fifth dimension. The quality of energy we put forward will bring that quality back into our lives, more and more quickly as the energy magnifies. A key to the coming times is to put forward the energy we want to magnify for ourselves and All Our Relations. We can't "screw" our way to virginity, or war our way to peace. We must choose to live now what we want to magnify into our future. Those who are thinking that greed and rape and pillage are how to be secure, safe and happy will reap the benefits of that, which won't be very pretty.

How will this be reflected in terms of the planet itself and the earth changes that are already happening and even scientists can see will happen in the future?

That's an interesting one because what I've been told is that Mother Earth herself is graduating. She is Lady Gaia, growing and evolving to another plane. The prophecies say, and my highest and finest teachers say, that Earth will be in harmony. This is the decree. So, those who choose to be in harmony and live in a golden time will continue on with her and ascend to a new plane of beauty. In physical terms, it's almost like the rocket will go up and the launching pad will stay. Disharmony will be left behind, and those who need to continue to play in that game will move themselves off this planet and go to another place to learn.

Often, we think of ascension in terms of going somewhere else, leaving the planet physically, perhaps by our dying process, where the body dies and the spirit goes to another dimension.

I don't think any of us will know exactly what's happening until it happens. But, I do believe that Earth herself is ascending. That's a part of what my book, The Last Ghost Dance, *is about. It tells that in the old days of the Ghost Dance,* people saw the possibility of a renewed Earth — a place of beauty where there is joy and harmony and unity, and clean water, and plenty for all — an exquisite, golden, peaceful world. That's what they were dancing for and have continued to, in secret, over all these years. It's clear to me that all of us are being asked to join in that uplifting dance, that process of trusting and looking toward and working toward that golden world. And it's also clear that it will be manifest for those of us who are putting "our eggs in that basket." We can make the choices that will call it into reality for us, our children and All Our Relations.

Eight

Marilyn Sunderman

*The true artist is known by the use
he makes of what he annexes, and he annexes everything.*

— Oscar Wilde

Synchronicities often play a role in leading a writer to an interview, and the one that led me to painter and author Marilyn Sunderman was way off the meter.

As you've read in the introduction portion of Brian Weiss's chapter, he hypnotized me during one of our conversations while I was writing articles about him for *Omni* and other magazines. Instead of having a past life memory during this regression hypnosis session, I had a vision he called " a mystical experience," in which I saw myself and a male friend in two separate scenes. In one, I was wearing a white dress and swirling around in a garden. In the other, my friend was wearing a denim shirt and jeans, had a black leather satchel by his side, and stood on a rocky shore facing the sea all night while waiting for the sun to rise.

I had this hypnosis session in Brian Weiss's office in Miami on April 2, 1992. More than a year later, in May 1993, I was in a bookstore when a magazine I'd never heard of caught my eye. I didn't pick it up off the rack, and walked to another side of the store and continued looking at books. But I felt drawn to that magazine — I don't know why — and kept going back to the rack. Each time, I resisted picking it up. Finally, I said to myself, almost out loud: "Okay, okay, I'll buy it." So, I did.

That evening I did something I never do: I removed the books and magazines from the store's bag by turning the bag upside down and dumping out its contents onto the bed. That particular magazine flopped out and opened to photos of paintings on the left and right pages. The largest painting caught my eye immediately and I gasped; I couldn't believe my eyes...someone, a stranger, had painted the vision I'd had under hypnosis in Weiss's office a year earlier.

This stranger was Marilyn Sunderman, an internationally known portrait artist and painter.

Her studio's phone number was in the magazine article, so the next day I called and left a message for her. Within days, upon returning from an out of town trip, she phoned me back. When I explained who I was and why I was calling, she let out a sigh and a laugh.

"I can't believe this," she said. "I just today finished reading Brian Weiss's book *Many Lives, Many Masters*."

More than 20 years ago, long before it became fashionable to probe into past lives, Marilyn had begun having spontaneous past life memories, so she seemed more shocked by the Weiss coincidence than by the fact that I'd just informed her that she'd painted a stranger's vision.

"Oh, I've done *that* before," she chuckled good naturedly. "I've been told a few times that I've painted people's visions."

Oh. So, this was old hat to her, then.

Even though the magazine had printed the painting in black and white, I knew that Marilyn's colors would match my vision, too. The shoreline, the view of the ocean, the man and the woman, all were *exactly* as I'd seen them in that vision more than a year earlier, right down to the style of my white dress, the style and color of the man's clothes, his black leather satchel, the style and color of our hair, our body types, *everything*. In the painting, though, Marilyn had presented the two standing side by side on the shore, while in my vision, the man stood by the shore and I stood behind him "in another dimension" where he couldn't see me.

"Don't tell me the colors in the painting," I said. "I want to tell *you*." And then I described them all. They were all correct. The setting, the two people, the colors, the angles, the mood, the lighting, the style — it was as if she'd been sitting at an easel inside my head that day a year before with her canvas and paints. To add to the intrigue, Marilyn told me that she'd done the painting *nearly six years before I'd had the vision*. In fact, she'd sold it long ago, but did have numbered and signed serigraphs of it. These were not publicly displayed anywhere that I could have seen them prior to my hypnosis session with Brian Weiss (which was tape-recorded), or after it, so we knew that I couldn't have subconsciously incorporated a memory of her painting into my vision.

Since I was researching a magazine article about inspiration and creativity, I arranged to interview Marilyn. I then told Brian Weiss about this strange coincidence. He remembered my vision, and he was as shocked as I was. Two months later, Marilyn came to Miami to meet with gallery owners who were planning to feature her paintings. We had many conversations during that week, and I introduced her to Brian Weiss. Marilyn was as eager to have a past life regression session with Dr. Weiss as he was to conduct one, so a few days later, she had an appointment with him in his office.

She details all of this in her beautifully written first book, *Past Lives, Present Joy*, which she began writing a few years later, and which was published by Kensington in January, 1999.

The book chronicles both her career as a painter — her portrait of John F. Kennedy is in the Kennedy Library collection, she's been commissioned to paint the portraits of titans of industry, and her paintings hang in royal collections around the world — and her past lives, which she believes have dramatically affected her work and the relationships she's had in her present life.

She's as gifted a writer as she is a painter, and her story is a page-turner that also presents her philosophical views on the nature of karma, which differ from those most often tossed around.

Best-selling author Bernie Siegel, M.D. called the book "A story of great courage and ultimate wisdom." Author and former U.S. Senator George McGovern, who many years ago was one of Sunderman's college professors, said, "This book from the heart of a talented artist searching for the meaning of life and death, will sharpen your insights and quicken your imagination."

Marilyn Sunderman was born on December 11, 1935 in LeSeur (home of those famous baby peas), Minnesota to a dairy farmer and his wife. The third of four children, she was the only girl, and a precocious one at that. By three, she'd begun to paint, at seven she began to write a novel, and at 14, she completed her first commissioned artwork.

She graduated from the University of Minnesota with a degree in Art and Philosophy, and moved to Chicago, where she worked in the art department of a magazine and her adventures began. Although those adventures would take her around the world more times than most people go around the block, and have also included a brief marriage to an aristocratic man who made Dr. Jekyll and Mr. Hyde look like Bambi, one of her favorites happened close to home and touches upon a love of words that's as great as her love of art.

"When I was 21, and working at the magazine, my uncle Leland Case, who'd been an editor for *The New York Times* in Paris and had interviewed Lindbergh and Einstein, called me and said that he had a 21st birthday present for me," she recalls wistfully. "He said that I'd need to get away for a long lunch hour. I did, and we took a cab over to a very tall building in Chicago, and went up a private elevator to the top floor. I got off the elevator, a door opened and I was greeted by the poet Carl Sandburg."

Her 21st birthday present was lunch with one of the world's most beloved poets.

It was 1956, five years after he'd won the Pulitzer, and 11 years before his death. "I remember that he laughed a lot, and he was so gentle, like what people would love to think their grandfather would be like," Sunderman says. "He autographed a collection of poetry for me. Sometime later, someone wrote to the magazine I worked for saying that they couldn't understand one of his poems. I wrote a quick little analysis of the poem, and the magazine published it. Unbeknownst to me, they sent it to Carl Sandburg. And he wrote me this little note saying that any time anything of his needed to be interpreted, he'd love for me to be the one to do it."

She is still in awe when she tells me this story more than 40 years later. I'm in awe, too: He's my favorite poet, I have his entire collection, and I wish I'd had a conversation with him over lunch. But, alas, she met him eight months after I was born, and he died when I was only eleven.

In her twenties, Sunderman toured Europe for the first time. Over the years, she would study there extensively, and it would also play a large role in her spontaneous past life memories, which ran from The Spanish Inquisition through Nazi Germany, and included lifetimes as a mystic, a soldier, and a murdered painter in a royal court.

Her commissioned portrait painting took her around the world, too, and she also became known for her Impressionist-style paintings, which have been compared to Monet's. Her work is in galleries and collections across the country, and from Paris to Tokyo. She lived for a number of years in Honolulu, and now shares her Sedona, Arizona home and studio with her dog, Apollo.

She also holds a doctorate in Fine Arts from Dakota Wesleyan University; lectures about the links between creativity, inspiration and spirituality; and studies mysticism and native peoples' traditions, both of which she's recently expressed in a series of paintings.

We have had countless conversations since 1993, and the one presented here took place in August 1998 as she prepared for her book tour. Shortly after our first meeting, Marilyn sent me a serigraph of *Shared Horizons*, her painting of my vision.

The word inspiration is derived from the Latin for "in spirit." All people have inspiration. Some choose to express it, some choose not to.

Inspiration is when you have an idea and a passion behind it. I encourage people to look at their spirit and to use it. I truly feel that there is a divine inspiration. Creativity is one of the main bases in our lives. And I definitely believe that everyone is creative. I don't assign it only to those in the arts. You can do anything creatively, have creative relationships. In one of my workshops, I can show someone who denies they have any creativity that they do.

Maybe our Western society too narrowly defines creativity, limiting it to something that's just in the arts.

Absolutely.

And that you're not considered creative unless you're making your living at it.

And that is a most unfortunate attitude because ultimately, as far as I'm concerned, creativity includes that you create the package you are. Everyone creates themselves.

And quite literally we create other people when we have children. That's a big act of creativity.

Yes, and I think so often we forget that that little, wonderful creative being, that child running around, has things they want to accomplish in this lifetime, and has even brought things in from previous lifetimes, which, of course, is what my book, Past Lives, Present Joy, *is about. So, I think that the sooner each person can begin to take responsibility for themselves, the better. To understand that they're really they're own creators and co-creators with the universe.*

And that can be really difficult in our society, and in others too, where parents don't welcome the idea of just letting their children be themselves. There's so much control going on.

> *One of the things we must learn is to let go. I have a phrase I like to use: "Don't step on someone else's karma," meaning don't step on someone else's lessons.*

That can get kind of tricky because whenever we have interactions with people we're stepping all over each other's stuff all the time. We think we're helping someone when in fact we're actually preventing them from getting their lesson themselves.

> *It's a real big one — to get out of other peoples' way. I was just at a meeting last night with a particularly interesting healer. And what that made me think about was getting out of my own way. I was too much in my head, and not following my intuition or spirit enough.*

That's always a struggle because we live in a universe we've overlayed a set of logical rules onto, and then we expect it to behave by them. And when our intuition can't provide us with a whole set of logic to back it up with, we just ignore it. But, the whole idea of intuition is that it doesn't come with a "why" or a "how." We're supposed to take it on faith. And it's never wrong, but people have a rough time following it because it doesn't come with a "why." And in Western society, we can't do anything unless it comes with a reason.

> *That's been going on since the scientific age came in, that everything has to have an explanation. Spending my whole life in the arts, and attempting to understand creativity, one of the things that I've realized is that when you live artistically, there are no road maps.*

Yeah, there can't be, because that would certainly limit your artistic expression.

Yes, to the degree that you try to control it, you're not creating you're copying. There's a beautiful thing that Picasso said many years ago, and it's always stuck with me as a very profound thought. He said, you can copy this person, you can copy that person, you learn a lot by copying the masters, but when you begin to copy yourself you're in trouble. And that's about not just art, but in life.

That's great. That means that you'd be repeating yourself, plagiarizing yourself, becoming redundant. That's worse than copying someone else.

And you're not really living then. You've taken the aliveness out. If you get up each day and routinely plan your day to move along the same way, there is no aliveness in it.

There's no room for spontaneity.

Right. However, I've found that you do want some kind of order as a base. I'll apply it to art, and then to daily life: I have to have my materials in certain places, I have to have my paints readily available and know where they are, the same with brushes, the same with my canvases, so that I'm not spending all my time looking for things. Now, you can apply that to a person's day: Having breakfast can be a foundation, so can driving to work, but driving to work a different way now and then can add some spontaneity.

And spontaneity is important because without it we won't have new experiences.

Spontaneity is one of the main ingredients for being creative.

And then reacting to that spontaneity. I think fear stops people from being creative — it stops them from reacting and it stops them from expressing themselves. They're always afraid they're going to be judged because we tend to judge everything in our culture that's creative. We give out awards for movies, for music, for books, and for nearly everything else, and we're pitting everybody against each other in competition. So, people may think, "I'm not perfect at this, so why should I bother expressing myself creatively?"

> *You're right. And the greatest fear is not the fear of "out there," but the fear of what's within — how people judge themselves. Taking that first step is the most important thing. To not shoot yourself down before you even take that first step. Make that first step a small one so you're not overwhelmed. Because you're right — fear is one of the biggest things that people load on themselves. And they then come up with all the excuses about why they can't do something. I have a little four-part formula that I use about creativity. This is not about art, although that's been my profession forever and now I'm translating a lot of these same things to another profession of writing. Here's the formula: The first word is BEGIN., and when I do my workshops, I tell people: "Begin anywhere, begin somewhere, but begin." The second part is MAKE NO JUDGMENTS. It's like the story of the child learning to walk. First they get up, and they're so excited that they're on their feet, and they go to try and move, and they fall down. And they get back up and they do it again. And they get back up and they do it again. And they continue to do this. They don't sit there and judge themselves and say, "Oh, I'll never run a marathon, so I quit!" which is what a lot of people do with creativity and projects.*

And that's because a child hasn't been told yet by anyone outside of him that he "can't do it." He hasn't been judged by anybody, and nothing's affected his own opinion of himself yet.

> *Exactly. So, first we have BEGIN, then MAKE NO JUDGMENTS, and the third phrase is: MAKE NO COMPARISON. If your work, or whatever you're doing, was to be like someone else's, you'd be that person. (We laugh.) And the fourth part is: CONTINUE. And each one of those parts is just*

as important as the others. And, that's it! And that's the theme of my next book.

Which brings us to the topic of books. After decades as a painter, who also wrote, and created many other things, you have published your first book. You wrote it as a memoir, and it traces the impact of memories that were spontaneously popping up regarding past lives, and how that was affecting your present life. How that was teaching you why you were in the situations and relationships you were in. It made such an impact on you that you decided to write about it.

I'm not even sure I had a choice. The things that were happening became so pervasive in my life that I had to search them out and deal with it. And what I really came up with — and this is what everyone has to take a look at in order for them to come into being themselves — is what past patterns are running me? If you can recognize the patterns, you can then make a choice about whether you want to get rid of them or not.

And then you have to figure out how — by replacing that old pattern with something new.

My own experience with that is simple — the recognition of a pattern frequently is the end of it.

Do you think what stops people from making changes is that they don't know how to do what they're doing any differently? If they did, they'd already be doing it a different way. It's kind of a Catch-22, and I think that keeps people from making changes. They say, "I'd like to stop this, but what am I supposed to do instead? How do I do things differently?" Maybe if people began to think about how to do it differently, that would help them find the strength to stop the old ways, because they wouldn't be walking out into a void, they would have some healthy, better ways in mind, even if it's just a few little things to get them started. Maybe they haven't found the entire way yet, but a little something that gives them something to replace the old way with. It's like diet. When someone says, "You've gotta stop eating all these high cholesterol foods," you have to then tell them what healthy things to eat instead.

> *The first step is to recognize the pattern. Most people are walking around in denial that the pattern is even there. It's like a fish in water. Ask a fish what water is like, and it can't tell you because water is all they know. Many people continue to have relationships over and over with people who are alike. The first thing is to get in touch with that pattern. Just seeing you have a pattern can make it pop like a bubble.*

Assuming a person has gotten out of denial, and says, "I want to break this pattern," then what do they do?

> *I handle this in my book,* Past Lives, Present Joy, *when I talk about recognizing your karma, your patterns.*

This applies not only to past lives, but to patterns in this life.

> *Exactly. You can begin in childhood and see where you begin these patterns that you repeat over and over, and less of each day operates out of spiritual spontaneity and aliveness. More and more of each day is devoted to just doing what you're familiar with. You can do something a new way. How do you begin that? Using the example of driving to work: you start at the same place, you end at the same place, but you don't have to drive the same way every day. You don't have to begin each day with exactly the same breakfast. Add some variety; slowly breaking some of these patterns.*

In your particular case, you found that your patterns weren't just limited to this lifetime. You were getting spontaneous memories from past lives. What did that feel like?

> *It was quite frightening in the beginning. I was having memories. I was walking down the street and all of a sudden the street isn't made of the same material. You're in a different time and place.*

Did this have the quality of a very vivid dream, a daydream, a déja vu flashback?

> *It was more like a déja vu — I've been here before, it's not like it's in this present time, what's going on? I know what that person's going to say next. So many people, probably more people than not, have had that same feeling of "I've been here before," or "Gee, that person feels familiar." But, you know you've never met them before. So, that started happening. And then, I started repeating patterns of relationships.*

And you found from your past life memories that people from your present life were people you also knew from your past lives. And you were in situations with them now that were either identical to those from past lives, or exactly the opposite. So that you were playing out both sides of the patterns.

> *To a degree playing out both sides, but in particular allowing the same patterns to emerge again.*

There are two relationships you focus on in your book. One is the relationship that you had with your ex-husband in your present life, and he's very physically abusive and there's obviously something very wrong with him — he's deeply disturbed — he's not just a guy who loses his temper or is a garden variety control freak, he's someone who goes way beyond that. And you begin to have past life memories of knowing him. What kind of a relationship did you have with him in your past lives?

> *In the book , I do not dwell on past lives with him. What comes up is a past life pattern I've had where I relinquish all my control over to someone else.*

And whether it's to him or other people from the past or present, that pattern of allowing other people to control you is emerging.

> *Yes, and this is where even the person who doesn't believe in*

270

reincarnation can relate to it because it was my pattern of letting someone else shadow over me. And this was a pattern I had even if you only think in terms of this lifetime. However, what I found was there had been three other lifetimes where power and control was the issue. It began with a lifetime during the Spanish Inquisition where I was a person very much in control, a person with power, but with various traumatic things that happened during the Inquisition I relinquished my power because I became afraid of it.

In that Inquisition life, were you someone who was tortured, or were you doing the torturing?

In that lifetime, I was traveling as a female monk who was very spiritual and had a great deal of healing and psychic ability. And during the Inquisition I was tortured and killed because of my power. But, right before dying, I found my own mind twisting the power so much that I became afraid of being evil. So, when I was born into the next lifetime, I was afraid of my power and made myself a powerless person.

Right. Because power was something that had gotten you tortured in a previous life. So, you thought, "I'm not going to be a powerful person in this life because it got me tortured in the last one, so I'll play it safe."

Right. That was one part of it, and the other was that I was afraid that if I became powerful I could misuse it.

We all have the potential for evil and good.

Yeah, and we have to look at that in ourselves and then integrate our dark and our light, or else we'll be walking around in constant denial of parts of ourselves, which I think is part of the sickness of people right now. They do deny parts of themselves.

271

And this keeps someone from having a full, creative life.

You must have it all, you must eventually integrate it all. And I say eventually because I think life is a continuum. We're not just here on this planet; there's much more. And in that continuum, there are various lessons and various places. And I think one of the lessons for earth is that we must understand our entire "person" here and our lessons here, and then we get to go play and have lessons somewhere else, whether you want to call it heaven, as some religions do, or nirvana, as others call it. There are all sorts of words used to describe it.

Others might call it another dimension.

Yes.

You originally wanted to title the book *Born to Say Goodbye,* and that was because of this theme of saying goodbye to old patterns. One of the most important parts of your book, which ultimately was titled *Past Lives, Present Joy,* reveals what you believe is the real reason for karma. And it is quite different from what many other people write about and talk about in relation to karma. You talk about not repeating things over and over until you get it right, until you can make that tired old pattern work. Your feeling is that we're born to say goodbye — goodbye to the old patterns.

Originally, when I wanted to call it Born to Say Goodbye, *I was thinking in terms of born to say goodbye to a person I had known in three different lifetimes. And then it grew from there, and I felt it was born to say goodbye to past patterns, patterns that we operate out of that keep us from being in the now. It's only in the now, in the present, that you can be creative. Not out of yesterday, and not out of tomorrow. Then, I eventually realized that what I really felt was not just saying goodbye to past patterns, but saying goodbye to the whole package of ways of doing things, and what you get out of this is you get to just be.*

You get your freedom. Again, it's like you said before, you're breaking routine. Whether it's routine finely honed over an entire lifetime, or many lifetimes, or a seemingly harmless routine like eating the same thing every day for breakfast, it's still routine.

Yes, and it comes down to just being there, being who you are. Wouldn't it be wonderful to just get up and for each day to be it's own day, unlike any you've ever lived before.

Without any trappings left over from the day before.

And that is the goal.

So, when other people use karma as an excuse for continually repeating their patterns, that's a form of denial and a crutch. That's using karma as a reason to continue to live in an unhealthy way. What you're saying is use your karma, instead, to free yourself from those patterns and look at the fact that you've repeated this before, and say, "Well, I'm just not going to do this again."

And ultimately to not have to deal with karma at all. And to recognize that in that sense karma is just another belief system. Let's give an example: A person knows someone who has harmed them. They say, "Okay, I'm going to forgive you." Well, in saying that, they might be setting up a lesson for the other person, in the sense of taking on more karma. The classic example is: you killed me in a past life, so now you have to make it up to me. So, now you have karma you have to get rid of. If I'm going to wait around for you to make it up to me, to work off that karma, I'm gaining good karma, and now I have to use that in some way. Early on in my life, I noticed that when I behaved a certain way I didn't feel good about it, and I thought, "Oh, how can I make up for that?" that's operating like karma. But, somewhere along the line, I realized that what I should be doing instead, is either before or after the apology, is say to myself: "Well, I'll never do that again."

Right. That's breaking the pattern.

Yes.

Rather than feeling like you're stuck with it and have to constantly make up for it, and be at the mercy of this thing that happened. By saying "I'll never do that again," you stop that pattern and aren't linked to it or trapped by it anymore.

That's the main thing. The apology is nice, the retribution is nice, but the main issue is not doing it again. That's getting rid of the pattern, that's getting rid of the karma.

I think that if we look at what might sound on the surface like a ridiculous analogy — and I'm choosing one that is ridiculous to make this point that we tend to lead our lives this way, which is just as ridiculous — we can see how people have traditionally viewed karma. So, here's the analogy: let's say you accidentally burn your hand on the stove. So according to the way we view karma, you might say, "Well, because I touched something hot and got burned, that means now that I'm supposed to go stick my hand in ice every day for the rest of my life *(we laugh)* to make up for the fact that I once touched a hot stove." Well, that's really nuts, and nobody would ever think that way. And, yet, we use that exact same line of thinking when talking about our karma.

That's right. We say, "I have to make up for this, I have to make up for this." Your analogy is a good example. (We laugh.)

What we really should be saying is "That stove was hot. I don't think I should touch a stove again." And then, that's that.

That's a very good example. And that's exactly it: "I'm not going to do that again."

When people believe they have karma with a person, they say, "Well, this person is acting really badly towards me. I wonder if that

274

means that in a past life I once acted badly towards them. That must be it. I guess turnabout is fair play and we're supposed to even the score — karmatically speaking — so I'll just take all this abuse because I deserve it because I must've dome something to them in a past life. So, for the rest of my life, it's okay for this person to now be lousy to me."

Yeah, this is what a lot of people do. They get attracted to the familiar and they don't even know why. Like the person who continues to marry an abuser. They continue to be attracted to a role they're used to playing, instead of saying, "I don't want to play that role anymore." And that pattern is not that easy to break, but the first step is the recognition of it. What does this have to do with creativity, to bring us back to where we started? Of course, this is my theme. I've probably got a trilogy of books going. This first one — Past Lives, Present Joy — is about breaking past patterns; the second one will be about "what do you do once you've broken those patterns? You get to be creative."

And by that you don't just mean you get to go create a painting, but that you get to go create a great life for yourself.

Exactly. And the third book will probably be totally about what I've always wanted to do, and that is to be able to fly without a plane. (We laugh.) It's out there somewhere, and I haven't experienced it yet to write about it. My work, my art, is always changing in relation to what I've learned about life.

That gets back to what we said at the beginning about inspiration and spontaneity, and not being in a routine. How you express yourself — and in your case, one of the ways you do that is through painting — is going to be based on what you're experiencing, but only if you allow yourself to do that. Sometimes some people get into a rut and just paint the same apple, year after year.

And that must be terribly painful.

But, what if someone says, "I like apples, but I'm going to make this apple different based on how I feel and what I'm going through." And this year the person's painting abstract apples, and next they're inspired to paint square apples. It's like when you did portraits. You did them for many years and some people might think that you'd get bored with it. But, what you brought to the portrait was far beyond just mimicking faces. You were inspired by your experiences, which would then affect what you saw in the person sitting for the portrait and how you represented them on canvas.

This is very true, and more and more instead of looking at their surface and their features, I kept heading deeper and deeper into their souls. At the time I left the career of portraiture, I was painting so much into the soul that the recognizable outer surface of the person became so unimportant. Frequently, the portrait wouldn't even look like their features anymore (we laugh). At that point in my career, I'd counsel them even before I began the portrait that what I was going to paint was deep into the soul. And, generally, they would look at the finished portrait and say, "Am I really that beautiful?" Because everyone's soul is gorgeous, but we mask it with all this stuff. So, I found it was a time to look at most people who were asking me to do their portrait and say to them: "I think maybe what you want is a photograph taken." And I went from painting people's souls to the soul of the universe. And that took me through many stages. For awhile I was painting scenes of people walking through doorways — the seekers and the searchers. Of course, I was directly relating what was going on in myself. One of the paintings is called "The Awakening." It took me two or three years to realize what I was painting was my own awakening, going from an agnostic to a deep believer. Now, I have a series called "Portals" and they're the portals between the third dimension and other dimensions.

How do you take what is a particularly abstract concept, like that one, and find a way to represent that on a canvas?

Let me give you an example. I have one painting that has a glowing field of irises in the foreground, and the sun is sparkling off those irises and you feel that you could almost reach out and pick them. And past the irises is some steps, and they lead further and further and further into a distance that's only a brilliant glowing light. So, I'm leading you from the third dimension in the irises, wandering further and further down this path, and finally until you're off. The person who owns the painting now was here visiting me two days ago and she told me that she constantly drifts away when she sits in front of the painting.

She's drawn into that beautiful representation of that light of the other dimensions.

So, for quite sometime I've been doing paintings that lead the viewer down paths and into other dimensions.

Much like you felt like you were going down new paths in your life.

Exactly. I lived a great deal of my life starting in this dimension, and then I would go out into other dimensions. Interestingly enough, I am now spending a great deal of time in other dimensions, and what's happened with some of my paintings is that instead of painting from the third dimension out, I'm actually painting out there...

Looking in.

Yes, looking in to the third dimension. And I'm calling this series "The Sacred Sites." I frequently paint ahead of where I am in my own knowledge, so what's happening is now that I'm aware of this knowledge, another series will come to me. In the Sacred Site paintings, I'm giving the viewer an experience of a sacred site and the energy that they can glean from it going back and forth between dimensions. They won't maybe even consciously know that's what's happening, though as I said before the client who owns the painting "Stepping Stones" told me that

277

she's constantly being drawn in to these other dimensions when she sits in front of the painting.

Much like people can be affected when something else visual triggers that meditative or altered state — like staring at the water or a fireplace.

Exactly. It doesn't matter where it happens to you. The artist is always trying to share the experience, the writer is always trying to share the experience. I wanted to know what people got from reading my book. And so many tell me the same thing: "This triggered things in my life." That's what I also want my paintings to do.

And it can continue to do that. It doesn't just do it once. Did you ever watch a movie or read a book, and given where you were in your life at that point, the movie or book had a particular impact on you? And then, a couple of years later, you watch that movie again, or read that book again, and now it means even more to you or it means different things to you because of what you've learned since and where you are now.

Yes, yes — you're experiencing it from a new level. Exactly! There's something that artists have been screaming down through the centuries — and it's not just artists, philosophers have been saying it and even Jesus Christ said it — and that is, "You, too, will be doing this, and you will do it greater than I." What they've been trying to say is that it's the process. It's the process of living where you can find your aliveness, your creativeness, and ultimately just who you are.

And that's often found by expressing yourself creatively. You learn more about who you are.

Yes, it's one of the ways to go through this process of finding out who you are. But, it's not about the goal. So many people get too distracted by the goal.

Well, you know there can't really be a goal because we're always going to be in the process if discovering who we are. It's just like watching that movie many times — every time you see it, it will mean something different to you because you are different. We're always in process, we're never a finished product. We don't ever reach our goal, though ultimately you could say we get as far as we're going to get on the day we die, at least in this lifetime. But, by definition, everything has to be process because we never get to a point where we say, "Okay, this is the person I am, and from this point on I'm never going to change." Even if you don't want to change, things are going to change, and you will be modified by your daily experiences and thoughts.

You have brought up the most wonderful, profound point.

Oh, my. And on a Friday no less *(we laugh)*.

You've brought up a profound point about this process. And it's one of the sicknesses that's going on right now. The disease is that people have begun to focus so much on the outcome, the product, the stuff, the things. They believe that "If I buy more stuff, I'm gonna feel good. If I make this much a year, I'm gonna feel good." And they're concentrating on the things instead of where the real wonderful things will come from, which is when they connect with the source and when they connect with who they are.

And that's a process. It's continuing.

That's the process. All the stuff in the world is never going to make you feel complete. Things are nice. You can feel better driving a car than walking barefoot for twenty miles. But, where your heart is while you're driving or walking is much more important.

But, unfortunately, people are very afraid to be in touch with their heart because that sets up vulnerability and the possibility of "Ooh, I could get hurt." And people are so afraid of that possibility that they'd rather not take their heart out for a spin.

279

And think of the fun that they're missing. Anyone who's ever been in love knows that it's one of the most exciting states there is when you begin. But, then they start to put all those expectations in the way. Using the metaphor of process — if you continue to be loving, loving, loving, it continues to be exciting. But, we usually say instead, "Well, if you love me, you'll do this. And if I love you, I'll do that." And that's putting all that stuff in the way, gathering all the moss all over that poor little rock!

And I think that what makes it even worse is that we're always looking for some kind of validation of our feelings. And what women in particular do is to sit around with our female friends and constantly analyze our relationships. So, we've taken away the real qualities of the relationship and what we really have is "The Relationship As Seen Through The Eyes of Our Friends." And we mistake that for the real one. And we begin to react to the person we're having the relationship with based on the opinions and feedback of all these other people who aren't in the relationship with you. And those friends and family members are often the ones who will place these expectations in our heads or reinforce the ones that we may unfortunately already have there. For instance, two people start dating, and the first thing one of the woman's friends want to know is "Ooh, has he taken you to that French restaurant yet?" or wherever, and the woman says, "Well, no." and her friend says, "Ooh, that's not a good sign." And it's that sort of thing that leads you to think, "Well, if he really liked me he'd do XYZ," or "My friends say that if he doesn't call me every night that means he doesn't really love me."

That's the stuff getting in the way of the process. Absolutely.

And, in looking for someone on the outside to constantly validate what's going on in our life, we're looking for our friends to say, "Oh, he sounds great, he's terrific, everything he's doing is wonderful." And we're looking for someone with a crystal ball to tell us how it's going to work out: "Oh, I think he's going to ask you to marry him." And in the course of looking for that external validation, we're destroying the relationship.

What you've just done is give a real nice, little synopsis of how people can destroy the creativeness of relationships. You just gave a great synopsis of how not to live creatively with relationships, and this same sort of thing applies to everything across the board. We can live creatively, or we can live out of others' expectations, our own expectations...

And fears.

And past patterns.

And other people's fears. Very often these discussions we have about relationships trigger our friends' fears, and they just glue their fears on to us.

Well, we put all these judgments in there. I feel the quest of my whole life has been to discover what creativity, aliveness and being yourself really is. And, having discovered what works to get there, to do this, I now want to share it with others. And now we come back to the word you started this conversation with: Inspiration. I think the greatest thing a human being can be for anyone else is to be themselves so they can be, just by example, an inspiration to others.

The opposite of creativity, of creating something, is destroying something, so if we aren't living a life that is quite literally creative, then we are living one that is destructive. And any time you do something like we just discussed — friends giving input about a relationship — we may be adding to the destruction of something rather than adding to its creation.

And let's take that same thought — which I love to do because before being even an artist or writer, I'm a philosopher, a thinker — and remember that there is an appropriate time for destruction.

Well, sure. And let's take an example from your life. You were married to an abusive man. Obviously, that was a relationship that needed to end, not go, but to be destroyed.

Correct.

And it doesn't even need to be that extreme an example. There will always be times when certain things have to end.

Just like a battery has a positive and a negative, there are certain people whose mission is to be negative. And their negative keeps things twirling. Many years ago, someone said, "Oh, you want a comfortable life with no stress and no challenges. Okay, we can take your brain out of your body and float it in tepid water. It still can think, and now you have this no-stress, no-challenge, very, very calm existence. How would you like that?" No, thank you! I would rather have someone push my buttons now and then, I would rather have challenges. That same person who's driving you crazy, is what's giving you the impetus to look at making changes or to do something differently.

And you talk about a time for destruction in your book. The whole theme is to destroy patterns that don't work. It's all a balancing act. To have the proper balance between when we're creating and when we're ending. That's the tricky part.

And when we do things creatively, we always have to let go of this in order to have that. You have this gorgeous apple in front of you. In order to make the salad, you have to destroy the look that the apple has now to take it to a new form. And now you have this salad, this other beautiful form of a thing. But you destroyed here to create there.

You transformed.

Life is a continuum.

It's constantly transforming.

282

My true theme in the book, is that there is no such thing as death. There is transformation. We go from this existence to another existence to another existence. The closest analogy we have for that is: At night, we lie down and go to sleep. Do we die then? No! We go to another place for awhile, and then we wake up. We continue to live.

So, after we "die," we really are just going to another place, from which we will then ultimately "wake up from" here in another life, or maybe somewhere else.

The stream of life continues.

There are examples of that in nature, even though people are reluctant to admit that they're part of nature. We like to think that humans are different than a tree, an apple, or water, but we're not. This is how all of nature operates. An apple is on a tree. Nobody picks it. It falls. Eventually it'll decompose — that's a friendlier word than rot — and then it's just going to continue on it's natural course. It's seeds, even if they're blown away by the wind or carried off by a bird, will eventually find their way to burrow into the ground. Now it's growing into a tree again. Transformation. The ultimate recycling. We're the same way. And if the seed was eaten by a bird or animal, now it's part of that creature's body. Transformed into something else.

And that brings us to the basic thing: The spark of life is all the same. The spark of life that's in a tree, a bird or in us is all from the same source. Life is everywhere, even out there on other planets, in other galaxies. So, if life is everywhere, and it's all from the same source, what are we doing with this great big fear about aliens? Maybe we should be more afraid of the person walking down the street behind us (we laugh). That life is everywhere is so easy a concept to get. I was telling this to someone recently, and her eyes were getting bigger and bigger and she said, "But, they wouldn't look like us!" And I said, "Well, my dog doesn't look like me! So what?" (We laugh).

Exactly. Nothing on this planet looks like anything else, so why should something from another planet look like us?

An octopus doesn't look like us, and you could go on and on. So, what is that supposed to mean? (We continue laughing.)

Hey, a lake doesn't look like you but it doesn't make it any less valid that it's alive.

Exactly. I remember some years ago talking with a science teacher. And, you know, sometimes they're some of the most blocked people there are because many people in science haven't allowed for science to grow past what they've already learned. Well, I looked at her and I knocked on the table and I said, "Just like this table is alive!" She thought I was crazy. She had forgotten that the table has molecules that are dancing around, and now, as they've proved, more of that table is space than is solid.

And also, we need to re-define the word "alive," because we have a pretty narrow definition of "alive."

True.

And when we stop and realize that "alive" means more than what we traditionally think it means, then we realize that yes, quite literally, that table is alive.

The spark of life has been given to me, and I'm grateful for that. And I think it's the same spark that's in everyone and everything else. I have a passion to share the feeling of that spark, the wonderfulness of it, and that the major force of everything is love. I hold a humbleness and a reverence and a love for everything.

Nine

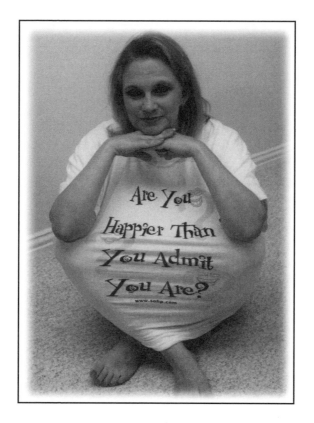

Pam Johnson

*Congress shall make no law respecting an
establishment of religion, or prohibiting the free exercise
thereof; or abridging the freedom of speech, or of the press;
or the right of the people peaceably to assemble, and to
petition the Government for a redress of grievances.*

— Amendment I, Constitution of the U.S.

*W*ho would've thought that the right to express happiness would need an advocate and spokesperson...and a national organization, no less?

At first glance, you may think that this is a frivolous non-issue, but, unfortunately, you'd be mistaken. And that would be because expressing happiness has become so politically incorrect that not only has Ann Landers, the advice columnist and etiquette institution urged her readers to keep their good news to themselves — she not so politely urged them to cease and desist sending those Christmas letters full of cheery year-in-review tidbits — but people all over the country are reporting that they've gotten into hot water at work for being, get this, *too happy.*

Enter Pam Johnson, founder of the Secret Society of Happy People. Well, of course you're laughing. As Johnson herself admits, "you can't say our name and *not* smile." But, this isn't a joke. The Society has quickly evolved into an advocacy group making headlines in support of some dead serious issues. Like the right (which we don't have) to free speech in the workplace. Get fired for having an attitude — a happy attitude, no less — and see if you're still laughing at the Secret Society of Happy People.

The Society got its name when Johnson noticed — and who hasn't? — that even the tiniest morsel of happy expression had been so demeaned that its bearers were forced into the closet, into the underground, into hiding, in order to escape the torrent of people eager to rain on their parade, says Johnson, who makes it clear that she's not telling people to *be* happy, just hoping to make it easier to *express* said happiness — without repercussions — should they happen to feel it from time to time.

It was this message that landed her in newspapers, on radio and television worldwide beginning in December, 1998, when she publicly challenged Ann Landers' call for a moratorium on holiday letters. Within a few weeks, Johnson found herself tackling the larger issue under which this expression of happiness stuff fell — free speech — when people from around the country began contacting her and relaying their tales of trouble in the workplace. Johnson contacted the ACLU, hoping to find a case in which an employee had been fired for "being happy," and much to her surprise was told that the ACLU hadn't handled any such cases because there were no legal precedents for them: you couldn't argue for free speech in the workplace when there was no such thing according to the law.

That sent Johnson in a broader direction, (including an appearance on ABC's *Politically Incorrect*) and the Secret Society of Happy People also became a beacon for those who were seeking justice in a whole new arena: Johnson put the word out that anyone who'd been fired, demoted or ever reprimanded by an employer for not just being happy, but for exercising what they erroneously believed was their right to free speech, workplace or not, could contact them for assistance (their website is sohp.com). The Society refers these to the ACLU and also supports lobbying and other efforts to create legislation resulting in freedom of speech in the workplace.

That Pam Johnson has become a public advocate doesn't surprise her, and shouldn't surprise anyone who has known her either personally or professionally.

Born in 1966 in Brownwood, Texas, and raised in nearby Abilene, Johnson is the daughter of a fireman and a homemaker who later worked in real estate. The oldest of two children, her family never knew quite what to make of the little girl whose commitment to public service baffled them. Growing up in this conservative, Bible belt community where girls were still encouraged to put all their efforts into either beauty pageants or landing the right husband right after high school graduation (what's a girl need college for?), Pam was the progressive, liberated one who didn't blend in — she preferred to be either the Governor of Texas, or a judge. Her ambitions weren't particularly encouraged, but that never deterred her. Despite the fact that she had a flair for fashion, and the poise to move easily within the realms of "the ladies who lunch," Johnson viewed that tea party world as just an effective part of the networking it would take for her to affect real social change.

She graduated from McMurry University in 1987 with a Bachelor's in Business Administration, and then entered the world of non-profit organizations, working in executive positions in fundraising, marketing and programming. She taught workshops in corporate and community settings, wrote, was active in public speaking regarding voting, health, social responsibility and other issues that led her to find ways to bring social issues into corporate awareness as her work took her around the country.

Based in a suburb of Dallas, Johnson created The Secret Society of Happy People in 1998. Her first book, *Don't Even Think of Raining on My Parade: Adventures of the Secret Society of Happy People*, was published in the winter of 2000 by PJ Press. I first met Pam Johnson in 1993 when I was writing a number of health articles for *The Miami Herald*. We have had countless conversations since then, and the one presented here took place in January, 1999 when she first began looking for potential free speech in the workplace cases.

❧ ❧

You've really stirred up a national debate.

It's not quite big enough yet! We want to get happiness out of the closet and make it acceptable again to be part of everyday conversation.

You were pretty shocked to find out that we don't have the right to free speech in the workplace.

I think most people would be. We believe the constitutional right to free speech applies everywhere, including the workplace, but it doesn't. It stops at your employer's door. We lose that right. You can't be arrested or fined by the government for what you say at work, but you could be reprimanded or fired. And unless it's linked to discrimination or sexual harassment, you have no legal recourse. Ironically, this includes being reprimanded at work for expressing your happiness. We heard reports about people being reprimanded at work for being too happy, so we checked into it, and that's how we discovered that the right of free speech doesn't extend to the workplace.

And you found out that the ACLU is looking into finding a way to change this.

They'd like laws to be created at the state level, but there's no legislation pending right now and we're a long way from having that.

It could get pretty tricky because someone could claim their right to free speech was violated if they were fired after they told the boss to drop dead.

Workers should have some right to free speech.

And it would be a difficult law to word in order to be practical.

Oh, absolutely. The ACLU gets a lot of calls from this, but that's why it's been so difficult to go down the path towards making it a law. Beyond what someone might say to the boss, you have to look at when and where he says it — at a stockholder meeting or in private — and somehow that has to be accounted for in the creation of a law. Someone expressing an opinion to co-workers in the breakroom shouldn't be fired for it. It will be difficult legislation that walks a fine line.

It won't be easy.

No, it won't. You have to protect a worker's right to free speech while protecting the employer from that free speech being used inappropriately.

That would make it a limited free speech.

At least that's ahead of where we are now.

When you started The Secret Society of Happy People, you probably didn't expect to come up against a civil rights issue, a constitutional issue of law.

It would have to be written as a separate law. And what's amazing is that people are simply not aware that they don't already have this right.

Do you envision some kind of test case will come up?

Someone will be fired for something they said, they'll realize they don't have the right to free speech, they'll contact a state legislator who supports the right to free speech in the workplace, and then he'll sponsor a bill to create that. That's how it's going to have to go.

This would have to happen state by state.

Unless it's a case that has enough publicity that it gets national attention leading Congress to make it a federal law. Federal laws are created like this all the time — from something that happens to someone.

What other areas do you see yourself becoming active in?

Any time we either see or hear about people receiving a social backlash or economic backlash because they've expressed something they're happy about, we'll be there, as consumer advocates for the right of expressions of happiness. Whether that's in the social or legal arena.

It's pretty surprising that something that sounds so innocuous could cost them their jobs.

Or cause them to be miserable at their job because there is a tremendous amount of peer pressure to complain about your job, even if you like it.

The focus on negativity is epidemic.

Well, that's because it's "in" to be miserable. And it's "in" to complain. And being negative is the best way you receive positive reinforcement these days.

People are ready to give you a shoulder if you've got something to complain about, some pain to share, but they tell you to shut up if you have something to share that you're happy about.

Exactly.

Our entire artistic and entertainment industry revolves around this wallowing in our wounds, now, too. And it's also the basis for nearly every TV talk show: They've become just publicly aired therapy sessions.

And so many of them are therapy sessions that aren't solution-oriented. They're not looking for answers, they're looking for ratings. Commercials are also a problem. They also show where our society has gone, and how the emphasis is on being miserable.

That's so they can sell you products to make you happy.

That's right.

You can control people a lot by keeping them miserable.

Oh, exactly. And miserable people control people. There's a reason to be miserable, cranky and the thorn on the rose. In some weird and sick way you are rewarded for this.

With attention.

When you want it. Or people will stay out of your way, which is what you might want. They just don't want to deal with you, so you get away with an awful lot. Like the bully at work, or the bully of the neighborhood.

This glorification of misery is really connected to humans' penchant for using intimidation and violence to get what they want.

Oh, definitely. You're not rewarded for being good-natured or happy. We've moved into an era where the bully gets what he wants because people are afraid not to give it to him.

This extends to the famous. We've had an epidemic of actors, sports stars and the like getting away with everything, even murder, often quite literally, and they are rewarded for being miserable and violent because it's in peoples' and companies' best interest to do so economically.

There are probably two reasons for that. People don't voice their outrage at this loud enough, and they don't voice it "economically." It's pure economics and if people want to continue to make millions from Mike Tyson, for example, and the promoters and sports businesses don't turn down the opportunity to make millions from him, then perhaps people will just stop watching him. That would put an end to his ability to make millions.

Unfortunately, we complain about people like this, but most folks still watch them, and this just perpetuates the problem.

You're right. If we would've boycotted the O.J. trial, for example, it wouldn't have been on every channel and people wouldn't have profited from it.

And the very same people who thought it was appalling ran out and bought all the O.J. books.

My gut instinct is that people who don't like this usually won't write letters to news stations and make their voices public. They'll just change the channel. People who don't want to watch Jerry Springer just don't watch him. They're not taking the time to voice how appalled they are at that show. Hopefully, the Secret Society of Happy People can play a role in encouraging people to speak up about these things.

The more we focus on being miserable, the more miserable we actually will be, and the more unhealthy.

Also, it's a power play. Being miserable has given people power. They don't want to lose what they perceive as their power. Think about it even with your friends. There's a certain amount of power a miserable person can create. They can control the communication. They can control things physically. They choose to use negativity as their power base. I think that most people really aren't miserable, they've just fallen into the social trap of talking about negative things, or dwelling on misery, just to fit in! They just want to be accepted.

The pendulum has swung way to the opposite extreme from the days when it was socially incorrect to say anything negative, when it was considered embarrassing to even admit you had any kind of a problem.

> *Right. Hopefully it'll swing more to the middle. It's necessary to acknowledge and heal your wounds, but we've created a society that does nothing but focus on them. And we don't focus at all on anything that makes us happy. And we don't want to hear it when someone is happy.*

Metaphysics and universal law says that you create whatever you focus on. Focus on misery and you create misery. Focus on happiness and you create happiness.

> *That's true. It's about increasing the possibility to create more of what you want, and that's gotten lost in all of this wound bonding we've been doing. Like attracts like. Express nothing but misery and you'll attract others who do that. Feel free to express happiness when you feel it — without feeling like it's politically incorrect to do so, and without worrying whether someone is going to rain on your parade — and you'll attract others willing to express their happiness.*

You've been getting a lot of response from around the world.

> *We've been featured in a magazine in India, and we've gotten a lot of members from India. We've been on the radio in Germany, England and Australia, in a newspaper in Israel. We've been all over. I got a letter the other day in a language I can't even figure out. We're attracting people from all professions, all socio-economic levels, all ages, though we seem to have struck a particular chord with the 40-plus baby boomers. I've had a couple of principals contact me because they're interested in recommending positive websites to students. We're going to be*

developing some special programs for elementary schools in particular, things that will be implemented in the classroom. And, of course, we have a corporate program under way, too. All of this is designed to make it socially acceptable to express your happiness should you have something happy you'd like to share.

As you say this, I can't help but laugh because this sounds like something from some scary, futuristic movie that might have been made 30 or 40 years ago. Something like: "As the 21st century dawned, it was illegal to admit you were happy…" and then we see scenes of the Misery Police arresting people and torturing them until they renounced their happy thought. Then we see the aftermath, when the rebels have finally won, and they're trying to re-educate people, teaching school kids and workers how to feel safe expressing the happy news or happy thought they may have from time to time.

(She laughs). Well, hopefully, we haven't gotten that bad yet, but that's where we're heading. People forget how to express their happiness because it's become "un-cool" to do so.

And they've also been told to believe that they can't be happy without Prozac or some other drug.

Life isn't all doom and gloom, but there are times when it's very appropriate to be blue or temporarily depressed — you've lost your job, you've lost a loved one, or had some other terrible thing happen — and you don't necessarily need to take medication. But, we've become a nation that wants the quick fix. "I'm having a bad day, give me Prozac." It's also become very profitable for companies to convince us that we need to take their happy pills. Plenty of companies have an economic incentive to convince us we're miserable. And it's not just the pharmaceutical industry, it's every industry. "Buy this lipstick, it'll make you happy." And it's not just the lipstick, you need to keep buying it, you need the latest shade. The latest car, the latest whatever. It's all the same vicious cycle.

We've had advertising for centuries, but not like we have it now: we are completely inundated by it 24 hours a day, it's everywhere around us, it's constantly in our homes on the TV, the radio, in our magazines and newspapers. Brainwashing, constant brainwashing. "You're miserable, you're not good enough — buy this and get happy, buy this and be worthy of people's love and attention." The slogan should read: "Buy this and make our stockholders happy."

You know, we talk about our right in this country to "life, liberty and the pursuit of happiness," and I think that in wording it that way our forefathers may have unconsciously tapped into something that's always been awry in the human condition — we know how to pursue happiness and other things, but we don't know what to do with it once we get it. We're not very good at having things, only at wanting them. And those who do get what they want always feel they have to be careful about showing their happiness because others around them may not have what they want and may be resentful. That all leads to guilt, and so it's no wonder nobody knows how to be content even after they've gotten what they want. What you're working for now is essentially nothing less than a complete overhaul of human nature.

I think some other cultures have mastered to some extent the art of contentment. They can appreciate the present. Western cultures have a hard time with that. Especially now that commercialism is ruling our culture. Their influence has gotten out of control. So, in some ways, yes, I'm trying to overhaul human nature, trying to show people how to be more Zen. How to not carry their negative baggage with them forever. You can heal your wounds. You may have a scar, but at least it's not the wound anymore and you're not actively wounded all the time. Things don't heal if you don't let them heal, if you stay only in the wounded, negative moments. We're defining ourselves now by our wounds, by the things that have made us victims or made us miserable or we're the victims of our bad choices. That serves no one. It doesn't serve you, or the ones you love, or society as a whole.

Our current pop culture, advertising, entertainment, and self-help psychology all works against that, and encourages the constant open wound. That's because there's profit for them in this at some level.

> *Advertising used to be a resource, just a tool that allows you to know what products or services are out there. But it's evolved into a measuring stick of the quality of our life — can I afford this, am I good enough, am I pretty enough, will this make me happy — and the advertisers aren't the only ones at fault, the consumer has played a role in this. We have brains, we can use them to make choices and we can decide what influence advertising has on us. We've chosen to let it control us, make us feel incomplete, make us feel like we're missing something. We'd rather give somebody else our choices.*

One of the more irresponsible aspects of human nature.

> *Our choices lead us into things, and new choices can lead us out of them.*

It all leads back to self-empowerment.

> *Yes, it does. No one can escape that.*

It seems as if the more empowered person who isn't using their wounds as their identity, and is comfortable sharing their contentment or happy moments or news — when they have them — is really the oddity in our current culture, the one people point fingers at.

> *As an example of that, I got an e-mail from a man who'd been an Army officer. He wrote, "I'm often found to be 'too casual,' or 'lacking a sense of urgency,' simply because I'm really optimistic and happy. Although I'm successful, I'd be more successful if I wasn't as happy, or so I'm told…isn't that twisted?" I believe that this is a widespread problem. People have lost their jobs because they didn't fit into the corporate misery culture, because they dared to show their happy nature. And where can*

these people go for help or support? Are there any legal, governmental, social or organizational groups that can shed light on this, or do anything about it? There aren't. So, essentially, that's one of the reasons why I founded The Secret Society of Happy People. And why I'm also supporting the ACLU in their efforts to bring to light the fact that we don't have free speech in the workplace. But, there's very little the ACLU can do at this point. This is all in the early stages of creating awareness. This is very important.

The Secret Society of Happy People is dead serious.

(She laughs). *We're dead serious with a smile. Despite the fact that it's funny, and it's meant to sound funny, it wouldn't even sound funny unless there was a real need for it, if our message didn't resonate with so many people who see how the pendulum has swung so dangerously to the other side. The other funny side to this is that people get hostile that such a group as this exists. I've heard from some very hostile people who've made threats. It's a small number, but they do exist.*

Just the notion of happiness makes some people downright violent.

To my downright shock and surprise, yes it has! That's what I didn't expect. I figured they'd just ignore this. But, I guess they have to have their own crusade. And this must be what, ironically, makes them happy. So, we're happy for them.

Ten

Gladys Seymour Davis

Where is the wisdom
we have lost in knowledge?
Where is the knowledge
we have lost in wisdom?

— T.S. Eliot

Gladys Seymour Davis sculpts bodies and dispenses wisdom. But just her own. She also reminds us that the body has its own inherent wisdom.

Picture this, if you can: one part Whoopi Goldberg, one part Deepak Chopra, blend and place in the body of someone who looks like an Olympic athlete. There is no other way to describe Gladys Seymour Davis, creator of The Seymour System, a body restoration treatment that focuses on contouring the entire body, while also improving the lymphatic, circulatory and other vital systems. This not only helps clear the body of the effects of what's been brought into it from the outside, but what has been created inside as well.

"We're allowing the body to heal itself," Davis says emphatically, "The body is a housing and transportation system. And it *is* self-healing. All it needs is a little help, a little nudge, so it can work its magic."

Davis has created what can essentially be called a non-surgical cosmetic procedure that not only sculpts the body by dissolving fatty deposits, but by doing so also improves the function of joints and vital systems. The overall result, says Davis, is a body that's "youthing instead of aging."

The treatment also aligns the body's internal energies and releases stored emotions and stresses. Results begin quickly, even after just a few treatments, and clients report not only the sculpting effects in the face and body and better skin tone, but also weight loss, improved circulation, increased energy, reduced swelling and pain, increased immune response, improved joint function and range of movement.

Her goal is to teach people to "do daily self-care, so they can do these treatments on themselves and their loved ones," she says. "this is the *real* physical education. It's educating ourselves about our physical bodies and taking care of each other."

Davis teaches her clients and students how to do these treatments themselves by showing them the sculpting and pumping techniques, which are easy to do yourself with soap in the shower or afterwards with body lotion.

The Seymour System is physician-approved and has been recommended by the World Congress on Cosmetic Surgical Rejuvenation as a non-surgical treatment. Perhaps its best example is Davis herself, who, though born in 1946 and the grandmother of four, looks half her age and feels it. A life-long athlete, Davis studied physical education at Concordia Teachers College in Illinois and at Allen University in South Carolina, and is the former wife of Pittsburgh Steeler offensive guard Sam Davis, who was part of the team's legendary four Super Bowl wins during his 15 years with the Steelers.

The Seymour System evolved, she says, when she "went on a hunt to find my body, and I found that you have to put your *hands* on the problem!" By the 1970s, Davis had plumped up to a size 16, and in her quest to restore her former physique, vitality and health, she researched oriental techniques, such as acupressure and acupuncture (thus discovering the meridians of the body's energy flow), sports medicine, holistic medicine, biology and human anatomy. Along the way, she developed what would become The Seymour System from her research and hands-on approach, then studied it and practiced it further in conjunction with health, bodywork and wellness centers, as well as medical professionals.

In the mid-1970s, she opened The Figure Contouring Salon in Pittsburgh, PA, where her clients included many from the professional athletic community. Then, in 1983, she founded the Institute of Biotherapy, which for two years served the Pritikin Longevity Center in Miami Beach, Florida, and further developed her treatments. All the while, she did them on herself, and the transformation has astounded even physicians. "They would always say that for my treatments to work this well it means that they're jump-starting all the body's systems," she says. Gladys Seymour Davis's slim, well-toned, healthy body remains that way, she says, because she works on her body every day. "It's all about maintenance, and just a few minutes a day makes a big difference."

Based in North Bay Village, an island just off Miami Beach, Davis now has clients from all over the U.S. and abroad, and her treatment has garnered attention from both the medical community and the media.

I first interviewed her in the summer of 1994. We've had, quite literally, hundreds of conversations since then, and an overview of her work was included in a chapter of my book of health reporting *Purify Your Body*, which was published by Crown/Three Rivers Press in 1997.

In the conversations presented here, which took place in the spring of 1995 and the summer of 1998, Davis takes a look at the world that's made a mess of our bodies, minds and spirits, and then offers her take on how to fix it.

You're in for a fun ride.

❧ ❧

You have some insightful, and very funny, things to say about how our society operates, and how ultimately this ties in to our health and well being.

Men have never been home. People act like women raising their children alone is something new. Women have always been the ones who've been there raising the children. It's only recently that the men have been around enough to really influence their children. Before that, the men weren't around to tell the women, "Don't teach my son to do this," or "Don't allow him to do that," or "He'll grow up to be a homosexual if he learns how to cook for himself." That's women's work in a man's mind.

And raising a son to be a kind person is considered by some men to be raising a son to be a sissy.

The men would say, "He's a sissy, he's not tough enough. What are you doing to that boy? You're gonna ruin him!" In the old days, they considered raising them to be tough was acceptable because they were raising them to go to war. You didn't want him to be too kind because then it would be very difficult for him to kill another human being to believe what the sergeant said: "That's not a person, that's the enemy!" We have a tendency to de-humanize people to make it okay to kill them. Like what we did to the Native Americans. They'd say, "Those aren't people, those are savages!" Or to the slaves. "Yeah, bring those people over on those boats. It's okay to make them slaves 'cause they're not real people, they don't look like us!"

So, when fathers were off at war, or working 18 hours a day...

They hardly ever saw their kids. All they knew about their children was what the mother told them. And all the kids knew about their dad was what the mother told them.

And back then, the women had more input into raising their kids in a more well rounded way.

And the fathers were used just for disciplinary purposes. "I'm gonna tell your father when he gets home!" That elusive person who came in and exacted the punishment when needed. He was the fear mechanism. The fear was always in the house. It wasn't about the law outside the house. People were concerned about their parents finding things out, 'cause I guess in those days they could kill you. There weren't any computers or social security numbers, so you could just pick up the whole family and move. Nobody knew who you were. Start all over again. Kill the wife, kids, bury 'em, and go!

So, this all began to change in the 1950s, when Dads were suddenly home in the suburbs, and only working from 9 to 5 instead of 18 hours a day. No war for him to be off at. So, now the guy's home all the time saying, "Don't raise my son to be a sissy."

So, the sons weren't raised the same anymore. The fathers said, "That's women's work, you let him go out and play." The sons went out to play. They were taught nothing. Nothing! So, how could he know? We expect men to be kind, sensitive and understanding. They haven't been taught that for years and years.

Can we undo the damage that was done to them in childhood? Can we teach an adult male to be kind and sensitive and loving?

Yes! I saw an interview on television, one of these National Geographic specials. They're in a little village in Africa. And there's this little woman sitting on a stump, with a pipe in her mouth. And they're telling her that in the outside world, men are in charge. And the old woman says, "WHAT?!!!!" In her own language, and they're interpreting. "WHAT?? HOW IS THAT POSSIBLE? THE WOMAN IS EVERYTHING, WOMAN CREATES MAN. HOW CAN MAN BE MORE THAN

WOMAN??" And I'm saying to myself, "Guns." (We laugh.)
That'll do it. 'Cause when you get a group of people together who
don't mind killing you to be right — They'll beat you into
submission. It's absolutely ridiculous! America's a wonderful
idea. You get all these people from the whole wide world living
together under one roof, and speaking one common language so
they can tell one another how they do things in their home
country. But, you get here and they want you to do things one
way, the white way. People resist because they don't want to be
in a melting pot. Who wants to melt? Now, to blend, that's okay.
When you look into a salad, you can still see the tomatoes, you
can still see the carrots, you can still see everything. You don't
have to give up your identity in order to be a part of something.

You've said that you think this current generation of children are
going to be raised better than the baby boomers were. Why?

Because the men aren't around again. They've jumped ship.

Where are they? They've left the women and we have so many single parent households, or they're not spending as much time at home
as their fathers did. So, now we're back to the women teaching their
sons how to be balanced human beings without the negative interfer-
ence from the fathers.

All that while they attempt to finish the raising of the men
they married!

So, the wives have to finish raising the husbands as if they're still
children.

Everybody's somebody's baby, and we're just big, old, tall kids
out here trying to get along with other people's children. It
doesn't work. We have a bunch of men who want to be king,
with all the benefits of the king and none of the responsibilities.
Women want to be queen, but with none of the responsibilities.
And men won't admit that they're the problem. They put some

special on TV about violence, and what are we gonna do about it...you don't see any women running around doing this stuff. Well, men, if this is your world, and there's a mess then you've made the mess and you'd better clean it up.

Many people talk about the return of feminine energy after the year 2000 and an eventual return to a matriarchal society.

We've always had peace when the women were in charge. Remember The Honeymooners? *There's the complete picture of men since they've been in charge. Ralph: "I am the king of this castle, Alice. You know what you are, Alice? Nothing!" Ralph gets in trouble, who always bails him out?*

Alice.

Yup, and he says: "Baby, you're the greatest!" Until he starts feeling good again, and then Alice ain't nothing again. How the woman lost reverence, I don't know. I come from a culture where the women are revered. In the Bahamian culture, the woman is revered.

People think that everyone thinks the way they do. That creates a lot of misunderstandings between men and women. Women say one thing, men actually hear another.

Well, women listen, men don't. I'll tell you another thing, if you want a man to hear you when you're talking to him, you have to touch him. Otherwise you might as well be in outer space as far as he's concerned. But the minute you touch him, you're real. Or you have to lay him down. Then he'll listen. Vertical and horizontal are two different worlds. The best relationship is someone you can stand up with in the vertical world and lie down with in the horizontal world. A lot of people you can lie down with and it's good, good, good, but you can't take him outside. And there are others that are magnificent out in the world, but you lie them down and there's nothing there (we laugh).

So, why weren't men taught to listen?

I think it has a lot to do with the way men were raised, the way they were spoken to as children. Almost like military-style orders: "You do this, you do that, da-da-da-da-da. You're not a man if you do this, you're not a man if you do that. You're never going to amount to anything!" It gets to a point where they...

Just tune things out.

They have to. It's like when mothers can tune out all the noise their children make. Same kind of selective listening. You can tune out anything.

I remember a study released this year (1998) showing that men and women listen differently. That women can listen to many things at once and follow them all, while men can only listen to one thing at a time and very effectively tune out everything else. And men can also tune out just that one person or sound, too. It might as well not even be there. These different abilities arise from the way a woman's brain processes things differently than a man's.

The women are going to have to just do what needs to be done. And if the men want to come along that's fine. We consider men fun to be with, they're fun for us. Better than a fishtank (we laugh). In America, money is the great equalizer. "Be all that you can buy." And once women had their own money, men lost control of them. It's not that men are any different now, it's that women don't have to take it anymore. Because men used to be the only ones with the money, they could have this in-house dictatorship. In the past, there were two modes of freedom, one for the male and one for the female. The man's freedom was his money. The woman's sign of value and her freedom was her looks, her body. She could be stupid as hell, but as long as she looked good somebody would buy her and put her on his arm. "I'll take one of those." A man could be the most handsome guy you've ever seen, but if he ain't got no money, he ain't got no woman. Not unless he just wants to be king of the trailer park. Or he could be "kept," bought by a woman with money.

Now, that whole system has been uprooted. Unless someone actively chooses to still live that way.

Yeah, and now we have another problem — we have adults acting like children, and children acting like adults. And now that people are talking openly about spirituality so much, men really get scared. Because as far as they're concerned, that's "airy fairy" stuff.

Because it's about feelings — that's the new F word — and no one ever taught them how to deal with feelings.

People are emotionally and spiritually drained. And that's why I do what I do.

You're committed to educating, and to bringing out the healer in everyone.

You know what happens when a hurricane's coming? Man's got nothing to do with it. All of a sudden we've got nothing but believers.

Everybody starts praying.

We are nature's children. And whatever runs nature runs us. That invisible realm. You can call it spirit, universal energy, God, whatever. People want to think of us as machines, but that's just so the boys can sell us some parts for repair (we laugh). *We are organisms. We were born. I don't know a person alive that can even knit a foot* (we continue laughing). *People are ridiculous. Money, money, money, money. That's all it's about.*

311

Let's talk about the body. Explain how The Seymour System works.

> *This isn't about what you weigh. The bottom line is freedom. Free up the fat deposits, the toxins, and let them go. The body made it up, trust it to know what to do with it once you free it up. The body knows two languages — chemistry and physics — and the body will use those to eliminate this stuff. The body's little globs of fat — adipose tissue — lie just below the skin's surface and aren't as stubborn as you might think. This stuff can go from solid as ice to fluid.*

How do you make that happen?

> *I use the bones in my hands — the side of my thumbs and fingers in particular — and you can do this, too. In effect, I'm turning them into knives without a blade, and following the natural outline of the body. That means don't make circles like they do when they're working on muscles in massage. This isn't about muscles. The body has seams that don't show. I follow those — the acupuncture meridians, the lines of the body's energy flow. Once the fat tissue is loosened, gradually after a number of treatments, it will be processed and eliminated naturally by the body.*

The first step of the treatment is to clear the body's lymphatic system because it's what acts as the body's filter, and you do this by an up and down pumping-like motion on all the lymph glands — on either side of the neck, under the jawline, under each arm, in the chest, and where each thigh meets the torso near the groin area.

> *These lymph areas become routinely clogged and keep the body from flushing out properly, leading to everything from puffiness and swelling, to impaired disease-fighting capability and a whole lot of other systemic problems. Accumulated toxins in the tissue spaces and muscles are also released in the process of clearing out the lymph glands. Then I work on the rest of the*

body, and pay particular attention to the joints, which can become partly clogged by fatty deposits. It's a holistic treatment, and a direct treatment, so you have to do the whole body, you can't just do parts. They're all interconnected. What good is liquifying the fat deposits if they can't get processed properly because the lymph system is clogged or sluggish?

As you contour the entire body, you're following it's form and also using vertical motions, not circular ones like in massage.

I'm following the body's form and it's functional energy flow, and it's easy to do this yourself, too. It's also a very invigorating feeling because you really are freeing up the body in so many ways.

Tell me about the hunt for your body, and what led you to create The Seymour System.

I just never believed I couldn't get my body back to where it had been. I just realized that science and medicine didn't know how to do it.

Did you go through some of the mainstream approaches first?

Well, yeah, I had been a physical education major, so the first thing I did was do the things they taught me. And I realized that all that did was make me more solid, not smaller. And my problem wasn't a muscular problem, it was a fat problem. And when you said the word "fat," people said, "Eeehhh, we don't want to talk about that."

At what point did you discover that this was about more than losing some weight, or being firm, it was also about the lymph system, the circulation, the joints, the entire health of your body?

Well, all of that came in eventually. It all started when I went to Beverly Hills, California because I ran into a woman who had worked in Beverly Hills, and that was the only place where people actually looked good after having something done! So, I went out there and had treatments. That was just when people were first beginning to talk about cellulite. And they were doing cellulite treatments and that sort of thing. And what I came away with from that was you actually have to put your hands on the problem in an effort to solve it. I saw people doing spot things, just focusing on particular areas of the body, like cellulite on legs, and I began to think that this was more than that, it was about the whole body. So, I came back to Pittsburgh and started a business. It was called The Figure Contouring Salon. And what helped the treatment to evolve was hearing from the clients. "You know, since we've gotten the fat out of my leg, my leg doesn't hurt anymore." And I thought, wait a minute, hold it, let's think about this. What's the common denominator in people as they get older? The body fills in with this fat stuff, and then the circulation gets bad and then everything starts to break down. Is this whole aging thing about the body filling in and slowing down and not being allowed to function? That's how I ended up in Florida. I came to talk to the people at Pritikin. At the time, they were the only people working on fat. I set up an institute here called the Institute of Bio-Therapy. One of the doctors from the Pritikin Center consented to oversee the program. I got an investor and opened the clinic to figure out why my treatments worked. We had watched the bodies changing and had some ideas about why. We thought if we used people from the Pritikin program, because they were on a controlled diet, we'd have a better chance to figure out why my treatments worked. We found out it was a natural phenomenon .

The body was being allowed to work without being impeded by extra tissue.

From there I decided to also take it to the cosmetic arena. It's not just about what you weigh. It's also about your skin looking and being healthy, it's about preventing and getting rid of wrinkles. Form follows function. If the body was working properly inside you wouldn't see so many of those changes on the outside. The basic problem you've got with the fat tissue is that once it settles, it begins to solidify. And once it does that, it begins to block circulation and to cause problems in the joint areas.

How can you prevent this?

By working on yourself every day, doing the treatment in the shower with soap, or afterwards with lotion.

So that you're keeping up with it on a daily basis and it doesn't continue to accumulate.

It's a continuing process. First you have to restore your body, then you have to keep it that way. It's restoration and preservation of the human form. Your body reflects the way you treat it. Nature knows what your body is supposed to do and what it's supposed to look like.

Tell me how this all fits in with your spiritual outlook.

Well, your spirit is living in this transportation and housing unit — your body. Intuitively, we know that we're slowly becoming incarcerated in our own bodies when they're not working right.

When people have these treatments done, they undergo not only physical changes and improvement, but emotional ones, too. And since the body physically stores everything that's ever happened to it not just physically but emotionally, this emotional release as a result of treatments would make sense. Through this intense bodywork, you're also freeing up an awful lot of emotional stuff, too.

The name of the game is freedom. We need freedom. That's what we're looking for and we want it from inside. When you're feeling good, then the whole world is different. The best people ever look is when they're in love. And that has nothing to do with diet and exercise. There's that loving feeling inside.

There's that glow.

Yes, that glow, that release, that freedom. And that's the kind of thing people get from this treatment because for the first time they're learning how to love themselves, learning how to understand themselves. Peoples' relationship problems stem from their relationship with themselves. And if you're gonna deny that you have a human body, that's a real bad start. You can't say, "I'm a loving human being, but my body doesn't count." Excuse me, but your body represents all that you've learned since you've been here. Learning how to take care of ourselves is one of the first things they teach us. What do people want? They don't care about what they weigh. They want a good, comfortable, easy life, they wanna have fun, they wanna play, they don't wanna have to take this planet so seriously. And when you're afraid of aging, which is the last fear that we've gotta face, and do something about, then you can live your life rather comfortably. But people are really afraid of aging, because we don't know how. We don't have adequate physical education. Literally an education about our physical being. People don't like the way the experts look either. Plus, the experts are telling us half-truths. They say, "Use my procedures, learn how to move, do this, do that." And the part they leave out is, "But, then you'll still need cosmetic surgery." People ask me if I'm training professionals to do this. If love is what it's about, then we need to train people that we love to take care of our bodies. To be that close to us, to transfer that kind of energy into us. Someone who truly cares. Professionals can only care so much. But Mom, now she can care about her daughter. We need active self-care, partner care, family care approaches to using this treatment.

How would that work?

Partner care is about choosing someone who you care about, who cares about you, who's willing to learn how to help take care of your body. Maybe it's your legs or your back in particular. And you learn how to do the whole body. And you work on one another. That way, treatment is at home. It's not a stranger. The body understands physical communication. It's about my mind using my hand to get something done to my body or someone else's body. It's not just idle movement, it's intentional thoughtful action. It's about the thought — the hands are just used as the tools. People look at this treatment and say, "It looks like a form of massage." But that's not the intent.

No, you're not working on the muscles.

Massage is another thing entirely, and there are some excellent massage therapists out there.

Okay, Gladys, let's unleash your wisdom...

The most un-tapped natural resource is human energy. People want to make the human body a machine. Excuse me...the human body was created naturally, it is not a machine, it is a living organism and it thinks for itself. I suggest we seek some wise counsel from it! If you just run to the knife for cosmetic surgery, you've done nothing to improve your body's function. You've gotta look at the skin as a spacesuit. The whole body, actually. The skin expands and deflates, especially with women because we were designed to inflate and deflate. The problem happens when the body gets too much excess tissue in it, more than the body needs for fuel, so it doesn't re-absorb it. It's fat we're storing.

And you're not just talking about obesity, but even just the extra globs we have stored here and there.

Yes, and it surrounds our muscular structure, and our joints. It's like jello, and the longer you let it set in your body, the more solid it becomes. And when you build muscle you're just trapping dehydrated fat cells in an armor around your body. This impairs the joints and affects the circulation. You have to get rid of the fat, liquefy it. Or else the body's locked in. Once this gluing process starts, and the body can't stretch its muscular structure, as time goes on even the bones get locked in place because the body doesn't stretch as far as it used to because it's bound by this stuff.

And this stuff is also in your joints.

From years of usage, it's like you've got a rubber band around the joints of your body. You can feel it when you work on the joints with your hands.

And pretty soon you're filling in everywhere.

It's like building a house of fat. First it lays the foundation, then you see a little something pop up over here, and then there, your body is depositing the excess fat. Genetics plays a role. Some people fill in more in the upper part of their body, some people get it right in the middle, right where the organs are and that's more dangerous, others get it in their arms and legs. And people call this normal again! It's not normal. It's common and it's unhealthy, so we've come to expect to see it. And modern medicine hasn't focused on how to stop it.

Anything they don't know how to fix...

They ask us to accept! Our outside reflects what's going on in our inside, and this can be prevented. The body doesn't have a limit — the more you put in the more it will store! It will expand just as much as you're willing to put into it. It's like a bank — the more you deposit, the more you save. People sit around and say, "I don't have any energy." You've got that food you've already processed and stored, and it's literally sitting there burdening your body's systems. That's why you feel so tired. You've got this weight on your body's structure and its systems.

And it has nothing to do with what your scale says. You can be at an ideal weight, but still have little globs of fatty tissue under the skin that can impair the function of systems, make you look puffy or older. Gum up the joints.

> *The good thing about using your bare hands for tools is that you can feel this under the skin. You're using your hands like a snowplow, to get the snow off the pavement. We get the "snow" off and expose the muscular structure. So, it's more of an artistic endeavor. Even the cosmetic surgeon knows that the fat is under the skin.*

When you cook a chicken, you see the fat, it's clinging to the underside of the skin.

> *I don't think people realize that fat is a part of the skin. I think they think it's a separate system somewhere, between hither and yon! When you literally step in with a manual override and release it, soften and liquefy it over time, the body will process it.*

After a treatment you feel completely different than after a massage. After a massage you feel very relaxed, but after one of your treatments you feel very light and energized.

> *The treatment releases energy as it's reconstructing the body, re-designing it.*

You're doing the same thing a sculptor does when he has a slab of marble.

> *Absolutely. And the form is already there, the treatment is just uncovering it. Any place there's skin, there's the potential to store excess fat tissue.*

So, even a thin person will have ripples of this and it can potentially slow circulation and clog joints.

Right. Because the longer it sits there, the more solidified it becomes. And you don't need much for this to be a problem. It just needs to be in the wrong place. The body is a self-healing organism, and we can manually assist it.

So, we need to clear this out so the body can do its job.

Right. Older people say, "I used to be taller!" Your body literally contracts as you age. You need to stretch, to free it up from whatever's constricting it, keep the muscular structure elongated. Your relationship to your body is your primary one —
"Til death do us part," that's the only relationship where that holds true (we laugh).

That's true.

It's not about how long you live, it's about how well you live.

Part Three

Eleven

Michio Kaku

String theory is 21st century
physics that fell accidentally into the 20th century.
— Edward Whitten

Listen, there's a hell of a universe
next door: Let's go! — e.e. cummings

For any speculation which
does not at first glance look crazy, there is no hope.
— physicist Freeman Dyson

*T*ime travel, parallel universes, wormholes, black holes, 10 dimensions, 24 dimensions — is this the stuff of science fiction? Not anymore.

It's the stuff of serious study by the most acclaimed physicists in the world, including Nobel laureates. In their quest for a "unified theory," one theory that would unite all the rest, including Newton's theory, Einstein's theory and quantum theory (one theory that would work for objects of *any* size at *any* velocity), scientists have come up with something so amazing that even *they* have been reluctant to accept it. Only in recent years has it gone from "This can't possibly be," to "It's the only thing that works."

It's called the superstring theory of hyperspace. And it shows that the only way that the vastly different mathematical descriptions for the universe's basic forces — gravity, electromagnetism, the strong nuclear force, and the weak nuclear force — all fit together is if these are forces of not just our three dimensions, but are forces that are simply vibrations, like the strings of a violin, in 10 and even 24 dimensions. Our universe, then, would exist in more than the dimensions we are aware of in our everyday life: it would exist in hyperspace, higher dimensional space.

Whether we are aware of them or not, we are immersed in these "extra," higher dimensions, even though we may not know how to access them yet, says theoretical physicist Michio Kaku, author of the best-selling *Hyperspace* (Oxford University Press, 1994), which delightfully discusses the scientific, cosmic and even spiritual implications of this likely candidate for the unified theory, and *Visions* (Doubleday/Anchor, 1997), which explores how science will affect the way we live in the 21st century.

Kaku has been the father of string field theory since 1974, when, at only 27, he took the pages and pages of mathematical scribbling and turned it into the simple, one-inch equation that may turn out to be the unified theory that every physicist, including Einstein, would've given his eye teeth to come up with.

"This was my dream since I was a kid," says Kaku, who took a six month sabbatical from City College of the City University of New York, where he is Henry Semat Professor of Theoretical Physics, to write part of *Hyperspace* in an office right above the one Einstein occupied at the Institute for Advanced Study at Princeton. "For more than ten years, my theory was in limbo. Then, finally, in the late 1980s, physicists at Princeton said, 'There's nothing wrong with this theory. It's the only one that *works*, and we have to open our minds to hyperspace.' We weren't destined to discover this theory for another 100 years because it's so bizarre, so different from everything we'd been doing. We didn't use the normal sequence of discoveries to get to it."

Kaku, who manages to explain the most complex physics in an easy-to-follow, engaging and gripping manner, offers his wide-ranging and progressive take on science not only in his research, to his students and in his books, but also to listeners around the country is his long-running nationally syndicated hour-long weekly radio program, *Exploration*, which broadcasts from the New York public radio station WBAI on Tuesday afternoons at 1 p.m.

Discovery and sharing knowledge have always been his passions.

Born in San Jose, California in 1947, his very name implied his destiny: In Japanese, Michio means "the way," and phonetically, Kaku means "nuclear." The middle child with two brothers, Kaku was born the year after his parents were released from the U.S. internment camps that forcibly held Japanese-Americans during World War II, in one of the country's worst civil rights blunders of the 20th century. The government confiscated his family's savings, and sent them to the camp at Tule Lake, California in 1942. When they were released, four years later, Kaku's father, a gardener, got a lawnmower and started again, and his mother became a maid.

Michio Kaku knew early on that he would be a scientist, and that research would be his mission, but not the kind of research that others had in mind for him.

"I got a four year scholarship to Harvard, and while I was there they wanted to groom me for work in the Star Wars program designing weapons ignited by hydrogen bombs," he recalls. "I didn't want to do that. I thought about how many scientists had died in World War II."

He graduated Summa Cum Laude in 1968, at the age of 21, with a B.S. in Physics, and, ironically, was promptly drafted.

Assigned to infantry training at Ft. Benning, Georgia, Kaku realized early in his training "the impact of technology," he says. "Here I was in machine gun training, calculating mortar trajectories in my head. And one day I said to myself: *What the hell am I doing? This is a bomb that's gonna kill someone, and I'm here figuring out its trajectory!* That's when I felt my first existential shock. Science is a sword — it can destroy, but it can also cut ignorance, poverty, and disease, and it can be liberating. It all depends on *who* holds the sword. I realized the power that science has."

He dealt with this, he says, "by opposing the Vietnam War. Science has been used by war to kill, but it doesn't have to be that way."

He requested a transfer from infantry to the radio signal corps, but the Army said no. A routine physical, however, did change the young scientist's course.

"They found too much sugar in my blood," he says. "And I was free."

While still in the Army, he'd entered The University of California at Berkeley, in 1968, and began working toward his Ph.D. Once discharged from the military, he became a full-time student.

"I realized that you must take social responsibility for what you create," he says. "I opposed the Star Wars system. I was part of a group of young scientists who revolted."

In 1972, he received his Ph.D. in Theoretical Physics. "String theory was just beginning then, and it was before we'd discovered 10 dimensions," he recalls. But, just two years later, he founded String Field Theory with his now-famous one-inch equation, "and around the same time, physicists realized that these little strings only vibrate in 10 dimensions."

He was teaching at Princeton, then, in 1974, but left for the City University of New York (CUNY), where "they were building a big string group working on hyperspace theories," and where he remains today.

His theory, he says, represents "a paradigm shift, and that's why at first it was resisted. We didn't use the normal sequence of discoveries leading up to this. And the math has to catch up to the physics. Areas of math that had no relationship to each other are now being unified. The barriers are tumbling down. Physics is forcing this. It's an historic reconciliation of these two fields: math and physics," he says. "We physicists are what I like to call 'revolutionary conservatives.' We cling to old theories until we can't anymore, and then we make a great leap. Evolutionary shifts usually are made by young scientists, so it's not surprising that I came up with this at twenty-seven. Dirac and Einstein were also in their 20s when they came up with their theories."

Kaku says he wanted to write his books so that the physics and its implications would be "exciting to people."

As a result, "lay people mail me their candidates for the Unified Field Theory every day!" he laughs.

He is very good at creating contexts, metaphors and analogies so that the non-scientists can fully understand even the most complex science.

"What keeps us going are new ideas," he says. "We have very few theories of the universe and all the new ones are built upon the old ones, they expand upon them. Our three main ones don't like each other or resemble each other. They summarize the last 2,000 years of physics, and the challenge is to unite the three. The simplest way is in ten-dimensional space as strings. Strings are a bridge between the quark and Einstein's theory."

Think of equations, he suggests, "as recipes." He sees these equations in his head, "all the time, when I'm walking, when I'm driving!" And while lay people may wonder how anyone can make heads or tails out of a bunch of letters, numbers and squiggly symbols, Kaku explains that these components of equations "are just manifestations of a picture." They are simply a language used to represent concepts.

In the matter of string theory, he explains that "the vibrating strings are literally a condensation of space into a kink. This means that matter is a condensation of higher dimensional space, and this would mean that we are pure vibrational energy and that *everything* is made of the same stuff."

Just like the ancient mystics claimed.

"Everything in the universe is connected just like everything inside an electron is connected," he says.

And he takes this connection very seriously.

"Unfortunately, most of our top scientists work on weapons, not on other things, and we can now literally destroy life on earth.

Humanity doesn't learn until it *has* to learn, and in the meantime we're still trying to justify the pollution and the violence," he says. "You know, Plato said that in the perfect world it would be the people who knew the most about nature who would rule countries."

Perhaps, then, Plato believed, leaders would better respect nature and the human lives that are part of it. Michio Kaku would like to believe that one day we will come around to respecting life and our inherent interconnectedness, which science, it seems, is on the verge of "proving."

For his part, he says, "science literally affects everything around us, and that's why I like to educate people."

Once you read these conversations, which took place in 1994, shortly after *Hyperspace* was published, you'll wish he'd been *your* college physics professor. I did.

You say that the best place to begin talking about hyperspace, also known as superstring theory, is with a child's questions about the universe.

Children ask cosmic questions, like did God have a mother, or what is the farthest star, and if scientists can answer either one of these questions then we may actually change the course of modern scientific history. And unfortunately, when we hit junior high school, this childhood curiosity is ground out of us. All of us are born physicists. All of us ask questions: Why is the sky blue? Why is there light? We're forced to learn about levers and friction and pulleys and things that have nothing to do with children's questions. And this is where Einstein excelled. Einstein asked himself questions that only children would ask. And this is why a mathematician at Oxford University, Charles Dodgson, decided to write a book for children, because he knew that adults would be prejudiced against wormholes, prejudiced against multiply-connected universes, so he wrote a children's book under a pseudonym, the children's book was Alice's Adventures in Wonderland, *and then the sequel* Through The Looking Glass. *Dodgson changed his name to Lewis Carroll.*

The simplest representation of a wormhole is the looking glass of Alice. That like two Siamese twins joined at the hip, we now have two universes — one, the bucolic countryside of Oxford, England, and the other one Wonderland, where animals speak in riddles and common sense isn't so common. He realized that the looking glass was the simplest representation of what mathematicians call multiply-connected universes, what we physicists now call wormholes, that may eventually become gateways to perhaps another universe or another time.,

You talk and write about how we can't access these other dimensions right now because we don't have the energy it would take to manipulate space and time. But, if we stop thinking of it in a physical way, limited by what we know now, and if we just open all the doors, can we conceive of another way to access these other dimensions besides using vast quantities of energy?

Think of Isaac Newton. Three hundred years ago, he was the first human who could calculate what it would take to put a man on the moon. A Saturn rocket, for example, has about a million pounds of thrust and accelerates to about 25,000 miles per hour. He must have cried, knowing that in the 1600s in Merry Olde England, all they had were horses! We physicists today also cry. We can calculate that the amount of energy necessary to bend time into a pretzel or punch a hole in space or leap into the tenth dimension is 10 to the 19 billion electron volts. That's one with 19 zeroes after it. We are very primitive on the scale of civilization.

Newton must have known that in the future energy would be harnessed on the scale that could create rockets that could go to the moon, or he must have known that in outer space there must be civilizations out there that are more advanced than us and would have the ability to access this kind of energy. Either we wait until we have rocketships that can journey to black holes, for example, and black holes is perhaps the simplest way to open up the looking glass of Alice, or perhaps we make contact with extraterrestrial civilizations that have already mastered the Planck energy, as it's called. But, at the present time, our feeble technology is too primitive, even though we can dream about these things.

We say it's too primitive because it's based on the laws that we follow, which we've set down arbitrarily. Now, what if tomorrow someone says, "Aha! I've found it, a way we can do this! It's all brand new. It's not going to take a gazillion units of this energy!" Also, the mystics believed that accessing these other dimensions is something you can do with your mind.

Take a look at it this way: Many times flat predictions are made, and then just a few years later we're seen to be fools, right?

A hundred years ago, Auguste Compte, and I mention him in Hyperspace, a great philosopher, said that humans will never be able to visit the stars, that we will never know what stars are made out of, that that's the one thing that science will never ever understand, because they're so far away. And then, just a few years later, scientists took starlight, ran it through a prism, looked at the rainbow coming from starlight, and said: "Hydrogen!" Just a few years after this very rational, very reasonable, very scientific prediction was made, that we'll never know what the stars are made of. The interesting thing here is that historically time travel, higher dimensions and wormholes were all considered to be outlandish figments of the imagination, or of crackpots and mystics and charlatans, and physicists used to scoff at anyone who would dabble in these things. However, the tide has turned. Now, this is the center of gravity of modern physics research. We have a bulletin board at Los Alamos National Laboratory, where they manufacture hydrogen warheads, in fact, and three to five papers a day are logged on that computer bulletin board from physicists all over the world looking at different dimensions, and looking at the possibility of space warps and time travel and things like that.

In some sense you're right — we are children in terms of understanding the full implications of what we are doing. A whole province of fantasy and science fiction is now fair game for serious theoretical physicists. That even Nobel prize-winners, such as Steven Weinberg and Murray Gell-Mann have stated that this is probably it, that little strings vibrating in ten-dimensional hyperspace is perhaps the simplest, most economical and most correct way of unifying the known laws of physics. The problem is that we are still children in terms of solving these equations, and it may turn out that we will find equations that are even more fantastic than anything discovered so far. We have an equation one inch long that describes how these strings vibrate in ten dimensions. The problem is to find the solution to all these equations. Some of these solutions have opened up our imagination to parallel universes and stuff like that, things that historically were scoffed at by scientists.

In *Hyperspace* you use the analogy of the carp who thinks the universe is just limited to his pond. We're like the carp who realizes that something may be beyond the water's surface, and who wonders, "How can I leap out of this pond, see what's beyond the water, and then once I'm out there, how can I go back and forth at will?"

Historically, if you look at a "scientist" carp in the pond, they would say that there is no third dimension, that there's nothing beyond what they can measure, and that's the prejudice that physicists have.

Every once in awhile, though, the carp would see something outside the pond when he looked up.

Yeah, a glimmer.

So, a carp scientist might say, "I want to know what this is," and try to get out there. Or, a carp who'd been picked up out of the pond would return and want to figure out how else to get out there.

Right. You see, the strength and weakness of physicists is that we believe in what we can measure. And, if we can't measure it, then we say it probably doesn't exist. And that closes us off to an enormous amount of phenomena that we may not be able to measure because they only happened once. For example, the Big Bang. The philosopher David Hume once said that scientists will never be able to use science to understand the Big Bang because it only happened once, and science depends on reproducibility. That means, in some sense miracles, and in some sense mystical experiences are beyond the province of science because you cannot reproduce them on demand in laboratory conditions.

Our strength is that we can verify these things by reproducing them, but it's also our weakness because certain phenomena, like creation itself, only happen once, and we cannot reproduce it in the laboratory, which makes us very myopic and in some sense closed off. That's one reason why they scoffed at higher dimensions for so many years. Now we realize that there's no alternative, that hundreds of alternative theories have been proposed over the last 50 years, and each one has been shown to be inconsistent — every single unified field theory except one has been shown to be mathematically inconsistent, and that one theory that has survived every single challenge by the severist critics is the Hyperspace theory: that these little strings can vibrate and they give us quarks, protons, neutrons and whatever, but they vibrate in a ten-dimensional hyperspace universe.

These are strings of energy.

Strings of pure energy, right. For example, the top quark was discovered last month (in 1994), and that made a lot of headlines, but a lot of people on the streets said, "What the hell is a top quark?"

He's the chief of all the little quarks, the boss, the head honcho!

(He laughs) Yeah, in fact on TV I saw them interviewing them on the street and asking them "What is the top quark?" All sorts of crazy responses came out! But, the simplest response is: It's the last of the quarks. And the inventor of the quark, Murry Gell-Mann, I had on my radio show in New York City as a guest, and I said, "Well, you're the inventor of the quark model. Is that the last word in particle physics?" He said, "Of course not!" There are 60 sub-atomic particles that they've discovered that can explain the thousands of other sub-atomic particles, and the model is too ugly. This is my analogy: it's like taking Scotch tape and taping a giraffe to a mule to a whale to a tiger and saying this is the ultimate theory of particles. It's ridiculous. We have so many particles that Oppenheimer once said you could give a Nobel prize to the physicist who did not discover a particle that year. We were drowning in sub-atomic particles.

Now we realize that this whole zoo of sub-atomic particles, thousands of them coming out of our accelerators, can be explained by little vibrating strings. They're like a violin string.

The Pythagoreans, the Greeks, believed that violin strings were in some sense a paradigm for the universe. They didn't quite know how it would fit, but the harmonies of the universe, they thought, would be manifest by the harmonies of a violin string. The Pythagoreans founded a school of Greek philosophy trying to find in nature harmonies and resonances. Well, that's the analogy today, too. In fact, the quarks, according to Murray Gell-Mann, the inventor of the quark model and winner of the Nobel prize, said that the simplest representation of the quark is that it's nothing but the vibration of a string, and these strings, in turn, can only vibrate in ten dimensions. If you have an 11-dimensional universe it decays back down to ten. Ten is the magic number that works. The irony is that western reductionism, which believes in smashing things apart in order to find the ultimate constituents of matter...these reductionists have always laughed at holists and the people who believe in Buddhism, Taoism, whatever, and the irony is that by smashing these particles to their smallest constituents, we then find strings that only vibrate in the ten-dimensional universe and all of a sudden we realize that you have to look at the whole universe in order to understand the quantum theory! So, in some sense now we're combining the best traditions of holism and reductionism.

It's nice to take a little thing and look at it, but you can't look at it out of context and in isolation. You must see how it connects to the whole larger picture.

Right. Take an ant hill. If you want to discover the laws of ant behavior you don't take apart an ant and look at the DNA of an ant (he laughs) *to find out how ants behave when they form colonies. But, that's what we physicists do, that's western science. And western science has been very successful by taking sledgehammers and smashing protons apart and out come the quarks. But, then the quarks themselves are nothing but vibrating strings which vibrate in 10-dimensional hyperspace. By smashing atoms apart we're forced to understand now that the universe is the smallest unit that you can quantize! And that*

335

is, of course, the essence of holism. On one hand we have these hard-nosed mechanistic physicists who have scoffed at holism, and then on the other hand we have the holistic people who have not had the advantage of looking inside the proton. Now we have the grand unification of the two outlooks.

Many people talk about how ultimately this grand unification will end up showing what the mystics have been saying all along, the idea that "we are one." A frog, a rock, a person, a planet...they're all interconnected.

Right. This is very important. In the last part of my book Hyperspace *I become very philosophical, and I say that we are children of the stars, and our bodies are made out of stardust. We're part of the natural order of things. I say to people who get depressed and have a dark vision of the world: We have a right to be here, with all our faults, with all our pollution, with all our problems. Our bodies are made out of atoms that were forged in the center of stars. It was Einstein who gave us this vision of unification that we're all one, that all these forces we see around us appear to be broken, just like, for example, if you have a beautiful crystal and you smash it apart and these beautiful pieces of crystal land on a table top, and you have these flatland people living on a tabletop trying to piece these pieces of crystal together. They see a broken universe, a universe where light and gravity and the nuclear force all seem very different, and all seem quite broken. But, gradually, as they put these pieces together, they begin to realize that they fit into two huge chunks. One chunk is the atomic physics, the quantum physics, and that's the quantum world. The other piece of crystal is the theory of relativity, which gives us the Big Bang and space warps and this beautiful cosmic picture of spacetime. But these two pieces don't fit together: the quantum and relativity do not fit together. The only way you can fit these two pieces of crystal together is to move one piece up off the table into the third dimension, and then these two pieces of crystal form beautifully into a beautiful crystal.*

So, my analogy is that, like flatland, you can imagine that in the beginning of time there was this beautiful crystal that shattered and the pieces landed in flatland, and over thousands of years the quest of these flatlanders has been the process of unification. Only in the third dimension can we fit these pieces together. The same way we now have the quantum theory and relativity. These are the two giant theories of physics and they don't fit together. Only in ten dimensions do these pieces fit together. Einstein was considered a relic by many physicists. Many physicists were enamored of the quantum theory, which gives us transistors and televisions and radio and so forth. They were almost hypnotized by the beauty of the quantum theory, the theory of atomic physics and nuclear physics. And they thought that Einstein was an old fool, working on unification. Even Wolfgang Pauli once said that "What God has torn asunder, man should not put together." If God shattered the crystal at the beginning of time, we should not have the audacity to put it back together. But, now we're realizing that Einstein had the correct instinct. His quest was the unification. But he missed the key — the key was that he wasn't radical enough. He gave us the fourth dimension, but he didn't go radical enough to give us the fifth, sixth, seventh, all the way up to the tenth dimension.

Where did he stand on the idea of more dimensions?

He had a problem with it. The fifth dimension was unraveled while he was alive. The fifth dimension gives us the simplest explanation of light. For example, when I was in college I asked my professor, "What is light?" and he said, "Well, it's a wave." But, I said, "Well, light can wave in a vacuum. That means nothing is waving. How can nothing wave?" and he said, "That's right — nothing can wave. You just get used to it!" (he laughs) And now we realize that what is waving is what the mystics called the fourth dimension, or what today we call the fifth dimension because we added time (as the fourth dimension). Einstein himself realized this, but he didn't go far enough. He didn't understand the nuclear force, basically. That's the thing that he missed. If he had lived longer he would have seen how physicists put together the nuclear force. But the nuclear force was the bad boy of physics, with these thousands of particles, and it took us many decades before we finally figured out how the nuclear force all works. Enrico Fermi once said, "If I had known there would be so many sub-atomic particles, I would have become a botanist rather than a physicist!" (he laughs) You can't blame Einstein for missing the nuclear force, because it was a zoo, it was horrible. We didn't figure it out until just about ten years ago when we finally figured out what is called quantum chromodynamics, which gives us the quark understanding of sub-atomic particles.

We have a description of each dimension we are used to and operate in. We have a conceptual framework for all three dimensions, plus time as the fourth. What is the conceptual framework for all the dimensions from the fifth on? How would you describe them?

There was a mystic, Charles Hinton, at the turn of the century, who spent a lifetime trying to visualize the next dimension. And he would have all these analogies. For example, if I take a cube and I unravel it, I get a cross. If I have a hypercube and unravel that, then I get a cross consisting of cubes. He coined a word for it, it's called tessaract. There's even a children's book called A Wrinkle in Time, that talks about tessaracts. Salvador Dali was so enamored of this tessaract that he painted a famous crucifixion of Christ that I re-printed in my book, where Christ is crucified on a tessaract, a four-dimensional hypercube.

Many PhD theses have been written about Picasso and about Dali, but I'm sure that not a single one of them understand the essence of what Salvador Dali and Picasso were trying to do, and that is, capture the fourth dimension. When you see these women with two eyes facing you from the side, that's impossible, but from a higher-dimensional point of view, a higher—dimensional person can see all around you simultaneously. Just like when we see a flatlander, a cookie man on a tabletop, we can see all of him at once. That's what Picasso wanted to capture in cubism — four-dimensional perspective. Nude Descending Staircase was an attempt to capture time as a fourth dimension. So, Hinton believed that perhaps ghosts lived in the fourth dimension, and his attitude was that if you could take this cross, this tessaract, and mentally reassemble it, which is physically impossible in our world, you would then attain nirvana, the highest state of consciousness.

Gee, that's a good project for the weekend.

(He laughs) Right...in fact, he used to manufacture these cubes, they're called Hinton's Cubes. I think you can still pick them up in stores. The object was that if ghosts lived in the fourth dimension, and if you have the capability of manipulating the fourth dimension, then you will be able to mentally commune with ghosts and spirits of long-dead ancestors.

What do physicists think of that logic today?

Well, we owe a debt to these people because in any math book, when they have pictures of higher dimensional objects, they use all the tricks that Hinton devised at the turn of the century.

He laid the groundwork, then.

He laid the groundwork for visualization of all these things. You visualize them by first opening them up, opening up a hypercube, that's one way to do it. Another way to do it is cross-sections. For example, if you stick your finger through a tabletop, the flatlanders will see a ring of flesh. If you stick two fingers, they'll see two rings of flesh, and if you bring your two rings of flesh together the flatlander knows he's going to be ripped apart and thrown into hyperspace. Now, one of these days, if you walk *down Fifth Avenue, and you see a sphere of flesh hovering in front of you* (he laughs)...

We're in trouble.

We're in deep trouble! You should turn around and walk the other way! And if a second sphere of flesh were to materialize behind you, and if these two spheres of flesh were to come close to you, you are now going to be flung into hyperspace.

Like a bowling ball.

Yes, like a bowling ball. Now, if you were to get a net and try to capture a hyperperson, you would throw the net around the sphere, but the person, of course, could simply lift his finger out. Similarly, if you stick your finger in a tabletop, a flatlander would draw a circle around it, and he thinks that the circle drawn around your finger captures your finger. But, it doesn't because we could just pull our finger out. However, as Hinton and many other people pointed out, there is one way of capturing a hyperperson, which is not the most pleasant. If you stick your finger in a tabletop, there is one way for these people to capture your finger. It's to stick a needle through it.

Sideways.

Sideways, right. To draw a circle around your finger would not work, and to throw a net around a sphere would not work because you can pull your finger out. What Picasso and Dali and the others were trying to do was gain a perspective on the fourth dimension. Leonardo DaVinci and the great Renaissance painters discovered the third dimension when they discovered the laws of perspective, the vanishing horizon and so on. If you go back farther, medieval painters have a two-dimensional universe, a very flat universe.
Because of this many people have speculated that maybe God lives in a higher dimension — What object is omnipotent and

can see everything in the universe simultaneously? What object can go through walls as if walls don't exist? That would be a supernatural being. If you had flatlanders who had gold in a safe, the safe is nothing but a square and inside the square is gold. But, we can see inside the safe, reach into it and pull out the gold. So, this means that a hyperperson could reach right into Fort Knox and just pluck out the gold, or reach into your body and perform surgery without cutting your skin. These are some of the powers a hyperperson would have when viewing our lower-dimensional universe. They could also scan the universe instantly and simultaneously and see all around us, and that's why many theologians have stated that Hyperspace is the proper residence for God.

So, what we're looking to do is to become hyperpeople, get ourselves out there so that we could interact with our universe but from a place where we have more dimensions.

In some sense, yes. People ask, "how come I can't visualize these higher dimensions more easily?" The reason is an accident of evolution. We've evolved on this planet to dodge saber-toothed tigers and charging mammoths, and we didn't need those extra dimensions. These extra dimensions are perfectly visualizable on a computer. I have a videotape of a rotating hypercube and a rotating hypersphere. For a computer, what's three dimensions? Any dimensions for them is perfectly fine.

Of course, we're looking at it from a 3-D perspective.

Yeah, we're looking at it in 3-D, so we see shadows, that's the other way to see these things — by looking at shadows projected down on our universe.

These other dimensions are out there. So, does that mean that one day when we find a way to communicate with that dimension or penetrate it, will it all of a sudden enter into our scientific realm and our consciousness. Will we be functioning within it? Are we already? We were always functioning in 3-D even when people thought the world was flat. We didn't suddenly look different or start functioning differently when Columbus came back and said, "Hey, I didn't fall off!"

That's right. In other words: Where are these higher dimensions? People used to ask Hinton this question, and why can't we see them? Hinton's answer was essentially the modern point of view, that these dimensions are, first of all, all around us — every point in the universe touches the fourth dimension (also known as the fifth, if you consider time to be the fourth). Think of the carp swimming in the pond. Every point in the pond touches the third dimension.

He just can't visualize it.

Right — he can't visualize it. And the energy necessary to lift the carp up to it is quite severe. What Hinton said is that these dimensions are very small, but they're there, and they vibrate. And these vibrations give us what is called light. The new wrinkle on this is that we think there are many more dimensions beyond what Hinton visualized.

Light, then, is being carried by this other dimension?

Well, that is what light is. Let's say that there's a rainstorm on this pond, and ripples forming on the surface of the pond. These ripples would be visible to the fish. The fish would see shadows rippling on their pond, and they would call that phenomenon light. Light isn't so much carried by these vibrations...that's what light is. Light is vibrations in another dimension.

So, we do have visual proof of another dimension.

Oh, yes. We have visual signals from the fifth dimension. When these dimensions vibrate they obviously affect our universe. So, in other words they are 1) all around us, 2) they affect our life in very important ways: these dimensions ripple, form light and form the nuclear force, and the nuclear force, in turn, is what makes the stars shine. So, in some sense the stars shine because of the sixth, seventh, eighth, ninth, tenth dimensions.

These other dimensions beyond the fifth are all tied to the nuclear force.

That's right. That was where Einstein didn't go far enough. Even when he was alive people were talking about the fifth dimension, but when you start to add the others, that's where the nuclear force comes out. You get what are called Yang-Mills particles, which are now known to be the glue that holds the quarks together. When you vibrate the fifth dimension you get light. When you vibrate the sixth, seventh and eighth dimensions you get Yang-Mills fields. They are the glue that holds together the quarks, which in turn are released when you have a detonating sun. When the sun shines you're releasing the force that is tied up in these Yang-Mills fields.

You said that once we go beyond the 10th dimension things begin to get messy.

The Universe is unstable beyond ten. Where does ten come from? There are two answers to that. First of all, ten is the smallest number of dimensions in which you can summarize all the laws of the universe. But, there's a more profound reason, and that goes to mathematics. In the history of mathematics, the strangest and most profound mathematician who was ever born was a guy called Ramanujan. He was an Indian mystic, and perhaps the smartest, most spectacular mathematician to walk the face of the earth. The tragedy is that he was born in India in total isolation of European mathematics. On his own he re-derived about a hundred or two hundred of European mathematics. So, here's this Indian postal clerk, and he writes a letter to Godfrey Hardy (famous Cambridge mathematician

— he received the letter in 1913, when Ramanujan was 26), *and Hardy says, and I'll paraphrase: "Holy shit! Either this guy is a fraud, or the greatest genius of the last 100 years!"*

Hardy calls for Ramanujan, and together they work out a whole blizzard of mathematical formulas. The most famous is the Ramanujan Function. This opens up a whole branch of mathematics called elliptic modular function, which only works in 24 dimensions. The number 24 is littered throughout Ramanujan's notebooks. It's one of the magic numbers of mathematics. That beautiful identities work in just 24 dimensions. We physicists independently discovered many of his identities, and we found a second magic number — eight. We physicists are different from mathematicians. We add two more dimensions to make them physical. So, in superstring theory, ten and 26 are the physical magic numbers, (eight and 24 are the mathematical magic numbers).

Why do you add two?

Because we physicists like to have our equations fully relativistic, and when we add relativity to any theory we always add two more dimensions. Why ten and 26? Well, we have these little strings vibrating, and these strings can break, and when they break and re-form that requires an enormous amount of mathematical identities to make the theory consistent. It only works in ten and 26 dimensions (the same as eight and 24 in mathematics).

If you say that beyond ten dimensions things get a bit funky, how do you explain why they also work so nicely in 26 dimensions?

There may be another universe out there in 26 dimensions. I didn't want to mention it in the book too much because it would scare people and also we physicists still haven't quite figured out the relationship between ten and 26. Remember, this theory is very young, and this theory is so fantastic that it has startled the world of mathematics. In the last hundred years, mathematics and physics separated. After Einstein, mathematicians went into studying hyperspace. But, physicists said, "That's a bunch of baloney! There is no hyperspace, there is no fourth dimension, that's for ghosts and charlatans and mystics!" So, physicists stuck to the quantum theory, which is, of course, in three spatial dimensions.

Now, mathematics and physics are marrying again — there's an historic reconciliation. The world of mathematics is now being bowled over — there's just no other word for it — by physics. A whole rush of ideas is now flooding into mathematics because of this hyperspace theory. And, at the heart of this theory is the work of Ramanujan. When people ask how this mystic worked, well, he would wake up in the morning and have visions, and he would see these equations dancing in his head, and he would write them on the blackboard so fast, that Hardy was just racing on his notepad trying to write them down. They're summarized in what are called The Lost Notebooks. Ramanujan only lived to be 33 years old, and he died of tuberculosis. To this day, we still don't know how his brain operated.

His brain was obviously in tune with other dimensions.

Yeah! Hardy, the great mathematician, used to rank other mathematicians on a scale of one to one hundred, and he used to place himself at 30, but he placed Ramanujan at 100. If you could look at one of Ramanujan's mathematical identities on a piece of paper you'd see on the left hand side of this equation an infinite sequence of products — this times this times this times this, each term being quite complicated — on the right hand side is an infinite sequence of sums — this plus this plus this plus this — and the two sides are equal to each other only in 24 dimensions!

And this just popped into his head.

This just popped into his head! It's sort of like music. We're *used to Western music — Bach and Beethoven — and all of a sudden we hear Eastern music for the first time, and we hear half-tones and harmonies that are totally alien.*

We hear things we call dissonant.

Right. And if we hear Eastern music coming from India we realize there's a whole new logic, an equally valid logic, that Western music hasn't discovered. That's sort of the comparison with Ramanujan's work. We're so used to Western mathematics, and here comes this Eastern mathematics that caught everyone by surprise.

It would make sense in the holistic picture of the universe, or we should say universes, that everything would connect: physics, math, dreams, music.

Well, it's quite surprising that in this work of Ramanujan, an Indian mystic, we have someone who would dream equations that it would take a computer to check. And that these dreams would only work in 24 dimensions.

What's going on between dimension eight or ten and dimension 24 or 26?

Those universes are unstable.

So, it doesn't stabilize again until we hit 24.

A universe in, say, 13 dimensions would de-stabilize and decay down to a ten dimensional universe where it's stable. The stable universes we can work in. The reason why they're stable is because you have to have an enormous number of mathematical identities that must be satisfied, and these identities are exactly the identities of Ramanujan, which were re-discovered by physicists. We said, "My God, these equations look familiar! We've seen them in history! They're the works of Ramanujan!"

What happens when we go up beyond the 24th/26th dimension?

Then things become unstable again. A universe in 50 dimensions would decay back down. Mathematicians have realized that there are magic numbers. In certain dimensions magic takes place. There's just no other word for it. That identities that normally don't work at all, all of a sudden work in these dimensions.

It's conceivable that one day we'll find out we've been wrong: that all this decay we've seen is only what we consider decay right now given what we have to work with, but that ten years from now we'll have new tools and we'll find that what we used to think was decay actually isn't.

That's possible. Physics goes by essentially one principle, and that is that any new theory has to be consistent with experiment and all previous theories. In other words, Newton wasn't wrong, Newton was incomplete. Newton didn't understand the speed of light and Planck's Constant or the quantum theory.

So, all new theories must be an expansion of the old.

Right. The old theories are correct in their domain. In the domain of small velocities and large size, Newton's theory is correct. Einstein comes along and says that when objects get into the speed of light, then we have to have a new relativistic theory. Then the quantum people come along and say that in the realm of the very small, Newton's theory also breaks down. So, Newton's theory is correct for big objects moving very slowly. Einstein's theory is correct for big objects moving very fast. And the quantum theory is good for tiny objects. The unified field theory is a theory for objects of any size at any velocity. The unified theory must then be consistent with Newton's theory, Einstein's theory and the quantum theory. Therefore, ten years from now, perhaps even a greater theory will be discovered. But it must be compatible with all the previous theories.

We could go on and on into an infinite number of dimensions then, couldn't we?

Possible.

Right now we believe that there's something about the way the universe is constructed that it's most comfortable in ten or in 26 dimensions.

Right. There's another way of looking at it, and this was mentioned by Steven Weinberg, who won the Nobel prize in the '70s, and that is that this theory gives you many solutions in ten dimensions — millions of solutions — and perhaps all these solutions exist as parallel universes. Stephen Hawking has also said this, too. That if you really believe the quantum theory, that means the universe is the smallest object you can quantize. This means that the universe can be in many states, just like the electron can be in many states. This means that there must be parallel universes. These universes may be unstable, they may eventually decay down to a universe that looks like ours, but in principle you cannot rule out the existence of parallel universes.

Another word for dimension, then, is universe.

Yeah. In fact, Stephen Hawking wrote a book last fall about what he calls baby universes or what most people would call parallel universes. These parallel universes are like soap bubbles. We believe that the quantum theory says that the universe is the smallest object you can quantize, therefore the universe must exist in different energy states, and therefore there must be parallel universes. Now, the question is: can you go between them? This is the subject of an enormous amount of controversy right now. Hawking says that there are wormholes, or tubes that connect these universes, like a spiderweb network connecting soap bubbles together. But, these tubes are very small and they open up very briefly. They're too tiny for us to go through. Quantum theory says that even the most bizarre things can happen if you wait long enough. So, if you wait long enough, perhaps a large wormhole will open up and you'll wind up on another soap bubble. Now, what will these other soap bubbles look like? Steven Weinberg speculates that these other soap bubbles are dead universes, that the proton is not stable in these universes so we have a soap bubble of electrons and neutrons.

Now, isn't that kind of arrogant? We always assume that everybody else's universe is dead but ours.

Right (he laughs), *right. So, Hawking says, not so fast, maybe some of these soap bubbles are dead, but maybe some look just like ours, except they're one quantum transition away from ours. So, this gets us back into the many worlds theory — the theory that there are many quantum worlds that look just like ours except that there's just one small quantum difference.*

How might that translate? The universe would look just like ours except that in that other universe, for example, you might have red hair?

Something like that. Let's say that you have red hair because just before conception a cosmic ray came in and hit your mom's DNA and turned brown to red. Well, a cosmic ray is a quantum event. And maybe the cosmic ray missed that DNA or maybe hit another DNA molecule (when it hit your mom in another universe). These are the kinds of things now that Hawking is working with. Hawking works with something called wave function of the universe. Remember the Schrodinger's Cat paradox? That paradox is: you write a wave function psi of cat; and you have to add psi of dead cat plus psi of live cat. Now, many people can't stomach that. Either a cat is dead or alive. You cannot add the wave function of a dead cat plus the wave function of a live cat. But, that's what we physicists do! Now, Hawking comes along and says that instead of writing wave function of a cat, we write wave function of universe we know plus universes that we don't know. Now, this blows your mind away.

Actually, Firesign Theater said it best in the '70s: "How Can You Be Two Places At Once When You're Not Anywhere At All?"

Right. And how can universes be two places at the same time! Remember, the philosophy coming out of this is that the universe is the smallest object you can quantize. If the string theory is correct it means that the strings vibrate only in ten dimensions and twenty-six dimensions. Hawking's point of view is that our wave function is the most likely. That these other wave functions decay with time, and they decay down to our universe. So, we do in some sense co-exist with other universes.

We just don't see them.

Yeah, we just don't see them, or our universe just happens to be quite stable. It's been stable for about 15 billion years, and that's an awful long time to be stable. These other soap bubbles may have expanded and then contracted again. This gets us into the death of our universe. Many philosophers have wailed at the fact that our universe must die, and that in some sense life is meaningless. Because no matter how many tears we shed, no matter how many heroics we achieve, it's all for nothing, because the universe will die, and we will die with it. There is one, and only one, way in which you can escape the death of the universe, and thereby make life worth living. In fact, Bertrand Russell wrote perhaps the most depressing paragraph in all human history, and I quote that paragraph in my book, where he talks about all the great achievements of humanity being for nothing. But, there is one way to get around it and that is hyperspace.

Just go to another universe where everything's fine.

That's right. If your apartment house is burning down, and you know that you're gonna burn with it, there is one way to get around it, and that's to go to the basement. Go to the "hyperfloor!" (he laughs)

Or go outside.

Right or go outside. And from the basement you can go outside. From the outside you can watch the apartment house burn down. And another one can be rebuilt in it's place.

And, while you're in that burning apartment, the outside has always been there. Just because you haven't gone there yet, doesn't mean it isn't there. Those parallel universes are out there, affecting us in whatever small or large ways they do, but we just haven't figured out how to go there yet.

Right. Yeah, we haven't figured out how to access this other dimension yet.

There must be little leaks, because using the analogy of the apartment building, air from the outside leaks into that apartment building all the time. So, there must be little leaks from other universes into ours.

That's right.

Could that be what's behind things like synchronicity?

Hawking writes about the little leaks. They're the wormholes, the little tubes. His opinion is that the size of the little leaks is ten to the minus 33 centimeters, which is a very small distance. It's the smallest distance you can write down, in fact, on a sheet of paper that has any physical relevance. These wormholes are very small, but once in awhile a big one's gonna open up — the Heisenberg Uncertainty Principle. Over the lifetime of the universe there is the possibility of big ones opening up. Hawking and the others who write about this say that the probability of leakage, according to the equations, is very small. However, as you pointed out, ten years from now many of the things that we are saying now may be obsolete. We're sort of like children now in understanding the full extent of these things.

It could be that this apartment house isn't built out of brick, but of screen, so that air can get in and out, and with that as an analogy to our universe, effects from other universes can filter into ours, even though there's a barrier of sorts there.

> *Possibly. Physics deals with what is reproducible, and what is reproducible in the laboratory is the quark model, and that takes us to strings, and strings takes us to higher dimensional travel. What is not reproducible in the lab are a lot of phenomena that are equally valid, like synchronicity. That's the problem that orthodox physicists have. Science has pushed the Big Bang theory to the limit now, to the point where it's intersecting with religion, but the Big Bang theory itself is a theory that can't be verified because it only happened once. We can only look at echoes of this thing. People always ask what this says about religion. Well, physicists are the only scientists who can mention the word God and not blush, so let me now tackle it directly: Theologians have always thumbed their nose at physicists by saying, "What happened before the Big Bang?" And at that point physicists have simply stopped, and are embarrassed. And physicists, of course, challenge the theologians by saying, "Did God have a mother?" Well, there is a partial resolution to this, I think. If this theory is correct it means we can go before the Big Bang, because this is a quantum theory, which goes before the Big Bang, and this modern-day theory is as follows, and it has now become orthodoxy in cosmology: In the beginning was Nothing, which a capital N, a state of no matter, no energy. All there was was ten-dimensional hyperspace, but it was empty. The ten-dimensional hyperspace obeys the quantum. So, in the beginning was the quantum, and the quantum existed in Nothing. The quantum means that things are unstable. That means that Nothing was unstable. That means that bubbles began to form, and in each little bubble you had a breakdown in this beautiful ten-dimensional Nothing. These little bubbles then began to expand very rapidly, and they became what is called The Big Bang. So, the Big Bang, in some sense, is a rather minor aftershock of a much more*

cataclysmic event, and that is the breaking of ten-dimensional Nothing down to the present day three-dimensional universe that we see expanding all around us. This means that there are other bubbles out there, and maybe these bubbles are constantly forming and contracting, and that we co-exist with an infinite sea of bubbles.

Therefore, there is an infinite sea of other universes.

That's right. The bible, for example, in the gospel according to St. John, Chapter 1, verse 1, says that in the beginning was the Word, and the Word was with God, and the Word was God. Well, physicists say that in the beginning was Nothing, and the Word was the Quantum. In Hindu mysticism, they say that in the beginning was the Mist, and in other Christian texts in the beginning was the Void.

These are just all different symbols of the same thing.

Essentially the same thing, right. So, when you push Einstein's theory until it breaks down, you have to add the quantum, and the quantum theory says that Nothing is unstable, because that's one of the essences of the quantum — you wait long enough and anything can happen, so things are unstable, so Nothing is unstable, too. This also means that all these symmetries you see around you are nothing but pieces of hyperspace. So when you see a crystal, a beautiful sunset, symmetry all around you, what is the origin of the symmetry? Hyperspace. Remnants of this crystal — this perfect ten-dimensional hyperspace universe — that was shattered at the beginning of time. So, why is a crystal beautiful? A mathematician or physicist would say it's so you can pack atoms together in an array. Well, why are atoms arranged in this array? Because they obey the Schrodinger equation. Because they have an inverse square potential with what's inside the atom. Well, where did the Schrodinger equation come from? Well, that came from the wave function of the universe. Well, where did the wave function of the universe come from? That came from hyperspace.

All roads lead to hyperspace.

That's right. All the symmetries you see around you — the symmetries of quarks, crystals, the sun — are nothing more than pieces of the original symmetry. The original symmetry of hyperspace. That's where everything came from: ten-dimensional Nothing. Space was there, time was there, but there was no matter or energy as we know it.

Hyperspace will most likely be the key to time travel when we harness a relationship with these other dimensions.

That's right. Even though most orthodox physicists say that time travel is not possible, they don't understand Einstein's theory, that as early as 1949 the first time travel solution of Einstein's equation was discovered. In fact, by a friend of Einstein, Kurt Godel, who is perhaps the most famous mathematical logician of the last thousand years. He worked at the Institute for Advanced Studies at Princeton. Einstein wasn't too worried about this solution for time travel. Well, he was worried, but he had a way to resolve it. In Godel's universe, the universe rotated; he had a huge swirling mass of gas. But, the universe does not rotate, it expands. Therefore, Einstein died thinking that time travel was not possible. Since then, we've discovered hundreds of more solutions, all of which allow for time travel. So, how do we explain this? Let me give you an analogy. Newton thought that time was like an arrow, that you fire an arrow and it never comes back. Einstein says time is like a river, it meanders around stars and galaxies, speeds up and slows down. We've actually measured this. One second on the earth is not one second on the moon. The new twist on this is that time can have whirlpools and eddy currents and it can fork. Remember, this is just classical Einstein's theory; forget the quantum for the moment. Since 1949 we've known that time can have whirlpools. But since then, we've found hundreds of solutions where we have eddy currents, and this thing peeling off and that thing peeling off, and time even forking. Now, how do we deal with this? The simplest time machine you can build is actually a wormhole. You take a black hole, and the black is spinning very rapidly, and when it collapses, it collapses into a ring of fire, or neutrons. This is the ring of Alice's looking glass, because inside the ring is another universe. This other universe can be our universe in a different time. If you were to leap through this ring of fire, you would, in fact, wind up in a different time era.

The question is: What does it take to build these things? In Back to the Future we had Michael J. Fox getting into a plutonium-fired car. Today we know that plutonium is not sufficient enough to give us this ability. As we mentioned earlier, the energy necessary is ten to the 19 billion electron volts, and that's far beyond the energy found even in plutonium. But, in principle, it means that an advanced civilization, maybe even a future civilization may have the ability to bend time into a pretzel. And this gets us into the problem of what happens if you go back in time and kill your grandparents before you were even born. The modern way of looking at this is that time forks — the universe, then, forks into a parallel universe. So, that if time machines were as common as car dealerships, so you could buy a Ford Taurus, a Toyota and an XK-1 Time Machine then perhaps you could save Abraham Lincoln from being assassinated. At that time, time would fork.

And you would go into a parallel universe, one in which Lincoln had not died.

Right. In that universe Abraham Lincoln didn't die and history became different, but you do not disappear. In Back to the Future, they said Michael J. Fox would disappear if his parents didn't get together. And he has a photograph of himself from the future, and the photograph slowly fades away. That's not possible, because time does not dam. There's no dam on the river of time.

All it would mean is that he would have split his known universe into two different ones.

That's right. The time-line for Michael J. Fox doesn't simply stop because his mother falls in love with him instead of his father. What this means is that again the quantum theory enters the picture. The quantum theory allows the forking to take place, and this means that time travelers from the future may, in fact, have entered our time now, and have interacted with us even. We can't rule that out. Stephen Hawking has published a criticism of this, saying that yes the equations do seem very convincing. However, he says, he gives empirical proof that time machines are not possible because we don't see tourists from the future. This is his famous objection to time machines. My attitude, and I think your attitude is the same thing, that tourists from the future are so advanced...

That they wouldn't show up snapping pictures...

(He laughs) Yeah, right! They're going to be so advanced that they're not necessarily going to want to change our history.

And even if they did it accidentally, they're not going to be behaving like tourists.

Yeah, not like us going to Yellowstone Park and throwing garbage everywhere. They're going to have a much more holistic relationship with their universe. They're not going to litter and trample over the natural wildlife that is us, the natives, the way we do when we go to national parks and such.

Yeah, we're really awful.

We're just atrocious. I think that the future is not going to treat us like we treat Yellowstone Park.

Future scientists and future humans in general probably won't be as arrogant and won't be the control freaks that we all are now.

Right.

We insist on being able to reproduce a phenomenon, and that's because we are still arrogant enough to believe that we should be able to have control over science, or therefore "it doesn't exist." You can't control nature, and you can't necessarily make sure something happens twice.

> *Right. So, this means that intelligent life in the galaxy —*
> *and I think there is intelligent life in the galaxy, and most*
> *astronomers believe that there should be on the order of a few*
> *thousand planets with intelligent life forms in our galaxy —*
> *may have the wisdom and the technology to tamper with this*
> *kind of energy and bend time into a pretzel. I think that the*
> *mathematics and the equations are rather convincing that it is*
> *conceivable that time machines can be built. By the time any*
> *civilizations can build one of these machines they will have the*
> *maturity and wisdom and harmonious relationship with nature*
> *so that they're not going to want to trample over things. So,*
> *Hawking's objection is only valid if time travelers were just like*
> *us.*

What do hyperspace possibilities tell us about long-held spiritual beliefs? The Eastern philosophy versus the Western? Eastern philosophers have operated under the premise, it seems, that there is hyperspace. Everything that they have espoused over the years is in keeping with hyperspace theory, whereas Western has not.

> *Western physics has been dragged kicking and screaming in*
> *this direction, in the sense that all alternatives have been tried*
> *— unified field theories of this and that — and in my book I*
> *quote this famous encounter between Neils Bohr and Wolfgang*
> *Pauli when Pauli presents his unified field theory and then Bohr*
> *says "We're all agreed that your theory is crazy, but what divides*
> *us is whether your theory is crazy enough!" This means that*

*Western science realized that it has not been crazy enough, that
it has been much too conservative, because nothing has worked.*

Maybe spirituality and metaphysics is just the ultimate physics?

*It could be. It could be that Western physics has exhausted
itself, in that it has exhausted everything you can do with four
dimensions, and it simply cannot do anymore. Therefore, as
Bohr said, and he had the wisdom to say this, we have to be
crazy. And what is simple, and crazy, is hyperspace. It's just
adding more dimensions — what could be simpler than that? It
does not require a great leap of mathematical complexity. We
have a simplicity with this which allows us to unite forces that
we never though could be united. The Eastern philosophy, on the
other hand, comes to this naturally. They say that you have to be
in a harmonious relationship to things, and that the universe is
much bigger than you realize and that we can't be arrogant to
think that what you can see and what you can measure is all
that there is. There is more than what we can measure in a
laboratory.*

*But, the mechanistic way is how Western science has
developed, and rather successfully, with taking things apart and
reproducing things in the laboratory. But, it has been successful
at a tremendous cost. And the cost is rampaging through the
environment, controlling nature and forcing nature to do
animal tricks, basically. Western science, from the git-go, has not
been in harmony with nature and has not been in harmony
with the larger universe. Einstein, in some sense, was not part
of the Western tradition of smashing things apart. He was more
in tune with the Eastern philosophy of unification.*

Do you think that accessing hyperspace is what's going to save the
planet?

*Possibly. People ask, "Of what use is hyperspace theory?" My
personal opinion is that we are in a danger period in our
evolution on our planet. We've looked out into space out to 100*

light years and we don't see intelligence, any hint of an intelligent life form. And I ask myself the question, Why in our little sector of the galaxy don't we see any intelligent life. And, my attitude is that ultimately coming out of the swamp, all intelligent life will discover element 92, and discover pollution, and with uranium and petrochemical plastics industry you now have the ability to blow the planet apart or pollute your planet to extinction. And I think that many civilizations in outer space may not have bridged this gap. The generation that's now alive, our generation, is the most important generation ever to walk on the face of the earth.

We're the most advanced.

Yes, and we're the only ones with the ability to destroy our own species. No other generation has had that capability. So, I think in outer space civilizations are tested to see whether they have the maturity and compassion to not use nuclear weapons to settle racial hatreds and sectarian differences. And on the earth it's not yet clear whether or not racial hatreds and sectarian hatreds will be fought out with nuclear weapons. If we bridge the uranium gap we will eventually usher in an Age of Aquarius, an age when we can have energy on demand, when we can have mastery of the four forces and work in harmony with the rest of the universe so that we don't corrupt or deform the natural order of things.

Is the way to get there by accessing hyperspace?

That's right. My personal belief is that even though immediately it's not going to give us a better toaster — people ask me can I get a better toaster, a better TV set, better cable with this theory — (he laughs) the answer is no, you're not gonna get better cable. On the other hand, I firmly believe that the ultimate destiny of all humanity will lie with hyperspace, in the same way that Michael Farraday, one hundred years ago, was asked by Gladstone: "Of what use are these contraptions for

England?" and Michael Farraday, tinkering with dynamos and generators, said: "Mr. Prime Minister, I know not of what use these machines will have for England. All I know is that one day you will tax them." (He laughs). And that's how we view this theory. We do not know how hyperspace will ultimately affect humanity. But we do know that because it is the unification of all forces, one day all humanity will tax this theory. One day we will be masters of our own destiny so we will not die in the big crunch, so that poverty and inequity will be resolved.

Is one of the ways we'll have access to hyperspace to abandon our old ways of doing things, and say, "This thing doesn't have to be consistently reproduced. Let's throw caution to the wind."

It may have to be because...well, you know the superconducting supercollider was canceled...

One of the biggest crimes of the century.

Yeah, so we will not be able to access these kinds of energies outside Dallas, Texas, so we will have to go where angels fear to tread.

So, maybe this was the universe's way of saying, "Nope, sorry. If I give you this superconducting supercollider you're going to just keep on doing things the old way. I'm going to take this away so you have to come up with a new way."

Perhaps, yes. Perhaps we physicists have been humbled, and will have to deal with things a different way. In the last part of my book I get into how physicists view other civilizations in outer space. For example, physicists look at type one, type two, type three civilizations in outer space. We look for energy. A type one civilization is a planetary civilization where they mine the oceans, have cities in the ocean, control the earthquakes, control the weather, and for energy they simply go to the center of the earth. They have unlimited energy on a planetary scale. A type two civilization gets energy from a stellar system. You just go to the sun and grab a piece of the sun. They absorb energy directly from the sun. A type three civilization is a galactic civilization where they get energy from star systems, not just one particular source. So, for example, in Star Trek, *that's a civilization almost on the verge of type two status. They have the ability to ignite dead stars. A type three would be like the Borg in* Star Trek, *or like Azimov's Foundation series. And that's why the Federation fears the Borg, because the Borg is type three. Where are we? We are type nothing, type zero. What do we use for energy? Do we mine the oceans, do we control the weather or earthquakes? No, we burn oil, we use decayed matter from the dinosaur era.*

We're hopelessly backward, aren't we?

Yeah, we're children on this scale. We're only perhaps a century or a few centuries away from type one status, because knowledge doubles every twenty years, energy is escalating enormously. Our grandparents lived in a world where you were lucky if you had a horse. One horsepower. Today we think nothing of getting in a sportscar at three hundred horsepower. Energy available to the average person has geometrically expanded in the last few decades. We will attain type one status very soon, but it will mean a planetary government, because if you can control the weather that means you have to have cooperation among all the nations of the earth. If you make it rain in Alabama, that means a thunderstorm in Bangladesh. So, this is what I mean by the Age of Aquarius. By that time we will have abolished wars, poverty will have been abolished, and there will be tremendous cooperation among peoples.

So, the essential problem in science today is overcoming human nature.

Sort of. Overcoming the nature to tribalize and factionalize.

And we'll have to overcome our desire for external power.

And to dominate — that's one of the banes of humanity. Technology, though, is democratizing. The computer revolution is very democratizing. Anyone can get access to the Internet. Once information leaks out to the earth it goes everywhere. If we can negotiate the next several decades, where we have a greenhouse problem, all these nuclear weapons that we have to get rid of, leaking nuclear waste dumps and chemical dumps, and all these pesticides in our diet, if we can make it through these next few decades we will be on our way to a type one status. And at that point we'll be able to access enormous amounts of energy in a harmonious way, and then I think we can assume our rightful place in the universe. I think ultimately our place in the universe is in the stars. And I don't say this in a naive, starry-eyed kind of way. If you look at it from the natural progression of how humans have mastered energy, sometimes atrociously, sometimes burning down whole forests in the process...

It is what it's leading to.

It is leading to a planetary civilization.

It wouldn't make any sense that we should be part of a universe that we couldn't interact with.

That's right. Our home is the universe and we should feel natural with it.

And all of it's functions, which includes hyperspace?

And hyperspace may be the key to seeing our true role in the larger nature of things. We're just prejudiced right now by thinking that what exists is what is measurable. Ultimately what is measurable is on a scale of energy far beyond anything that we can amass. And on that scale then you can begin to access higher dimensions.

Twelve

Deborah Mash

*All men will benefit if we can invoke the
wonders of science instead of its terrors.*

— John F. Kennedy

*W*hen people reminisce about where they rode out Hurricane Andrew, perhaps no one will have a more bizarre story than Dr. Deborah Mash.

That night — August 23, 1992 — as the storm approached, Mash rounded up 600 pounds of dry ice, her husband and mother, and headed for the University of Miami medical school campus. With the wind whipping up to 164 mph and the rain pelting sideways, Mash and family settled in for a long night snuggled up next to a freezer full of...human brains.

"There was no way I was going to let the souls of the dearly departed and six years of my life go down the drain," says Mash, an internationally prominent neuroscientist and the director of the University of Miami Brain Endowment Bank, one of only three general brain banks in the nation.

Brains are scarce, and Mash made sure the nearly 400 in her charge would survive the storm, still frozen. When Mash and her family emerged at seven the next morning, August 24th, Miami was a wreck. But, Mash's brains were fine, much to the delight of researchers around the country who depend on these banks to provide much-needed brain tissue for their study of neurological disorders and diseases.

Why all the fuss over gray matter?

"The brain is the last biological frontier," says Mash, who is also one of the world's leading addiction scientists, the university's Jeanne C. Levy Professor of Parkinson's Disease Research, and a Professor of Neurology, Neuroscience and Pharmacology. "We need to study the human brain post-mortem — diseased brains and healthy ones for comparison."

Studying them, looking for treatments and cures, is the easy part. The hard part is getting the brains. When you agree to be an organ donor and it's noted on your driver's license, you pledge everything but your brain. The brain is endowed separately and directly to one of the three banks that accept all kinds of brains (Miami, Boston, Los Angeles), or to one of the handful that specialize in one disorder.

These main banks make brain tissue available to their own researchers, as well as distribute samples to researchers across the country, and one brain can provide enough tissue for 50 researchers.

Brains are needed because there's a lot to study: causes, treatments and cures for Parkinson's disease, Lou Gehrig's disease (ALS), mental illness, depression, Down's syndrome, and many others including AIDS.

Researchers are also looking into what has happened to our brains because of alcohol, drugs, chemicals, stress, trauma and injury. And they want to study what part genetics play in the brain's day-to-day job. "Normal" brains are as much in demand as those that aren't because they are used as "controls," to compare to the diseased or impaired brain. All brain banks have a shortage of normal brains.

Yet just because you've pledged your brain doesn't mean researchers will be able to use it. A brain can't be harvested from someone who's been dead more than 12 hours or from someone who was on a respirator. The ideal brain comes from people who die quickly of natural causes or in an accident. Brains for donation are removed by pathologists, coroners and funeral directors. After removal, the brain is frozen.

"We need baby boomer brains," says Mash. Drug abuse studies in particular required brain tissue from the age 40-55 crowd, many of whom first indulged in chemical recreation during the 1960s and early 1970s. They're ideal candidates for studies on the long-term affects of drug use.

Finding treatments and a cure for addiction has been one of Mash's main professional crusades, and her research in this and other areas of neuroscience have been widely published to substantial acclaim in science journals. She leads the way, also, in combining the best of modern medicine, with the best of what alternative and herbal medicine has to offer, and coined the term *neuroshamanism* to describe this approach in her landmark work with the drug ibogaine, which is being studied as a possible cure for addiction.

Despite the U.S. government's historic queasiness about sanctioning mind-active drugs, ibogaine penetrated the bias and survived to become only the second psychoactive drug to get the green light on the long road to FDA approval (MDMA was the first), and Mash heads the team conducting the FDA human safety trials.

Paradoxically, ibogaine's curative power seems to derive from its consciousness-altering properties. It's derived from the roots of *Tabernathe iboga*, a shrub native to equatorial Africa, where tribes have long used it in small doses to remain alert while hunting, and in larger amounts during sacred rituals. Since the 1960s, addicts have found that using ibogaine causes them to lose their craving for the drugs they were addicted to, and does this *without* any withdrawal symptoms.

How it works has led Mash to label it "a chemical bar mitzvah" because that's pretty much how it was used in African tribal cultures — as a rite of passage. "It's a psychoactive drug, but not a hallucinogen like LSD," she explains. "It puts you into a 36-hour waking dream state. During this altered state of consciousness, you relive your childhood experiences, get to the root of your addictions." In Africa, this was done as a clearing of the old, to make way for adulthood, and therefore acted as a preventive: get rid of your childhood baggage so you don't end up in adulthood with emotional dysfunction that could lead to many unhealthy situations, including addiction. Now, says Mash, it can be used to reprogram an addict's life. Those on ibogaine report that they are detached from childhood recollection, but are reexamining it, coming to grips with it, perhaps understanding it for the first time. All neuroses are potentially solvable this way. Mash and her team always keep in mind that "drug addiction is an illness of the spirit, and if you're going to cure it, you have to do so at that level."

On ibogaine, one may confront experiences long ago swept under the emotional carpet. Scientists have been startled to see that ibogaine cures the anxiety of decoupling from a long-term habit, prevents withdrawal symptoms, and relieves — although not completely eliminates — cravings. Follow-up doses weeks, months, or years after the initial treatment may be necessary for some patients.

Mash began the human safety trials in 1994. So far, the only side effects reported are slight nausea and imbalance at the treatment's beginning, and those can be alleviated. In monkey studies Mash found no brain toxicity. "Toxicity showed up only in a study at Johns Hopkins University and it was only toxic in near-lethal high doses."

Mash and her team are fighting an uphill battle for funding, despite their FDA approval for human safety trials, and attribute some of that to the negative bias that has evolved surrounding the use of psychoactive drugs because of recreational uses and abuses of substances like LSD. They believe it's a mistake to label psychoactive drugs as bad because they're mind-active, and hope that ibogaine will change some misperceptions and open the door to research with psychoactive drugs.

"Treating drug dependence with a *drug* is still considered ironic," say Mash. "So is the fact that the first FDA safety trials take place in Miami, the premiere transit point for cocaine in this country."

As part of her work testing ibogaine on addicts, Dr. Deborah Mash has become the Director of Research at Healing Visions Institute for Addiction Recovery. In this capacity, Mash studies addicts undergoing treatment with ibogaine at an offshore clinic, and incorporates this data into her overall quest for a cure.

Those who've been treated with ibogaine say that it's the equivalent of thirty years on a therapist's couch, and Mash agrees.

Dr. Deborah Mash's journey in science has been almost as long. Born in Chicago on September 30, 1952, Mash moved to Hollywood, Florida in 1956 where she grew up. At South Broward High, teachers fast-tracked her in math and science when she showed both interest and tremendous talent. A competitive kid, she won science fairs with her biochemistry projects, and as a senior in high school, she "discovered brain science while studying psychology." She knew then, she says, that it would be her life's work.

"I briefly toyed with being a medical doctor," she recalls. "But I wanted to devote 100 percent of my life to research."

Mash has never fit the stereotype of the stuffy scientist who's quiet, prim and unaware of life outside the lab. Far from it. In college, in the '70s at Florida State University, where she received her B.A. in Psychobiology, she looked like Cher did back then, with waist-length black curls, an exotic aura, and eye-catching, funky leather outfits. Mash spoke out against the Vietnam War and whatever other social causes stirred her passions. Her husband, Joe Geller, is an attorney and has long been the chair of Miami-Dade County's Democratic Party. At his FSU law school graduation years ago, he blurted out an impromptu plea to stop the death penalty while on stage receiving his diploma. They were — and still are — quite the couple.

I first met both of them — nearly 25 years ago — when I was an undergraduate at FSU and Mash was doing graduate work, and it has been fascinating to chronicle her work for *Omni* magazine, *The Miami Herald* and other publications throughout the 1990s.

Mash received her Ph.D. in Pharmacology at the University of Miami in 1984, and then had a two-year fellowship with Harvard Medical School at Beth Israel Hospital in Massachusetts. In 1986, she joined the University of Miami as a neuroscientist and professor. She has also remained politically active and from 1988 to 1998 served on the North Bay Village City Commission, in the Biscayne Bay island town off Miami Beach that she and her husband call home. Mash is also the Secretary of the Health Council of South Florida. All of this while frequently traveling the globe to meet with other scientists, lecture, and present her research at conferences and meetings where she is in constant demand.

Her work, she says, is "like reading chapters of a very good detective story." She shies away from the term "workaholic." Instead, she likes to say that "science is a way of life. You don't walk away from this." Her life is primarily consumed by her scientific crusade. "Intellectually, I never grow weary of it. I love the discovery. Every day I'm faced with something new. I learn every day."

Now, her main crusade is to understand, prevent and treat drug and alcohol addiction, both scientifically and sociologically. "I pore over research at home, I design experiments in the car on the way to the lab. To combat abuse, we have to understand brain changes and dependency. Then we can design specific therapeutic intervention. When we understand craving, we can know how to block it. We want to stop the progression, to keep people off drugs and alcohol. We all pay, and it's a hefty price tag: just look at the crack babies."

While Dr. Deborah Mash plays the role of internationally prominent neuroscientist, she has also extensively studied metaphysics, shamanism and spirituality — the new combination discipline she termed neuroshamanism — so that she can take a total approach to understanding the brain and human consciousness. Our conversations in these areas began in 1992 and continue today. Those presented here took place in the fall of 1995 and the winter of 1999.

❧

How would you describe your mission?

It's something deeply personal, and it's something very silent. And there's something very sacred and close to me that drives me. It's something that I hope to see come to fruition in my lifetime. And simply stated, it's just a mission to learn something fundamental that either has an impact directly, or somewhere down the road, to alleviate human suffering. And that arena for human suffering is something that's very fundamental because it goes to the roots of basic behavior, and that is that it deals with the brain, the central nervous system, and the phenomenology of the soul — the way it interacts with the array of neural architecture that we call the central nervous system.

When did you realize that this was what you were going to dedicate your life to?

I knew early on that my pull was in the direction of science. At the same time that I was grounded in math and physics and biology, I always had a phenomenological link to something a little more macroscopic than the nuts and bolts of the sciences. When I decided I wanted to go into neuroscience, the discipline was called psychobiology. I actually started out thinking I wanted to go into psychopharmacology or psychophysics because they really didn't have neuroscience as a discipline until some years later when I got closer to my graduate training. I knew I was going to do a mindscape type of discipline starting in my last year of high school.

It's so bizarre to think that neuroscience has only been called that for a little over two decades. It's so obvious that it should've been called that from the beginning. Instead brain science was lumped in with psychopharmacology, a term that quite literally means how drugs effect the psyche. It was drug-oriented instead of the study of the brain and the central nervous system.

> *Right. And this showed how scientists really knew very little about the brain and behavior. Psychopharmacology is how drugs affect behavior, and that was one of the main tools for getting to define consciousness.*

How was neuroscience born?

> *It came out of two things: one, the recognition that this is the last frontier of human biology, and two, that the time was right, historically speaking. What we had was studies of the mind — brain science — although brain, as a discipline, goes back over one hundred years. We've had neurology, neuroanatomy, and people who were actually looking at the brain and describing neurons, which are the basic building blocks of the brain. That's about where it stood. Then that fell away, and we went more into philosophy, then into psychology. When we began to design ways to measure behavior, then it began to move in a way that became really a science. But there was this dualism: there's the psychology movement of the ghost in the machine, and there's the reductionists who looked to explain everything with a single neuron or DNA molecule that encodes everything about human behavior.*

How do you explain the difference between neurology and neuroscience?

> *Neurology is focused on the study of diseases of the brain. Neurology gives us a window into explaining brain function. The interesting thing about neuroscience is that it's a little bit of all disciplines. And that makes sense. If you're going to try to understand behavior, you've got to come at it with everything you've got: chemistry, anatomy, physiology, pharmacology, molecular biology, and genetics.*

So, you're studying the fundamental basis of the brain and the central nervous system in general, as opposed to from the point of view of disease or malfunction.

> *Right. You're laying the fundamental groundwork of what gives rise to consciousness: How do we perceive color? How do we remember a loved one's face? From where in the brain does language arise?*

In the study of consciousness, we have a point where the study of ancient mysticism and science are overlapping. Scientists, even the most skeptical, are saying, "Hey, wait a minute, this is beginning to look like what the mystics used to talk about." What's your take on that?

> *I think that scientists aren't all that enlightened yet in terms of being able to have a language where they can begin to see a fundamental overlap with much of the mystical traditions and the spiritual truths. They're just not there yet because they want to reduce it all down to...*

What they can measure in a lab.

> *Exactly. They want to take it apart to the specifics of the nervous system where they can measure an input/output arrangement. In the process of doing that, they lose out on the bigger picture.*

They're willing to believe there's a soul when it shows up in a blood test.

> *Probably right. I think that's probably the best way to say it. Now, even so, there are plenty of historical accounts of neurobiologists or neuroscientists who think of life in a way that can be described by physical laws of chemistry and hard science, but the constant tension is that they want to be able to describe it, but they haven't evolved the language (beyond the scientific), so what do you do? You reduce it. How do you describe human*

behavior? You reduce it to a cell membrane, an expression of a neurotransmitter phenotype. In the process of reducing it, they still can't explain it. Then, we add on human emotion, because every aspect of human behavior is colored by the emotion of human existence. And that to me is encoded in the DNA. That goes back to the first sea slug that came out of the primordial soup. That will and desire to live, to survive, to create, to procreate.

As someone who is scientist, but also as someone who views spirituality as an important part of her life, how would you define spirituality?

For me, there's no distinction between the two. I'm someone who would go up against those who would say, "If you can't prove it, it doesn't exist." For me, it's the wonderment of looking at a brain. From having the experience of actually being able to hold brain tissue in my hands and to study it, to see the diversity and to look at the life of the human being and then see it reflected in the architecture of a brain, there's no question that there's some type of emergent reality that is manifested in the central nervous system. Why evolve a central nervous system? Why have this ability to perceive and express a view of reality and have all of the free will that this gives us — because this is virtually limitless — so why evolve a complex brain, why go to all this trouble?

If we weren't capable of some pretty extraordinary things.

Correct.

Do you see spirituality as the question mark, the mystery behind all things?

To me, spirituality is, well, the fundamental truths about why we're here and what is humankind's mission and why have we evolved all of these magnificent capacities to reflect upon the

373

universe. I've been very influenced by Teilhard de Chardin and his writings. He studied evolution and was there when they found the "Peking Man" right at the time when the Catholic Church was censoring the idea that indeed we evolved from prehistoric man, and here was this wonderful mystic, who was also a Jesuit priest and a scientist. And history puts him right at the right place and the right time, because he was right there, able to challenge the church and say, "Wait, there's no conflict here. We do evolve from primitive man; it's a fact. And here I am at the site in China when they find Peking Man, one of the main missing links." And he's able to look at evolution and to say, "Well, this is a plan. We are all rising to a level where we can look back on where we came from. We are the manifestation of the creative principle in the universe and we are returning back to that source." That makes sense to me. Spirituality is something else. Spirituality is how we perceive it. It's the serotonin, the serotonergic link, or peptide probably coming from the pineal gland and we're just beginning to understand it. I'm certain that when one goes into very deep meditative and mystical states that there's a neurobiological correlation to that. I don't think we understand yet what neurochemical systems are activated, but when you talk about the alignment of the chakras and directing of energies and healing energies that can be distributed to different parts of the body, we're activating systems in the brain and the immune system, the spinal chord, and going right out to the peripheral nervous system. That interaction is very much an interplay between the universe that's manifest as well as the universe that's invisible.

There are a lot of things that are lumped under the heading of spirituality that ten years from now may be considered science. When you talk about chakras, people may say, "Oh, that's that spiritual stuff." No, we're talking about energy. We're talking about what's in the realm of hard science, and when it's demystified, it will one day be considered one of the sciences just like other things that used to be considered myth or religion. Like the sky. That wasn't always considered a science, that was the thunder god. Then a couple of hundred years later it's astronomy, it's cosmology, it's hard science.

No doubt.

One day, these things that are now under the umbrella of spirituality will be absorbed by other, scientific disciplines.

I think that's correct. One of the interesting things about the alternative medicine movement is that those who are healers and who are well-grounded in medical science, who are a bit more open-minded, can go back and look at history, and look at things that have been written in medical treatises that are thousands of years old — if you go back to the Vedas and the Upanishads — and if you think about these things what you realize is that although they didn't have our scientific terminology, they were describing phenomena that were grounded in physical science. And whether we recognize that or not depends upon how open-minded we are.

Everything is grounded in physical science, but until we can find a way to measure and test and so-called "prove" it, we lump it under something else.

We can't take a picture of the heart chakra.

And there was a time when we couldn't take an X-ray, so people could say that that didn't exist then either!

Correct. We can't take a picture of the heart chakra, but anyone who has stumbled upon a situation that's very threatening, where their heart is racing and when all their stress hormones are acting on the heart muscle to make it beat very quickly...and the links between the central nervous system and the heart...you understand that there's energy, there are actual relays of neural inputs that go from brain to heart that can make someone die suddenly. That's an energy field that's putting chaos into the system. Well, in the same way, if you meditate and you use certain techniques to re-route neural signals, you can change distress and dysfunction in an organ. Now, is that a spiritual center that's linked to the heart? Well, in religious traditions, in Christianity, they talk about the "sacred heart." They show pictures of icons and religious symbols of ancient mystics with beams of light coming from their heart. And when one feels good — and everyone's had this experience — they know they can actually feel sensory inputs within their heart. You're filled with love in your heart. You suffer from a broken heart. We describe these things. There must be a pathway, an energy flow.

And, eventually, we'll figure out how to measure it.

The same thing with your gut. If you look at the lower base of the spine, at the chakra that controls the organs that sustain life in terms of bringing nutrients into the body, that is a center where there can be disease or there can be healing energy. No, we don't know how to measure it. But, when you think about diseases, and how diseases affect our bodies, you see the impact of mind and behavior. And since mind and behavior interlaces with our concept of spirit, you're born with a collective consciousness that's encoded in every single cell in your body. So, there is a continuity to life at that level.

You coined the term "neuroshamanism" to describe the meeting of modern neuroscience with ancient or traditional mysticism and shamanism, and this includes exploring the use of herbs, botanicals and other natural substances and methods in healing. Let's talk about that.

A shaman is an individual who lives according to the natural laws of life — physical life and all the planes of existence above and beyond it. A shaman recognizes that the material universe is a school ground of all the dimensions of what IS. His or her frame of intellectual reference is a soul in a physical body, rather than a mind/body with a soul. And this way of living life creates a combination of freedom and responsibility that is a healing consciousness. Modern neuroscience has roots deep in the history of Western biology, medicine and philosophy, going as far back as ancient Egypt. The Egyptian works were amalgams of mysticism, superstitions and elaborate speculations. They considered the heart to be the most important organ, thought of it as the seat of intellect and wisdom, and the center of intellectual activity. Early descriptions of their work are cool and empirical, similar in tone to modern neuroscience. The attempt to bring back an interest in shamanic medicine to mainstream science, to study it as it relates to understanding behavioral states will no doubt at first be viewed as new age mumbo jumbo, just like our modern reconciliation of the ancient Egyptian scientists struggles with providing terminology and descriptors. But, we need to expand neuroscience. Modern neuroscience is a hybrid derivative science that emerges from the coupling of many disciplines, including behavioral science, genetics, immunology, anatomy, physiology, and others. And it achieves its role as an integrative discipline with one exception: Where it fails is in that neuroscience really struggles with its attempt to integrate behavioral science, which is by its very nature highly empirical and phenomenological. It implicitly views behavioral studies as pseudoscientific — far outside the range of mapping the neural topography of cells, chemicals and DNA coding.

The closest crossover point is psychoneuroimmunology — the study of the interactions among the immune, nervous and endocrine system, or what is called mind/body medicine. This includes the concept of behavioral immunity, or mind and immunity, how conscious thoughts can affect response to disease or play any number of roles in health.

So, modern science is inching towards the province of the shaman, even though mainstream scientists would probably rather use other labels for that.

And that's where this new term — neuroshamanism — comes in. The neuroshaman will further this type of integrational study to address complex behavioral states in humans. The neural mechanisms will begin to be understood, including the role of hormones and behavior and the role of sleep architecture in disease prevention. Consciousness, dreaming, sleep state, altered states, memory at a genomic level — all will be linked with a more humanistic view of the individual as part of the larger human family. An important part of the new neuroshamanism will be the study of indigenous peoples medicine and plants as a way to identify new products from the study of ethnobotany.

And using many of them in their natural state instead of synthesizing them as we do now with our plant-based pharmaceuticals. Already, nearly one-third of our over-the-counter and prescription drugs are derived from plants.

What will be a new addition here is the uncovering of the best kept secrets of the neuroactive plants — as a route to exploring novel brain chemicals that may unfold new, yet to be explored pathways to understand and describe for the first time the higher states of consciousness.

Progress is being made in neuroshamanism, especially as more people use alternative medicine and the pharmaceutical industry has had to finally come to terms with the shift. We now see mainstream drug companies putting out over-the-counter herbal products. And specialty pharmaceutical companies have been formed.

The neuroshamanistic approach is being used by the biotech firm Shaman Pharmaceuticals, which is based in the San Francisco Bay area. It's expected that health care economics in the 21st century will be a real driving force that takes this neuroshamanistic approach away from the purely mystical and into the practical. The integration of ancient and modern has already been legitimized by the formation of the Office of Alternative Medicine at the National Institutes of Health to provide taxpayer dollars to fund these studies. The neuroshaman will take back to the laboratory information from so-called alternative healers to design studies as part of new research programs that will pave the way for a revolutionary change in the way we view ourselves as neurobiological organisms. This approach will foster the emerging sense voiced in recent decades, that we need to re-connect with fundamental aspects of spirituality, from physical healing to higher consciousness.

At the risk of being tomatoed and pelted with stones, other scientists have talked about and written about the link between mysticism or shamanism and science, including physicist Fred Alan Wolf, who wrote the book *The Eagle's Quest* about his experiences with shamans. This is the science of the altered brain. That's what neuroscience studies — the brain in all of its states. Why should one state be given any more or less credibility than another?

Yes. And that's what's behind my work with ibogaine. We're also looking into the relationship between sleep states like REM (Rapid Eye Movement) and Post Traumatic Stress Disorder, chemical addition, and basic behavior and personality. You know, when you go into sleep states, that's when we begin to cross the mirror between waking reality and spirit. We're right there on the edge, which is why sometimes with lucid dreaming you can begin to bring some of this (spiritual or metaphysical experience) back. That's one of the intriguing things about ibogaine, apart from how it works on chemical dependency — it's acting on that edge of consciousness. Let's talk about detox mechanisms in the brain. In the course of human evolution, we've evolved what are called cytochromes, cytochrome P-450's...

Which is not a car. This doesn't come with a leather interior (we laugh).

Sounds like a car (she laughs), but most of these are found in our liver. Our liver is our detox system. And it detoxes literally everything. Some of these enzymes that are in our liver are always turned on. And some of these are induced. So,

379

nicotine, for example, induces a certain family of P-450s. So does alcohol.

To detox what you've just put in your body, in this case nicotine or alcohol.

Correct. It's our body's way of protecting us from internal and external toxins. Well, it turns out that not only are these enzymes in our liver, but our brain has a whole second set of them that are very poorly understood.

And the brain isn't a place where a toxin goes to get flushed out like the liver, so what are these enzymes doing in the brain? Are they there to signal somehow, in an administrative capacity as opposed to hands-on?

What they're doing in the brain is anybody's guess, but this goes back to the mind-body dichotomy, that there's mind and there's body. Well, it seems as if, biologically speaking, there is a barrier. There's an immune barrier, which we now understand can be somewhat leaky (we laugh), *because the brain/mind controls the immune system and vice versa. Now, it turns out that the brain has its own liver.*

Wow.

We have detox mechanisms upstairs (she's pointing to her head). *So, you can literally have a detox that's directed to the mind. So, these enzymes are in the brain. It's not understood how they express over the course of development, how they change with age, what their normal function is. What it looks like is that the reason we have evolved P-450s* (in the liver and elsewhere) *was as man came up and started to eat plants, and there are a lot of toxins in plants, man evolved these P-450s to protect us against plant toxins. At the same time, we have certain ones that are turned on in the brain to protect us. Different classes of brain chemicals are regulated by these P-*

450s, too, so you can spin off abnormal molecules — metabolic members of a pathway that these P-450s would get rid of. If, for some reason, you don't have these P-450s operating correctly, you could spin off some very strange molecules, and it could be these abnormal chemicals could lead to a Parkinson's Disease, for example. Food, environment, stress, many things interact with brain chemistry. And we believe that some of these P-450s are always turned on and some are induced.

Induced when something shows up and triggers the need for clean up.

Correct.

Now, if someone is defective in clean up, then they could end up with all kinds of problems, conditions or diseases, all kinds of brain-related problems.

Right. Everything, including the basics of personality, could also be wired up in terms of this.

Personality is created based upon what kind of brain chemicals we've got, what they're doing right, what they're doing wrong.

That's right. I think where the neuroscientific community has fallen short is that we fail to see the brain as part of an ecosystem. Food, environment, everything affects it.

The brain isn't in a vacuum, so of course what's going on in your brain has to be affected by what you eat, by your environment, as well as your body's internal environment.

Exactly. The other thing is that when you think of neurode-velopment and brain chemistry, I think it's pretty clear that from in utero until puberty, the biology of the organism is the driving force. When you make that transition from puberty into adulthood, you switch from the internal biology-driven system to a more externally driven system.

Why?

> *It's probably the natural course of human development. That's why mental illness emerges right around that time, why stress triggers abnormal brain chemistry.*

So, it's not just the hormonal changes in the body at puberty and onward. It's your body changing from A to Z, not just hormonally.

> *Yes. And I think that's why primitive societies marked that as probably the most important transition, why we have Confirmation, Bar Mitzvah and other rites of passage. Because that is the significant life event. And if we don't make that transition well, if we don't take our children through that transition, then we're guaranteeing that we lock in a state of pathology in the organism, ranging from anti-social behavior, to the gang mentality, and all the way to a serious mental illness.*

It's interesting that your work with ibogaine gets tied into this because it was originally used as part of a rite of passage, among other things, in West African tribes. People would take it, clear up their childhood stuff as a result of the psychological things that ibogaine would prompt them to recall and go through in a waking dream-like state, and clear out their old baggage. It was like saying, "All right, I'm moving on with a clean slate as an adult." So, here we have the root of a shrub that was instrumental in detoxing the body from its first 12, 13 or 14 years worth of stuff and then allowing it to go on with a clean state. It wasn't just a ritual like you might have in other cultures where you have a ceremony or a party, this was something that actually interacted with the body biologically, emotionally and psychologically. We don't have anything like that in so-called modern society.

> *No, no we don't.*

The closest thing we have is when teenagers take it upon themselves to experiment with drugs because they're looking for some mind-expanding experience, to escape from whatever is haunting them from their childhood. So, they're following, even though they don't know it, a road that's been there since time began. In that African society this was done consciously and purposely with guidance, not abuse (we both say abuse at the same time). And Western kids are now in a sense doing this ritual...

Trying to re-create it.

Trying to re-create this ritual and they don't even know that that's what they're instinctively doing. But, it's not with guidance, and it is abused. Nobody is carrying them through the transition, so they're grasping at straws.

Right.

They do it with drugs, sex, alcohol, anything that can help them spiritually and emotionally feel better.

Right.

And they can't explain it, so they can't come out and say, "Mom, I need a spiritual quick fix."

Right. "I need a spiritual wake-up call." And society gives them nothing. We're so bankrupt as a community. We've lost it. From organized religion on down. And certainly modern technology and science offers no solution for this. We turn up a cold palm to shake hands with youth as they come forward into adulthood.

They look to find it for themselves out of some kind of primeval drive.

Yes.

And they feel they're not getting the support they need and want at home, so they get it from their friends. And a pathology of that is getting it from a gang.

> *And, of course, it also depends on the drug. If you are using crack cocaine, which hits a certain neurochemical substrate, you're going to turn on the aggression, the power, the need for self-esteem — that's going to all be tied to that type of euphoria. If you take a hallucinogen, like mushrooms or LSD, like the 60s generation did, you go more towards a Prozac state...*

A "let's get happy" reaction.

> *Yeah. One triggers the dopamine, the other the seratonin. Our modern day "shamans," the psychiatrists, are over-prescribing Prozac or other antidepressants.*

Which just numbs everybody out.

> *Right, it numbs everybody out. So, we take our seriously mentally ill and sedate them with drugs like Haldol. We take our youth, who are lost and seeking to fill a spiritual void, and we numb them out by giving them Prozac. And this links into the whole pharmaceutical industry in the United States, and the spiraling up of the health care costs in our country. This is a hard one for me because obviously, as a neuropharmacologist, I support drug development, and I really do believe in the old axiom, "Better living through chemistry," so I know that there have been plenty of excellent medications that have been developed and the development costs have come entirely through the pharmaceutical industry. But, at the same time, American people are "paying" a lot for pharmaceuticals.*

They're also paying a lot to be doped up, and like Stepford people, they're wandering around aimlessly, with nothing bothering them anymore, rather than the medical community attacking the real problems these people are trying to deal with.

> *I think that's right. What's happened is about health care*

costs. *Our insurance industry won't pay, and wants to provide fewer services for lower fees. So, everyone is going to get less health care. And certainly, less mental health care, which in some ways we require most. Good mental health could stave off disease because we know that many of our illnesses are either stress and/or diet, and/or environmentally related. And yet, we continue to put a blind eye up to that, with no plan for how this is going to affect us in the future.*

Everyone's ignoring the giant elephant in the living room.

Exactly, exactly. And unfortunately, Science, with a capital "S", is much to blame for that because we know better than anyone, for example, that genes and environment go together, that the nervous system is not immune from toxins in the environment, everything from lead in the paint that children chip off the wall to pesticides in the food.

Doesn't this all get down to the fact that Science, with a capital "S" is a part of the System, with a capital "S", and so even though scientists may say privately, "We should be doing XYZ," they also know that the System is not set up to support that. That they have to deal with the government, and the funding, and they're wary of "rocking the boat."

Absolutely. It's fear. It's absolutely driven by the scientists' fear of losing their ability to do science.

Fear and economics.

Fear and economics drive it. And it's the new priesthood. With the Age of Enlightenment came the new priesthood and that new priesthood is Science and Technology. And so we have a consumer movement in America saying, "We want something more. We are now skeptical. We bought into this and we believed everything you told us. You were going to cure cancer — you have not. You were going to cure mental illness — you

385

have not. You were going to give us gene transfer — you have not. And we continue to see generations of youth being lost more and more to disease of the soul, to society-based illnesses from the toxic pollutants in the environment to the mental pollution in the environment. And you give us no road map, no strategy. And perhaps that explains the backlash and the turn to alternative medicine and spirituality.

In time, and probably not a long time, there will be a huge paradigm shift.

There has to be. It is the structure of scientific revolutions that when we become completely polarized there is a fundamental shake-up that allows us to go to the next level.

And we're bridging that right now.

And it's my belief that there are enough of us in the scientific movement who understand the complex phenomenology of the biological system but recognize at the same time that there may be other forces that we don't have descriptors for yet, that we don't have the terminology for, that we don't even begin to understand, that only the greatest of the great — like an Albert Einstein or a Linus Pauling — could begin to articulate. And from that fundamental paradigm shift there will be a new scientific movement that will come, that will begin to link the spiritual to the material, to help to guide this synthesis of the biological system with spiritual forces on the planet. I can only hope and pray that it happens quickly. Because I fear for the increased brain pathology that I see, the mental pathology, the brain-based illnesses that seem to be increasing for all age groups.

We were talking about that once before. Why are all these damaged people running around today in more numbers today than ever before? Not just the people who are physically ill, but the people who are killing their own children, abusing their spouses, kidnapping kids and killing them, the Jeffrey Dahmers who are eating the neighbors.

386

There just seems to be more of it. Every day there's a news report. Every day. Some horrible thing perpetrated by someone sick. And those are just the ones we know about. For every one we know about, how many don't we know about? Ten, twenty, a thousand?

Right.

And these aren't people who are just having a bad day (we laugh). It used to be that we'd hear about a sniper who stood on the tower in Texas, or Charles Manson, or Ted Bundy. These people were unique in that very rarely did someone like that pop up. Now, it's all the time. They're everywhere, they're everywhere. Even Charles Manson has noticed this. I read not long ago that he said in an interview — and I'm paraphrasing here — "These days, everybody's crazy. I remember a time when it *meant* something to be crazy!"

I think it's a kind of urban mania, and I think when you've perpetuated it along generations — generations of parent neglect, generations of sexual abuse, generations of drug and alcohol abuse — you can spend the rest of your life and millions of the taxpayers' dollars on finding which genes confer risk, but in actuality it's the environmental setting that's driving the emergent psychopathology.

And what about the psychopathology outside the urban environment? The abuse that goes on in "America's Heartland," in the suburbs, in rural areas? Where they're just as warped as people in urban areas. This isn't an urban phenomena of "too many rats in too small a space." This is all across the board.

I agree with that. I don't think it has to be just urban. I think its expression will be more pronounced as you come into the densely populated urban areas.

The pathology can happen anywhere. All it takes is a lousy environment of any kind.

> *It can. It comes from not being an integrated whole, from not understanding the mind-body-spirit.*

The people perpetrating this stuff felt empty, incomplete, power-less, worthless, a whole host of other things, you name it, and they went and abused their children, many of whom went on to do the same thing to theirs, and it went on and on from generation to generation.

> *Absolutely. They shame their children. It's a pattern of shame, a pattern of neglect, and in its worst manifestation it's a pattern of physical and sexual abuse. So it's a continuum. And these young people who are carrying it forward succumb to drug abuse and alcoholism. We see in our society that more and more people are self-medicating to numb themselves with the alcohol or drugs, although we know that there is a pretty strong genetic predisposition to that now. That's one of the areas where genes interplay with the environment. Depression, too. And then there are the other substance-abusing individuals who are, again, self-medicating because they are trying to fill a void. And it's interesting because the 12-step movement, which says, "Give it up to a higher power," is the one area in which modern addiction scientists say, "Yeah, we're going to buy into that behavioral approach, and say it's okay because it's been grounded, and it goes back many, many years, and there's some efficacy to it. Can't really put our finger on what it is, of course. And since society sanctions it, we're gonna use it." The Alcoholics Anonymous and other 12-step programs are a spirituality movement. And it works. Nobody's even begun to look at spirituality in treating serious mental illness. We know it works with cancer. We have so much — beyond medical anecdotes — for so-called "miracle cures" in cancer.*

Which is just the body healing itself.

> *Right. It's the body healing itself. There's the "body positive" movement for AIDS (patients.) We can point to the AIDS epidemic and say, "Has anything revolutionary come out of it's*

pain and suffering?" Now, in the face of one of the most hideous illnesses that has ever confronted mankind, here we have something that is a recognition that the organism is mind-body-spirit, and, yes, you can control a disease within you by the way you view yourself.

Which may account for many of the long-term survivors.

Correct. We're always going to be exposed to viruses, and what really concerns me now is what's being unleashed by digging up the rainforests. They have microbiological outposts on the edge of the rainforests, looking for bad viral organisms. As they tear up the rainforests and unearth all that stuff that has been buried for thousands and tens of thousands of yeas, viruses and bacteria will come into the air, the food chain, the drinking water.

And they're worried about viruses and bacteria being unleashed.

Yes. Before, it would be regionally isolated, but with today's transportation, you just get on a plane and move it across an ocean or continent.

And take the virus across the globe in 12 hours.

That's correct. And we don't have the antibiotics or treatments. The scary thing is that modern medicine, again, has given us a zinger because we're over-prescribed antibiotics to the point now where most of our antibiotics are not going to be effective. We have resistant organisms.

Also, we have bacteria and viruses leaving the neighborhood. I believe that the way the planet was set up, if you had something yucky "in the neighborhood," you also had it's antidote in the neighborhood. So, if you have a virus in a rainforest, probably the thing that cures it would be found not too far from there.

Sure. Yes.

Otherwise, we would have all been dead millions of years ago. And now we can transport viruses and God knows what else all over the planet, and we have no idea how to prevent, fix or cure this stuff. And if we would look at its origin, it's cure is probably a few blocks away.

Yeah, and I think that the problem is — and America is probably the worst offender — we charge into technospace without looking backwards to see where we've been. And we fail to pick up the clues along the path. We refuse, in fact, to do it. We think we can just start anew, when in fact, as you say, there are medicines in nature, and information from indigenous peoples, healers, the shamans, in and around the rainforests.

They certainly managed to live for thousands of years without modern technology.

They survived, exactly.

So, obviously there's plenty in their environment that's used medicinally.

Exactly. They know. And they have a verbal record of all this that should be archived and studied and written about by scientists, and yet we think that we can do it [heal] better, so we have a hubris that may cost us. That may cost us big. That's one of the benefits of the spiritual movement, too, that there's a sense now to look backwards and to honor native peoples and ask for their wisdom and their guidance, and help with what we've lost sight of as a result of our exponential technological speed-up on the planet.

And spirituality is nothing more than a system or a belief by which you acknowledge the fact that all of nature is interactive, and that extends beyond the planet and includes the cosmos. It's intangible: We can't see it, touch it, taste it, hence the word "spirit." Yet, there is always tangible evidence of it. We forget that. Yet, when somebody puts a fishtank in their living room, they're aware of it and respect it, they know that the fish are interacting with the water, and the algae that's growing on the gravel is affected by the condition of the water. We don't have any trouble accepting the concept of an interactive system when we see it in our fishtank. Why do we not want to believe it when we see it in the world at large?

Right. And I think that what makes us spiritual human beings is not just the knowledge of the interactive system, but stepping back and having the humility to honor the system.

To let it do it's thing.

Yes.

To realize that it gets back to all those cliches: "Don't fight Mother Nature," "Go with the flow." These aren't just oft-repeated words, they actually mean something.

It's old wisdom. It's the wisdom that preserves us. As a genus, as a species, as a family, as a race, as a nation, as a group of nations, as a planet.

If you look individually at different species of animals and see how they live with nature, you realize that from them we can learn when there's a time to go against the grain, and that there's a time when you go with the flow. When the bear hibernates in the winter, he's going with the flow. He's discovered that it's beneficial to him at that point to not fight the cold, but to go with the flow.

And the bear myths that go with that are deeply spiritual, because the time of hibernation is the time of introspection. And we don't sanction a time of hibernation in modern society.

Oh, no, we're too busy for that. We have to make use of every moment.

*We're verrrrry busy. So, we don't teach children the value of
down time. Of healing time. Of introspection.*

What else are you learning about the links between mysticism and
neuroscience? About the soul or spirit and the corresponding things
that go on in the brain and the rest of the body?

*It's very likely that there's a whole other tier of molecules in
the brain that are acted upon by the cytochrome systems. Two of
these classes of molecules that have gotten some interest lately are
tryptamines and the betacarbolines. The betacarbolines are
related to [the mind-active plant used by shamans] ayahuasca
and ibogaine. Ibogaine has a betacarboline "backbone," the
back of the molecule is betacarboline-like. Well, it turns out that
there are endogenous betacarbolines in our brain.
Dimethyltryptamine (DMT) is one of the active ingredients,
one of the primary psychedelic ingredients in the ayahuasca.
And we manufacture tryptamines in our own brain, too. So, it's
very likely that we are spinning off endogenously these molecules
that are very much involved in our ability to alter our state of
perception.*

Without taking any drugs or substances.

Without taking any exogenous [out of the body] substances.

So, we just have to figure out what triggers our body to make it
naturally. Do they have any clue?

*I think that right now we don't really have a clue. It's been
so poorly described by scientists thus far.*

Especially if it's a spiritual experience that triggers it, you'd have to
induce and measure it in a lab.

*The best example is the beta-endorphin example. We know
that when a mother gives birth, her body releases endorphins.*

That's part of the "afterglow" of birth. In the case of a Near Death Experience, there's some evidence that glutamate, which is a primary exitatory neurotransmitter, is released in a massive gush and acts on a certain chemical pathway in the brain that PCP (angel dust) also acts on, that the PCP receptor is associated with. So, that chemical system is thought to be associated with the Near Death Experience. Ibogaine has some similarities to the Near Death Experience, and it may be that it's due to the activation of glutamate.

The life review portion of the ibogaine experience is similar to the Near Death Experience's standard "Life Review."

Right. That flashing of your life. Those are some examples of what we're able to begin to discern about how the system is set up. I think that the bio-feedback technology, and what is learned from studying deep relaxation and sound are important. And sound will be even more important in the future — we know so little about the interaction between brain states and sound activation of the two brain hemispheres.

And the healing properties of sound is becoming a huge area of research.

The neurochemical correlates of that can give us bio-markers that can be mapped and measured. This is one type of experiment that I visualize as the scientific crossing over — the ability to formulate an experimental paradigm based on something that we can't necessarily measure, but we'll have a relevant bio-marker for the outcome. What this means is that if you've activated a certain neurochemical pathway in the brain, are there spillovers? And there usually are. There are spillovers into the bloodstream, so you can measure things in plasma. And there are spillovers into urine.

So, when you discuss bio-markers, you mean "a way to know that this has happened," a method to gather evidence of the event via blood, urine and other substances that play the role of bio-markers.

Right.

So, we can measure in urine or blood the level of brain chemicals to see what has happened after any number of different kinds of experiences.

And in addition to having blood and urine as markers, we can also look at immune system stimulation to see CD-4 counts going up, to see your lymphocyte markers increase under certain types of treatments with sound or light or other types of healing. Another example would be the ability to use functional MRI, and here's where I think it's really going to go: functional MRI mapping is allowing us to have a window into brain function that we never anticipated before. You're actually able to see very discreet regions of the brain activated and can look at it before and after a particular experience. So, we'll be able to look at people who have had deep spiritual experiences — before and after — or who have had meditative altered states.

And take a peak at it in the brain through an MRI.

And take a peak at the brain through an MRI scan (she snaps her fingers).

Are they doing that now?

No, but it's coming.

By scanning the brain of a patient or of someone during research, an MRI gives us a peek at the brain in action, and can quite literally show us so much new information or validate what we surmised before.

When you start asking questions about differences between male and female brains, the MRI shows us that a woman at rest [naturally] activates her brain's frontal lobes, which is the executive problem solving part of the brain. When a man is at rest he [naturally] activates the limbic portion, which controls fright, flight, rage and sexuality. So, women are always ready to solve problems, and men are always ready to procreate.

Or fight, or run away.

Or kill.

Which are exactly things women complain about: "He's afraid of emotional attachment," "He's running away," "He picks arguments," or "He wants to sleep with every woman he sees." And men complain about what we do naturally: "Why does she analyze everything all the time?" "Why does she always want to discuss our relationship?" because our brains are different.

And the MRI "showed" us what we "knew" already (we laugh).

It scientifically validated millions of years of anecdotal experience.

Right! (we laugh). One of the areas that is starting to open up, so that people begin to think about how energy flows along channels in the nervous system, has to do with acupuncture. So, here the East gives us an idea for a topographic map where you can actually stimulate and activate a network array. The beauty of the brain is its plasticity. We are a learning organism. So much of our behavior and so much of our pathology is learned behavior. Can we use energy technologies to unlearn and to reprogram in a healing way? And I think the answer is yes.

There is incredible work going on regarding the effects of sound on the mind-body, and on healing.

I'm fascinated by the importance of sound. I've always thought that sound therapy could also be potentially very beneficial for schizophrenia, where you have an example of an illness where people aren't able to access both hemispheres of the brain — the left and the right — in synchronicity. The two parts aren't firing in an integrated way. There are blocks to electrical impulses that keep the information from being integrated, it keeps it segregated. So, can you use sound to activate the right hemisphere of the brain, the part of the brain that perceives music?

Vibrational medicine addresses the use of many energy systems besides sound, including light and smell.

Smell is extremely important — aromatheraphy. Light is an easy one because there you have an example of something that's very well accepted.

Light as the ultimate healer.

In terms of neurochemistry, light turns off melatonin production.

Babies who are born with jaundice are put under a blue light. That triggers a healing effect. It would also work with full-spectrum light, but you can't put the baby out on the beach for two days. Different colors trigger different parts of the body to produce chemicals, to heal and right itself. These are energy frequencies.

Also, electrical stimulation is being used when you have a severe bone fracture that won't heal. The same technology is being applied now to the possibility of reducing breast tumors. Those are two very concrete examples, with good scientific protocol, of taking an alternative approach in a healing way.

It's become mainstream to use that blue light on babies. Thirty years ago, before they discovered this in research, they had to treat newborn jaundice with very dangerous transfusions. And there will be many other things like this that we will be able to "prove," even though we may not understand yet why they work. A lot of these things are inherently so simple that people are at first reluctant to believe that something as simple as light, as sound, could heal. They're locked into thinking that healing only come from pills or high-tech equipment.

We are highly manipulated by our technology, and all under the guise that "Scientific Reality" is indeed the true reality. And, when you think about it, that statement itself underscores the absurdity of it. Not to take away the importance of all of the modern advances that we've had.

But we should have balance.

It is about balance. It has shifted us so far into one direction that we've lost sight of the basics: of faith, of spirit, of emotion, of instinct, of intuition.

Of plants, of sunlight.

And all because we haven't been able to adequately measure it: "If we don't have a barometer, it can't be fact." So, I think that what will happen is the consumers will drive the industry, as they always do, and recent surveys have demonstrated that the American public will spend equal amounts on alternative medicine as they do on mainstream medical practices. Since the consumers are asking for more alternative medicine, they probably will get more. Even though we may not yet have a way to measure something, we do have relevant bio-markers and health outcome measures. And I think the scientific community as it begins to adapt and as it begins to go back to thinking about the organism — the body — as a whole, not just its DNA, not just its receptors, not just its chemicals, but rather as a system, an integrated system, that we will begin to design studies that will have relevant outcome measures. And it will be that transition that will allow us to make causative statements about the effects of light and sound, for example, as specific healing modalities.

An example of this might be if you were to take a Chinese healer who can sense and direct his body's chi energy and his patients' body's chi energy, and draw blood from this healer, do a urinalysis, an MRI, whatever it takes to measure levels of everything from A to Z, and then measure all of these levels again while he's in a healing session. Then you could see what may be different in his levels. That would be the first step in how to measure this chi energy, by first measuring the effects of the energy — its bio-markers, its health outcome measures — as you term it.

Yeah, and the other thing, too, and this gets us into the realm of the role that faith plays in healing, is that "miracles" do happen, and whether or not it's...

We call it a miracle because we can't explain it.

Right, we call it a miracle because we can't explain it.

These people who've been doing Chinese healing energy for centuries, that's not a miracle to them, that's their medicine. It's not the same as an evangelist "faith healer" who nine times out of ten isn't real. This chi energy is real. It's the body's energy, and we are an electrical energy system, we already know that. How can one measure that except for by its bio-markers? It's not like we have a Geiger counter kind of device.

No, we don't, but we have Kirilian photography.

It's heat radiation. It measures the energy emanating from a living thing: a plant, a person, whatever.

That's right, it measures heat fluctuations.

In that case, at least they knew what kind of energy they were looking to measure, so they eventually came up with a device to do it. But in the case of chi energy, they can't figure out what kind of energy it is, so they can't figure out what kind of device to build. It's the body's energy, of course, but not necessarily the heat-generating kind. I suppose they could try to measure it with Kirilian photography and other methods that measure thermal energy, or they could try to measure it the way they would sound waves, or other vibrational sources. Let's measure it in every way we understand up to this point that energy works, and see what happens.

> *My guess is that it's going to be detected as an alteration in the electromagnetic field. The ability to have a device to measure that and to see energy transfer from the healer to the person being healed could possibly be done along those lines.*

So much of what we know and can measure now, we couldn't measure in the past. Like electromagnetic energy.

> *And it wasn't that long ago, actually.*

And when we discovered new things before, and eventually figured out how to measure them, it must've been as shocking to scientists as the concept of human energy is today. We have a tendency to feel in each generation that we already have all the knowledge in the world.

> *Right.*

And that everything we learn from now on will merely be expounding upon what we already have. We're very egocentric in that way.

> *Yeah, scientific hubris.*

Yeah, we always figure, "If it was really out there, why wouldn't somebody have found it by now?" (we laugh) Look how long it took to figure out that the world wasn't flat, or to recognize the electromagnetic field, or to discover penicillin. It's just that nobody got to it until they got to it. We didn't have television and radio until just within the last 100 years. It was another kind of wavelength that was out there that we previously didn't know about and hadn't measured yet. What will it take to measure human energy?

> *[To measure chi life force energy], you'd have to work with a bio-electrical engineer.*

It's time for a big discovery, isn't it? It feels like it's been awhile since we've had a huge, landmark discovery. We've been just doing damage control: trying to cure diseases, trying to stop the effects of pollution...we're "putting out fires." In terms of discovering new things, most of that has been astronomy, cosmology — the Hubble brings back pictures of something we never knew was there, or we discover this or that from another telescope, or something comes out of a Shuttle mission. But, in terms of something radically brand new, what have we come up with lately?

> *The most important thing has been finding the genes that are linked to diseases, and working towards the ability to use gene therapy for treatment. That stalled during the Reagan and Bush years, but it's also been stalled because it hasn't met the promise. Even in the simplest cases, like Duchene muscular dystrophy, where you should be able to transfer the defective muscle gene — it hasn't worked. We don't know enough about the regulation of genes yet to be able to use them for treatments.*

Again, a lot of this comes under the heading of damage control or learning how to manipulate the body or its systems. But, what have we "discovered" lately that's new? Not much. During the last century, we got used to discoveries coming quickly on the heals of one another, one right after another, of something brand new. But it's been awhile since that's happened. I think that's because we give scientists a specific job to do. We don't say, "Go sit in a corner and ponder and see what you come up with." The way so many of the previous discoveries were made was that someone was looking into this or looking into that, and in many cases accidentally discovered something else. It wasn't structured, he wasn't limited by some government grant. He — or she — was free to do things out of curiosity.

Definitely, the run to get government grants will prevent you from discovering anything!

Exactly! But, now we've categorized our scientists, and said to them: "This is your goal." Nobody's got the time or the money to just sit around and ponder and discover things.

That's absolutely true. The way the federal funding is, now you have to adhere to a very strict script. Also, the competition is such that everyone attempts to show how productive they are, and if you're lucky while you're generating lots of published studies you might stumble upon the eureka, but the truth of the matter is most of us are struggling to keep our publication rate high, and that's damaged our creativity.

Because now you've got the tail wagging the dog.

Yes. And that's not going to change in the near future.

That's why I like the MacArthur "genius grants."

There should be more of these. And more think tanks. I think that science is going to need to be restructured in our society. The model that we have now may not be the best model for the 21st century.

Do we have any true scientific think tanks anymore?

Not many. Los Alamos National Laboratory is probably one of the last great think tanks. That's still a think tank.

And now with computers we can do things more rapidly than we ever could before.

The ability to survey and categorize has been greatly enhanced by computer technologies. We can handle large volumes of data in a way that allows you to do simultaneous analysis that could never be done before.

So, we could actually come to conclusions so much quicker. Nobody has to sit there with a blackboard for 20 years. They hit a button on a computer and get the answer in five minutes. But, of course, we aren't paying people to be creative.

Which is too bad. In research today, the old saying is really true: the answer is pre-figured in the way that you've asked the question.

When you're going to embark on a new research project, how do you get around that? Can you keep the questions vague and open-ended, so that you can remain open and not go down some preconceived path?

You do have an experimental plan, and it has a rationale that is based on the state of the field.

Now, is this to justify it to the government for the funding, or is this in your own mind?

Even in your mind you have an experimental plan, a set of ideas or hypotheses that you're going to test. And you know that there are a certain number of experiments that you need to do to test your hypothesis. The beauty of the scientific method is that while you're in there testing your hypothesis, you may come up with an angle that's completely oblique to the way that you were going forward with your research. In the old days, you might change tracks very rapidly to go after that other angle. Today, I think, because of the funding crunch, scientists will be less likely to go down these other paths. Every time we've done something that has led us to something new, it was a detour, often it wasn't our main road.

And all our great discoveries have been either detours or completely accidental.

And there is that moment of intuition, that moment of true discovery when you know you've hit upon something that you didn't anticipate.

Have you ever been influenced by any dreams?

I think that every scientist has taken daily residue into the dream realms, and certainly I have done the same. But, I've never had that fundamental eureka come about during a dream state. You know the benzene molecule is the classic example of that. The scientist, Kekule, discovered the structure of benzene during a dream. He'd been working on trying to figure out the structure of benzene for a very long time. Benzene is a six-member carbon ring with double bonds, and he dreamed of snakes lining up mouth to tail, mouth to tail, mouth to tail (she laughs)...it's structure came to him in a dream.

What role have dreams played in your work?

Not so much sleeping dreams, but I think waking dreams. I do scientific daydreaming. I will sit back in the chair, and go into a light dream state at my desk, and use that to try to get an angle, get a thought going that will help me to gain some insight into how something works.

You let your subconscious work on it.

And that's a luxury that I really should take more advantage of.

It really should come under the heading of necessity more often than we realize. Very often problems are solved when we stop thinking about them, when we let the mind drift and wander, and then the answer pops in. This brings us back to neuroshamanism.

The neuroshamans will be the ones who make the leap of faith. They'll be the ones to say, "We don't have enough empirical knowledge now to be able to really thoroughly describe and understand these other domains of human consciousness and existence, but we're willing to study them, we're willing to bring the tools that we have from the laboratory setting to apply them to begin to describe this." There's going to be a revolution. It's become polarized enough now. It's Kuhn's Structure of Scientific Revolutions, like when we went from the particle to the wave, same kind of idea. When you get polarized far enough in one direction, then there's another movement that comes up to jerk us back. Kuhn writes how there have been great breakthroughs, how science gets to a point where a great breakthrough moves the discipline in one direction or another, and then a lot of people work on the new idea and lay down enough pieces of the puzzle. Then, there's a shift again in our worldview, and there's a polarity and it fosters another major scientific shift in our worldview. And we haven't had one of those in the brain sciences in a long time.

At what point did you come up with the term neuroshamanism?

It was when I began studying and working with ibogaine. I had the recognition that there really is a human discipline that pre-dates modern science, that is valid and historical and has efficacy, and we don't even begin to understand shamanism. And I was thinking about the possibility that we would move away from creating synthetic drugs to plant-based natural product medicines that have as much efficacy or even more than synthetics. Many of our primary drugs, including aspirin, are derived from plant substances.

It's all economic. Companies want to synthesize the substances so they can patent them, own them and corner the market.

Right. And a lot of the natural products have already been studied and their structures are known. But it's easier for the pharmaceutical companies to just have a library of all their different compounds on a shelf, and then come back and screen their library of chemicals based on some new target that's been discovered that's relevant to disease X, Y, or Z. Researching plants in the drug discovery phase is expensive. In the case of the shaman healers, they have a living library of information that's based on their own "drug discovery" in their own environment, and they have empirical data that's been handed down from generation to generation.

What's been well-guarded and kept secret is the psychoactive plants. Perhaps it's easier to get in and learn from indigenous people what they know about anti-bacterial agents, anti-viral agents, and other plant medicines that may be good for digestive disorders or respiratory infections. What's going to be difficult is to learn about the most sacred of all the plants, which are the psychoactive plant teachers. And I think that those psychoactive plants hold the keys to understanding consciousness, as well as what goes wrong in serious illnesses of the brain. Not only will we have an idea of a plant compound that may interact with our own underlying neurochemical patterning, but they may lead to the discovery of other novel classes of chemical compounds in the brain. This happened with the opiates. First we had morphine, which comes from a plant — the poppy —then we found that we have a receptor for that morphine, and finally we understood that our brain makes its own morphine, including endorphin.

Do you think that shamans and medicine men also knew ways of preventing brain disorders through the use of mind-active plants?

One thing about the central nervous system that is unique unto itself is that it has this great deal of redundancy, and it has a great deal of regenerative capacity. And it's not just one neurochemical system, it's actually a cascade of neurochemicals that are signaling across certain temporal and spatial domains. There's a lot of opportunity for chaos in the system. So the brain has probably evolved — this is probably how evolution shaped behavior and consciousness and perceptions of the universe — through these network arrays that have a lot of irregularity in them. So, we have redundancy, irregularity, and regenerative capacity. In the case of a defect in the neurochemical loop, we think usually of a specific — one chemical, one defect. This is true for Parkinson's Disease. For schizophrenia we don't even begin to know what the real defect is, but we make some assumptions based on the psychopharmacology of consciousness — you take a medication and you get a change in a behavioral profile, and you say, "Aha! It must involve the dopamine system," which is the case for schizophrenia. So, we really don't even begin to have a good idea for any of the serious brain-based mental diseases — psychiatric disorders — of what is the ultimate chemical substrate that's affected that gives rise to the disease symptoms.

In many neurodegenerative and neuropsychiatric diseases, we don't know yet if there's a genetic link, but there are some assumptions that there may be genetic vulnerability. Now, can those be prevented? Can there be a way in which we use a plant substance to slow down the progression of the disease or retard the expression of its symptoms? Probably so. You may be at risk for a brain-based illness, but whether or not it expresses may be dependent upon whether or not you're taking the right botanical extract. Now, in terms of serious mental illness, we know that there's a link to stress and the environment. So, it may be possible that there may be categories of plant substances that are going to change the way a person treats or responds to the stress in their environment. We just don't know what those plant compounds are yet.

One of the things that's always annoyed me is that mainstream medicine takes this approach: "We're going to partially kill you first, with the radiation and the chemotherapy, and then if we find that you're not responding to that, then we'll try 'alternative medicine.'" Well, it's too late. They've damn near destroyed your body. The odds of anything helping at that point — alternative medicine or anything else — is so remote because your system is so compromised. Logic would say — and modern medicine doesn't operate on logic, only power and economics — let's try the natural, less toxic "alternatives" first, and then if they don't work we'll go in for the kill with radiation and chemotherapy.

One of the things that I think that modern medicine has really failed on — and with computer technology now, there's really no excuse for — is the ability to chart the natural history of an illness in a diverse group of patients. In other words, depending upon your gender, age, ethnicity and genetics, you're going to respond to an illness and a medication differently. We don't study the anatomy of a disease, it's progression. We don't chart the natural progression. One of the things that's beginning to be done now — in severe neurodegenerative diseases like Parkinson's and Alzheimer's disease — where you've got an illness that runs a course, as you chart it you see that maybe what originally you thought was the best way to treat the illness may actually speed the illness up. And I think that's probably true for cancer, too. We take a hit or miss approach.

And, by and large, they're poisons.

They are poisons. They try to poison the tumor without seriously poisoning the host. But, in actuality, you end up poisoning the host to some degree, too.

I've heard from scientists and doctors that one day we'll look back at the way we practiced "modern medicine" it the late 20th century, and we'll think that it was very barbaric. Including the fact that we'd poison the host in order to poison the disease. The fact that we did so many invasive procedures, when there were other ways to go. The same way we look back now at the way medicine was practiced a hundred years ago and shake our heads.

And you don't even have to look back as far as 100 years ago. In the 1950s, we had psychosurgery.

Giving everybody a lobotomy, as a matter of course.

Just take a look at the youngest medical discipline, which treats the nervous system, and look at how we treated mental illness. In the 1950s, we were doing pre-frontal lobotomies and pre-frontal leukotomies. Both of them are directed at the frontal lobes. Dr. Munoz won the Nobel Prize for the development of this procedure, and now, only 45 years later, scientists consider it barbaric although some procedures are still done today. There's a story that goes around the pharmaceutical circle, and I've heard this story many times, that there was a Native American who went from university to university, and from medical center to medical center, saying that he had a treatment for serious mental illness and no one would pay attention to him. And, apparently, what he had was rauwolfia alkaloid, which is what gave rise to the medication reserpine which was the first major tranquilizer. Rauwolfia is a plant. The whole plant, apocynacea, was used for centuries in India as a tea, for treating madness, hysteria and restlessness. This was in the 1950s. Hard to believe that we didn't have a medication until four decades ago, and that prior to that we routinely did psychosurgery on people to treat mental illness. It's not that many years ago. Now we have the drug clozapine.

Now, you look back and it's shocking. But, the way we thought of things then was, "When in doubt, cut it out" (we laugh). I always looked at the basics. We were put on this planet, no matter how you may believe we all got here: whether you believe literally that within seven days God created everything, or whether you believe in evolution. Either way, we're on a planet. Logic would tell you that for any kind of creature, including humans, for any kind of life to survive in any kind of environment, there must be life-supporting stuff in that environment. We've got air, we've got water, we've got stuff to eat. Logic would tell you that we would've all died off within a generation if we didn't somewhere in our immediate environment also have everything we needed to keep us thriving, in the form of things that would prevent us from becoming ill and dying off, and things that can treat and cure us. Things that would give us somewhat of a fighting chance, even keeping in mind the theory of "survival of the fittest."

There were no scientists with labs and synthetic drugs for millions of years, and we managed to get by. So, you've gotta figure that everything we need is somewhere in nature, in our environment.

I think we're going to push the envelope as we move into the 21st century, and we're going to push the envelope on two fronts: one is that we've abused our antibiotics to the point where we now have so many resistant organisms out there, and as we cut down the rainforests and allow some of the microbes that have been buried for literally millennia to come back up into the atmosphere...

Not only are we destroying nature's pharmacy, but we're unleashing God-knows-what.

Dinosaur germs! Literally (we laugh). We may be unleashing a plague that makes the bubonic plague pale by comparison. So, that's one possible push on the biological envelope. It's very likely that there are species of natural antibiotics and natural antimicrobials there in the plant and trees of the rainforest that need to be discovered. That's what the company Shaman Pharmaceuticals is going after. The other thing that's going to push the envelope is this: as the soul sickness on the planet begins to manifest, this disconnectedness of people at the same time that the technological pace is speeding up, we're seeing more rage and violence and anger because we're losing the unifying mythologies that keep the tribe sane. So, the need to heal that inner sickness, and the need to protect us — and it's not going to be jails, they can't contain it and we couldn't build them fast enough — means we'll have a need for medications to treat these anti-social personality disorders and mental illnesses that are emerging in the population.

Let's talk prevention. Not only are there plants and botanicals that can be used as medicines to treat physical and psychological conditions, but there are certain ways of living that help prevent illness of the body, of the mind, of the soul.

And give one coping skills.

Right.

Where that comes into play is the idea that you can use exercise, meditation, sound, music, light therapy.

And I think you have to believe that it's going to work for it to work, because of the concept of the self-fulfilling prophecy. Like when people say, "Oh, this won't work, but I'll try it anyway." We've become so negative.

There is an element of "purity of intention" needed for all of these approaches.

Science knows that intent works. That's what's behind the placebo effect. Scientists use it to prove a negative. But, the placebo effect equally proves the positive. If you tell people, "I am giving you something that's going to cure you," but what you're really giving them is a sugar pill or some other inert substance, and this person is cured, science makes that a negative by saying, "See, it's all bullshit, it's all in his head." When, actually scientists should be excited that it's all in the patient's head. That's a good thing. That means that he had the intent in his head to heal. And with the inert substance that you gave him, he really healed only because he *believed* he would heal. That shows you the power of intent, the power of belief, in healing. And science, instead, looks at it as a negative.

Now there's a push to understand how the way we respond to our illness affects the healing process. There is a real awareness, now, for the first time. For instance, that HIV-infected individuals who grieve seriously from the knowledge that they are HIV-infected will do worse than individuals who are able to maintain a positive mood.

As they decide to live with HIV, rather than conceivably die...

That's right, they haven't automatically signed their own death sentences. They do better, and this is known now. We may not understand yet precisely what the link is to the boost in immune response, but it's there.

And, fortunately, that's the kind of thing you can prove in a lab.

If there has been a blessing that has come out of the HIV-AIDS epidemic, it's been in the area of psychoneuroimmunology, and this large sector of the scientific medical community being able to suspend their belief systems, at least for a short amount of time, to be able to look at this in a creative way and say, "Gee, we don't really understand yet how this works, but it doesn't matter. We see it working, and we see it working in enough of this affected population to be able to sanction it and be able to say that there is something to this."

Where do you think neuroscience is going in the future?

With all of the significant advances that we've seen in neuroscience in the last 20 years, it's coming up to some dead ends. We've moved from describing the neuron, which is the fundamental building block of the brain — there are more neurons in our brain than there are stars in the Milky Way galaxy — and charting these, which is like going around the galaxy and trying to put each and every star in it's place and say whether it's a red star, a blue star, or a white star, to assigning chemicals and assigning input and output relationships, and we know that certain parts of the brain have discreet functions, but nowhere in doing all of this have we learned how and where consciousness originates.

That's the next logical step, and we'll have to try to find some way to please this scientific hang-up we have about the way in which we "prove" the existence of something, or prove how it works. To apply that to the study of consciousness, may require us to re-invent our idea of "proof."

That's true. I think that's true. The type of evidence you get, the answer you get is pre-figured in the way you ask the question, and if you don't know how to ask the question, then you can't answer it. So, I think we're going to come up against a blank wall every time we go for the bigger picture. Now, what's been exciting is the introduction of chaos theory into the description of the nervous system. And now we're using a whole vernacular that's completely foreign to the neuroscientific community. There have been meetings in which the chaos theoreticians are sitting down with the neurophysiologists and developing a vernacular so they can communicate with one another. The idea here is not to look at the single neuron with the single chemical with the single pattern of firing, but instead you look at networks of neural activity, and you look at irregularities in the way the brain functions in terms of its signaling across time.

You look at something we may term chaotic, and you find patterns in the big picture.

Exactly.

Rather than breaking it down and looking at something in isolation.

Exactly. This is truly in its infancy. There haven't been large-scale national meetings on these topics yet. It's been very small think tanks that are beginning to point the way, that this may be an alternative way to get at brain function and dysfunction, by using these types of approaches to describe how the brain works and to begin to model how the brain works. So, they actually now have computer simulations where they can begin to model certain simple aspects of human behavior, like memory and learning. My expectation is that the payoffs to using chaos theory and computer modeling will be really significant.

In areas outside science, we've acknowledged the ideas of group dynamics and context for a very, very long time. In group dynamics, for instance, if we want to understand how complex interactions among people work — in a country, a community, a group — then you study the interaction of the elements of the group with each other. If you want to know why a group is getting along or not getting along, you wouldn't just look at each individual's personality, you'd look at the way each individual acts with the others when they're brought together. Why, then, do we find it so difficult to accept in science that the idea of context and "group dynamics" works when we look at anything else, including the parts of the body? Science says that nothing exists in a vacuum, then contradicts itself by studying everything in a vacuum, in isolation, without regard to context. And there is no way to escape context. Everything exists in context. You can't study a liver in isolation. You have to remember it's interacting with other parts and systems of your body. And they can't just look at one neuron in the brain; they have to remember that it's part of a community.

> *Right. That's true. One example is in studying the cocaine epidemic, and looking at why cocaine kills some people and not others. It's been a real mystery to us. We continue to look at cocaine overdose deaths and found that individuals are dying with recreational blood levels of cocaine. Why are they dying? Why are they dying? Why are they dying?*

Was it from cocaethyline?

> *No, we thought it was, but it wasn't. So, what it must mean is that for some people, it really is a fatal arrhythmia. It's some chaos between the way the brain regulates heart rate and rhythm that throws a monkey wrench in there. And certain people who are susceptible, for an as yet unidentified reason, will die a sudden death.*

Everybody's body chemistry is different — I could OD on one cup of regular coffee — so it makes sense that some people might OD on a "recreational" level of cocaine. And you're finding this in significant numbers? Can this be attributed to these peoples' chemistry being particularly sensitive to a stimulant?

Maybe, or it may be that there's something about the mood they were in at the time they were using the cocaine, the brain state they were in, perhaps paranoid, just like what might occur in voodoo death.

You mean that they were in a negative frame of mind?

Maybe. Paranoid, anxious, fearful. In some individuals, cocaine is linked to paranoia, and so while these low blood levels would suggest that it's not direct cardiac toxicity, there must be something more at play to throw chaos into the heart rhythm that makes someone pre-disposed to a fatal arrhythmia. The fatal link could be in the brain.

Thirteen

Christine DeLorey

*To every thing there is a season,
and a time to every purpose under heaven.*

— Ecclesiastes

cientists and artists alike will tell you that much has come to them through dreams: inspiration, ideas, questions, answers, even metaphors that lead to inventions and discovery.

While recovering from a car accident in 1978, then 27-year-old Christine DeLorey began to dream about numbers. And more numbers. And numbers and emotions. And the cycles represented by numbers. With no prior interest in higher mathematics or numerology, DeLorey was initially puzzled. But, when the dreams continued, she paid even closer attention and then began her research.

For the last 20 years, DeLorey has significantly advanced the study and practice of numerology, specifically with the creation of her Life Cycles approach. She calls herself a Cyclic Analyst, and that title reflects the deeper nature of her work, which focuses on the healing powers of emotion, not only for the individual, but for every society.

Born and raised in London, DeLorey began writing non-fiction for magazines in England in her twenties, and traveled extensively, which led her to make the U.S. her home by the 1980s. Now based in Boston (www.numerology.freesoul.com), DeLorey is a columnist for *Aurora Rising* magazine, and has private clients in the U.S. and abroad. Her groundbreaking book *Life Cycles* will be published in April, 2000 by Osmos Books.

"There's nothing fatalistic about numerology," she says. "That's where I differ from other numerologists, those from 'the old school.' They believe that numbers rule our lives and there's no free will. I believe free will is *everything*. And numbers are the symbols for cycles that show you how to make things happen."

DeLorey uses numerology to facilitate a better understanding of current affairs and history in every arena, both globally and personally, and she is as much a social commentator as anything else you could find a label for.

She does this with much warmth and effervescence, in a sweet voice whose British accent holds none of her native country's famed stiff-upper-lipped reserve. An impassioned and articulate writer, she's funny and sincere, and takes her work very seriously.

"The cycles of our lives, and the life of the world, are about growth and healing," she says. "The goal, essentially, is peace through emotional healing."

One look at individual lives and relationships, and the world's constant state of turmoil shows exactly what she's referring to. These cycles are natural, progressive cycles of nature, she explains, and science is one of the languages used to describe nature, so these cycles are a science, even though it may not be currently grouped with the major scientific disciplines.

"We use numbers *mathematically* to understand and explain life's physical realities. That's how the sciences use numbers on that level," she says. "We use numbers *numerologically* to understand and explain the *non-physical* cycles and forces that make the physical possible. As to what these non-physical elements actually are, well, science has not yet found a way to prove them, but that doesn't mean that proof does not exist."

Regarding the nebulous nature of proof, DeLorey cites one of her favorite film moments.

"There was a wonderful scene in the movie *Contact*, in which Jodie Foster, as a scientist, questions theologian Matthew McConaughey's belief in God. She says that it's impossible for her to believe in something she can't see, and for which there isn't a shred of scientific proof. So, he asks her if she loved her late father. She says yes, of course she did. He calmly says: 'Prove it.'"

❧ ❦

I first interviewed Christine DeLorey in 1996, when we were introduced by a mutual publishing colleague, and we have had numerous conversations since. The one published here took place in the summer of 1998.

To enhance your reading of this conversation, on the following few pages you'll find the meanings of each of the numbers, one through nine, as provided by Christine DeLorey. In basic numerology, numbers are interpreted as having certain qualities, but these descriptions that follow are brief and merely scratch the surface of the cycle's implications. Regarding the destiny/personal numbers, Christine DeLorey reminds clients that 'what we call the destiny number contains some very factual information for the individual, but it does not determine who you are. It determines where you 'landed' on the day you were born, and directs you to the easiest possible path on which to fulfill your desires. This is also the path on which to discover what your desires actually are. And it is the path which will provide you with whatever you need to create your destiny or the destination that you, yourself, have chosen."

Your destiny or personal number is the sum of all the numbers in your birth date. The number of the year's , month's or day's cycle you are in is also arrived at by adding numbers of dates. The world, too, is also in a particular numbered cycle, which is arrived at by adding up the numbers of the calendar year. And the century also reflects a numerical cycle the world is going though.

THE NINE CYCLES
(courtesy of Christine DeLorey)

ONE: **Independence.** Taking the lead with innovative new ideas. Creative appreciation. Setting trends instead of following them. Learning how to adapt to drastic change.

TWO: **Relation.** Bringing people together through cooperation, intuition, partnership, peacefulness, patience and tact. Feeling your way through life rather than relying solely on intellect.

THREE: **Creativity.** Communication, developing friendship, appreciating beauty, feeling happiness, learning to see beyond the surface of things, creating a diverse network of associates.

FOUR: **Breakthrough.** Knowing that one's work must be what one loves. Learning how to overcome obstacles and limitation and turn it into opportunity. Being able to work hard for what one wants. Taking care of details.

FIVE: **Freedom.** Change. Expanding your experiences of life by learning from mistakes. Being aware of the material aspects of life, including the physical body and sex. Traveling through life's diversity and learning to appreciate different cultures.

SIX: **Responsibility.** Love, family, parenting, education, community, and the fine arts of entertainment. Understanding equality. Receiving validation from one's peers.

SEVEN: **Wisdom.** Inner development, spirituality, wisdom. The ability to analyze. The tendency to criticize. Learning to be at ease with the imperfect. Gathering expertise and being sought for one's knowledge.

EIGHT: **Power.** Learning to take and give back. Enterprise. Understanding the meaning of power. Using power constructively. The ability to influence others through your powers of material and financial manifestation.

NINE: **Completion.** Giving because you want to and not because you think you should. Tying up loose ends. Becoming an expert and not a Jack-of-all-trades and master of none. Deciding what you are meant to give this world before you leave it.

YOUR DESTINY OR PERSONAL NUMBER
(courtesy of Christine DeLorey)

ONE: An independent person whose journey focuses on independence. They may be independent in one area of their life, but dependent in another, and must learn to let go of that dependence.

TWO: A facilitator who brings people together. The theme is cooperation.

THREE: The creative, artistic person who can also be frivolous. Their lesson is to take themselves seriously.

FOUR: The achiever, through very hard work and total belief in what he or she is doing. They overcome obstacles.

FIVE: People who have a need to travel and understand the world. They are also very physical and resourceful people.

SIX: They have a need to heal, love and educate. They have to learn to let go of the need to be right all the time and the fear of being wrong.

SEVEN: An orchestrator, someone whose mind is constantly working. They seek perfection and are very critical of imperfection in themselves and others. They have the potential to be very wise.

EIGHT: Enterprising. Here to learn about material abundance, and once that's achieved, what to do with it.

NINE: Giving and enhancing person who has to be careful not to be a self-sacrificing martyr.

FINDING YOUR NUMBERS

We'll be using Christine DeLorey's birth date as the sample for these calculations.

TO DETERMINE YOUR DESTINY/PERSONAL NUMBER:
Add all the numbers in your year, month and day of birth, until you end up with a single digit.
November 27, 1951
Add the month — 11 1+1=2
Add the day — 2+7=9
Add the year — 1+9+5+1=16 1+6=7
Then add those three numbers from the month, day and year, and keep adding until you have a single digit: 2+9+7=18, then 1+8=9.
Christine's destiny/personal number is 9.

TO DETERMINE WHAT YEAR (CYCLE) YOU ARE IN: Add all the numbers in the day and month of your birth to the calendar year you are in now, until you end up with a single digit.
November 27 — Christine's birthday
2000 — current year
Add the month — 11 1+1=2
Add the day — 2+7=9
Add the current year — 2+0+0+0=2
Then add those three numbers from the month, day and year, and keep adding until you have a single digit: 2+9+2=13 1+3=4.
In 2000, Christine is in a 4 year.

TO DETERMINE WHAT NUMBER/CYCLE MONTH YOU
ARE IN: Add your cycle year to the number of the month you are in, until you end up with a single digit.
Christine's cycle year is 4.
To find out what the number/cycle she'll be in during the month

of October, which is the 10th month of the calendar year, add 4+10=14 1+4=5. She'll be in a 5 month (cycle) in October, 2000.

TO DETERMINE THE GLOBAL YEAR: Add the year's digits until you end up with a single digit.
2000 — 2+0+0+0=2

NOTE: Using these calculations you can also determine your numbered cycle for any calendar year or month in the past or the future.

❧ ❦

How does Life Cycles differ from traditional numerology?

Well, there's a tremendous difference between what traditional numerologists express as numerology and what I do. Generally, the biggest difference is that I have found a direct link between numbers and emotion. From this standpoint alone, I tend to see numerology as one of the most important and vital sciences on Earth today. It needs, therefore, to be separated from its old labeling as "new age" and "occult." My intention is to bring this knowledge into the mainstream, as an important branch of mathematics. I try to use language that can be understood by everyone, and I strongly assert that there is nothing supernatural about numerology. We use numbers to measure and understand everything on this Earth. So, it stands to reason that numbers can also be used to explain what is happening to us on the inside, too. Numbers are the very pulse of nature, human nature included. Numbers themselves are a science. Numerology is simply a branch of that science, the importance of which, despite its ancient origins, is only just beginning to be understood.

So, what you do with Life Cycles is incorporate our modern knowledge with the old, as well as place emphasis on the emotions.

One of the things I've discovered with numerology is that it's directly linked to the human will, which I've further discovered to be emotion. And that's where Life Cycles differs from traditional numerology. Life Cycles focuses on this will, this emotion. Psychology doesn't really deal with emotion. It deals with the mind and the brain. The subject of emotions is in its infancy. We can know so much more about them, learn so much more about them. The work that I put out there enables people to feel what is happening to them, not just have a mental concept of it. We know that emotion exists, and yet science, as it stands today, offers no way to prove the existence or purpose of our feelings.

Ironically, feelings probably get in the way of being subjective about that.

> *If science is still serious about understanding life, then it must remove its own self-imposed limits and acknowledge emotion as an unexplored megapower which sets the course of humanity's journey. For instance, governments are voted in and out by the way people feel about issues. Expressed emotion is the power of creation. This is why the most creative people are also the most emotional. Numerology brings us heart to heart with the power of emotion that is within each of us. Emotion, in all its diversity, is the human will. When we experience this connection for ourselves, we realize that we have spent our whole lives learning how to suppress our emotions instead of expressing them. Consequently, the will of humanity is anything but free.*

Feelings can sometimes be scary to people, and that's why they avoid them. They avoid the whole subject of emotions, and even in psychology they ignore the very thing they should be looking at, which is the emotions, and instead view the mind as some concrete, cold thing they can dissect, and treats emotions in a condescending and patronizing way. Traditional numerology and astrology can be guilty of that as well. But, with Life Cycles, you feel very strongly that emotions are the key to everything.

> *Yes. Life Cycles will show you what's happening in your outer reality, but it also shows you that what's happening out there is only happening because of what's happening inside. You create your reality simply by the way you feel. Your feelings drive you. They drive you to do certain things, or not to do certain things. To me, numerology and emotion go hand in hand. The numbers are simply a way of measuring or identifying what those emotions actually are, which is helpful since most people are in total denial about what they're feeling.*

Many cultures have assigned meaning to numbers since ancient times. When we look at certain numbers, their meaning is obvious. Like the number one — it's solitary, it's independent, it's the first number, the beginning. So, to say that the number one signifies those qualities makes sense. And the number nine is the end. So, seeing nine as a time to wrap some things up makes sense because it's completion, the end of a cycle. The number two — the joining of two separate energies, people, things, ideas. Makes sense. And three, that makes sense — two people together can create a third person.

Yes, and most numerologists, ancient and modern, agree that numerology is the study of the mathematical imprinting each of us was born with. From Pythagoras to Einstein, to today's exciting new appreciation of mathematics, it's widely believed that "all is arranged by number." There is no way to dispute this. This evidence is everywhere. But, I believe that we have only just touched the surface of how numbers and imprinting affect life, and that a new quality of life exists beyond numbers and imprinting. In my 20 or so years as a professional numerologist, I have found that numbers, when understood on a deeper level, are not the end of the story. Rather, they are a tool for understanding and telling the story. A tool which provides a road map out of the maze imprinting and into free will. Numbers are part of nature. They are an extension or an effect of time and space. To me, numerology is the most natural thing there is.

Is that because nature, all of life, operates in cycles? And cycles can be numbered and then better understood?

Yes, I study and practice numerology as it relates to life today, rather than rehash ancient understandings which have since been proven inaccurate or incomplete. Yes, wisdom can be found at all stages of the human journey. But if the "ancient ones" held all the answers, then by now this world would be a most enlightened and peaceful place. Instead, it is more volatile and dangerous than ever. As time passes, we experience more of life, and through new experience we learn new things. Knowledge, like everything in creation, evolves. But we must be careful not to get stuck at one particular level of understanding. There is so much more to learn in every field. Very often, a new understanding is simply a step closer to the truth — but not the truth itself. What needs to evolve along with modern knowledge is our intent to use our knowledge creatively rather than destructively. And, in this world of "experts and authorities," we must also learn to say "I don't know" far more frequently than we currently do. In my field, which is so ancient and yet so young, I find myself saying, "I don't know" to questions that were once considered basic. What I do know is that we travel through life on a sea of numbers. If we strive to understand these intricate forces, which both drive and confine us, we cannot help but learn more about ourselves, each other, and our purpose in the universe.

These cycles are just natural progressions.

Oh, absolutely. And that is one of the differences in my work. I see these as spirals. If they were just cycles, you'd go around in circles and that's not good. The point is to progress through each cycle and go on to the next level, like going up a spiral staircase. Even though cycles do repeat themselves, they repeat themselves at different levels of understanding. Until we learn what each cycle has to teach us, all we do is repeat them over and over. This is why so many people live their lives as if they're going around in circles and never getting anywhere. They do not have enough free will to be able to do what they really want to do. They are focused on making a living instead of creating a life.

And this is because we're locked into a system in which we elect others to make laws and decisions for us. Those in control cannot help but become addicted to their power over others. Even with the best of conscious intent, they find ways to manipulate the masses to protect their leadership roles. In their race for supremacy — and this goes as far as world domination — they are denying the basic needs of the planet itself. As someone once said, "When elephants fight, it is the grass that suffers." And that pretty much sums up the hopelessness, the lack of freedom in our lives. Life's numerological cycles also explain the timing and the motivation of political strategy in any era, economic movement, scientific discovery, everything. We can even use numbers to understand the fear-based mind set of those who, it seems, will do anything to prevent peace and freedom. We're also realizing that humanity must slow down. If we don't, nature will do it for us. Einstein said, "It's become appallingly clear that our technology has surpassed our humanity."

Using numbers to understand the cycles we are in means that this year, for example, I'm in a 5 year, and the goal is to have a 5 year at a higher level of understanding or wisdom than the last time I had a five year, which was 9 years ago. We hope that I've evolved so that I'm not just repeating the same stuff every nine years. I may be repeating concepts, but I'm doing it in a more evolved manner.

Absolutely. That is the point of interpreting numerology. It is a way of understanding our own evolution. In fact, if you look at the different scenarios of each yearly cycle, you'll see that there are only nine stories. There are only nine stories in the world. Of course, there are billions of people, and each of those nine stories is told differently. And we get the chance to write the details of those stories ourselves. These are the cards we are dealt within a year. How you play them makes all the difference, what you decide to learn, how deeply you decide to learn.

Which all gets back to our own evolution of consciousness.

Yes, well, one of the things I find happening is that although we've all been going within, and it's been a wonderful experience, we can't go within any further because we've stumbled across this thing, and it's emotion. And now what consciousness has to do is make room for it. Our lives are becoming extremely emotional, things are happening all over the world that are stirring the emotions in everyone. We are learning how to feel. We've spent the last thousand years learning how not to feel.

Trying to put emotion aside in favor of what we call rational thought, which, of course, is not human, and expects people to act like machines — totally devoid of feeling, desire, will, opinion, you name it.

Absolutely, and I think that what we're learning now is that the other extreme — living by consciousness alone — can be very enlightening but also just as cold and lonely as the rational extreme. Without the emotional involvement in life, life is just that: cold and lonely. We need to get emotionally involved in our world, not just our private lives, but our world. Only by knowing exactly how we feel about something can we tell the difference between what we desire and what we don't desire, what is good for us, and what is not. Emotion is neither positive nor negative. Only our intent can be categorized in that way. We either have loving intent or we have unloving intent. We support control by either wanting to control or wanting to be controlled. Or, we support freedom by wanting to be free and wanting others to be free. And that is the principle question I pose to my clients and readers: "What do you want?"

If it's freedom, then a personal journey begins — out of control and in to freedom. We are not free, not one of us. There are many people out there who already understand these principles and ideas, even if it is just subconsciously. They know in their hearts that there has to be more to life than war, disease, disaster, technology, fear, taxes and death. But even those who have reached this conclusion cannot help but feel hopeless because, after all, what can one person do about this? Any attempt to bring down this heartless system of ours has always resulted in massive loss of life. Violence, we know, is not the answer. I believe that the answer is in nature, and in the numbers that exist in nature. Numbers exist so that we can better understand what nature actually is. Numbers are a language used to express ideas, like any other language.

We can start to break away from this imperial system we have on this planet, one person at a time. Not by going into seclusion and living on a mountain top or something, but by choosing to make every decision for ourselves, by being who we really are. We can only know who we really are — rather than what this systematized society tells us we are — by allowing our feelings to tells us who we are. You can break from the system by doing what our feelings desire us to do, by feeling how you would like to live your life, and by finding the courage to take the steps that will lead you to your ideal, and by deciding for yourself what is right and wrong instead of being paralyzed by guilt, and instead of denying the guilt we all feel, reversing it, and turning it to blame. And by knowing that you cannot just grab freedom at the expense of someone else's. It's going to take a very long time for us to achieve or even understand freedom, but a start must be made somewhere. It can only start within and to be more specific, it can only start within the feelings of an individual. That's where everything in the world starts. I believe that we are living such emotional lives these days because we are in the process of learning about emotion. We are starting to give our feelings the freedom to be felt.

That's the cycle the world is in now.

Right. You know, people think that evil is rising all over the world, but it's not really the case. We've had worse times. I think it's just that we're seeing evil exposed more broadly and frequently than ever before.

Thanks to instant media communication, so we get to hear about it more than we ever used to.

Exactly. And I think that evil is not so much on the rise as on the run. Because it is being exposed.

When we look at history, we see that we're not living in a particularly violent era. Look back at the Spanish Inquisition, The Middle

Ages, The Wild West, even, and the Holocaust. Every era has had a lot of violence, it's just that now, instantaneously, we can see it on the screen and hear the details.

> *Which brings us back to cycles again, because each era of history has been a cycle that we did not learn from. And if you don't learn from a cycle, and from what a cycle of time is trying to teach you, history repeats itself. And that applies as much to our private lives as it does to events that go on in the world.*

In school, if you don't learn what you're supposed to in the third grade, they don't promote you to the fourth. You have to repeat the third "cycle" again. And our lives are like that — if we don't learn what we need to learn, and do what we need to do, we'll just have to do it over and over until we get it right.

> *Absolutely. I think that some people live very shallow lives simply because they were unable to learn a particular lesson in life.*

They were probably too afraid to deal with it.

> *Fear is one of the things we all have to deal with. There are a lot of important things going on in the world that can be frightening.*

And sometimes those aren't being dealt with because of people's petty emotional fears, ego stuff.

> *Well, that's the important thing about learning about the emotions — learning how to feel. When you go through this process — and it really is a process of unraveling how you really feel — you get stronger. Yes, you might have to cry and yell, and all the rest of that for a little while, but when you get through that, when you realize, "My God, that is what I was feeling," and you let that out of your body, rather than hold it in, you become stronger and realize that most things in life really aren't worth complaining about. One of the most important things to*

understand is what emotion is — it is will energy. To me we only have an illusion of freedom. We don't have freedom in this system we live in because it is a system.

A system doesn't allow its participants to be free because they have to follow the system. So, our system may be freer than other people's system, but it's still not freedom.

Yes, precisely. And that's terrible. When you do realize the extent to which we are not free, we can see the ridiculousness of today's politics, we can instantly see through the lies and rhetoric, and we have the urge to make every decision for ourselves. And that is what free will is about. And I think that's why governments are so frightened at the moment: They are losing control. And we're seeing governments get very, very dirty in order to regain the control they've lost. People are breaking free. It's frightening and wonderful.

And you incorporate this free will theme into Life Cycles in what manner?

To me, free will and emotion are exactly the same thing. Life Cycles merely gives one a road map. Not something you're supposed to adhere to at all costs, but a road map out of the system that doesn't allow for freedom.

The 4 year, for example, is a year of obstacles, so Life Cycles will show you how to deal with obstacles in that year, the way out of them. Is that the kind of thing you mean?

Well, the 4 year is definitely a very difficult year, and it is a year full of obstacles, but what that 4 year does is help you to build your ability to surpass yourself, to break through your own limits — what you believe are your limits, that is. When you get to that stage, what the 4 energy teaches you is to believe in yourself, to believe in what you're doing to such an extent that your personal energies push out, and push those self-imposed limits away from you. You will still have limits, everybody has their limits, but in this way they just won't be crashing down on you and preventing you from achieving anything. For instance, someone is trying to achieve something, but they're getting nothing but distractions, people are annoying them, they're getting delays. If this person believes strongly enough that they will succeed, the things that are annoying them and distracting them and interrupting them are going to have less significance. Those limits stop pushing down on you. They aren't such heavy burdens.

Because you've redefined what you view as a limit.

Exactly. I call that expanding one's limits.

So, instead of labeling it a limit, you call it a minor annoyance.

Yes.

So, in Life Cycles, you're teaching people how to get through the particular things that come their way during these years.

And more. Because when one gets an understanding of free will, every single decision you make is your own. You stop blaming other people. That's the first thing you do. Yes, you may be surrounded by people who annoy you, or who deliberately put obstacles in your way. That is their prerogative, too. You can find ways to get around this, to get around them. There is always a way to get around things, instead of feeling that you're stuck. When you feel stuck, and like there's nothing you can do about it, what you're really saying is "I don't have free will." Free will comes from within, so even someone sitting in a prison cell for the rest of his life can still achieve free will.

Within each cycle in nature, there are seasons, there are times for things. Times when a flower is growing, when it's in bloom, times when it's not growing, times when leaves fall and trees are dormant. And these Life Cycles are the same, aren't they? When people think that if they're not going a mile a minute, 24 hours a day, they're not accomplishing anything, we're reminded by nature's cycles that that's not true. There may be times, whether it's a month or a year, when you're in one of those cycles that a tree is in when it's bare and dormant for awhile, and building up its strength. Or you may be in a cycle where you're blooming all over the place.

My work is specifically designed to bring people to their own natural pace.

The 7 cycle is a time of introspection and slowing down, for example.

Yes, and it's only the society and system that we live in that tells us that we can't move according to our own natural pace. We are made to feel guilty if we don't appear to be constantly achieving.

We've even created products to force flowers to bloom when they don't naturally bloom and we're trying to do that with people, too.

Yes, yes. In fact, the very idea of cloning, to me, is the last ditch effort to kill free will. There's a lot going on in science right now that's terrifying.

What the implications of these things really are.

Like I said earlier, Albert Einstein believed that technology has surpassed our humanity. Just because we can do something doesn't mean that we should or must do it.

And our technology is also messing with our natural cycles.

Oh, most definitely. A lot of the technology out there that ordinary people are using every day — there seems to be no point to it. Of course, there are wonderful technologies out there. I'd be lost without my computer, but I've been in the middle of working, writing on my computer, and I've had people who know me interrupt me with a silly little message they've sent. And that's what so many of these people do — they sit on their computers sending silly little messages to each other, and it's one of the most boring things I've ever seen in my life.

I think it keeps people from actually communicating with each other in a more intimate way. People don't talk to people anymore, they e-mail them.

We're going into the 2000's, which is another cycle. And I think the reason I get so agitated about the use of technology is that everything in the one cycle is coming to a climax in 1999, and once we go into the two energy of the 2000's everything has got to slow down. And I know a lot of people can't even imagine that. One of the ways it might slow down is this Y2K glitch we're expecting with the computers. That will slow down the whole system, the whole bureaucracy. But, I think it'll be slowing down because of other things, too, like weather anomalies and war.

Explain what the one energy that we've been in for a thousand years means and what the two energy we're going into the year 2000 means.

In the last thousand years it's been a man's world. One is a very masculine energy. The 1000's were supposed to have taught us independence. But look at us, a will-less society that is totally dependent on such things as money, computers, electricity, oil, drugs, processed foods, technology and on other people to provide these things for us. And, yet, we continue to destroy those aspects of nature with which we are interdependent, such as air, water, animals, vegetables and minerals. Even space is littered with the debris of our quest for more control. The purpose of the 1 cycle is to teach us to be independent entities, with minds and wills of our own. That the mind and will have separate and independent functions — the mind being consciousness or spirit, and the will being emotion or intuition. The mind is masculine in nature. The will is feminine. The 1 energy teaches the real

436

meaning of leadership. This means that each of us must possess enough free will to be able to lead one's own life according to one's own unique desires. And yet, here we are, chained to a system in which the freedom to do so is mere illusion.

What will the 2000's bring, with its 2 cycle?

The end of the 1 millennium marks the end of a cycle in which we learned about our masculine energy. The energy of the mind/consciousness/spirit. The beginning of the new millennium, which is led by the 2 energy, marks the beginning of a cycle in which we will learn about the feminine energy within all of us. The reason that women's issues became such a major topic as we went into the last hundred years of this past millennium era, as we went into the 1900's, and continue to be a major topic today, is because we are living in a cycle of time in which a deeper understanding of sexual balance is finally possible. By heading towards the feminine 2 energy, these issues emerged. In the 2000's, we will experience everything from the perspective of the 2 energy, which is emotional, caring, peaceful, intuitive, partnership oriented, patient, nostalgic, and much slower than the 1 energy. It's emphasis is on the connection between all life, only a part of which is human. Until these connections are made, we will continue to experience the consequences of our trying to resist this evolutionary process. These include terror situations imposed by those who cannot accept the responsibility that comes with freedom, and those who cannot let go of their addiction to control.

There can be no freedom for any of us while others are destroying life in the name of some cause or other, and, worst of all, in the name of God. All they are doing is imposing their beliefs in place of another. Einstein said that "peace can never be achieved by force. It can only be achieved by understanding." Here are some words from the past that were too simple, too brilliant, to be understood by the mainstream at the time they were spoken. They will finally sink in during the new millennium because the 2000's is a cycle in which peace will become paramount — I mean first and foremost — to our survival. But not just peace among ourselves. Peace with nature is included here. I believe that a new and extensive look at numerology provides some of the understanding through which peace, on this level, can be achieved. At least that is my intention.

What else will the 2 energy of the 2000's bring?

It's a cycle in which emotional awareness will lead to spectacular creativity. It's quality will be determined by our willingness to feel who and what we are rather than rely on others to place us in some category or other. Emotion, feeling, is the source of all creativity. It is our ability to feel that fuels our minds and our imagination.

And emotion is seen as a feminine quality or energy, as is the number two. Are certain other numbers also interpreted as feminine or masculine, and what are the implications in that?

Masculine energy is reflected in all the odd numbers, and feminine energy is the even numbers. Masculine energy is by nature aggressive. One is the number of independence, progression, racing ahead, competitive. We've thought that progress means competition and surging ahead. But, all progress means is taking one step at a time. How that progression moves in entirely up to us. We've had 1,000 years of war and domination. We can start to feel the feminine two energy coming in now, and all of this will change. Women's issues are a big thing right now, and have been in the last 100 years as we moved toward the end of the one energy and toward the two energy of the 2000's.

And the two energy is cooperative, rather than independent and aggressive like the one energy.

It is cooperative, and we have misinterpreted that in the past to mean subservient. The two energy certainly doesn't seek superiority, but...

Quite the opposite, it seeks balance and equality.

Equality is the essence, and that's what's happening now — the world is beginning to balance itself. Humanity needs to balance itself among individuals and peoples, and it needs to balance itself with nature. And the female needs to be balanced with the male.

Mankind erroneously believes that because we've evolved into a dominant species that can make things and tries to conquer nature, that we are actually separate form nature. We think we can control nature. And every time we have a hurricane, we're reminded that that's a load of bull.

Yes, right. (we laugh).

How can people use their knowledge of these natural cycles, as you present them in Life Cycles, in their own evolution?

I think the ultimate goal is free will, which basically means doing what you love. But, if your freedom takes away from anybody else's freedom, then that's not freedom. People have to understand that doing what you want to do is not a matter of bulldozing your way through. With this two energy emerging, we're also learning how to control or balance ego. During the 1000's we've been affected by the one energy, and part of that is discovering who you are instead of what society tells us we are. That's been one of the biggest mistakes we've made throughout the last thousand years — we've allowed society to tell us who and what we are supposed to be, we've had no free will in this. There are fashion-makers out there, there are people who tell us what is "in" and what is "out," and life is not supposed to be like that. The one cycle is full of rules, and when we're in a one cycle we're supposed to learn to relax those rules, and simply be ourselves. And allow other people the same freedom.

During this one cycle we have first experiences of many things, and that can be frightening, so ultimately we're learning the meaning of courage, too. Which is why men have put courage before everything else. We teach little boys that they must not be cowards, they must not show any emotion — there have been an awful lot of misunderstandings within this one energy. And that's why for the last 1000 years it's always been a man's world. Women have been oppressed globally, and this is from those misunderstandings.

When we're aware of what cycle we're in on a particular day, month, year and even 1,000-year era, that better enables us to understand what we're going through in the natural course of our own personal as well as societal evolution.

Yes, and it tells us where we actually stand in the course of the journey towards free will.

Fourteen

JoAnn Morgan

What do you mean you've never been to Alpha Centauri?
For heaven's sake, mankind,
it's only four light years away, you know.
I'm sorry, but if you can't be bothered to
take an interest in local affairs, that's your own lookout.

— *Hitchhikers Guide to the Galaxy*
by Douglas Adams

JoAnn Morgan probably won't retire for at least another two decades, but she already knows where she'd like to spend her golden years. It's a place she picked out long ago, a place that won't surprise her family, friends and colleagues.

They won't be dropping by for Sunday visits, though, because her ideal retirement spot is a bit out of the way. Well, 118 million miles out of the way, to be exact. You see, JoAnn Morgan hopes to retire on Mars.

"I'd volunteer to be a part of a geriatric research project. We have a lot to learn about humans living a long period of time in space," says Morgan, her voice still bathed in the southern lilt of her native Alabama. "And if they leave me, I could mentally accept that, even if it meant I was going to die there. It would be fun, it wouldn't bother me at all. I would be happy to die on another planet or in a space capsule, but I wouldn't want to go there as long as my husband's alive."

Larry, her husband of more than 35 years, has no intention of accompanying his wife to Mars. "I wouldn't mind visiting, but I wouldn't want to live there," he actually says, in all seriousness. But if she wants to move there after he's gone, that's okay with him.

"He doesn't want to go to Mars because he couldn't hunt or fish there," JoAnn says of her husband, who as a music teacher and bandmaster, is grounded in more earthly pursuits.

JoAnn Morgan, however, has spent her entire professional life sending hardware and people "*....where no one has gone before.*" In 1998, at the age of 57, she celebrated her 40th year with the space program. That's not a typo, you read it right, that's 40 years. Morgan was NASA/Kennedy Space Center's first female aerospace engineer, then the first woman to be named chief of an operating division, then out of some 30 directors, she was the first and only woman when she served first as Director of Payload projects Management ("If it leaves the ground and goes up into space, I'm involved with it"), and then as Director of Safety, Reliability and Quality Assurance. Now, she's a first again, the first and only woman to hold one of the top four executive positions as Associate Director for Advanced Development and Shuttle Upgrades. The only person above her is the Director of Kennedy Space Center.

She's always been an executive who's very hands-on because she rose in the ranks through engineering, and now, after more than 40 years, she is one of only a very small handful of people at Kennedy Space Center who have been there since day one. "I've seen the whole space program unfold since the first launch."

She has worked on every mission since joining the space program as a 17-year-old student engineering aide in the summer of 1958, a few months before NASA was even created, when the space program was still under the direction of the Army Ballistic Missile Agency.

In her spacious, airy office at Kennedy Space Center, Morgan works among the memorabilia of the space race, including detailed spacecraft models and historic photos.

"That's me," she says, pointing to a photo taken in the firing room — the launch center — during the countdown for the Apollo 11 mission, which landed the first men on the moon. It's a familiar scene — rows and rows of computer consoles manned by guys wearing short-sleeved white shirts, skinny ties, pocket protectors, short hair and clunky black plastic-framed glasses. They all look like *Dennis the Menace's* father. All except one pretty guy with suspiciously long hair and no tie. Wait, that's no guy, that's JoAnn Morgan. If you watched Apollo 11's lift-off live on TV the morning of July 16, 1969, you would've seen 500 very happy men and one very happy woman slapping each other on the backs in celebration and passing out the traditional cigars.

No one had ever treated JoAnn Morgan any differently from the rest of the NASA engineers just because she's female, and that morning was no exception. She got a cigar just like everyone else. "And I smoked it!" she says, proudly, adding that she was too busy to light up right then and there, so she brought her stogie home that night and shared it triumphantly with her husband.

JoAnn Hardin was born in Huntsville, Alabama near the Army's Redstone Arsenal, on December 4, 1940. Her father, Don, was a pilot in the Army Air Corps during World War II, and would go on to be a chemistry teacher and then an army administrator at Redstone, coordinating the disposal of ordnance left over from the war. Her mother, Laverne, was a statistician after the war, and then turned her attentions to raising JoAnn and the three children who followed. Both

Don and Laverne had gifted science and mathematical minds, and balanced them with a deep love of the arts, insisting that his children learn to play musical instruments, JoAnn recalls, because "he said that music was using a different part of your brain, and that it makes you think differently."

JoAnn would eventually graduate number two in her class, encouraged by parents who "took it for granted that all their kids were going to be A students." She loved math and science, and from an early age wondered about the universe.

"I liked astronomy, and field trips to the planetarium, and I loved science fiction," she recalls. "I always like experimenting. In the fourth grade, I got a chemistry set. I built bombs and blew them up on the patio!"

Quite a hobby for a shy, quiet young girl who was never a tomboy, but preferred reading Jules Verne and her set of encyclopedias to playing with dolls.

In 1956, when JoAnn was a high school junior, her family moved to Titusville, Florida, where her father began working in ordnance administration for the Army at nearby Cape Canaveral. "The town had only about 3,000 people then, and half the kids in high school had dads who worked at the Cape," JoAnn remembers. "The Navy and the Air Force had much more funding for their rocket programs than the Army, but they failed, and only the Army had a rocket system that could put something into orbit. I knew this just from being in the homes of families who worked 'in the business.' Most of the launches were at night. All secret, all classified. Watching launches from the beach was a big thing for high school kids to do on a Friday or Saturday night. A lot of rockets would blow up and it was very exiting."

JoAnn Hardin met her future husband, Larry Morgan, that first year in Florida, when she was a junior at Titusville High School, and Larry, who had graduated the previous year, was in the Navy. It would be seven years before they'd marry, but Larry knew she was special right away. "She was always more interesting to talk to and to be around than anyone else," he remembers.

During her senior year, while Larry was off studying music at Florida State University, JoAnn and her friends continued to watch the secret night rocket launches near the Cape. "The Russian submarines would be right off the beach watching, too," she laughs.

On Friday night, January 31, 1958, the Army Ballistic Missile Agency began another secret countdown to launch. In Florida, the scientists and technicians, the kids on the beach, and the Russians submerged off the coast watched with anticipation. Would this one be the one to finally go into orbit?

A year earlier, the Russians had successfully made it into space — the first ones there — with the launch of Sputnik 1, and the race was on. In the Pentagon's War Room, Wernher von Braun, the German rocket scientist who would be recognized as the father of the American space program, and his colleagues, nervously awaited the launch, chugging cup after cup of strong coffee.

At 10:48 p.m., as the rocket rose from the launch pad, 17-year-old JoAnn Hardin watched from a beach less than three miles away, holding her breath. Nothing exploded or crashed, and the rocket went higher and higher, and out into orbit. America was finally in space.

"It was Explorer I, our country's first satellite," Joann says with the same awe she felt more than 40 years ago when she witnessed the historic launch. "I knew that this was going to change the world. I knew it was an enormous accomplishment. And I knew at that moment that I wanted to work in the space program. I wanted to touch the hardware, see how it works."

The day after she graduated from high school, in June, 1958, Joann joined the Army Ballistic Missile Agency as a civilian, one of only two students chosen from the entire country to work as engineering aides. During the next five years, she studied math at the University of Florida while working summers at NASA, what the Agency evolved into when it was no longer part of the Army. Her mentors included Wernher von Braun and his team of German and American scientists and rocket pioneers who divided their time between NASA facilities in Huntsville, Alabama and Cape Canaveral, Florida.

During her summers at the Cape, she helped design and build a new industry. "We had to build our own computers then," she recalls. "Even as a student, I worked hands-on, including the design and building of Launch Complex 39." She plotted trajectories, researched the effects of lightning strikes, designed a system that would protect mission computers from power outages and surges, and presented engineering projects and budgets to the bigwigs form Washington. With only a few hundred people employed at the Cape, a student engineer was as valuable a member of the team as a professional. She worked on the instrumentation for the Mercury missions, and back in Gainesville at the University of Florida she watched Alan Shephard, the first American man in space, as he was launched in Mercury MR-3 on May 5, 1961, narrating the live TV coverage for her fellow students in their sorority house. She did the same when John Glenn became the first American in orbit in Mercury MR-6 on February 20, 1962.

By the time she graduated in 1963, because of her summer work at NASA, she had already met all the requirements to be an aerospace engineer. She was Kennedy Space Center's first female aerospace engineer, "and the only woman there for a long time," she remembers. By that year, with Kennedy Space Center under construction, there were a few other women around, but they were in clerical positions or part of the astronaut nursing staff. JoAnn worked with the team that designed the Space Center. Previously, as the only woman at the Cape, she found no women's bathrooms. A security guard would stand outside the men's room when JoAnn needed to go in. The new Space Center would have plenty of women's bathrooms, even though she'd have them almost all to herself for years to come.

She laughs when she recalls that it was in the bathroom at Kennedy Space Center 23 years later where she developed a brief but important friendship with Christa McAulliffe, the teacher turned astronaut who died in the 1986 Challenger explosion.

Christa and Barbara Morgan (no relation), the back-up teacher/astronaut, had been around the Kennedy Space Center for months. "They came to watch the previous launch with Congressman Bill Nelson" going into space, "so I had the chance to talk with them a lot. We'd always seem to be running into each other in the ladies room, too." Christa , who was also a musician, wrote notes for JoAnn's husband's music students. The one thing she never talked about was any fear or concern about going up in the space shuttle.

After the Challenger disaster, though, "sometimes now crew do voice concerns," JoAnn says. "They're always really positive about it, but it's a risky business for people to go up in space. It's a hostile environment. And nothing can change that. Lift-off is a controlled explosion and landing is a controlled crash."

Back in the '60s, JoAnn says, it didn't seem to matter to anyone she worked with that she was a woman. They were *all* pioneers on a new frontier. The only hassles were brief and happened very early on, when she was still a student engineer and "heard catcalls in the cafeteria from some of the soldiers who were stationed at the base near the Cape." Although she brushed it off, she admits that to this day she gets a twinge on the rare occasions she goes into the cafeteria.

Immersed in planning the Apollo missions as a newlywed in 1965, JoAnn Morgan never considered becoming an astronaut. Why? "Because I don't like to drive." And in the early days, being an astronaut was "nothing more than driving in space. It was even worse than that. They were just inert bodies. But, they got past that and to the point where they had important tasks to perform." Her interest, she says, has always been in how things work, in creating the systems, designing the hardware.

By the mid-1970s, Morgan's career was at a crossroads. "I looked around and thought I could decide better what we should be doing. I was a lead engineer, and I was being noticed in a different way by management. They saw I was a leader and that I could handle management, money and politics," she says. "Besides I knew my department better than anyone else out there. I thought I could make things happen better than someone brought in from the outside."

Senior management agreed, and Morgan received a Sloan Fellowship to Stanford University, where she received her Masters in Science in 1977. Two years later, she was the first woman selected to lead an operating division at Kennedy Space Center, as the Chief of the Computer Services Division, the first of many executive promotions. She was also the first woman to receive a NASA Exceptional Service Medal, and has since received several more. On the occasion of her 40th anniversary at NASA, she received perhaps its most prestigious honor, The Curt Debus Award, and again she was the first woman so honored, and among only 10 other people to have received the award.

I first met JoAnn Morgan when I interviewed her for *Sunshine*, the *Ft. Lauderdale Sun-Sentinel's* Sunday magazine

One of the first of our many conversations took place in February, 1993 at NASA's Kennedy Space Center. Below her office in the Operations and Check-out Building (OCB), technicians dressed in the sterile garb of surgeons work in the High Bay 100,000 Class Clean Room, an enormous, brightly lit, warehouse of a room with exceptionally high ceilings. JoAnn Morgan points out the various projects being built for future missions. These spacelabs, she explains, are "independent spacecraft that will be latched down into the payload bay of the shuttle." Astronauts enter these labs though a tunnel. The labs don't have propellant systems, and cannot fly on their own, but they're called "spacecraft" nonetheless. Here in the clean room, "reusable pieces of flight hardware — racks, modules — all these pieces are configured any way you need them in order to build a mission to conduct experiments," she explains. "We're working on building spacelabs that will be used in missions anywhere from 10 months to 10 years from now. Cells, tissue cultures and other fragile items are installed at the last minute into the experiment racks, on the launch pad on the day of the mission."

This building was previously used for the Apollo spacecraft and lunar module. "You're standing in a very historic place," she says. "All the Apollo capsules were prepared here. The chambers down at the end is where the Apollo astronauts trained. The only thing new in here are the test stands to put the equipment in, and the canister to transport the payloads out to the shuttle."

It looks like a room full of a child's colorful Lego pieces. Morgan walks past Spacehab, a commercial venture that will fly in the shuttle. Designed to hold 20-30 small experiments, Spacehab will fit — self-contained — into the shuttle' payload bay. "This almost quadruples the space available on the shuttle for small experiments. In the middeck they can only do a few small experiments. The Spacehab company pays for this and they have sold to foreign governments, industry, universities, anyone who wants to perform an experiment in space. It's a global enterprise."

She was the Director of Payload Projects Management at the time of my 1993 visit, and was already coordinating payload for the

International Space Station. Two promotions later, as one of Kennedy
Space Center's four top executives, her position as Associate Director
for Advanced Development and Shuttle Upgrades keeps her involved
with the Space Station, but from a wider perspective, as we discussed
in the conversation presented here, which took place in December,
1998, just weeks after Senator John Glenn, the first American astronaut to orbit the Earth, returned to space on October 29, 1998 aboard
the space shuttle Discovery. Naturally, we talked about Glenn's historic mission, as well, and Morgan's excitement about a string of
upcoming missions that will lead up to man's arrival on Mars as soon
as 15 years from now. If we stay on schedule, that means that JoAnn
Morgan will be in her early 70s then, and just may get her wish to
retire on Mars.

❧☙

You're now the Associate Director for Advanced Development and Shuttle Upgrades at Kennedy Space Center, and have been in this position since 1996.

This is now my second promotion since you visited me here in 1993 when I was Payload Projects Director. I did spend almost three years after that as director of Safety and Mission Assurance, and then moved up to Associate Director, which is one of the four executive positions that run the Space Center, and my area of responsibility is Advanced Development — all the new things we work on — and Shuttle Upgrades. The shuttle is our only re-usable launch vehicle going into space now, and we have to keep it sound and reliable because it's going to be essential to building the space station and taking care of the folks that will be living in the space station until another re-useable vehicle is designed and deemed safe enough for people to travel into space on.

So, upgrade means improving the existing shuttle.

Yes, mostly technology insertion.

And is that developed within NASA, or is that contracted out?

Some of the technology is developed within NASA, and, in fact, Kennedy Space Center works on some of that now, like taking advanced sensors and packaging them into a system to understand how certain things perform that we couldn't measure when the shuttle was designed 20 years ago. We've been flying the shuttles since 1982, and some of the systems are old and the way they were designed didn't include imbedded measuring techniques so you could understand performance. Think about one of those home bread-making machines. The sensors are imbedded in the metallic structure of the bread-

making machine. When we built the shuttle, we couldn't do that, those kinds of techniques didn't exist.

Which means that our bread-makers are more advanced than the 1981 shuttle.

Well, in terms of a machine thinking for itself that's correct because technology has come a long way since then.

It must be mind-boggling just to keep up with the computer technological improvements, which happen daily, weekly and month-ly. The computer systems that ran the shuttle in 1981 must not be anything like what you have now.

No, that's true, and we've already had one major upgrade of the shuttle flight computers and even after upgrading them, which was many years ago, my computer on my desk has more power than one of the five flight computers in the shuttle. We have a long way to go to modernize and we're only limited by money, obviously. The amount of money that NASA has to spend on upgrading the shuttle is limited to $100 million a year, and we have to use that to both find the technology and develop the technology, and then packaging the systems. So, they can only do so much each year, and it's a fairly complicated kind of thing to implement because you have four orbiters and they have their schedule of flights, and you can't always be tearing them apart and working on them. It's exciting, it's a lot of fun, and it's a real challenge.

Is it possible to keep the shuttle computer system and the one it links with at NASA as state-of-the-art as someone's home computer?

They can not always be state-of-the-art. Some of them are always going to be lagging a little. One of the things that the flight crew has been able to do is adapt to using little laptops, and they've got enormous power in them now, so for some unique functions they can use those, especially as interfaces with some of the experiments and payloads. But, the basic core functions of running the shuttle itself, the avionic functions as the flight people would say, those will probably always lag. That's one of the hardest things to upgrade, by the way, the avionic systems, to take out the computer and the software. And now we're using custom software that not a lot of other people in the world use, so then when you go to change it, it's a big deal. You have to get all the applications programs and then the certifying so they meet the reliability standards. But, that's just one part of it. There are also many other things, like the opportunity to insert non-toxic propellants, that are enormous changes.

Every day, people face strange computer glitches, just because the software has decided it's going to do it. All of a sudden, today, it decides to go nuts. That's a possibility with every piece of software, in every computer, everywhere. It must be an awfully scary prospect that that could happen in the shuttle. What safeguards do you have to keep that from happening, and why can't people get that for their personal computers (we laugh)?

The way we deal with that on the shuttle is that we have four out of five of them running all the time, simultaneously and parallel, and the fifth one is voting on which one's the healthiest and using that information. And, of course, you can't do that in your house. You can't just line up five PCs and have them running, with the fifth one off to the side saying, "Oh, number three, you look a little sick here, we're gonna shut you down for awhile and operate off of number one and two." And that's how we have to do it. We have to bank them and have that built-in reliability by having one computer checking on the others.

So, if one just decides it's going to crash, you have four others that could take it's place.

And one of them is checking up on all of them, and saying, "Ooh, this one's about to crash."

During the past few years, NASA began the transition to an International Space Station.

> *I think it's wonderful that they're naming the different pieces as they're going up. The first piece is Zarya, which means sunrise, and for astronauts sunrise is one of the most beautiful events that they see, and it's every 90 minutes or so as they orbit. And then Unity is the node, the piece that all other pieces can attach to, sort of like a funny-looking hexagon. And one piece is named Leonardo, and was built by Italy, and it's a logistics module. They're constructing an outpost, and the Pony Express can go there now! Building the Hubble Telescope, a repairable observatory on orbit, was a magnitude lower than this space station. The International Space Station is the biggest construction project ever in space. Just two pieces are 70 feet high. When you stand at the bottom and look up, it's a long way!*

That's seven stories, I live on the 7th floor, that's up where I am.

> *And we have another 38 launches to go to get the rest of it put together.*

When do they expect people to be able to inhabit the space station?

> *It'll be late in the year 2000 before they actually move in and start to live there. And it'll have an escape vehicle that can bring them home in case of an emergency.*

How far out there is it, and how long does it take to get there?

> *It would take a day and a half to two days to rendezvous with it. It's out beyond where the shuttle usually orbits.*

People can go back and forth with relative ease. With this space station, now, you're getting closer to your goal of retiring on Mars.

I know, it's wonderful, and they're actually finally talking about people going to Mars.

How long does it take to get there? And when will we go?

Well, between 2009 and 2013 we could go to Mars. And now that John Glenn has flown again, and shown that a 77-year-old man can withstand it, and we all know that women live longer than men and are healthier in old age (she laughs)...

When you're 73 and want to go retire on Mars, they probably aren't going to argue with you *(we laugh).*

We have this little joke around here. The Kennedy Space Center director, Roy Bridges, is in his 50s, a couple of years younger than me maybe, and we were kidding him — he's an astronaut, he's flown twice — and we said, "Gosh, Roy, you could fly again in a few years if they have a geriatric program with astronauts going to Mars." And he did some quick calculations, and he said, "Well, I actually won't be old enough!" (we laugh). *They want you to be in your late 70s for that. It takes about a year to get there. And then you'd want to stay for awhile. A mission to Mars, with humans, as envisioned by some of the folks I've been talking to — I've been doing a lot of work with that because Advanced Development is my responsibility — is more than a two year project. It takes a year to get there, you spend some time there and do some work, and then it's another year to get back.*

If you go all that way, you want to stay awhile.

You want to stay for six months, you want to see it. This is like when Columbus went to America. It's a long voyage, and you want to stay awhile so you can learn as much as you can. We're sending robotic missions to Mars now every 26 months. They're robot scouts, they survey the climate, some land. They'll show us where's a good place to potentially site hardware so that we have an outpost ready there so that when people go there's a habitat.

The robots build the habitats.

Right, and we'll have a factory there that produces oxygen out of the carbon dioxide atmosphere and stores it so that you have plenty of oxygen stored there. We'd have everything ready.

So the first time man sets foot on Mars, they'd be arriving at an outpost already built by robots.

Yes. And they'll start building this probably between 2005 and 2010. That is, if people care, if Americans care about doing that kind of exploration.

How long does it take to build the outpost, a couple of years?

Yeah, because you have to send about 80 metric tons of hardware out there to build the village.

Just out of curiosity, in the space program what can you buy for $40 million dollars? I'm just wondering how much we could've done instead of giving it to Ken Starr.

Oh, gosh...(she laughs), *well for $40 million dollars you could've done the design, development and set of space suits for astronauts to wear on Mars; you could've gotten new computers designed for a Mars Rover; you could've gotten a food factory for fresh vegetables on Mars, one that would operate as a closed ecology system; there's just no end to the things you could've gotten for that kind of money. I know, isn't it a waste?*

It is.

Pathetic.

No matter what your politics, you have to look at this impeachment in a reasonable way and say, "You must be kidding." We're making some strange history. Looking back at what you've done over the last 40 years at NASA, you've been a part of history, you've watched it unfold. You're a walking history book *(we laugh)*. Not that I'm trying to make you feel old, you started there at 17 and you're only 57, but for one person to have participated in 40 years of the space program is pretty incredible. There aren't that many other people with 40 years there, are there?

> *No, there aren't. One of the last contractors to be here for four decades retired, and he and I were talking about that, and it's a wonderful feeling to have seen it and I enjoy sharing it with young people. I tell them, "You have this ahead of you if you're committed to a career in this industry because there is always going to be change. Exploring the universe is endless and offers you maybe the greatest breadth of knowledge and awareness of change of anything that you could do."*

I think that's why John Glenn's recent return to space was so very important. Even if they learn virtually nothing about aging in space from this one particular set of experiments, that's not as important and there's time to send other older people up there. The most important thing is that it brings awareness so that people support the continuation of exploration. If it takes putting a hero back into space, to do that, that's fine. I don't have a problem — as many others in the press do — with the idea that sending him up there was just a gimmick. Some gimmicks, if it's fair to call them that, do have a valid purpose behind them. Maybe it is a gimmick, but it's a very valid one. John Glenn took this very seriously, it was NASA's motives that the press was questioning, not Glenn's. Well, of course, NASA did this for publicity. You have to, in order to keep the public awareness up, or we'll quit exploring because the public will quit supporting funding.

> *Well, he is absolutely an inspiration to talk to, and has been great for the work force because he's re-invigorated interest in some areas that maybe people weren't very serious about before.*

His personal integrity and personal sacrifice — he offered himself as a guinea pig in all of this.

It could have been a life or death mission.

Yes.

A 77-year-old man just sitting on Earth having lunch can be a problem, let alone shooting him up into space.

Yeah, and to offer himself as a guinea pig...Back in January, 1998, after they announced his mission, before he'd even gone into training, he came down here and spent a few days, and talked to some of my engineers who were working on experiments that would go on that mission. He has such knowledge of technology. We were working on these experiments with these new sensors I was talking about at the beginning of this conversation, and his knowledge of technology was something. He had studied so much. And then he was talking about human biology and aging. And I tell you, he'd been studying aging from a medical standpoint for years. You could tell by his quotes, what he'd been reading, the doctors he'd talked to. He was so serious in his desire to bring new medical information into the system.

That has always been his way — as an astronaut, he was extraordinarily thorough, and he had the reputation in the Senate for being that way, too. And, so, what better person to send back up in space at any age, whether he was 77 or not.

In light of everything that happens in politics, it's also nice to have a real hero.

A real one, not a manufactured one, and that realness has always been John Glenn's appeal. His commitment to his craft, which he's always displayed, is something we rarely see these days in any field. We used to see it, but not much any more. People's motivations are different now. They do what they do to make more money, or for their ego, not for the love of the craft, whatever it is. He's from an era when people thought of themselves as craftsmen, and you could even call an astronaut that. Whether you were making a widget or flying into space, in those days people put a lot of pride and love into what they did and they cared about quality and about knowledge. And, unfortunately, that's not a big priority these days. Money outweighs everything now. So, that's why I think people find him so refreshing. What was it like the day he lifted off in the shuttle?

Well, it was a madhouse, it was a complete madhouse!

You told me a funny story five years ago about how you got your cigar when they passed them around in the control room after Apollo 11 lifted off — the mission where men first walked on the moon. Did they pass around cigars when Glenn took off in the shuttle, and did you get one?

No, they didn't pass around cigars, there were no cigars (she laughs). *There's no smoking allowed in federal buildings anymore. And the young launch team wouldn't even think of it.*

But, it's been tradition! What do they do instead?

We eat beans and cornbread. That's the good-luck after launch thing, and everybody goes down to have their beans and cornbread. It was a wonderful day, a gorgeous, clear day with no haze, no clouds, just beautiful blue sky.

Where were you during the launch?

I was taking care of all the senators who were here. We had a special place for them to watch the launch from. All my experiments were ready. I'd given my go-for-launch the day before. So, I was hostess that day. And the senators had one of their own flying with John Glenn flying, so it was an emotional day for them. I think everybody there had tears in their eyes.

There was one very moving moment about five minutes before launch. This public affairs officer came over and said, "Would you stand for 'The Star Spangled Banner?'" and the P.A. system started playing "The Star Spangled Banner," and then a few people started singing. And by the end, the whole crowd was singing, everybody all around, it was echoing. And it was amazing because there were a lot of people from other countries there. We had a lot of guests. And there was a Japanese astronaut on the mission. And the people from other countries were humming along. It was an incredible experience.

The kind of thing that gives you chills.

Oh, it did, it still gives me chills when I think about how it felt. Several of the senators had never seen a launch in person. They were just beside themselves, they were so thrilled.

What was it like at Kennedy Space Center while Glenn was out there in space?

It was well-planned, well-rehearsed, the astronauts had trained so much. The mission was well-conceived and thought out. Once in awhile there was a little minor adjustment of things, but I never sensed anywhere — here or with my colleagues at Houston — that people were feeling frantic or worried or anything. The mission was a great mission. And, as a matter of fact, I don't think NASA people felt nervous about it. There might have been some doctors fretting and worrying about how the experiments were going. And there were two doctors on board who knew what to do in case of an emergency, so, to tell you the truth, I never gave that a thought at all during this mission. He was wonderfully fit, both intellectually and physically. He was prepared for this. And that's the way I felt. He was prepared, the team was prepared, the crew was prepared.

What do you think is the most important thing that will result from his mission?

In the long run, the most important thing to come from this will be our awareness of the raw talent we have in our aging population, and how it's been underestimated. In this country, we have been so oriented towards valuing youth that this is the paradigm shift coming.

Especially with the baby boomers aging. The baby boomers like, and are used to, being the center of the universe, so there's no way we're — I'm a boomer, too — going to let anyone tell us we can't do something. And some of the boomers are in to their 50s now.

Yeah, and there's enormous intellectual and physical capability that this whole older population has, and they may now have a profound influence. And five years ago, nobody would've ever dreamed how powerful that could be.

Do you think that will affect how people view things like mandatory retirement at particular companies?

Possibly. And this could become a big factor economically and make a lot of difference on many fronts. I think the sociological side of this is probably the real long-term influence of John Glenn's shuttle mission. I think the implications for people flying in space is that it reinforces something I told you a long time ago — the physical is one of the less important factors in what you're able to do because the power of the body is less important in a no gravity environment. What counts is what you're able to do with your intellect. The learning capacity of the mind is so key. And this mission just reinforced that.

It's not like anybody needs to do any heavy lifting out there *(we laugh)*.

Yeah, and look how easy it was for these two guys to build this seven story building out there at the space station this week! I'm exaggerating the ease of it, because it is complicated, but they're doing it with a robot arm.

And they're floating. They don't need to lift it against the forces of gravity. And by comparison, look what it takes to put up a seven-story building here on Earth.

Two people can't do it.

And certainly not in a week *(we laugh).* Did you get the chance to talk privately with John Glenn?

I did, I talked with him privately on a couple of occasions. I had lunch with him before the mission, too. About two weeks before launch, I had a wonderful conversation with him at the beach. He was here to do his final countdown rehearsal test and practice his emergency egress from the vehicle. It was a wonderful conversation and I enjoyed talking with him about music and things other than space. He had enormous calm and confidence.

Did you reminisce? You know him from way back when.

Yes, I wasn't a close friend back then, but a part of the launch team.

But, you're one of the few faces he's seen here for 40 years.

Well, yeah (she laughs).

There's a sense of continuity when he can have lunch with someone that he knows was there even before he went up into space the first time.

Yeah, we did get quite a laugh because I didn't work on his launch, but I did work on Gus Grissom's, which was the one before John's. We got a laugh talking about our memories of Gus Grissom. And I worked the day of the Apollo fire [that killed Grissom] in the block house. When several of us had dinner with Glenn before the shuttle mission, Roy Bridges, the Kennedy

462

Space Center director asked Curt Brown, the commander of the crew if he wanted to say anything, and Curt made a few comments and then said, "Let me ask Senator Glenn if he'd like to say anything." John Glenn, with enormous humility, turned to his commander, the payload commander and he said, "I'm gonna do whatever these guys tell me." It was like he was communicating, "I'm part of a crew, I'm not in charge of anything other than discharging my technical duties." It was turning into The John Glenn Mission, and he was so aware of that, and wanted to share this mission with the rest of his crew, and to remind people in the room that there's a whole crew going, that he's not the only one going. And I think it was wonderful that he had that insight, the wisdom of age. It reminded me of my grandmother — how older people have that wisdom and remember how important it is to share glory, to share what the accomplishment means, and to give that power away, to give it to other people.

When you're older, perhaps you're not so propelled by the ego and insecurities of youth anymore.

They can still be competitive, but they don't have to be competing against their crewmates.

Your background and hands-on approach make you quite unique to NASA, or to any group — that you can administrate, but also know the technology and are an engineer. This gives you a perspective that others won't have. Has that played a role in your career, that you offer something that not that many others can?

It's possible, but I think that a greater contribution to my continued value here is my ability to change and to get other people to change and evolve. When you're about to enter your fifth decade (she laughs) working in a place that's as dynamic as this, I reflect back and see that a lot of the people who left did so because they couldn't change, or because when given an assignment they couldn't get other people to change in order to accomplish it.

And you're in an arena — the space program —of constant change.

Right. And I think this is as much a personal quality, being comfortable with change, and to keep learning.

Have we all but abandoned the moon?

No, no, but I think the commercial world is going to drive a return to the moon. We'll use the resources of the moon — the chemicals that are there — and there's also the opportunity for a telescope on the other side of the moon, which could be the grandchild of the Hubble Space Telescope, but be located on the moon, and that would mean that we'd need a little relay satellite around the moon so we could get the data back to earth. There are opportunities out there, it's just that with no gravity on the moon, and not near the kind of chemistry you have on Mars to sustain life, industry needs to figure out how to mine some of the chemicals and minerals on the moon that would enable them to create a sustainable infrastructure. The other thing the moon would be very useful for, and this is related to Mars, is it would be a good place to test some of the technologies to see how robust and rugged they are.

Some of the ones we would be using on Mars.

Yeah, you could put something there to see how it functions on the moon for six months, and it's a lot easier to manage the data, get the data back to earth and understand what it's telling you. And that would give you a higher comfort level in the reliability of the equipment.

What can be done to increase awareness and get people excited about continuing the space missions?

I think we have to get women involved in understanding this. Women make up 52% of the population, and they're predicting that by early in this next century 60% of the workforce will be women. But, I don't think women feel connected to the space program. Having the bulk of half your population disinterested...

That does put a damper on things.

Yes, and I don't know the answer to this, but we really need for women to take an interest in this. There's an underlying issue of women studying math and science less than men. Women have so many issues — medical, health care, educational, family — and so this is at the bottom of the priority list, but exploration is hope for the future and is the future. But, somehow, because it's so far out there and not affecting women's day to day lives, therefore many of them feel it can't be worthy of investing in.

And what they may not realize is that NASA spin-off technology has affected them more than anything. Without space exploration, they wouldn't have the breakthroughs in medicine and daily technology if it hadn't been developed for NASA first.

And they wouldn't even have what's in their homes, the appliances and materials in their daily life. They need to be educated about this. I notice that with the Mir accidents and John Glenn mission, for the first time magazines like Vanity Fair *are writing about these things. Every magazine ought to be helping to educate. This is at the bottom of why kids don't study math and science — because there's no hook, no vision presented to them.*

And it's also taught and presented to them totally out of context. It isn't taught very well.

I do worry about that.

Maybe the way to educate both men and women is to give them

a context within their daily lives that they can relate to, so they'll see that everything within their personal and professional life has been improved by the technology of the space program — their care, their computers, medical technology, you name it — and that's a good starting point. From there they'll need to see the big picture, see the importance of space exploration itself.

Even though we have a lot of women astronauts who are achievers and hold many degrees...

The average woman doesn't relate to them.

Exactly. They might be a role model for a few, but there's no connection for the rest.

And it's unfortunate that the one person they could relate to, a teacher, died in the Challenger explosion. And I'm sure that scared a lot of people away from supporting exploration. Do you think there will be another non-astronaut in space?

I think we will someday. Especially after the space station is built. That will encourage industry to take advantage of the laboratory side of the space station and use it for developmental projects. When that happens, they're going to want their own people to be involved. And they'll want their own marketers to be involved, and the media. And that'll bring the public back in.

In the not too distant future people will be traveling to the space station the way they travel to Europe now for a meeting. There will be a lot of traffic back and forth.

Absolutely.

And they'll need to find a way to bring down the cost of shuttling people back and forth.

That's right. When another reusable launch vehicle comes along that's low cost — and there's a lot of investment into technology like the Venture Star, to be able to do that — in about ten years going there will be a routine kind of thing. Then people will think differently about it. And it'll be perfect as an international laboratory and education center, too. And we'll be going on to other explorations, like Mars.

Wait until we get out to Mars and find out there are already locals up there *(we laugh)*. We'll arrive and they'll say, "Aw, jeez, we've got company."

Publication Acknowledgements

Portions of the introduction and/or conversations in each chapter have been previously published in narrative or Q&A format in the following publications:

Omni
    Brian Weiss, M.D. (*Interview* Q&A feature)
    Deborah Mash, Ph.D. (two *Mind* column features)

Body, Mind & Spirit
    James Redfield (two Q&A feature articles)
    Deepak Chopra, M.D. (Alternative Medicine feature article)
    Brian Weiss, M.D.(feature article/pseudonym feature article)
    Brooke Medicine Eagle (Alternative Medicine feature article)

The Miami Herald
    Deborah Mash, Ph.D. (*Health Beat* feature article)

The Fort Lauderdale Sun-Sentinel's Sunday magazine, *Sunshine*
    James Redfield (feature article)
    JoAnn Morgan (feature article)

The Orlando Sentinel's Sunday Magazine, *Florida*
    JoAnn Morgan (feature article)

Tallahassee Magazine
    James Redfield, Arun Gandhi, Brook Medicine Eagle, and Michio Kaku (together in feature article)

South Florida Magazine (now *Miami Metro* magazine)
    Brian Weiss, M.D. (Q&A feature article)
    Deborah Mash, Ph.D. (feature article)

Palm Beach Life
    Brian Weiss, M.D. (feature article)

Palm Beach Jewish World/ Miami Jewish Tribune
    Arun Gandhi (feature article)

ABOUT THE AUTHOR

Nina L. Diamond is also the author of *Purify Your Body*, a book of health reporting. As a journalist and essayist, she has written hundreds of articles for dozens of magazines and newspapers, and has been a regular contributor to *Omni*, *The Chicago Tribune*, and *The Miami Herald* among many others. She extensively covers the arts and sciences, media, and current affairs, and she publishes social commentary, humor and essays.

She was a writer and performer on *Pandemonium*, the National Public Radio satirical humor program, for its entire run in Miami and select markets nationwide from 1984–1998.

She is also a contemporary pianist and composer. *New Places*, her debut album of piano solos, which she also produced, will be released in 2000 by Serenada Records. Her music has been featured as the soundtrack on documentary and television news broadcasts.

She lives on the bay in Miami.

Herbs and other natural health products and information are often available at natural food stores or metaphysical bookstores. If you cannot find what you need locally, you can contact one of the following sources of supply.

Sources of Supply:

The following companies have an extensive selection of useful products and a long track-record of fulfillment. They have natural body care, aromatherapy, flower essences, crystals and tumbled stones, homeopathy, herbal products, vitamins and supplements, videos, books, audio tapes, candles, incense and bulk herbs, teas, massage tools and products and numerous alternative health items across a wide range of categories.

WHOLESALE:

Wholesale suppliers sell to stores and practitioners, not to individual consumers buying for their own personal use. Individual consumers should contact the RETAIL supplier listed below. Wholesale accounts should contact with business name, resale number or practitioner license in order to obtain a wholesale catalog and set up an account.

Lotus Light Enterprises, Inc.

P O Box 1008 VT
Silver Lake, WI 53170 USA
262 889 8501 (phone)
262 889 8591 (fax)
800 548 3824 (toll free order line)

RETAIL:

Retail suppliers provide products by mail order direct to consumers for their personal use. Stores or practitioners should contact the wholesale supplier listed above.

Internatural

33719 116th Street VT
Twin Lakes, WI 53181 USA
800 643 4221 (toll free order line)
262 889 8581 office phone
WEB SITE: www.internatural.com

Web site includes an extensive annotated catalog of more than 10,000 products that can be ordered "on line" for your convenience 24 hours a day, 7 days a week.